CONTROLLING THE WAVES

CONTROLLING THE WAVES

* * *

Dean Acheson and
U.S. Foreign Policy in Asia

* * *

RONALD L. McGLOTHLEN

W · W · NORTON & COMPANY · *New York* · *London*

Copyright © 1993 by Ronald L. McGlothlen

Printed in the United States of America

First Edition

The text of this book is composed in Times Roman,
with the display set in Perpetua.
Composition and manufacturing by The Maple-Vail Book Manufacturing Group.
Book design by Jacques Chazaud.

Library of Congress Cataloging-in-Publication Data

McGlothlen, Ronald L.
Controlling the waves : Dean Acheson and U.S. foreign policy in
Asia / Ronald L. McGlothlen.
p. cm.
1. Acheson, Dean, 1893–1971.   2. United States—Foreign relations—
Asia.   3. Asia—Foreign relations—United States.   4. United
States—Foreign relations—1945–1953.   5. Reconstruction
(1939–1951)—Asia.   I. Title.
E748.A15M3   1993
327.7305—dc20   92-38848

ISBN 0-393-03520-4

W. W. Norton & Company, Inc., 500 Fifth Avenue, New York, N.Y. 10110
W. W. Norton & Company Ltd., 10 Coptic Street, London WC1A 1PU

1 2 3 4 5 6 7 8 9 0

To My Wife, Elvera
My Daughter, Carrie
and Our Dachshunds, Punkin and Velvet

⚡ Contents

AUTHOR'S NOTE   9
ACKNOWLEDGMENTS   *11*

Chapter One   Dean Acheson   *17*

Chapter Two   Acheson and
the American Reconstruction of Japan   *23*

Chapter Three   Acheson and
the American Commitment in Korea   *50*

Chapter Four   Acheson and
the Amercian Comitment on Taiwan   *86*

Chapter Five   Acheson and
the American Cold War with China   *135*

Chapter Six   Acheson and
the American Commitment in Vietnam   *163*

Chapter Seven   Acheson and
the New Co-Prosperity Sphere   *202*

NOTES   *207*
BIBLIOGRAPHY   *278*
INDEX   *307*

Author's Note

Controlling the Waves is a narrative history. To keep its narrative format uncluttered and direct, I have restricted all discussions of research methodology and most collateral evidence to the notes—which therefore contain far more than the customary quantity of additional information. For example, some researchers have assumed that most Asia-related documents bearing Dean Acheson's name actually emanated from his subordinates. Acheson, however, utilized a simple document code, and it, along with other evidence, indicates that he personally wrote and received some of the most critical documents on Asian issues. This code and many similarly important research issues are fully discussed in the notes. I have chosen the discipline of a painstakingly strict narrative format for one reason: to balance the demands of scholarship with those of readability. As for the lessons of my narrative, I leave them for my reader to discern.

✎ Acknowledgments

A book of this complexity hinges on the support of a number of people, all of whom I would like to thank. First and foremost, let me thank my wife, Elvera, and my daughter, Carrie, for their constant encouragement, assistance, and advice. (My wife can probably recite much of this book from memory.) I would also like to extend a special thank-you to our good friend Deena Mistretta, whose exceptional intellect and insight have contributed to both the research and the writing phases of this book. Another special thank you goes to my parents, Lamont and Betty McGlothlen. If I have been able to spend a little more time at the National Archives than many researchers, the reason is simple: my good friends Jerry and Elaine Rubin have provided not only a place to stay but important moral support as well.

For their expert counsel on matters of history, writing, and publishing, I would like to thank Carl Parrini, Jordan Schwarz, William Logue, and William Stueck. For their expert assistance with archival and library research, I would like to thank Thelma Davis, Earl Shumaker, and Dennis Bilger. For helping me to develop a deeper understanding of the State Department during the Acheson years, I would like to thank Max Bishop, Paul Nitze, Dean Rusk, and Lucius Battle. For help with proofreading, I would like to thank Marianne Miller, Morgan Burkett, and Ladisca Tegnelia.

CONTROLLING THE WAVES

The State Department Hierarchy
with Respect to the Far East in 1950

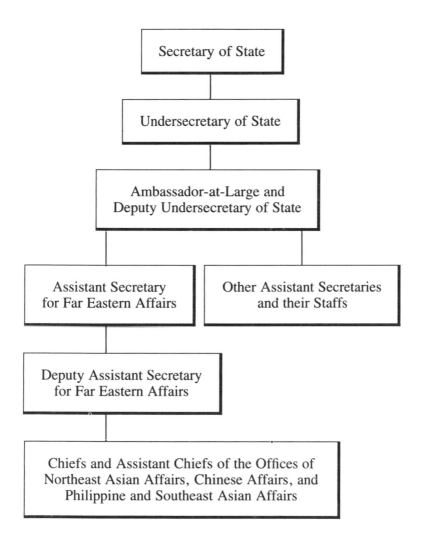

NOTE: Before 1950, there was no Deputy Undersecretary of State, and the Office of Far Eastern Affairs was run by a Director, who carried less authority than the Assistant Secretaries who ran other offices.

Dean Acheson

B<small>EFORE</small> W<small>ORLD</small> W<small>AR</small> II, the Japanese Empire provided the political and economic superstructure for much of the Far East. During the war, the United States dismantled this superstructure, and afterward American planners replaced it with a new one—essentially the same edifice which still stands today. To a large extent, these planners followed the vision of an extraordinary chief architect—Dean G. Acheson. Initially as Undersecretary of State and later as Secretary, Acheson orchestrated the U.S. State Department's efforts to rebuild Japan and its regional trade network. In Acheson's paradigm, Japan was the natural "workshop of Asia," and its trade with Korea, Taiwan, China, and Southeast Asia provided the logical starting point for regional economic recovery. Accordingly, Acheson tailored U.S. policies in the most critical areas of the Far East to fit a single, overriding objective: the restoration of Japan's political stability and economic power. The rapid rehabilitation of Japan, he hoped, would eliminate Japanese dependence on American aid, promote a broad-based Asian recovery, safe-guard the expansion of U.S. trade throughout the region, help secure America's recent recovery from economic depression, and contain the expansion of communism in Asia. This Japan-centered strategy, however, entailed serious risks. Acheson ultimately laid the foundations for a dramatic resurgence of Japanese power, but in the process, he initiated America's awkward commitment on Taiwan, its twenty-year feud with the People's Republic of China, and its costly involvement in the Korean and Vietnam wars.

The son of an English-born Anglican bishop and his Cana-dian wife, Acheson enjoyed an affluent childhood in Middle-ton, Connecticut, graduated from Yale University and Harvard Law School, and served in the U.S. Navy during World War I. A two-year apprenticeship as law clerk to Louis D. Bran-deis, a Supreme Court Justice and leading economic theorist, rounded out Acheson's education. He married Alice Stanley, and they eventually had one son and two daughters. In 1921, Acheson accepted a lucrative position with the well-connected Washington law firm of Covington and Burling. When he was not practicing law, Acheson dabbled in presidential politics, campaigning in 1928 for Alfred E. Smith and in 1932 for Franklin D. Roosevelt. A victorious Roosevelt made Acheson his Undersecretary of the Treasury, and he became Acting Secretary shortly thereafter. Roosevelt, as part of his New Deal, experimented briefly with the theory that monetary inflation could spur consumption, thereby lifting the United States out of the Great Depression. Accordingly, he ordered Acheson to implement a complex gold-buying program designed to devalue the dollar. Acheson objected, calling the order illegal and unworkable, and Roosevelt fired him. The gold scheme soon dissolved in failure, but it was not until 1940 that Roosevelt brought his wayward sheep back into the fold—this time as Assistant Secretary of State for Economic Affairs. Acheson became Assistant Secretary of State for Congressional Affairs in 1944, and he rose to Undersecretary of State when Harry S. Truman succeeded Roosevelt the following year. Desirous of a change, Acheson left the State Department in mid-1947. At Truman's request, however, he returned as Secretary of State in early 1949 and remained in that position for the duration of the Truman presidency.[1]

As Acheson's authority grew, so too did his abilities. He learned to deal effectively with superiors, subordinates, and the U.S. Congress. When General George C. Marshall became Secretary of State in 1947, he issued a single, blunt instruction to Acheson, his Undersecretary: "I shall expect of you the most complete frankness, particularly about myself. I have no feelings except those I reserve for Mrs. Marshall." Acheson, though much amused, took Marshall at his word, and they became one of the most successful teams in State Department history. Acheson also forged a warm friendship with Harry Truman. The off-year elections of 1946 ended in disaster for the Democrats; they lost control of the Congress, and Truman took much of the blame. Bone weary at the end of a grueling campaign, Truman arrived back in Washington to find just one person waiting for him at the train station—Dean Acheson Marshall, staggering under a heavy work load, often left the job of briefing the President to his Undersecretary, and Truman came to rely on Acheson's intelligence and insight. Later, when Acheson served as Truman's Secretary of State, the two men grew even closer. Truman sometimes referred to Acheson as his "number one brain man," and Acheson made his admiration for Truman evident to everyone around him. "In relations between the Secretary of State and the President," Acheson once remarked, "it is very important for both of them to recognize at all times which one is President." To be sure, Acheson was not above an occasional bit of manipulation, but he never forgot who was President, and Truman repaid Acheson's loyalty with his own.[2]

Acheson earned a similar respect from his subordinates.

Lucius Battle, Acheson's personal assistant, later remembered that when Alger Hiss (a State Department colleague) was accused of espionage, Acheson stood by him—despite the fervent objections of his staff. Dean Rusk, one of Acheson's closest advisers, recalled, "I was completely devoted to Dean Acheson. He had a brilliant mind. He was loyal to his colleagues, and he elicited from them an extraordinary amount of loyalty." Max Bishop, another close adviser, observed, "Acheson had the kind of mind I suppose we would all like to have." The genuine esteem of the President guaranteed Acheson strong support from above; the genuine esteem of his advisers guaranteed him equally strong support from below.[3]

But Acheson received mixed reviews in Congress. Early in his career, when he was Assistant Secretary of State for Congressional Affairs, he ingratiated himself with the congressional elite by personally arranging their junkets abroad and doing other special favors. As he rose through the ranks, he cultivated a number of important friendships on Capitol Hill, but he made enemies as well. Acheson never learned to suffer fools gladly. His barbed wit often incurred animosity, and some members of Congress found him imperious. As a Democratic Senator from Texas, Lyndon B. Johnson cooperated closely with Acheson, but later, as President, he could scarcely resist poking fun at his old friend. Dean Rusk, who served under both men, mirthfully recounted, "Lyndon Johnson later acted out in pantomime the impression Dean Acheson made on senators when he came to testify. Dean Acheson was impeccably dressed, and he had that bristling mustache. He looked around the room as though he was sniffing a skunk. Lyndon Johnson used to act that out in pantomime, and it was really a hilarious affair!" Nevertheless, for all his foibles and idiosyncrasies, Acheson had a gift for legislative strategy, and his programs seldom suffered defeat at the hands of Congress.[4]

Acheson's Republican critics in Congress frequently accused him of not paying enough attention to Asia. Their rallying cry was a simple rhetorical question: "Has the State Department got an Asian policy?" Even Acheson's friends acknowledged that he never made the Far East his top priority; Europe and only Europe held that position. On June 3, 1959, long after he had retired from government service, Acheson delivered an address at the U.S. Naval War College as a favor to Max Bishop, his onetime Chief of Northeast Asian Affairs. Afterward, while chauffeuring his former boss to the airport, Bishop probed him about his emphasis on Europe. "With Europe," Acheson responded, "everything was possible; without Europe, nothing was possible." "I think he gave full attention to Asia," Bishop subsequently elaborated, "at least the attention that it was due in relation to the European countries. After all, there was just one nation of real strategic importance in Asia back then, and that was Japan." Dean Rusk, Acheson's Assistant Secretary for Far Eastern Affairs, likewise remembered him as "a North Atlantic man" who relegated the Far East to a secondary role. But Rusk also recalled, "Our general attitude in those days was that it was important for the United States to have control of every wave in the Pacific Ocean . . . ."[5]

In Acheson's thinking, if the United States needed to "control every wave in the Pacific Ocean," it would have to begin with the reconstruction of Japan. There were two reasons for this. First, since Japan was the only industrialized nation in the Far East, the United States could best expedite regional recovery by rebuilding Japan and its prewar trade system. Second, Acheson's own experience with the Far East centered on Japan and its prewar empire. From the early 1930s through the end of World War II, Japan aggressively pursued economic ascendancy in the Far East under the guise of creating a "Greater East Asia Co-Prosperity Sphere." In the postwar years, Acheson sought a surprisingly similar ascendancy for Japan, but one in which Japan exchanged its failed militarism for American tutelage, protection, and domination. There was, of course, some irony in fighting a savage war to crush Japanese power, only to rebuild it in the postwar years. "We used to joke a little," Dean Rusk candidly recounted, "about this revival of the Greater East Asia Co-Prosperity Sphere." Yet, ultimately, the deeper irony of Acheson's diplomacy would lie not in its contradiction of the past but in its transmogrification of the future. For decades to come, the United States would be rocked by the hidden costs of Acheson's paradigm—and of his intricate machinations in Japan, Korea, Taiwan, China, and Indochina.[6]

CHAPTER TWO

Acheson and
the American Reconstruction
of Japan

ON SEPTEMBER 6, 1945, President Harry S. Truman appointed General Douglas MacArthur to the new post of Supreme Commander of the Allied Powers for the Pacific Theater of Operations—thereby giving him command over the U.S. occupation of Japan. In theory, MacArthur would rule Japan in cooperation with two agencies set up to represent the victorious allied powers—the Far Eastern Commission (FEC) and the Allied Council on Japan (ACJ). In reality, MacArthur took his marching orders from Truman, the Joint Chiefs of Staff (JCS), the State-War-Navy Coordinating Committee (SWNCC, pronounced "swink"), and, later, the National Security Council (NSC). SWNCC, first organized in late 1944, coordinated U.S. postwar planning, and on September 6, 1945, Truman approved its "Initial Surrender Policy" (SWNCC 150 / 4). In this policy, SWNCC charged MacArthur with two primary tasks: to ensure that Japan would never again become a menace to the United States and to establish a new government in Japan which would "support the objectives of the United States as reflected in the ideals and principles of the Charter of the United Nations." To these ends, MacArthur carried authority to reform Japan's political system and restructure its economy, but he also carried instructions to exercise his power through the existing Japanese government.[1]

MacArthur swiftly moved his headquarters—the Supreme Command for Allied Powers (SCAP, pronounced "scap")—to Tokyo, and there he found a nation in crisis. William J. Sebald, a State Department adviser to MacArthur, later remembered, "In uncertainty and confusion, the Japanese seemed well on their way toward political fragmentation." Throughout 1946, MacArthur and his staff waged a desperate struggle to pull the war-ravaged nation back from the brink of anarchy and economic collapse. Japan's political situation gradually stabilized but not its economy. Japan had lost over 88 percent of its merchant fleet, and its industrial production for 1946 came to just 30.7 percent of the prewar average. Japan depended on trade for its survival. It imported the bulk of its raw materials, including 93.5 percent of its oil, 93.4 percent of its iron ore, and 100 percent of its wool, cotton, and rubber. To pay for these imports, the island nation exported manufactured goods—chiefly textiles, which made up 58.2 percent of its prewar exports. Japan's Asian trading partners (particularly those in its prewar empire—Korea, Taiwan, and Manchuria) had accounted for 53 percent of its imports and 64 percent of its exports. But the war decimated Japan's foreign trade. Wartime developments (including the widespread substitution of nylon for silk) rendered many of Japan's products redundant in Western markets. Japan became overwhelmingly dependent on U.S. imports and lacked the means to pay for them. In the period 1930–34, the United States had received 23 percent of Japan's exports and supplied 24 percent of its imports; in 1947, the United States received 12 percent of Japan's exports and supplied 92 percent of its imports. The resulting deficit balance of payments (which many other nations also suffered) became known as the "dollar gap," and it soon threatened to destroy what little remained of Japan's economy.[2]

Yet, overshadowing even this problem, was one of far greater urgency—impending starvation. With less than 15 percent of its rugged geography suitable for agriculture, Japan had long imported over 30 percent of its food, primarily from its empire. Now, there was no empire, and Japan's former trading partners had no food to spare. To compound the problem, Japan's population, experiencing the effects of repatriation and a high birthrate, actually increased during the war—from 73 million in 1937 to 78 million in 1946. Only Japan's former enemies could prevent widespread famine. In 1946, the United States sent Japan 700,000 tons of food (mostly wheat) at a cost of $142 million, but with many other nations to feed as well, American planners could provide no more than starvation rations. Sangyo Keizai, a well-known Japanese newspaper reporter, declared, "If we can be fed, we don't care who has political power." In May, enormous food demonstrations broke out in Tokyo, Yokohama, and other large cities. MacArthur's bureaucracy redoubled its efforts, and the Japanese Government launched several new programs, but the shortages only grew worse. On a fact-finding trip to Kyoto, Max Bishop, Assistant State Department Political Adviser to MacArthur, saw throngs of hollow-eyed Japanese men crowded around the garbage cans behind a U.S. Army mess tent. As American soldiers filed past to empty the refuse from their plates, the Japanese would scramble after every morsel. By year's end, the State Department openly acknowledged that Japan's food crisis was "leading toward starvation."[3]

About this time too, the State Department recognized that it could no longer simply leave Japan's problems to Douglas MacArthur; it would have to intervene. First as Undersecretary of State (1945–47) and later as Secretary of State (1949–53), Dean Acheson orchestrated this intervention. Earlier, Acheson had employed his talents against Japan, supervising economic sanctions in 1941 and economic warfare operations from 1942 through 1944. Now, with the help of his advisers, he set to work rebuilding Japan. At his disposal were five principal means for addressing Japan's economic crisis: (1) the development of a U.S.-sponsored recovery program, (2) the revision of the industrial restrictions and reparations obligations imposed by the Allied powers, (3) the replacement of MacArthur's economic advisory team, (4) the negotiation of a peace treaty, and (5) the restoration of Japan's regional trade. With varying degrees of success, Acheson employed all of these, and his role with respect to Japan can best be understood by examining them one at a time.[4]

The Development of a U.S.-Sponsored Recovery Program

Toward the end of 1945, a special committee surveyed the effects of U.S. strategic bombing on Japan, and Paul H. Nitze, the committee's Vice-Chairman, used its final report to spotlight Japan's economic crisis. Nitze joined the State Department a few months later, becoming Deputy Director of the Office of International Trade. There he discovered that many other nations shared Japan's problems, and colleagues in the Treasury Department confirmed his belief that "a continuous progression of countries" would soon be "unable to meet their financial obligations." In February of 1947, Nitze pushed his concerns up the chain of command to William L. Clayton, Assistant Secretary of State for Economic Affairs, and Dean Acheson, Undersecretary of State. Only a massive infusion of U.S. aid, probably five billion dollars a year for five years, Nitze estimated, could prevent a worldwide economic catastrophe. Secretary of State George Marshall, heavily engaged with an upcoming foreign ministers' conference in Moscow, had delegated considerable authority to Acheson, and already he had begun laying the groundwork for aid to Greece, Turkey, and Korea. Now, at Nitze's urging, Acheson embarked on a far larger scheme. From March 4 to April 8, while Marshall was attending the Moscow conference, Acheson took charge of the State Department as Acting Secretary. On March 5, the day after Marshall's departure, Acheson met privately with Truman and broached the idea of expanding America's foreign assistance programs. Avoiding any discussion of cost, he requested only the authority to conduct a preliminary study, and he pointed out that the Departments of the Army and the Treasury backed his request. Truman, with no more than a murky understanding of Acheson's intentions, gave his consent.[5]

SWNCC promptly named an ad hoc committee to conduct the study, and Acheson set up a committee of his own to supervise the State Department's leadership role. In its first report (SWNCC 360, completed April 21, 1947), the ad hoc committee estimated that, for 1947, total U.S. exports would reach $16.2 billion, against imports of just $8.7 billion. The enormity of this imbalance meant that the rest of the world would "not be able to continue to buy United States exports at the 1946–47 rate beyond another 12–18 months." Furthermore, the committee noted, the President's Council of Economic Advisers had recently predicted a "slight recession within the next twelve months," and if even a mild recession coincided with a sharp drop in exports, "the effect on production, prices and employment might be most serious." By implication, the committee evoked the grim specter of a worldwide depression—reminiscent of the one the United States had just endured in the 1930s.[6]

Acheson immediately went to work with Nitze and others to fabricate a tentative plan, and with Joseph Jones, a speech writer, to fashion a major address. On May 8, at Cleveland, Mississippi, Acheson delivered the speech and unveiled his plan. With annual exports surpassing the $16 billion mark, he asserted, America's future depended on its foreign trade, and the nation could safeguard that trade only by rebuilding the economies of Europe and Asia. Since even the United States lacked the resources to accomplish such a task all at once, Acheson exhorted his fellow countrymen to "push ahead with the reconstruction of the two great workshops of Europe and Asia—Germany and Japan." Their rehabilitation, he reasoned, would eventually lead to a general recovery. Surprisingly, Acheson's speech aroused little interest, and within a few days he ordered his subordinates to write a new one.[7]

Thus far, Acheson had accepted Nitze's premise that the Far East would have to play a major role in world economic recovery. The nations of Asia, which had once accounted for over 15 percent of all world trade, accounted for only 8 percent in 1947, and their total trade volume stood at just 41 percent of the pre–World War II level. Japan, Asia's only industrialized nation, had earlier accounted for 5.4 percent of world trade and had ranked fourth in the world in total exports. But during the postwar years, Japan's imports dropped to 18.6 percent of prewar levels, while its exports sank even further, to 4.3 percent of prewar levels. To Nitze, these figures meant that Far Eastern recovery was critical to world recovery and that Japanese recovery was fundamental to both. But not everyone agreed.[8]

Acheson won high marks for his handling of the State Department's day-to-day affairs; not so for his part in organizing Marshall's preparations for the Moscow conference. The Secretary of State returned from the conference piqued about the inadequacy of his briefings, and he gruffly told Acheson to make sure that it never happened again. They solved the problem by creating a State Department Policy Planning Staff (PPS), and Marshall selected George F. Kennan to be its first director. Kennan tried to make Nitze his deputy, but Acheson vetoed the appointment. After conducting his own investigation of the balance of payments problem, Kennan concluded that the United States should adopt a Europe-first strategy, and the initial report of his Policy Planning Staff (PPS 1, completed May 23, 1947) reflected this conviction. William Clayton, Assistant Secretary for Economic Affairs, backed Kennan, and together they converted Acheson. Marshall followed suit. Nitze's two-front strategy, the theme of Acheson's Cleveland speech, fell from favor, and Kennan's Europe-first strategy replaced it in the follow-up speech. Acheson spared no effort to create media interest in the new address, and the Secretary of State himself delivered it at Harvard University's commencement ceremony on June 5. The speech was a success, and the State Department eventually dubbed its new economic equation the Marshall Plan. Even given this shift to a Europe-first strategy, however, Acheson did not simply forget about Japan; he scaled down, rather than eliminated, his nascent plans for a Japanese recovery program.[9]

Acheson left the State Department (as earlier agreed) on June 30, 1947, and returned to his former law firm. Three weeks later, the State Department completed his economic rehabilitation plan for Japan (SWNCC 381, completed July 22, 1947). The new plan focused on the revival of Japan's regional trade, and it anticipated the return of Japanese economic independence by 1950. Funding would come from a U.S. grant of $400 million, plus another $150 million to be raised from the sale of Japanese assets. MacArthur naturally wanted more, and in his own "Green Book Plan" he called for a four-year program costing $1.2 billion. The Joint Chiefs of Staff objected strenuously to both the regional emphasis of the State Department plan and the price tag on MacArthur's proposal. After trying first to amend the State Department plan, Pentagon planners fielded a third plan (SWNCC 384), which dispensed with the State Department's regional approach. Some State Department analysts continued to insist that "a 'Japanese plan' standing by itself" would be of "doubtful value," but Marshall accepted a modified version of the Pentagon's proposal. Marshall, MacArthur, and the JCS reached agreement on a one-year, $180 million recovery package for Japan, which would be in addition to the U.S. Army's existing $350 million-a-year relief program. Congress then pruned the recovery package down further, to $165 million. Thus, although Acheson and his advisers originally envisioned a $550 million, regionally oriented recovery program for Japan, the end result was a $165 million program with little regional orientation.[10]

The Revision of Industrial Restrictions and Reparations Obligations

In early 1947, at about the same time Nitze began directing Acheson's attention to the economic reconstruction question, he also urged the elimination of punitive restrictions on Japanese industrial production. The Soviet Union, Nitze counseled, would accuse the United States of remilitarizing Japan, but only for a few days. Acheson, then Undersecretary of State, adopted Nitze's suggestion and quickly sold it to Secretary of State George Marshall. Together, they pushed a brief statement ("Assured Production Capacity Levels for Japan") through the Far Eastern Commission (FEC, which represented the Allied Powers), followed by official notification that Japan's industrial production would henceforth be allowed to reach a level commensurate with its standard of living in 1930–34. Moreover, on February 28, the State Department notified SCAP that it should use the new FEC statement as a pretext for designating those facilities which would "in no circumstances be subject to removal" as part of Japan's reparations. MacArthur swiftly complied. As Nitze predicted, the Soviet Union objected vehemently for several days and then tacitly accepted the State Department's fait accompli.[11]

This, however, still left Acheson with only a partial solution to the reparations problem, and his advisers cautioned that anything short of a full settlement would prevent "the stabilization of the Japanese economy" and increase "the burdens of the American taxpayer." Throughout 1946, the State Department advanced a succession of proposals on reparations, but the FEC refused to take up the issue. Acheson instructed American embassies around the world to circulate the U.S. proposals and protest the FEC's inaction. Their efforts accomplished nothing. In January of 1947, George Atcheson—the State Department's Political Adviser to MacArthur—predicted that Japanese recovery would continue to be "obstructed by non-settlement of the reparations question." Japan's economy was "bankrupt," George Atcheson emphasized, and its industrialists could not even begin the rebuilding process until they knew what equipment would be "left to them" after the payment of reparations.[12]

Seeing no other choice, Dean Acheson joined with other top policymakers in a straightforward power play. The State Department presented the FEC with a new reparations proposal (SWNCC 236 / 35) and warned the commission that if it failed to act, MacArthur would "issue this same policy as an interim directive." As usual, the FEC procrastinated, and on April 4 the JCS ordered MacArthur to issue the U.S. proposal as an interim directive. Having secured control over Japan's near-term reparations, Acheson set up a secret committee, the Advisory Committee on Development of Japanese and Korean Trade. The committee recommended that reparations removals be limited to Japan's "war supporting industries." Acheson and Marshall launched another offensive in the FEC, and on June 19, 1947, it adopted a new "Basic Post-Surrender Policy." This policy, which was essentially written in the State Department, limited reparations removals to "primary war industries" and specified that no removals would be allowed to "prejudice the cost of the occupation and the maintenance of a minimum civilian standard of living" in Japan. Acheson left the State

Department on June 30, 1947. During his absence, the United States fielded one more comprehensive proposal on reparations, but the FEC rejected it and remained deadlocked.[13]

On January 7, 1949, the Truman administration announced the appointment of Dean Acheson to replace an ailing George Marshall. Acheson, upon assuming office as Secretary of State two weeks later, found that Japan's economy had improved only slightly during his absence, while its population continued to soar. The island nation muddled along on a virtual flood of imports from the United States—mostly food, fuel, fertilizer, and raw materials—while its exports remained severely depressed. Current estimates showed that Japan's annual trade deficit had mushroomed from $180 million in 1946 to $352 million in 1947, and its trade deficit for just the first half of 1948 stood at $271 million. Equally alarming was Japan's foreign trade indebtedness, which Acheson himself described as "the huge sum of $790 million." The cost of American assistance, according to Japanese figures, reached $404 million in 1947, $461 million in 1948, and $535 million in 1949. Since U.S. taxpayers could not indefinitely redress Japan's deficits, Acheson once again found himself heavily involved in Japanese affairs—beginning with the reparations issue.[14]

The policies which the United States forced upon the FEC in 1947 had effectively minimized Japan's reparations payments—particularly with respect to machinery transfers. Japan possessed 700,000 machine tools, of which approximately 225,000 had been used in war industries and were therefore subject to transfer. Japan actually transferred just 14,000 machine tools to its former enemies. In late 1948, however, the U.S. Army floated a new proposal designed to both permanently resolve the issue and dramatically increase the rate at which Japan doled out its machine tools. MacArthur at once argued that such a program would sabotage U.S. efforts to stabilize the Japanese economy and that all reparations payments should be terminated.[15]

Max Bishop, now Chief of the Office of Northeast Asian Affairs, vigorously echoed MacArthur's arguments and added that further reparations might produce serious psychological and political consequences in Japan. In opposition, Paul Nitze, Deputy Director of the Office of International Trade, projected that any move to cut off reparations payments would "provoke international reactions so hostile as to embarrass Japan's trade prospects in the Far East." W. Walton Butterworth, Director of Far Eastern Affairs, backed Bishop, while Charles Saltzman, Assistant Secretary of State for Occupied Areas, threw his support behind Nitze. In mid-February, the two sides outlined the debate in a joint memorandum to Acheson. Agreeing with MacArthur, Bishop, and Butterworth, Acheson reasoned that the "inability of the Japanese economy to provide even a subsistence level of life for its people" created a burden for U.S. taxpayers which additional reparations payments would only increase. Acheson and his advisers framed a revised policy (NSC 13 / 3, approved May 6, 1949) which indefinitely postponed Japan's reparations. By the time the United States actually curtailed reparations in late 1949, Japan had disbursed $3 billion in overseas assets and $35 million in industrial equipment. Much later, in the mid-1950s, Japan reopened the issue and negotiated a series of final settlements which cost another $1 billion.[16]

The Replacement of MacArthur's Economic Advisory Team

From the very beginning, Douglas MacArthur got along quite well with George Atcheson, his State Department Political Adviser, and even better with Max Bishop, Atcheson's assistant. Indeed, the General saw to it that both men received the Congressional Medal of Merit, but he allowed them precious little influence on occupation policies. Dean Acheson, then

Undersecretary of State, quietly accepted this state of affairs until early 1947. On January 5, George Atcheson cabled a warning to the State Department that the Japanese economy was virtually bankrupt and that the importance of Japan's difficulties could not be overemphasized. Acheson and Secretary of State George Marshall, in cooperation with the Departments of War and Agriculture, responded by sending out a large mission, headed by Colonel Raymond Harrison. Harrison, an Agriculture Department analyst and a respected veteran of earlier fact-finding trips to the Far East, ostensibly carried orders to study the food situation in Japan and Korea; actually, he studied far more. In a preliminary report issued on February 15, Harrison offered extensive recommendations on Japan's industry, agriculture, and foreign trade. He also threw in a bombshell: MacArthur's existing staff was inadequate to carry out any of the recommendations. Harrison ended his treatise with an exhaustive list of all the experts that would be necessary for a complete overhaul of MacArthur's bureaucracy.[17]

Several weeks later, Acheson received the final version of Harrison's report, as well as the reports of Clifford Strike and Edwin W. Pauley, each of whom led missions to Japan to investigate the reparations issue. On April 14, Acheson reacted with a long memorandum to Secretary of War Robert Patterson. After citing Japan's "increasing difficulties," Acheson contended that the findings of the Harrison and Strike missions indicated "the necessity for making available to General MacArthur civilian personnel of outstanding skill and experience to deal with the economic and financial aspects of the occupation." In particular, Acheson elaborated, MacArthur needed much more highly qualified personnel to handle "food and agriculture, rationing and price controls, restoration of trade and industry, allocation of raw materials, currency and public finance, labor relations and the effectuation of the reparations program." Acheson concluded his missive with a bold appeal for joint action: "I should like, as a matter of great urgency, to explore with you all possible steps to introduce into the staff of the Supreme Commander a quality of personnel and experience comparable to that which has been made available to the Office of Military Government in Germany. The State Department stands ready to assist the War Department in all practicable action to this end. . . ." Patterson, however, proved to be in no hurry to impugn MacArthur's competence, and when Acheson left the State Department in mid-1947, the matter remained unresolved.[18]

Worse still, the issue of upgrading MacArthur's staff soon became intertwined with the equally vexatious question of what to do with the *zaibatsu,* Japan's family-owned business conglomerates. By some estimates, the *zaibatsu* controlled as much as 75 percent of Japan's industrial, financial, and commercial activities, and many U.S. planners held the *zaibatsu* system partly responsible for what Acheson once called Japan's "will to war." In 1945–46, SWNCC and SCAP formulated a series of policies (centering on FEC 230) which mandated the complete dissolution of the *zaibatsu*—including such corporate giants as Toyota and Mitsubishi. MacArthur, after some initial resistance, set up a sweeping *zaibatsu* dissolution program and made the whole concept his own. Over the next two years, the *zaibatsu* suffered serious losses, but MacArthur's program never came close to achieving its objective.[19]

Beginning in late 1947, a close-knit group of high-level policymakers began to challenge the efficacy of the *zaibatsu* dissolution concept. This group consisted of James V. Forrestal, Secretary of Defense; Paul H. Nitze, Deputy Director of the State Department's Office of International Trade; William H. Draper, Jr., Undersecretary of the Army; and George F. Kennan, Director of the State Department's Policy Planning Staff (PPS). Before entering government service, Forrestal, Nitze, and Draper had all worked at Dillon, Read, and Company, a prestigious Wall Street investment firm. Forrestal was the firm's president, Nitze its vice-president, and Draper a senior partner. Forrestal first drew Nitze into government service and then handpicked Draper to be his Undersecretary of the Army. In early 1947, Forrestal also made himself the chief mentor of George F. Kennan, eventually helping him to become Director of the PPS. Although Acheson blocked Kennan's attempt to make Nitze his deputy, the two men set up an informal working relationship within hours after Acheson left office, and thereafter Kennan frequently turned to Nitze for economic advice.[20]

Through a well-planned series of special missions to Japan and high-level reports on its problems, the team of Nitze, Draper, Forrestal, and Kennan gradually amassed sufficient evidence to challenge MacArthur's handling of the Japanese economy. In April of 1948, Draper announced that the United States intended to dismantle most of MacArthur's *zaibatsu* dissolution program, and in September a team of experts, the Deconcentration Review Board, arrived in Tokyo to accomplish the task. MacArthur complained bitterly about the Wall Street "tycoons" who were whittling away his authority, but the "tycoons" still had a few more surprises. First, they constructed a new policy on Japan (NSC 13 / 2, approved October 9, 1948) which ordered MacArthur to shift some of his power to the Japanese government. Next, Nitze and Draper drew up a new blueprint for the Japanese economy ("Economic Stabilization in Japan"), which centered around "fiscal, monetary, price, and wage stability, and maximum production for export." Finally, when their plan was nearly complete, Draper wondered aloud whom they should put in charge of its implementation. Nitze suggested Joseph M. Dodge, a longtime friend and prominent Detroit banker. The National Security Council (NSC, which succeeded SWNCC) approved the Nitze-Draper plan on December 10. Before the day was out, President Truman added his approval and publicly announced the appointment of Dodge to be a senior adviser to MacArthur.[21]

Thus, by the time Dean Acheson returned as Secretary of

State in January of 1949, Nitze, Draper, Forrestal, and Kennan had created a new economic policy for Japan and chosen Joseph Dodge to oversee its implementation. They had not, however, brought MacArthur himself to bay. On the contrary, the General swiftly created a committee of high-ranking officers to which he expected Dodge to report. This arrangement, if left unchallenged, would have rendered Dodge impotent and left MacArthur's authority intact. In a meeting on January 26, Kenneth Royall and William Draper, Secretary and Undersecretary of the Army, cautioned Acheson that he would immediately have to find some countermove for MacArthur's bureaucratic gambit. Acheson, working closely with W. Walton Butterworth, his Director of Far Eastern Affairs, devised a three-part solution. First, he persuaded Truman to bestow upon Dodge the rank of Minister, the highest rank available and one which Dodge himself requested. Second, in a cordial and carefully worded letter, Acheson personally apprised MacArthur of Dodge's mission and credentials. Third, Acheson ordered Max Bishop, his Chief of Northeast Asian Affairs and perhaps the only man in the State Department still on amicable terms with MacArthur, to serve as Dodge's escort. All three parts worked to perfection, and Dodge received the complete cooperation of MacArthur and his minions.[22]

Yet, even after MacArthur accepted Dodge, he still resisted the transfer of his own political authority to the Japanese government—particularly in the area of economic reform. Bishop, during his visit to Japan, investigated the problem. In a two-hour interview on February 3, 1949, MacArthur told Bishop that the State Department could best help Japan by backing a U.S. commitment on Taiwan, blocking Pentagon efforts to rearm Japan, and curtailing Japan's reparations payments. Bishop cabled all of this back to the State Department and then added one thing more. At the end of the conversation, MacArthur emphasized that while he had not always agreed with recent State Department policies, he felt that "the Far East in general and Japan in particular had been given a full hearing when Mr. Acheson was Undersecretary of State; and that he welcomed Mr. Acheson's appointment as Secretary because he felt once again Japan would receive its full measure of attention."[23]

General William F. Marquat, Chief of SCAP's Economic and Scientific Section, shared MacArthur's hope that Acheson would be open to SCAP's point of view. In a private meeting, Marquat even tried to convince Bishop that the State Department was still "100% behind" the *zaibatsu* dissolution program. Bishop, as tough as he was affable, coldly disabused his old friend of such illusions. The time had come, Bishop admonished, to " 'call off the dogs' and give the Japanese a chance to run their own business." Bishop concluded his investigation with a personal tour of the Tokyo-Yokohama area. Upon returning to Washington, he reported to Butterworth that although the Japanese economy showed some signs of improvement, housing was "in desperate need," transportation was "woefully inadequate," and industrial activity was "a pygmy compared to prewar days." Japan was "at a crossroads," Bishop asserted, and the State Department needed to immediately "bring about a change in the character of the occupation," even if it took the intervention of the President himself to break the "impasse" with SCAP.[24]

Butterworth forwarded Bishop's report to Acheson, along with a warning that "excessive interference and assumption of governmental responsibility by SCAP" were already "making the Japanese increasingly restless." Acheson agreed completely and worked closely with Butterworth and Bishop to clarify U.S. objectives. The resulting policy (NSC 13 / 3) re-scripted MacArthur's role in the most unequivocal terms: "Henceforth, emphasis should be given to Japanese assimilation of the reform programs," while SCAP itself should proceed to "relax pressure steadily but unobtrusively on the Japanese Government in connection with these reforms." In effect, Acheson lined up his own authority and that of the President behind Bishop's simple demand—"call off the dogs." He also reiterated the Nitze-Draper theme that recovery, not reform, should be MacArthur's chief priority: "Second only to U.S. security interests, economic recovery should be made the primary objective of United States policy in Japan for the coming period." Truman and the NSC approved the new policy statement on May 6, 1949, and on the tenth, Cloyce K. Huston, the State Department's Counselor of Mission in Japan, forcefully enunciated it to an assemblage of MacArthur's top administrators. This time, they listened. On July 28, MacArthur decreed that the Military Government Section of his Eighth Army and all forty-five of its civil affairs teams would be abolished by the end of the year. Six days later, he announced the "completion" of his *zaibatsu* dissolution program.[25]

The process which Acheson had begun two years earlier was now complete. MacArthur rapidly relinquished his authority, passing it to Joseph Dodge and the Japanese government. Nitze, soon to replace Kennan as Director of the PPS, felt that Dodge should receive only the State Department's support, not its interference. Acheson agreed. Dodge—backed by Acheson, the Pentagon, and MacArthur —expeditiously pressured the Japanese government into accepting balanced budgets, modern accounting procedures, and a reduced rate of monetary growth. Dodge likewise persuaded the Japanese to adopt a long series of measures (including a revised monetary exchange rate) which were designed to foster the steady expansion of exports. This "Dodge Line," together with SCAP's earlier reforms and the well-timed election of a much stronger Japanese government, dampened inflation and created financial stability. Dodge's tight monetary policy triggered a mild recession, but it quickly gave way to sustained economic growth. The Japanese standard of living had reached 70 percent of its prewar level by mid-1950. Japan's industrial production, which stood at just 54.6 percent of its prewar level in 1948, reached 71 percent in 1949, 83.6 percent in 1950, and 114.4 percent in 1951. Industrial production would continue to rise, attaining more than twice its prewar level by 1956. The trade situation improved as well, but much more slowly. Japan's total foreign trade had climbed to only 40 percent of its prewar level by mid-1950, and trade deficits remained a serious problem. The Japanese trade deficit dropped from $425 million in 1948 to $154 million in 1950; it then shot up to $640 million in 1951 and remained high for the rest of the decade.[26]

The Negotiation of a Peace Treaty

The framing of a peace settlement to end the technical state of war in Asia also necessitated a long and difficult campaign. In late 1946, Acheson, as Undersecretary of State, ordered work to begin on a draft treaty, and at the Moscow conference in early 1947, Secretary of State Marshall pressed the Council of Foreign Ministers to take up this issue "in the near future." To further expedite the process, Acheson and John Carter Vincent, Director of the Office of Far Eastern Affairs, secured the cooperation of MacArthur's staff and reassigned the treaty-drafting process to a special six-member working group. In June, the State Department invited the ambassadors of several key nations to a special meeting, and when it opened on July 1, 1947, the U.S. representative proposed an eleven-nation peace conference to be held in San Francisco on August 19, 1947.[27]

Acheson left the State Department the day before this meeting took place, and, in his absence, his plans for a treaty began to unravel. The U.S. proposal for an eleven-nation peace conference received a mixed response. Ten nations expressed varying degrees of interest, while the eleventh, the Soviet Union, withheld its cooperation altogether. Max Bishop, who had then just completed his tour of duty as the Assistant State Department Political Adviser to MacArthur, tried to revitalize the

U.S. effort. His logic could not be denied: "It is impractical to attempt measures to revive the economies of the Far East until the existence of a state of war has been resolved." Hugh Borton—Chief of the Office of Northeast Asian Affairs and one of the planners Acheson had originally assigned to the issue—finally completed a draft treaty on August 5, 1947, but it ran into heavy criticism from John Davies, a Far East expert on Kennan's Policy Planning Staff. Davies argued that Borton had concerned himself too much with "drastic disarmament and democratization under continuing international supervision, including the U.S.S.R." Kennan promptly backed Davies, and the PPS reported that it could find "no satisfactory evidence that Japanese society would be politically or economically stable if turned loose and left to its own devices." Once the United States terminated its occupation, Kennan warned, it would not be able to prevent the "communist penetration" of Japan. In the ensuing showdown, Kennan, Davies, and the PPS simply outgunned Borton, Bishop, and the Office of Northeast Asian Affairs. The NSC adopted a new policy on Japan in October (NSC 13 / 2), and it specified that the United States would "not press for a treaty of peace at this time."[28]

The peace treaty issue remained dormant throughout 1948, but when Acheson returned as Secretary of State in January of 1949, MacArthur asked the State Department to draft a new treaty based on the complete demilitarization of Japan. Three years earlier, MacArthur had all but dictated a constitution to the Japanese government. (Dean Rusk later quipped that the document's chief flaw was that it did not translate well into Japanese!) Included in the new constitution were numerous restrictions on future rearmament, all of which the war-weary Japanese people warmly embraced. Max Bishop, now the State Department's Chief of Northeast Asian Affairs, understood Japanese sentiments and exhorted Acheson to accept MacArthur's approach. The JCS, however, immediately objected. Japanese industry and the American bases in Japan, according to Pentagon planners, were vital to U.S. security, and the JCS refused to accept any formula which might leave the former at risk and sacrifice the latter. The Wall Street team of Nitze, Forrestal, and Draper might have made short work of this dispute, but in March, Louis A. Johnson replaced Forrestal as Secretary of Defense and Tracy S. Voorhees replaced Draper as Undersecretary of the Army. Both men threw their support behind the JCS, and Johnson soon manifested an overweening animosity toward Acheson.[29]

Acheson, though he accepted Bishop's arguments, hesitated to challenge the Joint Chiefs of Staff on a matter of strategic planning. Indeed, he even joined with other members of the NSC in early May to forge a new Japan policy (NSC 13 / 3) which further postponed the treaty debate. Before the month was out, however, Acheson formally requested the JCS to reexamine its position. In a terse response ("Strategic Evaluation of United States Security Needs in Japan"), the Pentagon contended that a peace treaty was still premature, since "aggressive communist expansion" made it "essential that Japan's democracy and western orientation first be established beyond all question." In July, MacArthur again asked Acheson to push for a peace treaty, and William J. Sebald, the State Department's adviser to MacArthur, followed up with an even more cogent appeal for action. On September 9, M. E. Dening, Britain's Assistant Undersecretary for the Far East, held a special meeting with Butterworth, and he too recommended an early peace conference. The Soviet Union and the People's Republic of China might refuse to cooperate, Dening conceded, but, if necessary, a treaty could be approved without them. Acheson took up the issue with Ernest Bevin, the British Foreign Minister, four days later. In a candid exchange, Bevin promised to line up the British Commonwealth behind an early treaty, and Acheson agreed to draw in the Joint Chiefs of Staff. Acheson and Bevin also ordered their staffs to jointly produce a general scenario for treaty negotiations before the upcoming

Commonwealth conference, subsequently scheduled for January 9, 1950.[30]

Acheson needed three things: the Pentagon's cooperation, a draft treaty, and a rock-solid base of support within his own department. On October 3, 1949, he asked the JCS to again review the issue. Ten days later, Butterworth and Kennan completed a draft treaty. Acheson then assembled a conclave of experts, "The Consultants on the Far East," and worked closely with them to establish a general consensus on Asian policy. The United States, the consultants reaffirmed, should seek to "bring about a peace treaty as soon as possible." But the Pentagon still held out. In its third review of the issue, forwarded to Acheson on December 22, the Joint Chiefs of Staff rehashed all of its old arguments and added one more: neither the Soviet Union nor the People's Republic of China would accept a peace treaty which allowed the United States to retain its bases in Japan, and U.S. strategists still deemed these bases indispensable. On the twenty-fourth, Acheson and four of his advisers took up the matter directly with Omar N. Bradley, Chairman of the JCS, but Bradley held firm.[31]

Acheson pulled back and reorganized his campaign. First, turning to the British Foreign Office, he explained that while unresolved security problems had slowed his progress, he would "continue to work intensively at formulating a definite United States Government position." Next, when the NSC adopted a comprehensive policy on the Far East (NSC 48 / 1 and NSC 48 / 2), Acheson made certain that it included no statement of any kind on a Japanese peace treaty. Finally, in a private session with Truman on February 20, Acheson secured permission to commence work on a new NSC paper dealing exclusively with the treaty question. By these actions, Acheson kept the issue alive while his advisers searched for some way to get the upper hand against the JCS. The solution took everyone, including Acheson, completely by surprise.[32]

One evening in March of 1950, Lucius Battle, Acheson's

personal assistant, received an unexpected phone call from Carl W. McCardle, a newspaper reporter, who had just finished a long conversation with John Foster Dulles. Dulles, a leading Republican foreign affairs specialist, had once worked in the Truman State Department but had since blasted the President during a failed bid for the governorship of New York. In the course of a long-winded narrative, McCardle told Battle that Dulles now regretted his attacks on Truman and desired a new position in the State Department. The next morning, Battle recapitulated this to Undersecretary of State James Webb and suggested that giving Dulles a post would help to foster a bipartisan foreign policy. Webb, absolutely astonished, replied tartly, "Have you lost your mind?" A few weeks later, while traveling with Acheson, Battle opened a telegram from Webb to the Secretary which recommended bringing Dulles back into the State Department. Battle, smiling inwardly, passed the message to Acheson, who muttered aloud, "Has he lost his mind?" Acheson, though he loathed Dulles, eventually succumbed to Battle's logic and cabled Webb to take the issue to the White House. Webb plucked up his courage, ventured over to the Oval Office, and eased into the question. "Have you lost your mind!" Truman exploded, donning a look of utter consternation. Undaunted, Webb pressed his case, and Truman agreed to take the matter under advisement.[33]

Senator Arthur Vandenberg, the Republican mainstay of administration efforts to sustain a bipartisan foreign policy, weighed in on March 31 with a letter urging Acheson to support the Dulles appointment, but, contrary to much that was written later, this letter did not play a major role. In a telephone conversation with Acheson on April 4, Truman declared that after "thinking the matter over," he had decided to give Dulles a position; only then did Acheson relate the details of Vandenberg's letter. Dean Rusk, who replaced Butterworth as Assistant Secretary for Far Eastern Affairs in March, quickly persuaded Acheson to assign Dulles to the Japanese peace treaty.

Dulles objected that he had little expertise on Japan. Acheson replied that he did not need an expert, only someone with good judgment. Dulles accepted the appointment and persuaded John Allison, now Chief of the Office of Northeast Asian Affairs, to take on the additional responsibility of serving as his deputy. Thanks largely to the catalytic charm of Dean Rusk, these strange bedfellows—Acheson, Rusk, Allison, and Dulles—not only worked well together but became a formidable team.[34]

The Dulles appointment instantly gave Acheson the high ground he had been seeking in the peace treaty debate, but Tracy Voorhees, Undersecretary of the Army, countered Acheson's maneuver with one of his own. On March 23, Voorhees offered a token compromise: the State Department could negotiate a treaty covering all political and economic issues, as long as it left the U.S. occupation of Japan otherwise unchanged. Acheson, his patience at an end, girded his loins for battle and scheduled a meeting with Johnson, Voorhees, and the entire JCS for April 24. When the meeting opened, Acheson fired the first volley. He rejected the Voorhees proposal out of hand and accused the JCS of deliberately setting up requirements that would make "the conclusion of a peace treaty impossible." The choice the United States faced in Japan, Acheson warned angrily, was not between a satisfactory situation and an alternative but between "a deteriorating situation and an alternative." Johnson jumped in to defend the JCS, but in the end even he hedged on one significant point. The JCS wanted to table the question for another six months; Johnson, who had just scheduled a fact-finding trip to Japan, asked only to postpone the debate until he returned in early July. Acheson grudgingly agreed.[35]

One month later, on June 24 (Washington time), North Korea invaded South Korea, radically altering the whole situation in the Far East. Acheson, making skillful use of the crisis, immediately won Truman's support for an early treaty with Japan. The JCS thereupon gave its approval as well, provided that

Japan agreed to rearm and accept U.S. bases on its soil. Japan promptly did just that. Truman, faced with a stack of recommendations on the treaty itself, brushed them all aside, penned his own prescription for a brief instrument of reconciliation, and sent Dulles out into the world, briefcase in hand, to negotiate a settlement. According to John F. Melby, an analyst in the Office of Philippine and Southeast Asian Affairs, Dulles quietly stretched his authority to make "a lot of shady deals." The war-ravaged Philippines, for example, insisted on a strong reparations clause, something Japan steadfastly opposed. To the Filipinos, Dulles offered assurances that a weak clause would suffice, since the United States intended to force Japan to pay up; to the Japanese, he offered assurances that they could continue to ignore their obligations to the Philippines. By early 1951, Dulles had put together a comprehensive understanding with Japanese Prime Minister Shigeru Yoshida. Corollary understandings with other governments soon followed. On July 20, Acheson sent out invitations for a fifty-one-nation peace conference, and with them he enclosed copies of a newly completed Anglo-American draft treaty.[36]

The San Francisco peace conference opened on September 4, 1951. Acheson, who personally served as its presiding officer, confronted two formidable foes—an intestinal virus and the Soviet Union. Acheson's intestinal malady struck just two days before the conference, and it seriously threatened his pivotal role. Almost from the opening gavel, reporters speculated about a mysterious young man who occasionally approached the podium to whisper in Acheson's ear. Was this at last one of those communists that Senator Joseph McCarthy warned about so often? In fact, the young man was Lucius Battle, Acheson's personal assistant; his sedition consisted of regular reminders for Acheson to take his medication. But that was not all. The President himself attended the opening of the conference, and on the evening of the fourth, Acheson gave a special reception for him in the Pied Piper Room of the Palace

Hotel. Somehow, Acheson survived the reception without incident, but just when his ordeal seemed over, Truman invited him and a number of others up to his private suite. The President played requests on a convenient piano with smiles and laughter; an assortment of the well-heeled and the well-connected savored the moment; and Acheson suffered in silence. Battle repeatedly urged Acheson to retire to his room, but his loyalty to Truman would countenance nothing of the kind. Finally, Battle discretely apprised the President of the situation. Truman, without a moment's hesitation, abandoned his piano, marched across the room, and vociferously ordered his Secretary of State off to bed, as if he were a small boy up past his bedtime.[37]

By comparison, finding an antidote for Soviet designs proved a simple matter. The first item on the agenda was the rules of procedure. When the Soviets offered motions to amend the Anglo-American draft treaty, Acheson ruled them out of order until the rules of procedure had been adopted. Then, once the rules were in place, the Soviets discovered that their motions to amend were still out of order because Acheson's team had pushed through a set of rules which confined all deliberations to the existing draft treaty. "It took the Russians," Dean Rusk later recounted, "about three days to discover what had happened to them; we really boxed the Russians in with the rules of procedure for that conference." On September 8, 1951, Prime Minister Yoshida signed the peace treaty, followed by the United States and forty-seven other nations. (The Soviet Union, Poland, and Czechoslovakia refused to sign; Indonesia and the Philippines signed but subsequently withheld final ratification pending a reparations settlement.) The same day, Yoshida also signed a mutual security treaty with the United States, which Dean Rusk had negotiated in secret over the preceding months.[38]

The Restoration of Japan's
Regional Trade

Acheson's final option for dealing with Japan's economic crisis—the restoration of Japan's Asian trade—was both the most complicated and the most important. In 1934–36, over 64 percent of Japan's exports and 53 percent of its imports resulted from regional trade. In 1947, regional trade provided just 6 percent of Japan's imports, while all of Japan's exports, including those within the region, dropped to a mere 4.3 percent of their prewar average. Acheson, who understood Japan's regional trade system from his experiences as Assistant Secretary of State for Economic Affairs, came early to the conclusion that this system would have to be rebuilt. Japan's prewar trade in the Far East had three principal parts. First, China received 18 percent of Japan's exports and supplied 10 percent of its imports. Second, all of Southeast Asia received 19 percent of Japan's exports and supplied 17 percent of its imports. Third, and most important, Japan's other Asian trading partners—chiefly its imperial possessions, Korea and Taiwan—received 27 percent of its exports and supplied 26 percent of its imports. Acheson therefore designed his policies on Korea, Taiwan, China, and Southeast Asia to support his plans for Japanese recovery, but the full story of these policies must await subsequent chapters.[39]

Conclusion

From the outset, Acheson recognized that Japan held such strategic and economic importance that the United States would have to rebuild it as quickly as available means would permit. Initially, he intended to include Japan in the Marshall Plan, and even after he abandoned this approach, he continued to assign a very high priority to Japanese economic recovery. First as Undersecretary of State and later as Secretary, Acheson consistently worked to establish a recovery-oriented U.S. assistance program, relax restrictions on Japanese industry, develop a lenient reparations settlement, replace MacArthur's economic advisory staff, negotiate a comprehensive peace treaty, and reconstruct Japan's Asian trade network. After innumerable and hard-fought battles, he succeeded—to one extent or another—in each of these areas, and while his policies did not generate a full-blown Japanese recovery in the near term, they rescued Japan from impending economic collapse and gave it the means to achieve its long-term economic resurgence.

✔ CHAPTER THREE

Acheson and
the American Commitment
in Korea

To FULLY UNDERSTAND the origins of America's commitment in Korea it is necessary to recognize, first, that Korea was bound to Japan by the fetters of history and, second, that U.S. policy on Korea was neither consistent across time nor consistent within the branches of the Truman administration. There were, in fact, five successive Korean policies between 1947 and 1950, three of which were long-lasting and substantial: a policy of strong economic commitment during Acheson's tenure as Undersecretary of State, a policy of liquidating this commitment following his resignation, and a policy of renewed economic commitment after he became Secretary of State. During the two periods of commitment, American policy focused primarily on Korea's economic and psychological importance to Japan—with the implications of ideology, the exigencies of American politics, and the imperatives of U.S. prestige all confined to subsidiary roles. Differences between Acheson's regional economic vision and the Pentagon's global strategic vision led first to the eclipse of America's commitment in Korea following Acheson's 1947 resignation and then to tragic inconsistencies in the renewed commitment following his 1949 return. Ultimately, of course, Acheson's approach to Korean policy prevailed, but at an unanticipated and terrible price.

The First Stage:
September 1946–June 1947

Toward the end of the Second World War, Britain, China, and the Soviet Union agreed to join the United States in a four-power trusteeship for Korea, the modus operandi of which was a pair of U.S.-USSR committees. As part of this arrangement, the thirty-eighth parallel became a temporary demarcation line between the U.S. and Soviet armies of occupation. The State Department—according to Dean Rusk, who as a young army colonel helped to draw the demarcation line—initially favored stationing U.S. occupation forces "as far north on the mainland as possible, including some major points in Manchuria." But the U.S. Army refused to commit any substantial force on the Asian mainland, compelling the State Department to settle for that part of Korea below the thirty-eighth parallel. Unwittingly, U.S. planners chose the same line which had separated the Russian and Japanese spheres of influence prior to the Russo-Japanese War of 1904. The Soviets, given what must have seemed a restoration of their former position, thereafter refused to administer Korea as a single entity, and the two U.S.-USSR committees became deadlocked. The temporary demarcation line slowly evolved into both a political border and an economic boundary. A State Department report summarized the economic situation:

> Two-thirds of the agricultural resources, over two-thirds of the population, 90% of the textile plants, 65% of the food process-

ing plants, and 60% of the machine industry are located south
of the parallel. On the other hand, 90% of the iron and steel
industry, 85% of the chemical plants, and 90% of the electrical
generating power are located in the north.

Exacerbating these economic and political problems, the
American military government in southern Korea soon proved
itself poorly staffed and chronically ineffectual.[1]

By the time George C. Marshall became Secretary of State,
on January 8, 1947, the entire economy of southern Korea was
in serious trouble. John Carter Vincent, Director of the Office
of Far Eastern Affairs, recognized the problem and urgently
recommended a new diplomatic overture to Moscow, coupled
with a $50 million stopgap reconstruction grant for Korea. If
this failed, Vincent proposed to submit the entire Korean issue
to the UN. Secretary of War Robert H. Patterson supported a
similar aid formula for Korea, and the State-War-Navy Coordinating Committee (SWNCC) created the Special Interdepartmental Committee on Korea to consider the matter.[2]

But these were not the only options. Marshall, absorbed in
preparations for the upcoming Moscow conference, delegated
much of his policy-making role to his Undersecretary of State,
Dean Acheson, and during the period of the conference itself,
March 4–April 8, Acheson enjoyed still more influence as
Acting Secretary of State. Having served nearly four years as
Assistant Secretary of State for Economic Affairs, Acheson
had a superb grasp of world economics, and this included the
economics of Japan's prewar empire. He thoroughly understood the importance of Korea to Japan, and in 1946 he twice
told the press that it was "essential" for the United States to
rebuild Korea. This, of course, put Acheson (probably backed
by a few lower-level analysts) at odds with the limited assistance schemes of Vincent and Patterson. Acheson also held
the UN in much lower esteem than Vincent did. To examine
the assistance needs of both Korea and Japan, the Departments

of State, War, and Agriculture sent out a joint mission headed by Colonel Raymond Harrison. On February 15, 1947, the Harrison Mission issued a preliminary report which buttressed Acheson's position, and SWNCC's Special Interdepartmental Committee on Korea took up the issue just ten days later.[3]

The special committee considered four options: maintaining a policy of limited assistance (Vincent's primary plan), recognizing an independent nation in southern Korea as a means of liquidating the U.S. commitment (the concept favored by the Joint Chiefs of Staff), referring the issue to the UN (Vincent's alternative plan), and adopting "an aggressive, positive program for South Korea" (Acheson's approach). In a clear victory for Acheson, the committee selected his "aggressive, positive program" and specified that any mutual U.S.-USSR troop withdrawal would have to be based on adequate safeguards for Korea's territorial integrity. Fleshing out the details, SWNCC's special committee produced an astounding $600 million, three-year economic rehabilitation plan, which included $250 million for fiscal 1948 instead of the $137 million originally budgeted by the War Department. The committee also called for a "high commissioner" to replace the military governor and for the dispatch of a high-level business and industrial group to produce recommendations on facilitating Korean recovery. Of this $600 million, three-year package, fully $350 million would be earmarked for the revival of Korea's economy. (It puts these figures in some perspective to note that SWNCC then expected to spend roughly $500 million over several years to rebuild Japan.) Acheson's subordinates swiftly set to work molding the committee's aid figures into a bill that they could present to Congress.[4]

At the same time, Britain gradually abdicated its strategic osition in Greece and Turkey, and this issue became closely linked to Korean assistance. On September 8, 1946, Acheson had publicly declared that the United States should ''proceed in South Korea with the solution of urgent social and economic problems." He began work on aid to Greece and Turkey on September 24, and took that issue to the public on October 15. The Special Interdepartmental Committee on Korea endorsed Acheson's "positive program" for Korea on February 25, 1947; Truman endorsed Acheson's "positive program" for Greece and Turkey on February 26. The 1947 portion of the three-year Korean aid package came to $250 million; the aid proposed for both Greece and Turkey for 1947 totaled $400 million.[5]

In addition, Acheson chaired a committee charged with writing a speech to explain his aid strategy. At his insistence, the speech included sweeping language to the effect that American assistance should be primarily economic and should "assist free peoples to work out their own destinies." Truman delivered the speech to Congress on March 12, 1947, announcing at the same time Acheson's $400 million program for Greece and Turkey. The next day, Acheson went before the Senate Committee on Foreign Relations to defend what the press quickly dubbed the "Truman Doctrine." There, Senator H. Alexander Smith, a Republican, questioned the wisdom of the new policy's broad rhetoric and asked if it might not be more prudent to limit American commitments to "certain strategic areas." Acheson began his reply by enumerating countries where U.S. assistance would indeed be ill advised, but then, shifting suddenly to the offensive, he declared, "There are other places where we can be effective. One of them is Korea, and I think that is another place where the line is clearly drawn between the Russians and ourselves." Acheson mentioned no other nations. His intention was unmistakable—to closely follow up his aid package for Greece and Turkey with his aid package for southern Korea. Thus, from its earliest inception to the day of Truman's speech, Acheson expected immediately to apply the Truman Doctrine not just to Greece and Turkey, as many later assumed, but to Korea as well.[6]

Yet, before the other shoe could fall, Acheson had to bring

his developing Korean aid legislation into line with budgetary constraints. In a March 28 memorandum to Secretary of War Patterson, he revised the total three-year aid figure to $540 million and the portion for fiscal 1948 to $215 million. Acheson also indicated that he wanted the Pentagon to rapidly transfer its administrative responsibility for Korea to the State Department. Patterson, who considered Korea to be little more than a drain on army resources, replied that, in his view, the United States should "get out of Korea at an early date." He expressed doubts that Acheson's aid plan would prove to be either "feasible or remunerative," and he predicted an "adverse reaction" in Congress. Even so, the Pentagon had already lost this debate in the SWNCC special committee on Korea, and Patterson resigned himself to supporting Acheson's aid program—provided that it would eventually lead to "at least a very substantial reduction in our [the U.S. Army's] commitments in Korea." At the same time, Marshall, who was in Moscow, sent Acheson the first draft of a letter to the Soviets on Korea. Acheson thoroughly rewrote it, adding some very strident language, and Marshall submitted Acheson's version to the Soviets. Subsequent negotiations produced a brief renewal of talks in one of the two U.S.-USSR committees, but these talks achieved nothing.[7]

By this time, Acheson and Paul Nitze, his longtime friend and the Deputy Director of the State Department's Office of International Trade, had already begun to grapple with the worsening trade deficits which afflicted America's trading partners. In a sketchy initial version of what later became the Marshall Plan, they devised a scheme to rebuild the economies of America's trading partners in order to safeguard America's own record exports and, indeed, America's whole fragile economy. Their plan focused on "the reconstruction of the two great workshops of Europe and Asia—Germany and Japan." In mid-May, Acheson abandoned Nitze's two-front version of the nascent Marshall Plan in favor of a Europe-first version, as advocated by George Kennan, Director of the Policy Planning Staff. Nevertheless, Acheson ordered work to continue on a scaled-down aid program for Japan, and he made no change whatsoever in his exorbitantly expensive plans for Korea.[8]

Even Paul Nitze, the principal exponent of a larger U.S. assistance role in the Far East, saw Korea as a hopeless "basket case." Acheson, however, had come to understand Japan's prewar trade system while implementing sanctions against it in 1941; he knew that Korea was Japan's most important source of imported food. Acheson also knew from the findings of the Harrison Mission that Japan needed food now more than ever. Harrison reported that, before World War II, Japan had imported approximately 30 percent of its food, primarily rice. Between 1937 and 1946, the war nearly eliminated these food imports, while repatriation and an extremely high birthrate ballooned Japan's population from 73 million to 78 million. During 1946, Douglas MacArthur, Commander in Chief in the Far East, narrowly saved at least 11 million Japanese from starvation, but even so he provided a daily ration of only 900 calories per person—less than half the prewar 2,200. The desperate Japanese, according to Harrison, ground up various waste materials—including silk cocoons, nearly worthless following the advent of nylon—to supplement their meager supplies of flour, and still tens of thousands of people roamed Japan's riverbanks searching for roots and grasses to eat as "stomach fillers." Overall, Harrison estimated, only about 45 percent of Japan's population could be described as "self-suppliers" in food. To feed the rest, American planners predicted, the United States would have to supply 1,891,000 rice-equivalent tons of food in 1947 alone, accounting for most of a relief assistance bill that would exceed $330 million.[9]

Before the war (1938), Korea exported 1,865,000 tons of rice to Japan annually, about two-thirds of Japan's prewar rice imports and 98.6 percent of the total food imports the United States would have to provide in 1947. Southern Korea had grown 77 percent of Korea's rice, and when domestic consumption was factored into total production, it was clear that the South provided nearly all of Korea's exportable surplus. Moreover, the Koreans had used only limited amounts of fertilizer, each ton of which could yield approximately seven tons of food. If the United States could first restore and then increase the availability of fertilizer, southern Korea alone might eventually meet most of Japan's food import requirements. Acheson's Korean aid program therefore centered on "fertilizer plants, hydro and steam generating plants, and additional mining facilities." State Department planners projected that much of the additional mining and generating capacity would service the fertilizer plants, which in turn would facilitate the level of agricultural production necessary to restore Korea's rice exports to Japan. Acheson and his subordinates also hoped to rebuild southern Korea's sizable fishing industry, which had earlier exported large quantities of fish to Japan.[10]

Only slightly less important was the Korean market. The United States would have to support Japan until it achieved a favorable balance of trade. But in 1947, U.S. trade accounted for 92 percent of Japan's imports and only 12 percent of its exports. Clearly, Japan's Asian markets would have to be restored. On February 25, 1947, the Harrison Mission reviewed its findings before a subcommittee of the House Appropriations Committee, and Colonel Harrison forcefully summarized its conclusions: "You are not going to get industrial recovery in the Orient unless Japan is permitted to resume, in part at least, its prewar role of an industrial supplier of Korea and that area." Since Acheson's economic rehabilitation program for Korea would restore not only its exports but its markets as well, Acheson saw this program as nothing less than the cornerstone of his Japan-centered plan for regional economic recovery in the Far East.[11]

By reducing the Korean aid program's overall cost to $540 million, and the cost of its first year to $215 million, Acheson

barely managed to secure the approval of Truman's noto-
riously tightfisted Bureau of the Budget. Then, on May 20,
Acheson took his plan in person to the Senate Committee on
Foreign Relations as a first step toward presenting it to Congress. The War Department had earlier proposed to limit U.S.
assistance for Korea to a basic relief package costing roughly
$137 million. Calling this proposal insufficient, Acheson
pleaded, "We have got to do more, and my guess is that it
would probably be about $78 million more [equaling the $215
million of his plan's first year], in the direction of establishing
some sort of plants for the manufacture of fertilizer and a few
other things of that sort." After elaborating on the importance
of fertilizer in Korean agriculture, he concluded with a stark
warning that unless the United States acted firmly, the Soviet
Union would "take over the whole business." Unmoved, the
Senate Committee on Foreign Relations decided for procedural reasons that the bill would have to go to the Armed Services Committees in both the House and the Senate.[12]

Realizing that the House Armed Services Committee would
probably not have time to consider his Korean aid bill during
the current congressional session, Acheson next paid a visit to
Senator Arthur H. Vandenberg, a Republican and the Chairman of the Senate Committee on Foreign Relations. Faced with
a Republican-dominated Congress, Acheson and Marshall had
already devised a secret strategy. First, they raised "the banner
of bipartisanship," Paul Nitze later recounted, and then they
looked for "a fracture in the other party." "The fracture they
located," Nitze recalled, "was that between Vandenberg and
[Senator Robert A.] Taft." Hoping to widen this split, Acheson and Marshall quietly began to "build up Vandenberg, who
had been a thoroughly second-rate politician," and in time they
managed to "make a statesman of him." Vandenberg recipro-
cated by helping Acheson secure congressional approval for
the aid to Greece and Turkey, but, according to a contemporary memorandum, when Acheson approached him on the

Korean aid bill, the two men settled upon an "alternative procedure." If Acheson's initial plan to bring the bill before the
House Armed Services Committee proved "impracticable," the
Democrats would start it in the House Committee on Foreign
Affairs. From there, it would proceed to Vandenberg's committee in the Senate, though not before the next congressional
session. Even if Acheson could find a way to bring the bill
before the Senate in the current session, Vandenberg sternly
advised against it. Having thus gone to extraordinary lengths
to ensure that his Korean aid program would be considered in
Congress by early 1948, Acheson left the State Department,
as previously scheduled, on June 30, 1947. Thereafter, the
Korean aid bill, minus its only important advocate, foundered
in a sea of indifference. The State Department—"due to the
rush of business at the close of the [1947] session and the
feeling of congressional leaders that the program could not
then be passed"—withdrew the bill from further consideration
before the end of the year.[13]

The Second Stage:
July 1947–January 1949

With Acheson's departure, the American commitment in
Korea commenced a precipitous decline. SWNCC created an
ad hoc committee to write a complete policy statement on Korea
and designated John Allison, the State Department's Assistant
Chief of Northeast Asian Affairs, as its steering member. Allison, in a July 29 memorandum, recommended calling a meeting of the four nations of the Korean trusteeship in order to set
up elections for a unified Korean government. If the Soviets
rejected this idea, he postulated, the whole issue could then be
submitted to the UN. Allison also urged the State Department
to continue supporting Acheson's "positive program" for
rebuilding southern Korea. Utilizing Allison's diplomatic sce-

nario but omitting any reference to Acheson's aid plan, the ad hoc committee rapidly formulated a new Korean policy (SWNCC 176 / 30, adopted on August 4, 1947). This policy called for a continuation of U.S. economic assistance to southern Korea (at unspecified levels), and acknowledged that U.S. withdrawal would lead to communist domination. But the new policy's principal statement of purpose clearly reflected the agenda of the Pentagon: "Every effort should be made, however, to liquidate or reduce the U.S. commitment of men and money in Korea as soon as possible without abandoning Korea to Soviet domination."[14]

Translating policy into action, Marshall implemented Allison's diplomatic scenario step by step—only to find the Soviet Union unwilling to negotiate. Moreover, Joseph Jacobs, the American Political Adviser in Korea, warned that the situation there had become so serious that the United States might have to "abandon this country willy nilly." Finally, on September 17, Marshall submitted the whole issue to the UN. The Soviets countered by calling for the immediate withdrawal of all foreign troops from Korea. Anticipating this move, SWNCC had already requested the Joint Chiefs of Staff (JCS) to evaluate the effects of a complete U.S. military withdrawal from Korea on the security of the United States. The JCS, led by General Dwight D. Eisenhower, produced an unequivocal response: "The United States has little strategic interest in maintaining the present troops and bases in Korea." The Joint Chiefs added that the two divisions stationed in Korea were sorely needed elsewhere. President Truman had slashed his defense budget from $81.6 billion in 1945 to only $13.1 billion in 1947, and the JCS saw withdrawal from Korea as one means for bringing its attenuated resources into line with its expanding commitments. But Syngman Rhee—a contentious, right-wing political leader who was beginning to consolidate power in southern Korea—instantly demanded an ongoing U.S. military presence.[15]

In the ensuing debate, the Joint Chiefs of Staff found an extremely important ally inside the State Department—George Kennan, Director of the PPS. Kennan, whose meteoric career owed much to the sponsorship of Secretary of the Navy James Forrestal, began organizing his staff in April, and when Acheson left the State Department in June, Kennan inherited most of Acheson's role in policy formulation. Already, Kennan had spoken out against the expansive wording of the Truman Doctrine, and now he opposed its application to Korea as well. Furthermore, Kennan's friendship with Forrestal (who in July became the first Secretary of Defense) provided him with a clear understanding of the Pentagon's implacable opposition to a long-term commitment in Korea. On September 24, in a memorandum to W. Walton Butterworth, Director of Far Eastern Affairs, Kennan outlined his position in the strongest terms. Since the JCS had deemed Korea "not militarily essential," he argued, "our policy should be to cut our losses and get out of there as gracefully as possible."[16]

On September 29, 1947, Marshall held a special meeting with his top advisers, including George Kennan; Walton Butterworth; Robert A. Lovett, Undersecretary of State; and Dean Rusk, Director of the Office of Special Political Affairs. They reached a consensus, after only a brief discussion, that the U.S. position in Korea was "untenable even with [the] expenditure of considerable U.S. money and effort." But since they also felt that America could ill afford to "scuttle and run," they decided to seek a settlement "which would enable the U.S. to withdraw from Korea as soon as possible with the minimum of bad effects." Two weeks later, Kennan's staff summarized the State Department's position with respect to Korea in a report on the world situation: "Since the territory is not of decisive strategic importance to us, our main task is to extricate ourselves without too great a loss of prestige."[17]

Obligingly, the UN facilitated this approach. It expeditiously approved a U.S.-sponsored resolution which called for

UN-supervised elections in Korea on March 31, 1948, and the withdrawal of all occupation forces within ninety days thereafter, "if possible." Meanwhile, SWNCC evolved into the State-Army-Navy-Air Force Coordinating Committee (SANACC, pronounced "sanak") and began to reexamine U.S. policy in a number of areas. On January 14, 1948, SANACC replaced the existing policy on Korea (SWNCC 176 / 30) with an expedient umbrella policy (SANACC 176 / 35). This combined the conclusions of Marshall's September meeting with the elements of the newly passed UN resolution. Just eight days later, the Soviets categorically rejected the UN resolution. General Charles Helmick, the Deputy Military Governor in the U.S. occupation zone, cautioned that if the elections proceeded only in the South, Syngman Rhee might receive 70–100 percent of the vote. Any government formed by Rhee, Helmick projected, would be inherently unstable. Nevertheless, to Marshall and Kennan, the creation of a separate state in southern Korea—even an unstable one—seemed the only way to unload an unwanted and increasingly embarrassing burden. Niles W. Bond, Marshall's Assistant Chief of Northeast Asian Affairs from late 1947 onward, supervised the actual implementation of Korean policy. Neither the State Department nor the Defense Department, Bond later recalled, thought that the United States "had any long-term interest in Korea," and both departments were "thinking then of how to liquidate this involvement." "There was a general tacit agreement between State and Defense," Bond reiterated, "that we should eventually disengage."[18]

But in spite of this "tacit agreement," W. Walton Butterworth (who had been appointed to replace Vincent at Acheson's insistence) continued to espouse Korea's regional importance, and he commenced a rear-guard action to slow down the withdrawal process. On March 4, 1948, Butterworth cautioned Marshall that most UN members expected the United States to withdraw only after "the creation of reasonably adequate native security forces" and under circumstances which would "bequeath to the newly established government at least an even chance." The United States, he expostulated, was therefore "obliged to take measures to prevent the economic collapse of South Korea." Dismissing these arguments, the JCS swiftly produced a new study which recommended, first, that the United States should accept as a "probability" the "eventual domination of Korea by the U.S.S.R." after American withdrawal and, second, that the Pentagon should subordinate its military aid for Korea to that for "countries of greater strategic importance." SANACC, meanwhile, had given way to the National Security Council (NSC). Unlike its predecessor, the NSC boasted a semipermanent staff, the members of which came from the departments represented on the NSC itself. This staff, drawing material from all relevant departments, fashioned an entirely new policy on Korea—NSC 8—which Truman and the NSC approved on April 8, 1948.[19]

When put to the scales, NSC 8 tilted heavily in favor of the Pentagon. On one side, Butterworth found his concerns barely acknowledged. The United States would continue to provide southern Korea with "at least minimum relief and rehabilitation," but only to "forestall economic breakdown." On the other side, the Pentagon achieved all of its objectives. First, in keeping with the recent JCS study, the United States would provide southern Korea with only enough military aid to handle internal—but not external—threats to its security. Second, the new policy specifically precluded any direct U.S. military intervention: "The U.S. should not become so irrevocably involved in the Korean situation that any action taken by any faction or by any other power in Korea could be taken as a *casus belli* for the U.S." Third, the new policy's central statement of purpose virtually embodied the Pentagon's primary goal: the State Department would henceforth direct its efforts toward establishing a government in southern Korea *as a means of facilitating the liquidation of the U.S. commitment of men and money in Korea with the minimum of bad effects."* (The NSC's italics here indicate centrality.) In early 1947, it should be remembered, Acheson and the Special Interdepartmental Committee on Korea had specifically rejected the idea of developing a government in Korea as a means of liquidating the U.S. commitment there. Now, in 1948, exactly the same concept became the principal tenet of American policy. By this time, too, Acheson's carefully laid plans for rebuilding the economy of southern Korea had been largely forgotten.[20]

On May 10, UN-sponsored elections took place in southern Korea, with 80 percent of those eligible registered and 92.5 percent of these actually voting. It was a surprising success. Joseph Jacobs, Marshall's Political Adviser in Korea, at once turned bitterly critical of the Pentagon's contention that Korea was "expendable," and he implored the Secretary not to "let Korea down." Marshall ignored this appeal and instructed the U.S. Army to begin troop withdrawals on August 15, although at Butterworth's insistence he urged the JCS to remain flexible on its projected December 31 completion date. As military withdrawal proceeded, the State Department took over the general administration of Korea, but not the army's economic assistance program. Following the demise of Acheson's 1947 aid plan, Congress had appropriated just $113 million for basic relief assistance in Korea during fiscal 1948, and the army soon transferred this small program to the newly formed Economic Cooperation Administration (ECA).[21]

The President and the Congress created the ECA to administer the bulk of the U.S. foreign aid budget, and Truman, acting on Acheson's advice, made Paul G. Hoffman its director. Hoffman did not expect to assume his responsibilities until January 1, 1949, but in the late summer of 1948 Charles E. Saltzman, Assistant Secretary of State for Occupied Areas, paid him an unofficial visit. Charged with the implementation of NSC 8, Saltzman suggested that its aid provision might be interpreted to justify at least a modest reconstruction program for southern Korea. Hoffman replied that he would gladly follow the State Department's lead, but he doubted whether Congress would prove as tractable. Undeterred, Saltzman wrote a long memorandum recounting the history of Acheson's 1947 aid plan and pressing for a scaled-down version of it. He meticulously couched his proposal in the language of NSC 8, but even so he envisioned a three-year program costing at least $410 million—a rather roundabout way to achieve the "liquidation of the U.S. commitment of men and money in Korea." Recognizing this inconsistency, Undersecretary of State Lovett quickly attached a note to the plan which read, "I'm not sure the conclusions are sound—a four-year plan [*sic*] for Korea is too rich for my blood. Let's talk this over." Marshall, the final arbiter, opted for a compromise; he leavened Saltzman's plan with Lovett's caution. First, Marshall asked the ECA to draw up an economic development program which would put Korea "as near as possible on a self-sustaining basis." Then he added three important stipulations: the ECA's program should "require the least drain on the American economy"; it should "avoid the implication of any commitment to Korea"; and it should be funded one year at a time, with the full plan kept secret to minimize any risk to U.S. prestige.[22]

But economic assistance alone would not be enough. As General Helmick had earlier predicted, Syngman Rhee swept the Korean elections only to form an unstable government besieged by serious uprisings. Butterworth repeatedly asked Marshall to postpone the final withdrawal of American troops. Faced with the prospect of an embarrassing political collapse in South Korea following hard on the heels of U.S. withdrawal, Marshall finally acceded to Butterworth's requests on November 5. Officially, the State Department cited UN inaction as its reason for postponing military withdrawal, but that pretext evaporated on December 12 when the UN recognized South Korea as a lawful nation. By the terms of NSC 8, this was the cue for a hasty American exit. Even though Marshall had agreed to additional aid for Korea, and even though he had postponed the final phase of military withdrawal, he still intended to pull out. Marshall believed, as he testified later, that Korea's "close relationship with Japan" made it of "very material importance," but Korea was "not absolutely vital." Others, however, held a different opinion.[23]

To everyone's surprise but his own, Harry S. Truman won his bid for reelection on November 5, 1948, and on the twenty-second he invited Dean Acheson to Blair House for a casual discussion of world affairs. In the midst of this, and with his usual impish humor, the President buoyantly interjected, "I want you to come back and be Secretary of State. Will you?" With Acheson's acceptance, the pendulum of America's Korean policy began its backward sweep.[24]

During the election campaign, Walton Butterworth endured a maelstrom of Republican charges, not the least of which was that his Office of Far Eastern Affairs had few real experts on Asia. At Butterworth's urgent request, therefore, Marshall ordered Max Bishop, a seasoned Japan specialist, to take over Northeast Asian Affairs. After the election, Bishop, with the help of Niles Bond, his assistant, wrote a cogent memorandum on the broader implications of Marshall's Korean policy. In it, Bishop graphically depicted the disastrous psychological, political, and economic consequences which could befall Japan if South Korea fell to the Communists. Bishop, who had recently served as Assistant State Department Political Adviser to Douglas MacArthur, believed that Japan's "communal" society would gravitate toward communism and suffer serious unrest if it became surrounded by communist neighbors. Any unrest, he posited, would prolong the American occupation and prevent Japanese economic recovery. To safeguard Japan's future, Bishop concluded, the State Department should immediately request a review of NSC 8. Marshall postponed the question for over four weeks—probably so that he could discuss it with Acheson (already appointed to succeed him) before reaching a decision. In due course, Bishop won his case, and, on January 17, 1949, Marshall requested a National Security Council review of NSC 8.[25]

The Third Stage:
January 1949–June 1950

When Acheson formally took charge of the State Department four days later, he inherited a U.S. commitment to withdraw militarily from Korea, an ongoing reassessment of U.S. economic assistance to Korea, and a policy on Korea (NSC 8) that was slated for review. Acheson found himself, in effect, well positioned to begin shifting U.S. policy back toward the type of commitment in Korea he had espoused in 1947. Niles Bond, Assistant Chief of Northeast Asian Affairs, later recounted, "Up to about the beginning of '49, the State Department had pretty much gone along with the military on not regarding Korea as within our area of strategic interest. . . . Then [in 1949], we began to think this was an area of our national interest, and we became more involved." From January through mid-March, Acheson worked closely with his staff to produce a new policy. Max Bishop, Chief of Northeast Asian Affairs, later recalled, "I admired his intellect and his grasp of things. For example, I could go in there [Acheson's office] with an NSC paper and go over the whole thing with him, and when I'd finished, he'd say, 'Now let's see this, this, and this,' and he had it just like that!" The NSC swiftly approved the resulting policy—NSC 8 / 2—and Truman followed suit on March 23. Sharply reversing the earlier goal of liquidating the American commitment in Korea, Acheson's new policy declared that "the United States must continue to give political support, and economic, technical, military, and other assistance to the Republic of Korea." Given the well-established UN resolution on military withdrawal and the Pentagon's intransigence on this matter, the new policy also confirmed that the United States would complete the withdrawal of its troops from Korea, but the NSC specifically tied this decision to the "National Military Establishment"—not the State Department.[26]

In the months that followed, Acheson promoted Dean Rusk to Deputy Undersecretary and appointed Max Bishop to be Rusk's assistant. Both men enjoyed considerable access to Acheson, and both grew closer to him. After Bishop left the Office of Northeast Asian Affairs, Acheson made sure that his own emphasis on Korea's economic importance to Japan took center stage. Bishop's depiction of Korea's psychological importance to Japan became a secondary, but still important, motivating factor in U.S. policy.[27]

Although Acheson at once accorded Korea a much higher priority, the Defense Department did not. As part of NSC 8, General John Hodge, Commander in Korea; General Douglas MacArthur, Commander in the Far East; and General Omar Bradley, Army Chief of Staff, had agreed to develop only a lightly armed 50,000-man constabulary force in South Korea, even though they knew that the North Korean Army was fully equipped and had roughly 125,000 men. Nevertheless, by a surreptitious agreement, General Hodge allowed the South Korean Army to reach a strength of 65,000 men by the time NSC 8 came under review. Syngman Rhee then proposed a six-division, 100,000-man army with full equipment, augmented by a 350-plane air force and a 67-ship navy. Hodge, who had himself originally favored six divisions, undoubtedly agreed with Rhee, but General MacArthur stated bluntly that he saw little hope for South Korea in general, and none for creating a South Korean army capable of resisting a North Korean invasion. Bradley sided with MacArthur and opposed any addition to the authorized 50,000-man strength except for a few liaison aircraft and a small coast guard. As NSC 8 / 2 neared completion, the NSC staff circulated a compromise report authorizing full funding for the existing 65,000-man force plus the few aircraft and ships approved by Bradley. The JCS readily accepted this, though not before securing a final withdrawal date for American troops—June 30, 1949.[28]

Surprisingly, after the NSC approved these decisions as part of the new Korean policy, NSC 8 / 2, Bradley began to have second thoughts. The JCS had previously been influenced by Army Chief of Staff Dwight D. Eisenhower's assessment that the Soviet Union would avoid conventional wars for at least five years, but in late February of 1949 some CIA analysts began to predict that North Korea would attack South Korea shortly after the United States completed its military withdrawal. Bradley quietly asked his own staff to explore U.S. options in the event of North Korean aggression. His senior advisers concluded that a UN "police action" would be the only viable option, and with remarkable prescience they even predicated this scenario on the unlikely event of a Soviet abstention in the UN Security Council. When Bradley presented this to the Joint Chiefs of Staff, however, the other members dismissed it as too political and too impractical. Thus, when the last U.S. troops left Korea in June, Bradley had established neither an adequate South Korean army to replace them nor a contingency plan to deal with the possibility of a North Korean invasion.[29]

The State Department had extremely limited knowledge of— and even less influence on—the particulars of military assistance, but economic assistance was another matter. Picking up where he had left off in 1947, Acheson worked closely with Paul Hoffman and the ECA to design a new three-year economic rehabilitation program for South Korea. On June 7, Truman formally requested Congress to allocate $150 million for South Korea in the current fiscal year, and when hearings opened before the House Committee on Foreign Affairs the following day, Hoffman revealed the rest of a three-year, $350–$385 million program. Acheson, rejecting Marshall's secretive approach, allowed the full plan to be disclosed in public hearings, thereby firmly committing American prestige from the outset. The new aid plan concentrated on expanding South Korean production in fertilizer, coal, electric power, agriculture, and commercial fishing, with much of the increased mining and generating capacity allocated to the manufacture of fertilizer. Just as in the 1947 plan, Acheson expected that the additional fertilizer would restore South Korean rice production and that this, in turn, would revive South Korea's trade with Japan. Hoffman, in describing the aid program to the Committee on Foreign Affairs, carefully pointed out that while it seemed expensive in the near term, it would reduce Korean aid to $35 million per year by 1953. Much more, however, Hoffman stressed the "complementary" relationship between the economies of Korea and Japan. Considerable thought had gone into utilizing this relationship, he explained, and then he unveiled the early results: "In April of this year the Koreans closed a trade agreement with Japan, under which $29,000,000 in exports, mainly rice and marine products, will move to Japan during the coming year and Korea will in turn receive from Japan approximately $49,000,000 in imports, chiefly coal, machinery, and manufactures." Other markets for Korean exports, Hoffman projected, would remain quite limited, thereby simplifying U.S. efforts to encourage "maximum trade" between Korea and Japan.[30]

In follow-up testimony before the House Committee on Foreign Affairs, James Webb, Acheson's Undersecretary, emphasized Japan's "immense need" for Korean agricultural exports: "Shorn of overseas territories which formerly supplied her with food, raw materials, and markets—and which absorbed a large number of Japanese—Japan is faced with the problem of supporting a much larger population than ever before on her own relatively poor islands." Japan imported 25 percent of her food, Webb expounded, at a cost to the United States of roughly $400 million per year. Since South Korea had previously supplied most of this food, the State Department expected its Korean aid plan to be "a vital and integral part of our total effort in the Far East." Yet, even after many hours of testimony, some committee members remained unconvinced. Given the impending withdrawal of American troops, they suspected that the aid bill was merely a cover-up for retreat. Put simply, they ascribed to it Marshall's earlier intention. Acheson deftly parried by sending one of the chief exponents of the old policy to defend the new one—George Kennan. Between June 16 and June 20, Kennan repeatedly assured the House committee that the presence of U.S. troops in Korea was neither necessary nor desirable. On the twentieth, he even compared the situation in Korea to that in Greece, precisely as Acheson had done in 1947. Admitting that he had been "somewhat more pessimistic about a year ago," Kennan justified his sudden conversion by asserting, "The Koreans are doing much better now, and our people are doing much better than I ever thought they could in getting a local militia started." (Kennan reverted to his original position on Korea after he lost his PPS post in 1950.) Finally, Acheson, playing cleanup hitter on the twenty-third, told the committee that although he could make no guarantees, he thought there was "a good fighting chance" that the South Koreans could "take care of themselves." This—together with a brief explanation of the Pentagon's reasons for insisting on U.S. military withdrawal—clinched the committee's endorsement.[31]

The Senate Committee on Foreign Relations took up the same bill from June 12 through July 12, with the State Department's experts expanding on their House testimony. Acheson produced a few additional supporting witnesses, and Hoffman intensified his discussion of the "complementary" relationship between Korea and Japan, proclaiming at one point, "Japan can supply Korea with what it needs, and on the other hand, Korea can supply Japan with what they require." Likewise, Generals T. S. Timmerman and W. E. Todd added further assurances on the military situation. On the final day of testi-

mony, General Todd—Director of the JCS Intelligence Group—
declared, "If the Soviets would like to move by means of armed
aggression, Korea would be at the bottom of their priority list."
Tom Connally, a Texas Democrat who had recently replaced
Vandenberg as the committee's chairman, remained skeptical.
Since the South Koreans were "trading mostly with the Japanese," he reasoned, might not the Soviets "like to take over
and sort of 'gum up' the Japanese situation?" Todd thought
this "improbable," but the canny old Texan was not so sure.
Despite his deep reservations, Connally delivered an impas-
sioned closing speech which assured his committee's endorsement. It would be another six months before the full Congress
finally voted on the Korean aid bill, but it would be longer still
before the State Department heard the last of Senator Tom
Connally.[32]

Aside from its dubious planning in Korea, the Defense
Department had been slow to develop a strategic blueprint for
the Far East as a whole. In March of 1948, Kennan had suggested an offshore defense perimeter. Marshall passed the idea
to the Joint Chiefs of Staff, the JCS forwarded it to Douglas
MacArthur, and MacArthur drew a line extending from the
Philippines through the Ryukyu Archipelago and Japan to the
Aleutians. In keeping with earlier strategies (as well as NSC
8), MacArthur's line excluded Korea. No one bothered to submit this "Pacific Defense Perimeter" to the NSC, but it nonetheless became accepted policy by late 1948. MacArthur even
revealed it to the press in March of 1949. Paradoxically, just
as the State Department initiated the development of a comprehensive Asian defense policy in 1948, so too the Defense
Department initiated the development of a comprehensive Asian
foreign policy in 1949. On the face of it, Louis A. Johnson,
Truman's new Secretary of Defense, advocated only an over-
arching policy to facilitate the containment of communism in
Asia. But, behind this screen, Johnson waged a protracted
campaign to override the State Department's Taiwan aid pol-

additional military assistance for Chiang Kai-shek's discredited regime. By a series of shrewd maneuvers, Acheson won Truman's support, preserved his Taiwan policy, and substituted his own comprehensive Asian policy for Johnson's. The final policy statements, NSC 48 / 1 and NSC 48 / 2, both approved by Truman in the closing days of 1949, officially confirmed MacArthur's Pacific Defense Perimeter and reconfirmed Acheson's policy on Korea.[33]

Less than two weeks later, on January 12, 1950, Acheson delivered his much misunderstood speech to the National Press Club. "I am frequently asked," he told the assembled journalists, " 'has the State Department got an Asian policy?' " This had become the standard Republican query, and Acheson responded with what was now the standard Democratic Asian policy—NSC 48 / 1. The speech, then, was a defensive political gambit in which Acheson used a policy he had been forced to write by his bitter rival, Johnson, to counter his political opposition, the Republicans. Didactic as usual, Acheson included MacArthur's Pacific Defense Perimeter, but he also injected another element. Should an attack be made on a nation outside America's strategic umbrella, "the initial reliance must be on the people attacked to resist it and then upon the entire civilized world under the Charter of the United Nations. . . ." The Republicans later charged that by revealing the Defense Perimeter, with its exclusion of Korea, Acheson invited a North Korean attack. As was previously discussed, however, Acheson was neither the architect of this strategy nor the first to reveal it. Furthermore, although the UN reference may have seemed like a new element added to balance the discussion of the Defense Perimeter, Acheson had already instructed his embassy in Seoul, on December 14, 1949, to encourage the South Korean government to appeal to the UN in the event of a North Korean attack. Testifying before the Senate Foreign Relations Committee the day after his speech, Acheson maintained that the South Koreans could "take care of any trouble started solely by North Korea." If war came to Korea, he continued, the United States would likely consider military intervention only as part of a UN response, and while he personally "would take every possible action in the U.N.," the Soviet Union would undoubtedly use its veto to thwart his efforts. In short, Acheson's sentiments notwithstanding, the Defense Department retained the last word when it came to committing U.S. military forces in Korea.[34]

On January 19, 1950, a week after the Press Club speech, the House of Representatives defeated Acheson's Korean aid bill by a vote of 192–191. Acheson, who had lobbied persistently for the bill—even while testifying on unrelated legislation—became extremely upset. He immediately fired off a strongly worded letter to Truman, stressing that the bill's defeat would have "the most far-reaching adverse effects upon our foreign policy." Acheson's missive ended on the same emphatic note: "In our judgement it would be disastrous for the foreign policy of the United States for us to consider this action by the House of Representatives as its last word on the matter." With Truman's active support, Acheson adroitly fashioned a compromise bill which pruned the first year of his Korean aid program to $120 million and the two succeeding years to $100 million each. Then, for further insurance, he attached this scaled-down program to an extension of the 1948 China Aid Act, thereby securing support from the largely Republican China bloc in Congress. When hearings opened in the House on the revised bill, the Secretary reiterated his Senate testimony that South Korea could handle any attack by the North Koreans. Gone now was the more cautious "fighting chance" rhetoric of his earlier House appearance. The House readily approved the revised bill, followed closely by the Senate, and on February 14, 1950—nearly three years after its original inception—the President signed Acheson's Korean aid program into law. Quickly capitalizing on success, Acheson pushed through Congress a follow-up bill appropriating $100 million for the

Korean aid plan's second year, and on June 5 this too became law.[35]

Acheson intended no hyperbole when he called the defeat of his Korean aid bill "disastrous for the foreign policy of the United States." Indeed, as in 1947, not only the economy of South Korea but also that of Japan seemed to be hanging in the balance. American-sponsored improvements in Japanese agriculture had reduced Japan's food imports from 30 percent of total requirements in 1947 to 25 percent in 1949, but the cost of U.S. food assistance dipped only from $241 million to $239 million. The total cost of U.S. relief aid (including food, fertilizer, raw materials, and shipping costs, but excluding reconstruction funds) actually increased—from $350 million in 1947 to $468 million in 1949. Worse still, the cost of U.S. relief aid, particularly food assistance, seemed destined to soar far higher. Before and during World War II, Japan had exhorted its young women to provide more future soldiers for the empire. Slogans like "Bear and multiply" became the familiar refrains of Japanese propaganda. By 1949, the birthrate stood at a sobering 4.54 babies per woman of childbearing age, and if this continued, Japan's population would double with every generation. State Department planners predicted that the total number of Japanese would increase from 78 million in 1947 to 80 million in 1950; it actually rose to 82 million—twice the expected rate. When Acheson outlined this situation to the Senate Committee on Foreign Relations in January of 1950, he began by pointing out that Japan's population had grown by 8.5 million in just the past ten years. "Japan has a population," he elaborated, "which is far greater than can be supported on those islands and [it] is growing at a tremendous rate." The "great question," Acheson went on to assert, was whether Japan could find the raw materials and markets it required to maintain its precarious economic stability. Philip C. Jessup, Ambassador-at-Large, added in supporting testimony that the Japanese already faced extremely serious economic problems as the result of being "cut off from their previous food sources—Korea, Manchuria, Formosa, and some of the islands." Only by reviving Japan's foreign trade—particularly its trade with its Asian food suppliers—could the United States avert a Japanese economic collapse.[36]

"Japan was sort of floundering during this period," Dean Rusk, Acheson's Deputy Undersecretary, later recounted, "and we were scouring the earth to find just the elementary food stuffs that Japan needed." Before World War II (1938), Japan received nearly all of its annual rice imports from just three sources: Korea provided 1,692,000 metric tons, Taiwan 829,000 metric tons, and Thailand 25,000 metric tons. Neither China nor Southeast Asia had exported significant quantities of rice to Japan. In the postwar years, U.S. planners searched urgently for new Asian suppliers of food for Japan. The State Department, according to Rusk, looked first to Burma. With prewar rice surpluses even larger than those of Korea, Burma seemed like an ideal prospect until 1948, when a widespread civil war devastated its economy. Thereafter, to borrow Rusk's words, "it ceased to be an important food exporter." Indochina, whose yield of 22.4 bushels of rice per acre came to less than half of Korea's 51 bushels per acre, had nevertheless once managed to export rice in roughly equal volume. Between 1946 and 1950, however, France divided Indochina into three states, resisted full independence for any of them, and precipitated an intractable guerrilla war. Indochina, like Burma, ceased to be a major exporter of rice. Acheson even gave a reluctant and conditional blessing to direct trade between Japan and the People's Republic of China, but this too produced little result, and the State Department became increasingly pessimistic about its prospects. Taken together, all of these circumstances enormously magnified the importance of South Korea—the only one of Japan's major Asian trading partners that the United States could both control and rebuild.[37]

Moreover, Korea seemed to be in the midst of rapid political and economic stabilization. An election postponement and serious inflation threatened to reverse this trend, but State Department pressure eliminated both. Then, when general elections were held on May 31, some 86 percent of those eligible went to the polls, handing Syngman Rhee and his supporters a substantial majority in the nation's parliamentary assembly. At the same time, South Korea's annual fertilizer production rose from 2,340 metric tons in 1945 to 200,000 metric tons in 1949. This increase, combined with the beneficial effects of an earlier U.S.-sponsored land redistribution program, began to gradually revive rice production. In February of 1950, South Korea signed a contract to ship another 100,000 tons of rice to Japan. Total exports, according to ECA extrapolations, would reach $27,399,000 in 1950 and then soar to $51,773,000 in 1951—including $31,000,000 worth of rice and $10,998,000 worth of marine products. Additional increases would follow, and South Korea's markets, expected to absorb $49,000,000 worth of Japanese exports in 1950, would likewise continue to expand. This growing trade was still well below prewar levels, and no one expected Korea to achieve its full trade potential until the ECA completed the construction of new fertilizer plants. Even then, Korean trade alone could hardly sustain the Japanese economy. Before World War II, Korea had accounted for less than one-sixth of Japan's total annual trade and less than one-third of its annual trade in Asia. Other trading partners for Japan would have to be found. But in the near term South Korea remained Japan's most promising Asian trading partner, and in the long term the State Department expected it to play such a critical role that the Japanese economy might never fully recover without it.[38]

Just as Acheson's rhetoric on the importance of the Korean aid bill seemed justified by the economic situation, so too his confidence in South Korea's ability to defend itself seemed justified by the military situation. The Pentagon—making use of $110 million worth of equipment left behind by U.S. forces—

authorized U.S. support for a South Korean Army of 84,000 men, but that army actually reached 100,000 men by early 1950. To train this infant force, the JCS developed the Korean Military Advisory Group (KMAG), commanded by General William L. Roberts. Despite repeated requests to the Pentagon for more heavy weapons, Roberts officially reported that North Korea no longer had the capacity to conquer South Korea, and he publicly boasted that the South Koreans had "the best dog-gone shootin' army outside the United States." Even Mac-Arthur's skepticism faded, and more help appeared to be on the way. In the fall of 1949, Congress appropriated $27,640,000 in additional military aid for Iran, the Philippines, and Korea. Congress left the division of this fund to the administration, and in January of 1950 Truman allocated $10.9 million of it to South Korea.[39]

Appearances to the contrary, however, the Defense Department continued to accord South Korea an extremely low priority. Of the $10.9 million in additional military aid, only a few hundred dollars worth of radio equipment reached Korea by June of 1950, and most of the earlier U.S. military aid consisted of only light weapons. Where a comparable American force would have deployed 432 artillery pieces, including many heavy guns, the Koreans had only 91 light howitzers. The Koreans asked for tanks, but Pentagon planners—believing Korea's soldiers too ignorant and its terrain too rugged for heavy weapons—denied this request. General Bradley limited the South Korean Air Force to ten trainers and twelve liaison aircraft. Similar problems existed in training, communications, antitank weapons, and numerous other areas, all of which the Pentagon largely ignored. As Bradley himself later admitted, the "machinery" for determining military assistance in the Far East was seriously deficient.[40]

For a long time, the State Department remained blissfully unaware of these circumstances, but eventually KMAG officers apprised John Muccio, now the Ambassador to Korea, of the true situation. Muccio, in turn, promptly requested a major expansion of Truman's new $10.9 million military aid package for South Korea. On May 23, 1950, he specified that South Korea needed twenty F-51 fighters, ten training aircraft, and three C-47 transports, a shopping list which would cost another $6 million. The State Department forwarded Muccio's request forthwith to the Defense Department, but the JCS—citing Korea's low strategic priority—withheld final approval. The debate lingered on into late June, when the North Korean Army settled it in favor of the State Department.[41]

Unlike the State Department, Senator Tom Connally had long suspected that the Soviet Union would try to "take over" in Korea and "sort of 'gum up' the Japanese situation." The cover of the May 5 issue of *U.S. News & World Report* displayed his furrowed visage set ominously before a gigantic map of Korea. In the featured article, Connally's interviewer asked pointedly if the idea of abandoning Korea might be seriously considered. Connally responded that he was afraid it would have to be considered. "I'm for Korea," he declared, but then he went on to predict, "Whenever she [the Soviet Union] takes a notion she can just overrun Korea just like she will overrun Formosa when she gets ready." Once again, however, the State Department shunted Connally's warning to the side.[42]

On June 24, 1950 (Washington time), Acheson's three-year plan for the economic rehabilitation of South Korea—a plan which Acheson had fostered since 1947 and which had just begun to bear fruit—ran headlong into the plans of North Korean leader Kim Il Sung. An army of 135,000 men, supplied by the Soviet Union with 150 T-34 tanks, 60 IL-10 bombers, and 70 Yak-3 and Yak-9 fighters, launched a sudden, blitzkrieg attack against South Korea's 95,000 lightly armed frontline troops. With Truman's approval, Acheson swiftly requested a UN Security Council statement calling for both sides to return to their own borders. The following day, as Truman flew back to Washington from his home in Missouri, Acheson sequestered himself in his office. There, he concluded that although it would require a preponderance of American troops, UN action would be the best response. This would, in effect, not only seize the diplomatic high ground but also circumvent the Pentagon's long-standing opposition to committing U.S. troops in Korea. Later, in his memoirs, Acheson elucidated his reasoning: "Plainly, this attack did not amount to a *casus belli* against the Soviet Union. Equally plainly, it was an open, undisguised challenge to our internationally accepted position as the protector of South Korea, *an area of great importance to the security of American-occupied Japan"* (italics added).[43]

Others close to Acheson have verified the centrality of this Japan connection. Shortly after the attack, George Kennan, then a personal adviser to Acheson, told the British Ambassador that even though South Korea had little strategic value, "the symbolic significance of its preservation was tremendous, especially in Japan." A few weeks later, John M. Allison, who had replaced Bishop as Chief of the Office of Northeast Asian Affairs, summarized Acheson's policy on Korea in a brief memorandum. Japan was "the real prize in Asia," Allison explained, and the United States simply could not "allow a regime hostile to American interests in Japan to dominate Korea." The present author queried James Webb, the State Department's second-in-command, and Dean Rusk, Assistant Secretary of State for Far Eastern Affairs, about Acheson's decision-making process. "South Korea, in the hands of the North," Webb responded, "would have been a dagger pointed at Japan, and would have affected the whole economy of that region." Rusk offered a similar reply: "The Korean peninsula seemed like a dagger pointed at the heart of Japan, and we felt that if South Korea went to communism, this would have a profound effect on Japan."[44]

Tied closely to this concern was the matter of American prestige. In conjunction with his plan to rebuild South Korea's economy, Acheson had deliberately reversed Marshall's policy of minimizing the commitment of American prestige in Korea. Having thus himself put U.S. prestige at risk, he felt obliged to protect it. In his own words, "To back away from this challenge, in view of our capacity for meeting it, would be highly destructive of the power and prestige of the United States." Yet, in high-level meetings, planners from State and Defense focused not on whether to take action but on what action to take. After much discussion, the two departments concurred on three initial recommendations: additional military aid for South Korea, U.S. air support for the evacuation of American dependents from Korea, and the interposition of the U.S. Seventh Fleet between Taiwan and the mainland.[45]

During his long flight back to Washington in *Air Force One,* Truman reasoned that unchallenged aggression during the 1930s had led to the Second World War, and he resolved not to repeat that cycle. Dean Rusk, who in March had become Assistant Secretary of State for Far Eastern Affairs, took special note of Truman's decisiveness. He subsequently remembered, "Truman had the faculty of oversimplifying matters at the point of decision. . . . The problem would look like a heap of jackstraws, all intertwined and interlaced. He would study that, and then he would pull out one or two jackstraws that he considered to be essential to a decision. Then he would make his decision and go home and never look back." At the airport in Washington, Secretary of State Dean Acheson, Undersecretary of State James Webb, and Secretary of Defense Louis Johnson waited to escort the President to a Blair House dinner meeting which Truman had scheduled for that evening. Upon joining them in the presidential limousine, Truman immediately began to expound on the limitations of the Soviet Union's trans-Siberian Railroad. This single-track rail line would never be sufficient to supply the North Korean Army if the United States stood firm, he asserted, and then he thundered, "By God, I'm going to let them have it!" Demonstratively shaking Truman's hand, Johnson exclaimed, "I'm with you, Mr. President!" Given the Defense Department's previous stand on Korea, Acheson must have found Johnson's obsequious behavior particularly galling. Webb, cognizant of the hostility between the two secretaries, quickly interjected that Truman should carefully consider the recommendations that State and Defense had drawn up before settling on a specific course of action. Truman agreed. By a vote of nine to zero, with the Soviet Union boycotting over the issue of Chinese representation, the UN Security Council had approved a U.S.-backed resolution calling for both sides to return to their borders, and Acheson quietly relayed this news to the President.[46]

Once the group arrived at Blair House, however, it was Webb who buttonholed Truman in the cloak room for a discussion of the interdepartmental recommendations drawn up that after-noon—additional military aid for South Korea, air support for the evacuation of U.S. dependents, and the interposition of the Seventh Fleet between Taiwan and the mainland. Webb coun-seled that both he and Acheson thought it best to approve the first two and postpone the third. After a pleasant dinner, with a dozen senior officials in attendance, Acheson outlined the recommendations in detail to the entire assembly and pointed out that the jet fighters covering the evacuation of U.S. depen-dents could be authorized to knock out North Korean tanks. General Bradley expressed his support, observing that the United States would have to "draw the line somewhere," but he also voiced serious reservations about sending U.S. troops back into Korea. Johnson suddenly lost his early enthusiasm and declared himself firmly opposed to the use of ground forces. At the meeting's end, Truman—adhering closely to Webb's briefing—approved the first two interdepartmental recommen-dations and ordered the Seventh Fleet to steam toward, but not into, the Formosa Strait.[47]

On the evening of June 26, Truman again gathered a dozen of his senior policymakers at Blair House. Acheson, now somewhat more certain about the situation in Korea, asked the

President to expand American aid to Indochina, order the Seventh Fleet into the Formosa Strait, authorize full U.S. air support for the South Korean army, and seek a Security Council resolution requesting UN member nations to assist South Korea in thwarting North Korean aggression. Truman approved all four recommendations. In the days that followed, the State Department secured the necessary Security Council resolution, and the Pentagon dropped its resistance to committing ground forces in Korea. On June 30, acting in concert with the combined opinion of the Departments of State and Defense, Truman ordered U.S. troops into the war under the UN banner.[48]

Conclusion

America's Korean policy had come full circle: from commitment during Acheson's tenure as Undersecretary of State to liquidation after he resigned and back to commitment following his return. In the final stage, when Acheson was Secretary of State, he reversed Marshall's policy of gradual withdrawal, bypassed unrelenting Pentagon opposition, won a protracted fight in Congress, and committed the United States to the economic rehabilitation of South Korea. This, in turn, was fundamental to Acheson's plans for the long-term economic recovery of Japan. Acheson, his Undersecretary of State, his Ambassador-at-Large, his Assistant Secretary for Far Eastern Affairs, both of his Chiefs for Northeast Asian Affairs, the Director of the ECA, and several others have all been cited on this point, along with a cornucopia of statistics. But Raymond Harrison, Max Bishop, Paul Hoffman, and John Allison best summarized the core issues. In 1947, Harrison emphasized that Asian recovery could be attained only if Japan resumed its prewar trade with "Korea and that area." In 1948, Bishop contended that if Korea fell to the Communists, the psychological, political, and economic impact on Japan would prolong the

American occupation there and prevent Japanese economic recovery. In 1949, Hoffman insisted, "Japan can supply Korea with what it needs, and on the other hand, Korea can supply Japan with what they require." Finally, in 1950, Allison— explaining the American decision to defend Korea—declared that the United States simply could not "allow a regime hostile to American interests in Japan to dominate Korea."[49]

The ideology of containment and the exigencies of politics played a role in this process, but a subsidiary one. Containment could have begun—as the Pentagon clearly intended—at the Sea of Japan rather than at the thirty-eighth parallel, and given the Republican opposition to expanded Korean assistance, any political fallout generated by a full withdrawal from Korea would have been manageable. Secretary of State George Marshall's plan for pulling out of Korea while minimizing the damage to U.S. prestige might have been, and very nearly was, put into practice. But, as Acheson clearly understood, South Korea's regional economic and political importance could be ignored only at the risk of indefinitely postponing Asian recovery, resulting in serious consequences for both the U.S. position in the Far East and the future expansion of America's Asian trade.

In early 1950, Acheson finally managed to commit American money and prestige in Korea, but he had to rely on the Joint Chiefs of Staff to develop a viable South Korean army and to provide him with an accurate assessment of North Korean intentions. The JCS failed utterly on both counts. The outcome of Acheson's planning, therefore, was quite different from that which he had envisioned. Ironically, the Korean War played a far larger role in the initial phase of Japanese recovery than did Korean trade. Japan pulled its still formidable war industries out of mothballs, and the United States purchased four billion dollars worth of munitions from its former enemy. Nevertheless, Acheson did carry on with his plans for rebuilding South Korea, and American engineers eventually built the fertilizer plants that Acheson first began fighting for in 1947. By 1975, South Korea led the world in the application of fertilizer. This, as expected, resulted in dramatically improved rice yields, but a mushrooming urban population, combined with the effects of agricultural diversification, more than offset these gains—thereby eliminating South Korea as a net food exporter. The economies of South Korea and Japan did become heavily interdependent and did achieve a high rate of growth, but they developed in a way that was quite different from anything Acheson ever imagined.[50]

Acheson and
the American Commitment
on Taiwan

CONTRARY TO POPULAR BELIEF, Dean Acheson's policy on
Taiwan developed neither as an ideologically driven extension
of containment nor as a remedy for domestic political concerns. Rather, the Departments of State and Defense immediately seized upon Taiwan's strategic, economic, and psychological importance to Japan. The Joint Chiefs of Staff,
lacking the forces for a full commitment to defend Taiwan, at
first suggested that the State Department should do the job
with only economic and political means, and later offered to
support this effort with a limited show of force. Acheson, though
he tried without success to secure a full military commitment,
saw no advantage in an empty show of military force. His
policy therefore called for preventing, by the use of economic
and political means alone, the Chinese Communist domination
of Taiwan. The implementation of Acheson's policy pro-
gressed through five distinct stages. In the first stage, the winter of 1948–49, the State Department established its initial

Taiwan policy and made a few clarifications (NSC 37 / 1, NSC 37 / 2, and NSC 37 / 5). During the second stage, which spanned most of 1949, Acheson worked to implement these policies and supplant the tenuous political authority of Chiang Kai-shek. At the onset of the third stage, in late 1949, Acheson recognized (as indicated in NSC 37 / 8) that his schemes to replace Chiang had failed and that Chiang had established direct control over Taiwan. In response, Acheson curtailed U.S. military assistance to Taiwan—both to compel political reform there and to protect U.S. prestige if the island fell to the Communists. The fourth stage, which coincided with the spring of 1950, saw Acheson expand U.S. economic assistance to Taiwan in order to improve its political and military stability, while at the same time he and Truman grappled with new alternatives for getting rid of Chiang. The outbreak of war in Korea marked the advent of the fifth and final stage. Acting in concert, Acheson, Truman, and the Pentagon extended U.S. naval protection to Taiwan, approved a substantial aid program for the Chinese Nationalist Army, and abandoned the idea of eliminating Chiang Kai-shek.

The First Stage: November 1948–March 1949

The struggle for Taiwan began in late 1948, when the deteriorating position of the Nationalist government in the Chinese civil war put the United States on what strategist Liddell Hart might have called "the horns of a dilemma." On one side, the United States could ill afford to defend Taiwan and alienate the Chinese Communists, who would soon dominate all of mainland China. On the other side, Taiwan, with its strategic location and significant resources, was critical to the U.S. position in Japan. To deal with this dilemma, the administration of President Harry S. Truman developed not one but three separate policies: a China policy (NSC 34 / 2), a China trade policy (NSC 41), and a Taiwan policy (NSC 37 / 2). Surprisingly, Truman's State Department fabricated its two China policies—which will be examined in the next chapter—in almost complete isolation from its policy on Taiwan.[1]

The initial debate over Taiwan grew out of its uncertain status under international law. Technically, Taiwan was "a portion of the Japanese Empire awaiting final disposition by a treaty of peace," but at the Cairo conference in 1943 the United States had promised to return the island to China. The fact that the United States could still break its pledge and treat Taiwan in any way it pleased led inevitably to competing policy concepts, and these emanated from four independent groups: the Joint Chiefs of Staff (JCS), the State Department's Office of Northeast Asian Affairs, the Central Intelligence Agency (CIA), and the congressional supporters of Chiang Kai-shek's Chinese Nationalist regime.[2]

The JCS, in a report issued on November 24, 1948, found Taiwan to be of paramount importance—not to the United States itself but to Japan. This orphaned island, the JCS explained, dominated many of Japan's sea lanes and was "a major supplier of food and other materials for Japan." The facts bore this out. The Japanese, having ruled Taiwan from 1895 to 1945, had designed its economy to serve their own. By 1935, Taiwan accounted for 9.6 percent of Japan's imports and 6.6 percent of its exports, and the volume of this trade nearly doubled in the 1930s. Japan received 81 percent of Taiwan's exports and supplied 88 percent of its imports. In 1939, a fairly typical year, Taiwan shipped out 294,000 metric tons of rice and 903,000 metric tons of sugar; rice and sugar together made up three-fourths of the island's exports. Japan depended on Taiwan for one-third of its imported rice and nearly all of its sugar. The JCS nevertheless recommended against a full military commitment on Taiwan. "Communist domination of Formosa [Taiwan]," it asserted, "could be denied by such diplomatic and economic steps as may be appropriate to insure a Formosan administration friendly to the United States." Dean Rusk subsequently recounted, "They [the Pentagon's planners] said in effect, 'Taiwan is of strategic importance to the United States, but we don't have any troops to contribute to its defense, so you fellows in the State Department get out there and defend it by political and economic means.' And we said, 'Well, we don't have any muscle behind any such effort and that very likely won't work.' " The JCS then offered to base a few small naval units in Taiwanese ports, but without any corresponding military commitment. Robert A. Lovett, who succeeded Acheson as Undersecretary of State in mid-1947, rejected this idea on the grounds that it would further alienate the Communists without improving the situation on Taiwan, and he asked the Pentagon to hold open at least the possibility of full-scale military intervention. If such intervention proved necessary, he added, it would have to be "publicly based not on obvious American strategic interests but on principles which are likely to have support in the international community, mainly the principle of self-determination of the Formosan people."[3]

Like the Pentagon, Max Bishop, the State Department's Chief of Northeast Asian Affairs, focused primarily on Taiwan's importance to Japan. For Bishop, Japan's postwar stability hinged on the fate of its prewar empire. Bishop had already challenged the U.S. policy which called for abandoning Korea (NSC 8), and in so doing he had emphasized Korea's psychological, political, and economic importance to Japan. Now, making a similar case for Taiwan, Bishop argued that the United States should seize the island as part of the spoils of war, fortify its rocky western coast, and set up a local Chinese regime on the rest—possibly under some sort of UN supervision.[4]

A third approach emanated from the newly formed Central Intelligence Agency. In two successive reports, the CIA forecast that the Nationalist government would not be able to "recover its balance" and would seek "accommodation with the Communist power." If Taiwan then fell into Communist hands, the strategic effect in Asia would approximate that of "a Soviet penetration of Greece . . . in the Eastern Mediterranean." Korea and Taiwan together, the CIA added, had earlier provided 30 percent of Japan's food, and the loss of either area would force Japan to rely on "more distant and less dependable sources in Southeast Asia." Yet, even in all this gloom, there was a ray of hope. Some Nationalist officials on Taiwan, finding themselves "increasingly isolated," might request U.S. support for an "attempt to build up a regional authority." If such a local regime could break away from the Nationalist government, "the separation of the economy of Taiwan from the Chinese mainland and the re-orientation of that economy toward Japan would be beneficial to Taiwan, Japan, and the U.S." In response to this idea, John P. Davies, a China expert on the State Department's Policy Planning Staff, speculated that it might be more expedient to cultivate an independence movement among the indigenous Taiwanese than to promote a new regime run by their Chinese overlords. Both concepts rapidly gathered momentum.[5]

The Truman administration's fourth option was to maintain its support for the Nationalist government. In January 1949, John M. Cabot, U.S. Consul General at Shanghai, notified Washington that the Nationalists intended to fall back slowly toward Taiwan. Although the Nationalists found little favor in the State Department, they enjoyed the support of a militant China bloc in Congress and an equally militant China lobby. The China bloc, while never large, included several notables: Senators William F. Knowland (R-California), H. Alexander Smith (R-New Jersey), Kenneth Wherry (R-Nebraska), Styles Bridges (R-New Hampshire), Pat McCarran (D-Nevada), and Robert Taft (R-Ohio), along with Congressmen Walter Judd (R-Minnesota) and John Vorys (R-Ohio).[6]

On January 6, 1949, the National Security Council ordered its staff to formulate a policy statement on Taiwan. The initial draft (NSC 34 / 1) listed four alternatives: (a) occupying Taiwan with U.S. forces (Bishop's approach), (b) negotiating for "base rights" on Taiwan (the Pentagon's approach), (c) backing the Nationalist government (the China bloc's approach), and (d) supporting "continued *local* non-Communist Chinese control and using our influence wherever possible to discourage the use of Formosa as a refuge for National Government remnants" (the CIA's approach). The Departments of State and Defense settled on the fourth option. The United States would henceforth "seek to develop and support a local non-Communist Chinese regime" on Taiwan. As a backup plan, the United States would also "maintain contact with potential native Formosan leaders with a view at some future date to being able to make use of a Formosan autonomous movement."[7]

Dean Acheson took over the State Department on January 21, 1949. Two weeks later, he, the other members of the NSC, and the President approved the final draft of the new Taiwan policy (NSC 37 / 2). Acheson, however, had serious reservations. At his insistence, the NSC ordered the Pentagon to take another look at "the threat to U.S. security, in the event diplomatic and economic steps to deny communist domination of Formosa prove insufficient" and at "the military measures" this threat might necessitate. In its response (NSC 37 / 3), the JCS restated both its description of Taiwan's "great" importance to Japan and its conviction that the paucity of military resources precluded a full-scale U.S. commitment. The Pentagon also renewed its offer to station a few ships in Taiwanese ports.[8]

Largely on the basis of the recommendations set forth by Philip D. Sprouse, Chief of the Office of Chinese Affairs, Acheson drew up an aggressive new plan (NSC 37 / 4). In it, he proposed to "detail a high-ranking officer to Taipei" with instructions to approach General Chen Cheng, the Nationalist Governor of Taiwan. This envoy would offer sufficient economic assistance to develop a "self-supporting economy on the island," and the Economic Cooperation Administration (ECA) would draw up the plans for such a program. All of this would be done as quietly as possible, so as not to encourage "the further influx of refugees from the mainland." When the NSC again took up the issue on March 3, Acheson dominated the debate. Political and economic means alone, he cautioned, could not "guarantee a denial of Formosa to the Communists," but a limited show of naval force would accomplish nothing on Taiwan, while creating "an irredentist issue" for the Chinese Communists to exploit. "It is a cardinal point in our thinking," he elaborated, "that if our present policy is to have any hope of success in Formosa, we must carefully conceal our wish to separate the island from mainland control." At the meeting's end, Acheson, the Pentagon, and the President approved a new policy statement based entirely on Acheson's approach (NSC 37 / 5, which "supplemented," rather than replaced, NSC 37 / 2).[9]

The Second Stage:
March 1949–October 1949

For his "economic means," Acheson knew that he could draw from the remaining funds of the 1948 China Aid Act. The State Department had requested $570 million in economic aid for China, but the Republicans, who dominated the Congress, slashed this to $338 million and then appropriated just $275 million—leaving the rest unappropriated and unavailable. Congress also created a separate (and unrequested) $125 million fund for military assistance to China. The ECA, which administered the economic aid package, directed much of it to Taiwan, but the local authorities there stubbornly resisted political reform. To force a change, the State Department suspended all U.S. aid and restored it only after the appointment of a new Governor for Taiwan, Chen Cheng. Acheson, however, still not satisfied, persuaded the ECA to do no more than formulate plans for its program on Taiwan, and to base these plans on a figure of $17 million for industrial recovery and a smaller, unspecified sum for rural development. There should be no major expenditures, Acheson stressed, until his envoy had come to terms with Taiwan's new Governor.[10]

Almost at once, Acheson's strategy ran into trouble. Donald D. Edgar, U.S. Consul at Taipei, intensely distrusted Chen Cheng, and although Edgar held talks with Chen, they achieved nothing. In the weeks that followed, John L. Stuart, U.S. Ambassador to China, counseled Acheson to double American economic aid to Taiwan, while R. Allen Griffin, Acting ECA Director for Taiwan, found all such assistance futile and urged that it be terminated. Taking the middle ground, Donald Edgar exhorted Acheson to drop the ECA's industrial reconstruction program and concentrate entirely on agricultural aid, which could be channeled directly to the Taiwanese people. Acheson, unmoved by any of this advice, calmly persevered with his existing aid policy.[11]

Although Acheson could ignore his advisers, he could not ignore the congressional China bloc, which now challenged the administration's handling of the second portion of the Taiwan assistance package—the $125 million military aid fund. Based on a recommendation from the U.S. Army's Joint Military Advisory Group in China, Secretary of Defense James V. Forrestal asked the NSC to suspend all military aid to China. Approximately 50 percent of this aid had been delivered, and another 15 percent awaited shipment. All but $15–$20 million of the $125 million fund had been either allocated or spent. The NSC approved the military aid suspension (NSC 22 / 3), and Truman signed it on February 4, 1949. The China bloc, backed by the China lobby, instantly registered a strong protest. Acheson, at Truman's request, prepared a defense of the aid decision, but when he, the President, and Vice-President Alben Barkley met with congressional leaders on February 7, Senator Arthur H. Vandenberg did most of the talking. The military aid suspension, Vandenberg warned ominously, would lead to charges that the United States had given "poor China the final push into disaster," and he embellished this with depictions of an outraged public at home and a tarnished U.S. image abroad. The President, beating a hasty retreat, agreed to reconsider, and within days he lifted the military aid suspension. On March 10, Acheson informed Truman that out of the original $125 million military aid fund, $123,950,685.71 had been either allocated or disbursed.[12]

Unfortunately for Truman, tossing a bone to the China bloc did not put it off the scent. On February 7, fifty-one Republican congressmen petitioned the President to establish a commission to investigate U.S. policy on China. Truman again turned to Acheson, who offered to venture forth for an "off-the-record" discussion with the Republicans. This, Acheson reasoned, would minimize Truman's political risk and damage the Nationalists far less than going public with a laundry list of their transgressions. Truman agreed, and on February 24 Acheson met with thirty-one Republican congressmen. Reciting from an established State Department litany, Acheson described the sloth, corruption, and ineptitude of the Nationalist regime, and he admonished the congressmen that no amount of U.S. aid would make any difference. Then, unwisely departing from his script, Acheson depicted China as a backward nation with few resources, poor communications, little transportation, and an overabundance of illiterate and unruly peasants. Worse still, he ended his remarks by colloquializing the views of the U.S. Military Advisory Group in China: "We cannot tell what the next step is until some of the dust and smoke of the disaster clears away and [we] see where there [is] a foundation on which to build." The Republicans promptly leaked this to the press, which then described Acheson's whole approach as "waiting for the dust to settle."[13]

Despite a rather apathetic public response to the whole China issue, the China bloc stepped up its attacks. On February 25,

Senator Pat McCarran (a renegade Democrat from Nevada) introduced a bill giving China a $1.5 billion loan and authorizing U.S. military officers to take over direct control of some Chinese Nationalist military commands. Truman's supporters in Congress stalled the measure, but, in March, fifty senators from both parties delivered a letter to Tom Connally, the Texas Democrat who was Chairman of the Senate Committee on Foreign Relations, pressing him to take action on the McCarran bill. Acheson countered with a cogent epistle of his own. The Chinese Nationalists, he told Connally, had "lost no battles during the past year because of lack of ammunition and equipment," while the Chinese Communists had "captured the major portion of the military supplies . . . furnished to the Chinese by the United States." Additional military aid, Acheson concluded, would "only prolong hostilities." Connally smothered McCarran's bill, and in its place Acheson asked Congress to extend the 1948 China Aid Act (due to expire on April 3, 1949) to February 15, 1950. The ECA estimated that by this date, only $70 million would remain of the original $275 million economic aid fund. Congress approved the extension, and, on April 19, Truman signed it into law.[14]

Acheson thus preserved his Taiwan policy from the depredations of the China bloc, but steering it through the treacherous currents of Chinese politics would prove to be another matter entirely. Just before Acheson took office, the State Department had begun searching for a Chinese official who would "declare Formosan autonomy or ask to be taken under the wing of the United Nations upon Chiang's [Chiang Kai-shek's] fall." The prime candidates were Dr. Wei Tao-ming, Governor of Taiwan, and General Sun Li-jen, Commander of the Chinese Army Training Headquarters on Taiwan. But Chiang Kai-shek, the Nationalist President, did not fall. After appointing Chen Cheng to the governorship of Taiwan, Chiang resigned from the presidency and retained only his position as head of the Nationalist Party. Li Tsung-jen, Chiang's Vice-President

and political rival, took over as Acting President on the day
that Acheson became Secretary of State, and to court American favor, Li immediately offered to make Sun Li-jen the next
Governor of Taiwan. Acheson and his advisers in the Office
of Far Eastern Affairs received a full report on Li's overture,
but they overlooked it entirely in writing their supplementary
policy on Taiwan. As a result, Acheson's policy called for an
approach to Chen Cheng (a Chiang Kai-shek loyalist), even
though Sun Li-jen (a U.S. favorite) seemed likely to replace
Chen in the near future.[15]

Acheson selected Livingston T. Merchant, Consul at the U.S.
embassy in Nanking, to serve as his envoy to Chen Cheng.
After arriving on Taiwan in late February of 1949, Merchant
received instructions to press Chen Cheng for "certain assurances" in exchange for a U.S.-sponsored "industrial reconstruction program on the Island." Merchant at once recognized
Acheson's mistake. In a long telegram, he explained that Chen
Cheng was loyal to Chiang and would be unlikely to "provide
[the] liberal [and] efficient administration needed." The
replacement of Chen Cheng by Sun Li-jen, he suggested, would
be "the solution best suited [to] our interests." Acheson looked
into the matter and responded that while Sun had both a good
record and close ties to the United States, he lacked administrative experience. Acheson also feared that American support
for Sun might backfire and result in a governor even less qualified than Chen. Finally, even if Li did appoint Sun, Acheson
suspected, Chiang and his allies would "sabotage" the new
Governor as soon as he took office. In an item-by-item reply,
Merchant pointed out that Sun had willingly agreed to utilize
experienced administrative advisers, that Li Tsung-jen had
already indicated that he would replace Chen with Sun, and
that Sun's military position made him far less susceptible to
sabotage than any other candidate the U.S. might support.
Ambassador Stuart, Merchant concluded, should therefore
encourage Li to carry out the appointment of Sun Li-jen.

Acheson, persuaded at last, signaled his approval, and, on March 14, Merchant cabled back that Stuart, too, had accepted the revised plan.[16]

Although the name Sun Li-jen seems to have been entirely new to Acheson, it was well known in the State Department. A graduate of the Virginia Military Institute and the commander of the Chinese Thirty-eighth Division during General Joseph Stilwell's 1944 campaign in Burma, Sun had cultivated a fine reputation and innumerable American contacts. During the early stages of the Chinese civil war, according to Ambassador Stuart, the Communists considered Sun's First Army to be "by far the most effective force they had met." Threatened by such success, Generalissimo Chiang Kai-shek removed Sun from the First Army, which thereafter suffered defeat after defeat. Sun, promoted to Deputy Commander of the Northeast China Command but bereft of any real authority, drew ever closer to the U.S. State Department. In 1948, Sun became Deputy Commander in Chief of Ground Forces and Commander of the Army Training Center on Taiwan. In the former capacity Sun still lacked sufficient authority to influence the deteriorating situation on the mainland, but in the latter capacity he commanded some of the most important forces on Taiwan. All of this made Sun an excellent candidate for U.S. support. If Sun succeeded to the governorship of Taiwan, Acheson would have in place not only a leader who was prepared to break with Chiang and organize a new regime but also a gifted strategist who could defend the island thereafter.[17]

Throughout March of 1949, the Sun Li-jen appointment appeared imminent, especially since Chen Cheng seemed ready to resign. Chen even sent Ambassador Stuart an offer to ask Chiang Kai-shek not to interfere. Li Tsung-jen appeared resolute in his intention to replace Chen with Sun, and Acheson began coordinating his plans more closely with Paul Hoffman, Director of the ECA. The ECA, Acheson specified, would draw up plans for the economic rehabilitation of Taiwan, "including proposed capital expenditure for industrial replacement and reconstruction," but Hoffman would proceed only with fertilizer distribution and minor rural reconstruction projects. All major expenditures would be delayed until the "political circumstances" were "judged propitious for an all-out economic program on the island."[18]

Chiang Kai-shek, however, continued to control the Nationalist Party and a number of military officers, and he utilized these elements to neutralize Li Tsung-jen. Chiang's minions quietly blocked Sun Li-jen's appointment to the governorship of Taiwan, while Chen Cheng, despite his assurances to Stuart, surreptitiously consolidated his hold on that office. According to Donald Edgar, U.S. Consul at Taipei, Chen appointed "yes men" to every sensitive post on the island—thereby creating an administration that was "military, reactionary, [and] unpopular." Sun could yet become the Commander in Chief of Ground Forces, but Chiang's supporters in the Executive Yuan rendered this position largely irrelevant by giving Chen Cheng direct power over all civil and military organizations. Thereafter, Chiang and Chen conspired to keep their best military units outside of Sun's jurisdiction.[19]

In April, U.S. hopes for Taiwan commenced an agonizing roller-coaster ride. On the sixth, a downcast Livingston Merchant sent Acheson a virtual admission of defeat; a few days later, he indicated that he was inclined to believe a report that "Sun's string [was] played out." But just when Merchant seemed ready to open talks with Chen Cheng, Chiang Kai-shek held a cordial meeting with Sun Li-jen, and Li Tsung-jen reaffirmed his intention to appoint Sun to the governorship. Merchant held back. April faded into May, but still Li made no move to fulfill his pledge. Gradually, it began to dawn upon Merchant and Acheson that they were rank amateurs in the business of Chinese intrigue, and that they had been thoroughly outfoxed by one of the great masters of the art—Chiang Kai-shek. On May 4, Merchant cabled Acheson that the time had come for a complete revision of his policy, "rather than mere delay in its execution." The State Department, Merchant added, would have to "abandon [the] contemplated ECA reconstruction program on Formosa."[20]

Acheson immediately ordered Merchant to outline U.S. concerns to Chen Cheng and return to Washington. The meeting with Chen only confirmed Merchant's pessimism. In a final report on his mission, written soon after his return, he insisted that there remained "no possibility, short of the dangerous and risky effort to finance and promote a *coup d'état*," that the existing government could be replaced or reformed. On the one hand, Merchant observed, Taiwan had $90 million in gold reserves, sufficient food production to sustain itself, and a garrison of 200,000 troops. On the other hand, a locust-like immigration of "non-productive" Nationalist personnel threatened to demolish Taiwan's entire economy. Even if the ECA spent $25 million a year ($8 million more than actually budgeted), Merchant asserted, it "could not positively and constructively affect the Island's economy." The United States, Merchant reasoned, could maintain limited support, move to full support, or withdraw the bulk of its aid and rely on "the present Government's personal interest in resistance." Strongly recommending the third approach, Merchant suggested a scaled-down aid plan that would "reach and directly affect the little men of Formosa," coupled with preparations for raising the Taiwan issue in the UN. Any UN action, Merchant emphasized, should come as the result of an appeal by the native Taiwanese, although they would probably have to be organized by the "mainland elements on the Island." Merchant acknowledged that the Communists could conquer the island whenever they were ready, and he admitted that his plan constituted "a policy of calculated inaction colored with opportunism," but in his view there simply was no better alternative.[21]

Responding to these views on June 9, W. Walton Butterworth, Acheson's Director of Far Eastern Affairs, penned a similar list of options and likewise came out in favor of UN action. But Butterworth put no faith in the idea of an appeal to the UN by the people of Taiwan. Instead, he believed that the United States itself should go to the UN and candidly explain that the situation had changed since the days of the Cairo declaration, and that "the record of misrule by the Chinese authorities on the Island requires that the people themselves should have an opportunity to decide their own destiny."[22]

Finding his advisers once more at odds, Acheson called a special meeting for June 29—with Merchant, Butterworth, and four top ECA officials in attendance. The ECA officials did most of the talking. First, Allen Griffin, Acting ECA Director for Taiwan, expounded at length the ECA's efforts to restore Taiwan's trade with Japan. Then, Paul Hoffman, Acheson's longtime friend and the head of the ECA, analyzed yet another list of policy alternatives and concluded that they should completely write off the ECA program on Taiwan. Acheson promised only to give the matter further consideration, and he urged Hoffman and Griffin to redouble their efforts to expand Taiwan's trade with Japan.[23]

With Hoffman inveighing against any further assistance to Taiwan, Merchant espousing a radically new aid formula, and Butterworth pushing a high-risk UN strategy, Acheson decided to turn the whole question over to the State Department's Policy Planning Staff. Instead of clarifying the issue, however, the Director of the PPS, George F. Kennan, proceeded to confound it with yet another opinion. In an exhaustive report, he first explained that most State Department analysts felt that the United States should cut its losses and abandon Taiwan. Then, speaking only for himself, Kennan argued that President Truman should resolve the situation "the way Theodore Roosevelt might have done it"—by seizing Taiwan, abolishing the Nationalist government, and establishing "a provisional international or U.S. regime which would invoke the principle of self-determination for the islanders." "Formosan separatism,"

Kennan emphasized, was the only option with "sufficient grass-roots appeal to resist communism."[24]

Acheson, now bemused by a veritable kaleidoscope of opinion, selected the one alternative which no one recommended: he preserved his existing policy, continued to delay the implementation of its aid provisions, and gambled recklessly on future developments. In mid-May, with political tensions mounting on Taiwan, Sun Li-jen asked the State Department to apply more diplomatic pressure on the governorship question, even to the point of manipulating U.S. military aid. The State Department, anticipating a negative outcome, declined. Throughout May and June, Acheson and his advisers watched hopefully from a distance, while Chen Cheng tried to "shelve" Sun Li-jen and Sun plotted to "unseat" Chen. Finally, stalemated by Chiang's political infighting, and even a bit suspicious of Sun Li-jen's loyalty, Li Tsung-jen relinquished his plans to appoint Sun to the governorship of Taiwan.[25]

On May 17, David L. Osborn, U.S. Vice-Consul at Taipei, notified Acheson that Li Tsung-jen now intended to give K. C. Wu the governorship and transfer overall military authority on the island to Sun Li jen. Although Wu maintained somewhat weaker ties to the United States than Sun did, he had a long record of serving American interests, and his candidacy brought with it three distinct advantages. First, Sun's lack of administrative experience had made Acheson rather uneasy; K. C. Wu, the Mayor of Shanghai from 1946 to 1949, appeared to possess good administrative skills. Second, while serving as an economic adviser to Chen Cheng, Wu had acquired a broad understanding of Taiwan's problems. Third, and most important of all, Wu had always maintained cordial relations with Chiang Kai-shek, who would therefore be unlikely to block Wu's appointment to the governorship.[26]

As usual, however, Li Tsung-jen procrastinated. With his political struggle against Chiang Kai-shek still intensifying, Li held the Wu appointment in abeyance and delayed shifting more authority to Sun Li-jen. This allowed General Peng Meng-chi—the Taiwan Garrison Commander and a Chiang ally—to consolidate his control over most of the military units on Taiwan. In August, Li finally appointed Sun Li-jen "Commanding General of the Taiwan Defense Forces," but it was too late. Chiang Kai-shek, who had just moved his headquarters to the island, deftly shifted all real military authority into his own hands. Chiang, Chen, and Peng thwarted Sun's efforts to reorganize the island's defenses, and Sun's reports to the State Department became increasingly pessimistic. On September 16, 1949, W. Walton Butterworth, Director of Far Eastern Affairs; Dean Rusk, Deputy Undersecretary of State; and Fulton Freeman, Assistant Chief of the Office of Chinese Affairs, met privately with Li Tsung-jen's personal representative, Dr. Kan Chieh-hou. Kan, like Sun, seemed on the verge of despair. Chiang's viselike grip on the Nationalist gold reserves, Kan warned, had so depleted Li's resources that unless the United States immediately opened its pocketbook, Li would have to turn the entire government over to Chiang.[27]

Acheson, with feigned sangfroid, still held out hope. Dean Rusk later remembered, "Our general attitude in those days was that it was important for the United States to have control of every wave in the Pacific Ocean, and we tried to make good on this in a variety of ways, and that included the recognition that Taiwan was a very important strategic position." Acheson even presented his advisers with a new imperative: "You will please take as your assumption that it is a fundamental decision of American policy that the United States does not intend to permit further extension of Communist domination on the Continent of Asia or in the Southeast Asian area." Acheson also called for innovative ideas on implementation.[28]

Acheson himself came up with the first innovation; he would launch a new effort—this time by a flanking maneuver—to force the JCS into a full military commitment on Taiwan. Earlier, he had simply requested a reassessment of Taiwan's strategic importance; now he sent the JCS a memorandum (NSC 37 / 6) asking whether U.S. forces could defend the island in the event that he and the President deemed such action necessary for geopolitical reasons. To add a bit of urgency to this pregnant query, Acheson cited the findings of a recent CIA report: "Failing U.S. military occupation and control, a noncommunist regime on Taiwan probably will succumb to the Chinese Communists by the end of 1950." The JCS rejected Acheson's procedural ploy and reiterated its contention that Taiwan's strategic importance could not justify "overt military action . . . so long as the present disparity between our military strength and our global obligations exists." "The political importance of Formosa," the Pentagon added indignantly, did not "give rise to considerations of such importance as to justify overriding, on political grounds, the views of the Joint Chiefs of Staff . . . ."[29]

On September 13, Acheson once again assembled his top Asian policy advisers and asked them, with a hint of exasperation, what he should do about Taiwan. Philip Jessup and Dean Rusk made a vigorous pitch for taking the whole issue to the UN, but Acheson objected that this would only "show off the weakness of the United Nations." During World War II, Rusk subsequently recounted, the British derisively referred to the Indian Parliament as "the monkey house"; later, in 1949, "Dean Acheson tended to look upon the UN as the monkey house." Acheson disparaged any UN solution and, instead, created a special working group to revise his existing Taiwan policy. The working group ruled out a full military commitment, relegated the UN idea to further study, and amended only the implementation of Acheson's existing policy. Henceforth, the State Department would have to acknowledge the fact that Chiang Kai-shek was the "real source of authority on Formosa," and Acheson would have to employ his "diplomatic and economic means" to influence Chiang, rather than some potential successor. In particular, U.S. officials should notify

Chiang that once the existing aid funds had run out, any further assistance would be entirely contingent upon "the future
performance of the Chinese administration on Formosa." Despite
his unmitigated contempt for Chiang, Acheson decided to put
this new approach (NSC 37 / 8) to the test.[30]

The Third Stage:
October 1949–March 1950

The State Department immediately instructed John J.
MacDonald, U.S. Consul General at Taipei, to confront Chiang
Kai-shek with the warning indicated in its new policy, but
MacDonald objected that he would do better if he approached
Governor Chen Cheng. Among other things, MacDonald wanted
to put more pressure on Chen to expand Sun Li-jen's military
authority. Acheson accepted the idea of putting pressure on
Chen, but he ordered MacDonald to proceed as well with the
overture to Chiang—which MacDonald did on November 3.
Conspicuously delighted that the United States at last seemed
willing to talk to him (rather than replace him), Chiang nevertheless remained noncommittal. The next day, the U.S. embassy
in China apprised Li Tsung-jen of the overture to Chiang,
whereupon Li insisted that Chiang needed only to grant Sun
Li-jen "chief military responsibility" if he wanted to make Taiwan secure. MacDonald and K. C. Wu each in turn took this
same case to Chen.[31]

Yet, while MacDonald worked to influence Chen in Taipei,
Ambassador Stuart in Washington still hoped to replace Chen
with K. C. Wu. In an exhausting session with one of Chiang's
lieutenants, Stuart repeatedly implied that Wu should be
appointed to the governorship of Taiwan, and within hours
Chiang received a full report. MacDonald, once he understood
Stuart's game, fell into line. He cabled Acheson that, given
"the identification of K. C. Wu and Sun Li-jen with American

interests," their projected appointments to replace Chen Cheng and Peng Meng-chi, combined with a visit by "an American officer," might turn the whole situation around. At the same time, Sun dramatically underlined his own military prowess by repulsing a large Communist assault on Quemoy Island, and Chiang pledged, albeit disingenuously, not to interfere with Sun's command. Sun's erstwhile patron, Li Tsung-jen, moved his headquarters to Taiwan on December 6, but by this time he was only a powerless figurehead. Under heavy U.S. pressure, Chiang and his supporters finally gave K. C. Wu the governorship on December 7, 1949. Wu swiftly petitioned Chiang to remove Peng Meng-chi and expand Sun Li-jen's military authority. Chiang refused. Sun "begged" Donald Edgar, U.S. Consul at Taipei, to put more pressure on Chiang, but Edgar, narrowly interpreting his own authority, backed off.[32]

Sun Li-jen, however, had already begun work on an alternative plan—a military coup d'état. Suspecting as much, Chiang Kai-shek transferred General Liu An-chi and his forces from Hainan Island to Taiwan, thereby blocking Sun's coup. Then, in early January, Chiang summoned Sun and confronted him with an intelligence report on his conspiracy. Sun, thinking quickly, replied that the report must have emanated from Communist elements bent on dividing the Nationalists. If he had planned a coup, Sun protested, would he have been so naive as to tell anyone? Chiang accepted this logic, but Sun had to abandon his plans—at least temporarily. Acheson and his subordinates knew about Sun's projected coup and were undoubtedly disappointed when it fell apart.[33]

Chiang Kai-shek, with his usual cunning, grasped this moment for an all-out diplomatic offensive. He boldly requested additional U.S. assistance on December 23 and then followed up with a three-pronged campaign to "assuage the U.S." First, Wellington Koo, the Chinese Ambassador, delivered assurances to the State Department that the American favorites K. C. Wu and Sun Li-jen would soon receive substantially

increased authority. Second, Governor K. C. Wu set down a
long list of proposed reforms in a letter to Philip Sprouse, Chief
of the State Department's Office of Chinese Affairs. Third, in
response to American advice, Chiang personally replaced Yen
Hsi-shan, the Premier of the Nationalist government, with Chang
Chun. Robert Strong, U.S. Chargé d'affaires at Taipei, promptly
cabled Acheson that Chang Chun was "a real liberal" who would
"complete the triumvirate of American favorites, together with
Sun Li-jen as Defense Commander of Taiwan and Wu as Governor."[34]

But Acheson was skeptical. Since mid-October, the CIA
had been predicting that—barring U.S. intervention—Taiwan
would "succumb to the Chinese Communists by the end of
1950." On December 19, in conjunction with a new CIA study,
Acheson instructed Donald Edgar to reevaluate the situation.
Edgar replied that the Nationalist regime was fragmented and
unpopular; it did not seem susceptible to a coup d'état but
might suffer high-level defections to the Communists unless
the United States opted to pay off a few "selected generals."
Taiwan's economy remained sound, although imperiled by an
endless flood of refugees. In light of these facts, Edgar speculated that the State Department could probably sell either a
U.S. occupation or a UN trusteeship to both the Nationalists
and the Taiwanese, and he hastened to add that, without such
action, Taiwan would almost certainly fall within six to nine
months.[35]

Acheson had barely begun to deal with Edgar's assessment
when he suffered an unexpected attack from the Pentagon. The
State Department had determined (on the basis of the early
findings of the JCS) that it would be "futile" to extend the
existing U.S. military aid program for the Nationalists. But
Louis Johnson, Truman's new Secretary of Defense, disa-
greed. Under the guise of writing a comprehensive Asian policy, he set out to both extend and expand U.S. military assistance
for Taiwan, and he persuaded the JCS to follow his lead. With

the military portion of the 1948 China Aid Act nearly used up, Congress readily appropriated another $75 million in military aid for "the China area" as part of the 1949 Mutual Defense Assistance Act. Truman controlled the allocations for most of this fund, and Johnson wanted him to earmark part of it for Taiwan. The JCS forwarded a specific plan (NSC 37 / 9) to Truman and Acheson, but Acheson and his advisers would have none of it. They had already allocated the "China area funds" to Korea, Indochina, and the Philippines, and they believed that sending additional military aid to Chiang Kai-shek's regime would only delay its demise. On December 29, Acheson, his top Asian policymakers, and the JCS met to debate the issue. Omar Bradley, Chairman of the JCS, argued that, even if military aid only delayed Taiwan's fall, it would divert the expansionist energies of the Chinese Communists. Acheson retorted that since this might also involve U.S. prestige "in another failure for all to see," the strategic benefit would likely be exceeded by its geopolitical price. Bradley demurred, Johnson stormed off for a vacation, and the resulting comprehensive Asian policy (NSC 48 / 1, approved December 23, 1949) included no new military aid for Taiwan. Moreover, at Acheson's insistence, Truman and the NSC accepted a policy qualification (NSC 48 / 2, approved December 30, 1949) which reaffirmed Acheson's existing Taiwan policy and called for a stronger Pacific defense posture as a hedge against the possible fall of Taiwan.[36]

Acheson emerged victorious from this contest, however, only to plunge headlong into a new battle with the congressional China bloc and its China lobby supporters. Hoping to silence his critics, Acheson had suggested in March of 1949 that Truman authorize a public recounting of U.S. policy on China—an exposé to show that the Nationalist government, not the United States, was responsible for the triumph of communism. Truman approved it, Butterworth compiled it, Jessup edited it, and Acheson himself, with some help from Jessup, wrote a

15-page "Letter of Transmittal." On August 5, 1949, Truman released the completed project, 1,054 pages of tedium officially titled *United States Relations with China* but better known as the China White Paper. The press, rather predictably, ignored the white paper itself and focused instead on the harshest rhetoric in Acheson's letter of transmittal. Acheson tried to wait out the ensuing controversy, but it only intensified—especially after October 1, when the Communists formally established the People's Republic of China. Finally, in late December, the decision not to approve new military aid for the Nationalists left Truman facing a political firestorm.[37]

In the midst of frenzied press speculation, Butterworth and Rusk persuaded Acheson that a presidential press statement would be the most effective way to "straighten out the public record." Butterworth's office wrote the initial draft, the JCS made minor changes, and Truman issued the completed statement on January 5, 1950. Essentially, the statement ruled out additional military aid for Taiwan (after existing funds were used up) but left economic assistance intact. The Nationalists, Truman's press statement declared, already possessed sufficient resources "to enable them to obtain the items which they might consider necessary for the defense of the Island." Acheson secured in advance the support of John Kee, the Chairman of the House Committee on Foreign Affairs, and after the statement was released, he met with Senators William F. Knowland and H. Alexander Smith—the Republican leaders of the China bloc. The United States, Acheson explained, had to either stand ready to fight for Taiwan or accept "the real possibility of its collapse," and he offered two reasons for selecting the latter course. First, although the JCS viewed the situation on Taiwan with "considerable concern," it had decided that the island was *"not* of *vital* importance to the security of the United States." Second, any U.S. defense of Taiwan would raise the charge that the United States had begun to move in "the same orbit of imperialistic design" as the Soviet Union.

In his concluding remarks, Acheson emphasized that the Nationalist regime either possessed or could purchase everything it needed to defend Taiwan—provided that the political situation there did not "decay to a point where the invasion could be successful because of the sheer inability of the Nationalist Government to make its men fight." But Smith and Knowland remained unconvinced, and Knowland acidly described the Truman administration's military aid decision as "a policy of grave danger."[38]

Only a few hours later, Acheson delivered a remarkably different explanation to the Washington press corps. The United States, he asserted—with a perfectly straight face—had no designs whatsoever on Taiwan; the United States would uphold the Cairo and Potsdam agreements and continue to regard Taiwan as a part of China. A proliferation of words like "decent," "honorable," "integrity," and "principle" obfuscated the plain truth—that only a lack of military muscle had precluded a full commitment on Taiwan and that U.S. policy still called for separating Taiwan from the mainland by diplomatic and economic means. The Republicans, keeping up their offensive, forced Acheson into a tough fight in the Senate Foreign Relations Committee on January 10, followed by another in the House Foreign Affairs Committee on the following day. On the twelfth, in a much publicized address to the National Press Club, Acheson attempted a counterattack. Answering charges that insufficient U.S. aid had precipitated the "loss of China," he contended that the Nationalists had brought about their own defeats, despite ample quantities of U.S. weapons. He also outlined the Pentagon's Pacific Defense Perimeter (which ran from the Ryukyus to the Philippines and excluded Taiwan) in an attempt to show that the JCS—not the State Department—had ruled out a full-scale U.S. military commitment on Taiwan. But none of this stilled the critics.[39]

Within a week, the House of Representatives narrowly voted down Acheson's long-sought Korean aid program. In the Sen-

ate, Knowland and Smith introduced a bill to extend the 1948
China Aid Act to June 30, 1950, and they prodded the administration to allocate all of the act's remaining $105 million by
that date. On January 19—the very day of the Korean aid bill
defeat—Acheson secured Truman's support for a substitute
proposal on the China aid question, and on the twenty-fourth
he took his case to the Senate Committee on Foreign Relations. The ECA, Acheson admonished his Republican tormen-
tors, could not possibly spend $105 million on Taiwan in only
five months—"even foolishly." The Nationalist regime itself
had asked for only $55 million to cover the next eighteen
months, while the ECA projected a figure of just over $28
million for the same period. Congress, Acheson proposed,
should extend the 1948 China Aid Act to June 30, 1951, and
expand it to include the "general area of China," which
encompassed South Korea and all of Southeast Asia. Acheson
managed to convince Senators Connally, Vandenberg, and
Smith, but not Knowland. In a rough compromise (the Far
Eastern Assistance Act of 1950), Congress extended the 1948
China Aid Act to June 30, 1950, delegated the allocation of
its funds to the President, left its area of applicability unchanged,
and authorized a slightly reduced Korean aid program. Truman signed the measure into law on February 14, and within
a few weeks the political debate over Taiwan lost most of its
intensity.[40]

Throughout this process, Acheson insisted that the Nationalist regime already possessed sufficient means to defend itself.
His Office of Chinese Affairs reported that the Nationalists had
a 130,000-man army and a "surfeit" of armaments—including
at least twice as many small arms as needed, nearly 700 tanks
and armored cars, and ample stocks of artillery. They also
boasted an 85,000-man air force with over 500 aircraft, and a
30,000-man navy. Yet, the Nationalists remained vulnerable.
Only 60,000 of their soldiers were combat ready, less than half
of their aircraft were operational, and their largest ship, a U.S.-

supplied cruiser, had defected to the Communists. The problem was not munitions but leadership. By curtailing military aid, Acheson hoped to force a change in military leadership (in favor of Sun Li-jen), while minimizing the damage to U.S. prestige if Taiwan fell to the Communists.[41]

In addition to this new approach and the resulting political turmoil, January of 1950 saw a profound change in Acheson's Policy Planning Staff. As far back as 1947, George Kennan, the first Director of the PPS, had tried to make Paul Nitze his deputy, but Acheson had blocked the appointment. Nitze was only a "Wall Street operator," Acheson counseled Kennan, not a "long-range thinker." Kennan nevertheless continued to rely on Nitze's advice, and in September of 1949 Acheson relented and made Nitze the Deputy Director of the PPS. Shortly thereafter, Acheson began to push for a large nuclear buildup, while Kennan advocated the virtual abandonment of nuclear weapons in order to avoid an arms race. Nitze, somewhat to his own surprise, found himself first supporting Acheson and then, on January 1, 1950, replacing Kennan. Despite a deepening friendship with Acheson, Nitze never sacrificed his independence. To the contrary, he nurtured it. On one occasion, the wealthy Wall Street veteran bought his wife a fine thoroughbred horse for her birthday. Taking note of its unusually large equine nose, he named it "Mr. Acheson"—after his boss, whose prominent proboscis was surpassed only by his bushy mustache. Nitze later recounted, "We invited Acheson out to the farm for the weekend, took him out to the stables, and pointed out his namesake." Acheson "was not amused"—for which reason Nitze was all the more so.[42]

This kind of jaunty aggressiveness soon transformed the PPS, particularly with respect to Asia. Kennan, by his own account, left Asian policy alone except when ordered to produce a particular report. But Nitze observed no such conventions. He immediately set his staff to work on a replacement for Acheson's three-policy approach to China and Taiwan. The result was a single and unequivocal "two-China policy." Under this plan, the Nationalists would (as the result of American pressure) relinquish their claims to authority on the mainland and retain power only on Taiwan. The United States could then recognize both the Nationalist Government on Taiwan and the People's Republic of China. Nitze and his staff completed their proposal in a rare Sunday work session, and Nitze personally presented it to Acheson the next day. As Nitze looked on, Acheson skimmed through the paper thoughtfully. Suddenly, he stopped short and demanded to know exactly how many copies Nitze had made of his proposal. Nitze fumbled through a rough count, whereupon Acheson exclaimed, "Destroy them all but one; this is political dynamite!"[43]

Even so, Acheson was not satisfied with either his existing policies or the general performance of his Office of Far Eastern Affairs. He even considered establishing a second ambassador-at-large "somewhere in the general area of the Far East," but, instead, he sent his existing Ambassador-at-Large, Philip C. Jessup, on "a tour of the area." Jessup met privately with Chiang Kai-shek on January 16 at his secluded headquarters just outside Taipei. Chiang, adopting what the French school of fencing calls "the thrust direct," opened the discussion by interrogating Jessup on the Japanese economy. Citing Japan's exploding population and chronic inability to feed itself, he predicted that the Japanese would turn to communism when the United States terminated its occupation. The United States, Chiang astutely implied, could not afford to lose Taiwan's food exports to Japan. Furthermore, Chiang argued that the whole problem of communist expansionism would have to be "settled in Asia" and that the United States could not long avoid a full-scale war with the USSR. Although Jessup tried to play down both the dangers to Japan and the imminence of war, Chiang continued to insist that these factors would eventually force the United States to defend Taiwan. Jessup, in both an initial report and a follow-up meeting, warned Acheson that Chiang would stubbornly resist U.S. influence, while Sun Li-jen languished "in a pocket," from which he could not possibly organize a viable defense of the island.[44]

On December 19, 1949, the newly formed People's Republic of China (PRC) had signed a treaty of friendship with the Soviet Union, and in early January the CIA purloined a copy. It included an ominous secret provision: "The Chinese Communists must invade Taiwan in early spring, 1950. The USSR promises support if the United States intervenes." In addition, Stalin promised fifty combat aircraft and a special group of Soviet military advisers. A few weeks later, the CIA also reported that Chiang Kai-shek was merely "toying with local problems" while he waited for the United States to come to his rescue.[45]

The findings of the CIA, coupled with the results of Jessup's meeting with Chiang, touched off another State Department free-for-all. Like Jessup, Walter McConaughy, U.S. Consul General at Shanghai, argued that Chiang Kai-shek had become a major stumbling block. The Chinese people, the Consul General believed, had begun to hope for a "split within the Communist Party" and the rise of a "liberal . . . leader like Sun Li jen." The United States, McConaughy recommended, should withdraw recognition from the Nationalists and position itself to either recognize the PRC or "encourage new leadership." If Acheson chose to promote an alternative Chinese leadership, McConaughy speculated, it might "blossom" as the PRC's economic problems grew worse "in February or March." Livingston Merchant, now Deputy Assistant Secretary for Far Eastern Affairs, wanted Acheson to move even more aggressively. On February 1, 1950, he proposed that the United States occupy Taiwan, conduct a plebiscite, and create a new nation on the island. Merchant acknowledged that this would entail some geopolitical cost—particularly in terms of U.S. relations with the Chinese Communists—but he believed that the cost would be largely mitigated by his plebiscite strategy. Bluntly calling Merchant's approach "unrealistic," Philip Sprouse, Chief of the Office of Chinese Affairs, objected that Merchant's "plebiscite device" would neither mollify the Chinese Communists nor justify a U.S. occupation of Taiwan in the eyes of other Asians. In Sprouse's view, the cost of protecting Taiwan outweighed the benefits. Yet, even within Sprouse's own office, not everyone agreed. One analyst, for example, anticipated that the abandonment of Taiwan would cause other nations—particularly those in NATO—to seriously question American resolve.[46]

In mid-March, with the Taiwan debate moving toward a climax, Ambassador John Stuart injected a final assessment. Acheson's policy of treating China and Taiwan as "separate and isolated matters," Stuart contended, had become "increasingly difficult." The United States should therefore either accept the high geopolitical cost of offering full support to the Nationalists or abandon them completely and accept "the risk of accelerating [the] Communist seizure of Formosa." By Stuart's arithmetic, U.S. interests remained about evenly balanced between these two alternatives, but Acheson could not afford to dally. The Nationalists had begun to blockade and bomb the PRC's port cities, and the provocative nature of these actions multiplied the urgency of a U.S. decision. Stuart urged swift action in three areas. First, the State Department should withdraw de jure recognition from the Nationalist government, preserving only de facto relations. Second, Truman should cut off all arms shipments to Taiwan—even the final shipments of the 1948 military aid program. Third, Acheson should publicly warn the Nationalists that unless they ended their bombing campaign, they would be barred from further purchases of U.S. fuel oil and aviation gasoline.[47]

Conspicuous by his absence from this debate was W. Walton Butterworth. Butterworth was not an expert on Asia, and he had seldom exercised strong leadership, even within his own Office of Far Eastern Affairs. Acheson, far from comfortable with his own involvement in Asian issues, tried a number of remedies. He authorized several special committees on Asian questions; he considered creating a second ambassador-at-large to work exclusively on Asian policy; and he asked Dean Rusk, Deputy Undersecretary of State, to quietly assume a larger role in Asian affairs. But the problem only grew worse. Finally, Rusk offered to replace Butterworth and Acheson accepted. On March 28, Rusk left his prestigious number-four post in the department for a shallow foxhole in "no man's land." Acheson, Rusk wistfully recalled later, was "always a little grateful." Others remembered that Rusk at once made himself the first dominant voice in Acheson's pantheon of advisers on Asian affairs.[48]

The Fourth Stage:
March 1950–June 1950

Born into poverty in rural Georgia but educated at Oxford on a Rhodes scholarship, Rusk mixed boyish charm with Machiavellian guile. Acheson expected Rusk to help him deflect Republican criticism, improve relations with the Pentagon, and resolve the debate over Taiwan. They turned first to the political front. Although Acheson's Taiwan aid compromise had quieted the China bloc, Senator Joseph McCarthy soon opened a new avenue of attack. In a speech delivered at Wheeling, West Virginia on February 9, 1950, the Republican McCarthy began charging that numerous communist agents had infiltrated the State Department—particularly its Office of Far Eastern Affairs. "A great deal of nonsense," Acheson later noted in his memoirs, "has been written about the effect of the attack of the primitives, both before and during McCarthy's reign, on the China policy of the Truman Administration. Whatever effect it had on our successors, it had little on us." Nevertheless, McCarthy's onslaught prompted a two-part response. First, Acheson utilized the appointment of Dean Rusk to deflate McCarthy's rhetoric. Much to the amusement of the Washington press corps, for example, Acheson would whip through a list of conservative southerners on his staff—including Rusk—and then caustically pronounce them all "old-fashioned Southern Communists." For his part, Rusk cut such a conservative figure before Congress that McCarthy's bombastic accusations seemed laughable. Second, Acheson, with Truman's support, reestablished a bipartisan foreign policy by bringing John Foster Dulles, the leading Republican foreign affairs expert, into the State Department. Here again, Rusk proved invaluable. Acheson and Dulles intensely disliked each other, but Rusk kept them working harmoniously together. Taken as a whole, Acheson's political strategy proved extremely effective. At the end of March, Undersecretary of State James Webb reported to the President that Acheson believed that he was "over the hump" with respect to the Republican attacks on him.[49]

As a former army officer, Rusk proved equally adept at handling the Pentagon. Truman, to repay a political debt, had made Louis Johnson his Secretary of Defense in early 1949. The obstreperous Johnson exasperated Butterworth, but not Rusk. Despite standing orders from Johnson that all communications with the State Department go directly through him, Rusk constructed a private network of confidants within the Pentagon. Johnson, infuriated by Rusk's network, tried to get even when Acheson requested a military liaison officer. One day, Rusk answered a knock on his office door to find a thoroughly bemused Major General James Burns. Johnson, Burns announced with a touch of levity, had just assigned him to "defend the Defense Department against that fellow Dean Rusk." Instead of spying for Johnson, Burns allied himself with Rusk—especially in April and May, when Acheson began pushing for an increase in defense spending against Johnson's determined opposition. At the height of this struggle, Rusk once again found Burns at his office door, this time urgently requesting a drink. Rusk produced one from his private stock, whereupon Burns related that he had just accused Johnson of letting Acheson "be the Secretary of Defense." Johnson, Burns continued, had instantly exploded into an uncontrollable rage. On March 22, during a meeting between the top officials of State and Defense, Johnson exploded again. First, he lunged forward toward Acheson, banging his fists on the conference table and stamping his feet on the floor. Then he stormed out of the room, screaming hysterically that he would never meet with Acheson again. Johnson continued to be, in Rusk's words, "almost a disaster as Secretary of Defense," but he never overcame either Rusk's influence with Pentagon policymakers or Acheson's influence with the President.[50]

Acheson knew that if he won his struggle to increase the defense budget, it would, among other things, give the JCS the necessary forces for a full-scale U.S. commitment on Taiwan. Under his close direction, Paul Nitze and the Policy Planning Staff drafted a new policy (NSC 68), which restated the old concept of containing Soviet expansion and cited this as justification for building up U.S. military power. The annual defense budget, Nitze counseled Acheson, would have to be increased to roughly $40 billion. It would be an uphill fight. Truman and Johnson had already laid plans to reduce defense spending or, failing that, to at least keep it below $13 billion a year. Acheson outlined his plan to Truman in extremely general terms—avoiding any mention of Nitze's $40 billion figure—but even so, Truman balked and consigned the idea to further review. Only with the advent of the Korean War did Truman finally accept Acheson's new defense policy (NSC 68). In the meantime, the political situation on Taiwan continued to deteriorate. Acting President Li Tsung-jen journeyed to the United States for medical treatment in late 1949, and there he remained on February 28, 1950, when Chiang Kai-shek announced that he would re-ascend to the presidency on March 1.

Li initially hoped to challenge this illegal usurpation, but, finding no support from Acheson and Truman, he ruefully reconciled his differences with Chiang.[51]

The beginning of April found the CIA's analysts still anticipating a Communist invasion of Taiwan by year's end, and on April 10 they cautioned that no Nationalist regime would be likely to "effect political and military adjustments sufficient to defend the island successfully against a combination of internal and external threats." Chiang Kai-shek, responding to rumors of Sun's plans for a coup d'état, had withdrawn most of his troops from the strategic offshore island of Hainan. On the night of April 16–17, a sudden Communist invasion routed Hainan's few remaining defenders. On the nineteenth, the CIA reiterated its gloomy forecast, noting in the process that the Soviet Union had, as earlier predicted, begun sending combat aircraft and other military hardware to the People's Republic of China. The U.S. military attachés in Hong Kong and Taipei immediately asked Acheson to reconsider the curtailment of U.S. military aid to the Nationalists, and the assistant military attaché at Taipei even suggested giving the Nationalists $10 million a month in unrestricted loans for the purchase of munitions. Like an unstoppable juggernaut, the Chinese Communists Army made conspicuous preparations for an invasion of the Chusan Islands, forcing Chiang to order them evacuated on May 10. On the nineteenth, Robert Strong (the same Chargé d'affaires who had earlier expressed some optimism) reported that Chiang had denied Governor K. C. Wu the authority to initiate any significant reforms.[52]

Thus far, Acheson had assumed that the Nationalist regime possessed the weapons but not the leadership to defend Taiwan. Now, however, he began to reconsider. On March 7, Acheson reminded the Pentagon that although U.S. policy specifically disallowed new military assistance for the Nationalists, it permitted the completion of the 1948 military aid program. Out of an original $125 million, roughly $2 million remained unallocated. The Nationalists requested permission to purchase twenty-five medium tanks with these funds and twenty-five jet fighters with their own funds. This alarmed the British, who feared that the weapons might be turned against Hong Kong if Taiwan fell to the Communists. Acheson simply blocked the sale of medium tanks and jet aircraft, while leaving the storeroom door open for other types of tanks and aircraft. The Nationalists had no trouble revising their shopping list, but their U.S. military aid was still about to run out. Unable to reverse this without tying American prestige to the Nationalist cause, Acheson and Rusk devised an ingenious plan. The State Department, in cooperation with the ECA, quietly boosted nonmilitary assistance to Taiwan by over 90 percent. By "taking over" certain expenditures on Taiwan, Rusk explained later, the United States helped the Nationalists to "sustain their very heavy military budget." In effect, Acheson replaced in April the military aid he had precluded in January. At a special meeting on May 25, the State Department also urged the JCS to expedite Nationalist arms shipments and explore ideas for "the augmentation and intensification" of "covert action in support of resistance on Formosa."[53]

Yet, Acheson's official policy still called for political as well as economic measures to safeguard Taiwan, and, in the absence of the former, an expansion of the latter would likely prove futile. At the end of 1949, Acheson had nearly despaired of wresting power away from Chiang Kai-shek, but Sun Li-jen's aborted coup d'état raised hopes anew. Philip Jessup's Asian fact-finding tour in January included a tantalizing appraisal of Chiang's security arrangements. The road to Chiang's house, Jessup told Acheson, was guarded by one pillbox, a few soldiers, and "no great display of military protection." Livingston Merchant, Deputy Assistant Secretary for Far Eastern Affairs, promptly ordered W. W. Stuart, a veteran analyst, to study the prospects for "a United States cultivated *coup d'état* in Formosa." Stuart, in a late February report, examined all of the relevant factors and concluded that the full support of the Nationalist Army would be "the *sine qua non* of success." He then added, "General Sun Li-jen has himself indicated a disposition to overthrow the present Chinese Government on Formosa and has asserted that he would have the support of important Chinese military commanders. . . . It is believed that General Sun would be the best, perhaps the only, person who could carry out the military phase of the coup." The United States could initiate and guide this coup, Stuart speculated, through a clandestine liaison with Sun's representatives somewhere outside of Taiwan. Afterward, it would be necessary to recruit additional Chinese leaders for the "succeeding regime"— but not Vice-President Li Tsung-jen. Even though only Li carried sufficient legitimacy to preserve the Nationalists' seat in the UN, Stuart considered him too discredited and too "vacillating" to be useful.[54]

On March 9, Dean Rusk, Paul Nitze, and Livingston Merchant received an urgent message from Kenneth C. Krentz, U.S. Consul General at Taipei. Sun Li-jen had just informed Loris F. Craig, the ECA's new regional director, that he and "a liberal group" were planning to "overthrow the Government and set up one responsive to the people's will." A more democratic government, Sun argued, could successfully defend the island against the Communists, and he wanted to know if he "could anticipate U.S. support after such a coup." Craig, after consulting with State Department officials, told Sun that although the United States could not "express any opinion as to the advisability of this move," it would "continue assistance to any sound government, responsive to the will of the people of Formosa and capable of resisting Communism." Throughout April and early May, Acheson hesitated, waiting to see both what Sun would do and what his own advisers would recommend.[55]

First, Paul Nitze, in a report dated May 3, argued that the United States should quietly encourage Sun Li-jen to seize power but without becoming directly involved in the actual coup d'état. If the coup succeeded, the State Department could then step in with "a list of political leaders," followed within three days by a U.S. official who would provide Sun "with guidance from that time on." "Thence forward," Nitze advised, "the American hand in the running of Formosan affairs should be veiled but vigorous." Nitze also indicated that it might prove necessary to commit some U.S. air and naval forces to ensure that the new regime could withstand a Communist attack.[56]

Eight days later, Robert C. Strong, the U.S. Chargé d'affaires at Taipei, notified Philip Sprouse, Chief of the Office of Chinese Affairs, that Sun Li-jen was still considering a coup d'état. Sprouse drew up a short report on Taiwan, and although he neither discussed Sun's plot nor promoted a particular course of action, his overall analysis worked against any scheme that would increase U.S. involvement. On May 18, John Foster Dulles, Acheson's newly appointed Republican adviser, added his views to the mix and tried to glue the Taiwan question to the larger goals of American policy. If the United States continued "to fall back" before the advance of communism, he warned, the State Department could "expect an accelerated deterioration of our influence in the Mediterranean, [the] Near East, Asia and the Pacific." Moreover, communism would be seen as "the wave of the future," Japan would be rendered "untenable," and "the vast natural resources" of Indonesia and the Middle East would be left "in jeopardy." As an antidote, Dulles prescribed "a strong stand" on Taiwan to demonstrate America's "confidence and resolution." This, of course, might incur serious complications, including "a slightly increased risk of early war," but Dulles believed that a "resolute will" would suffice to overcome them.[57]

Dean Rusk, after assessing the views of Nitze, Sprouse, and Dulles, toiled countless hours to produce a report so exhaustive that it more closely resembled a book manuscript than a memorandum. After examining a broad range of options, he zeroed in on just one: a firm decision to "guarantee by American armed forces the status quo of Formosa pending its disposition by peaceful means either through a Japanese Peace Settlement or by the United Nations." Rusk, unlike everyone else, refused to confine his discussion of Taiwan's strategic importance to the dog-eared reports of the JCS; instead, he created his own balance sheet. On the negative side, he minimized the importance of Taiwan's trade with Japan. Immigration from the mainland had undermined the island's near-term potential as a food exporter. Furthermore, Rusk cautioned, if the United States took direct military action, it would risk "a 'shooting war' with the Chinese Communists—not the U.S.S.R.—while seeking to 'detach' Chinese territory from China." Rusk nevertheless put more emphasis on the positive side of his ledger. He reiterated Bishop's earlier analysis of Taiwan's psychological significance to Japan, Dulles's arguments on drawing the line against communism, and the Pentagon's depiction of the island's strategic location. Finally, Rusk noted that Taiwan would provide both "a pool of anti-Communist Chinese" and a base for "covert operations against China."[58]

Having thus established the desirability of a full commitment on Taiwan, Rusk turned to its chief difficulty: "So long as the Generalissimo and his group of followers remain on Formosa, they will be a source of embarrassment and trouble to the U.S. By experience we know that they will be ready enough to make promises of action desired by the U.S. and equally ready to fail in fulfillment of such promises." Rusk offered two possible remedies. The first called for offering the Nationalists both new military aid and full U.S. military protection in exchange for three things: the resignation of Chiang Kai-shek, the cessation of all air raids against the mainland, and the establishment of a new government run by "such Chinese and Formosan leaders as the U.S. may designate." Once this new government was in place, the United States would request a UN trusteeship for Taiwan. The Soviet Union would almost certainly play a major role in any UN settlement, Rusk acknowledged, but the United States would at least be able to keep Taiwan from falling under complete Soviet control.[59]

For his second option, Rusk outlined an American-sponsored coup d'état:

> The U.S. should inform Sun Li-jen in the strictest confidence through a private emissary that the U.S. Government is prepared to furnish him the necessary military aid and advice in the event that he wishes to stage a *coup d'état* for the purpose of establishing his military control over the Island. Sun should also be given ample funds (the total might run into several million dollars) to assist him in buying over the other commanders necessary to such an undertaking; he should be given firm assurances of whatever additional funds he might need in this connection during the early stages. Urgent preparations would have to be made to arrange for the shipment from Guam or some other nearby U.S. base of the arms and ammunition necessary to meet Sun's military requirements at the outset of such an undertaking.

Rusk included a rambling description of the "advantages and disadvantages" associated with each of his options. If Acheson and Truman chose the first, Chiang might refuse to step down. If they chose the second, Chiang's followers might prove recalcitrant once he was deposed, or, worse still, the coup d'état might fail and the U.S. role in it might be exposed. In the end, Rusk forthrightly and decisively recommended the second option—an American-sponsored coup d'état.

> Course (2), if successful, offers the better long-range possibilities in that it lays the ground for the same further action that would be possible under course (1) and at the same time provides possibilities which would not require further action envisaged in discussions with other governments. If the U.S. were

to strengthen Sun by military advice and assistance to the point where he was in a position to ensure a much more effective defense of Formosa than would have been possible under the Generalissimo, Sun would thus become a more important figure in relation to the scene on the mainland without the handicaps of the Generalissimo and discredited Kuomintang leaders.

Sun Li-jen, Rusk added, might even find a way to "make some kind of deal with dissatisfied Chinese Communist generals that would result in a break in the Chinese Communist camp." In any case, Rusk insisted that if a coup d'état could be "undertaken quickly and with the greatest skill and finesse," and if the U.S. Navy could safeguard Taiwan from invasion, the risks would be minimized and the prospects for success would be excellent.[60]

Rusk presented his report to Acheson on May 30, and at 4:30 P.M. on the thirty-first Acheson met with Rusk, Nitze, Jessup, and Dulles to discuss the issue. The meeting lasted two and one-half hours, with Undersecretary of State James Webb joining the group at 6:30 P.M. Unfortunately, no notes from this meeting are currently available. Soon after May 31 (probably during a private meeting on the following day), Acheson took up Rusk's recommendations with Truman. The President, according to Rusk, told Acheson that he would give the matter his full consideration.[61]

Audacious though it was, Rusk's proposal was not entirely unprecedented. During World War II, Franklin Roosevelt had discussed with General Joseph Stilwell the possibility of replacing Chiang Kai-shek with a more cooperative Chinese leader. General Frank Dorn and Detachment 101 of the Office of Strategic Services (OSS) then forged a plan to sabotage Chiang's plane when he made an inspection flight to India. Chiang and his wife would be given defective parachutes by an OSS flight crew, and Stilwell would find a new leader for China. After two months of planning, Stilwell forwarded the entire scheme to Washington, but Roosevelt declined to give it a final authorization. General Dorn, who supervised the operation, was Stilwell's Chief of Staff; Stilwell's Deputy Chief of Staff was a brilliant young colonel with a promising future— Dean Rusk. At about this time, too, Rusk first met Sun Li-jen, and, according to Rusk himself, they once dined together on shark's fin soup in the wilds of northern Burma.[62]

Thus, in May of 1950, a long chain of events led Dean Rusk to propose an American-sponsored coup d'état on Taiwan, and led Dean Acheson to believe that he had no other viable alternative. An entirely different chain of events, however, would shape the President's response. Truman, concerned about the political and diplomatic implications of the Taiwan issue, had already begun to conduct his own reconnaissance of the situation through two separate channels. The first of these consisted of the brothers Albert and William Jack Chow, two San Francisco businessmen who were also prominent figures in the Democratic Party. The Chows periodically traveled to Taiwan on business and reported back to Truman on conditions there. These reports generally reinforced those of the State Department, and Truman even forwarded one of them to Acheson with that observation.[63]

The President, however, kept his second independent channel entirely secret. Uncharacteristically, he utilized it to virtually bypass Acheson and the NSC. All of this began, innocently enough, at a formal reception on December 28, 1949. Convivial as always, Truman struck up a conversation with Karl W. V. Nix, an Ohio businessman whose father Truman had known socially for a long time. Truman and Nix discussed U.S. policy in some detail, and two months later Nix offered to serve as Truman's unofficial observer. Thereafter, Nix— whose business frequently took him to Japan, China, and Taiwan—intermittently reported his observations to Truman. In May of 1950, Truman sent Nix to Taiwan as his secret emissary to both Chiang Kai-shek and Sun Li-jen. Nix reported back to Truman at 5:00 P.M. on June 16, 1950. Neither Truman nor Nix left any notes on this meeting, but Nix undoubtedly described his discussions with Chiang in words similar to those he used in a subsequent memorandum.

> He [Chiang Kai-shek] told me in a private interview in May, 1950 that he was aware of his past mistakes and that if the President would send someone to Taiwan who would not insult him, he would do anything the President asked. Apparently American representatives in the past have ignored the important matter of considering the Generalissimo's face, and I appreciate his feelings in this instance.

Not only did Chiang offer to "do anything the President asked"; he also sent, at about this same time, a letter addressed to the President in which he offered to resign his office if Truman deemed that necessary.[64]

Nix may or may not have served as the mailman for Chiang's letter, but he clearly did hand-deliver a long missive from Sun Li-jen, dated May 23, 1950. Cautiously avoiding any direct mention of a coup d'état, probably for fear that his letter might fall into the wrong hands, Sun made only an oblique appeal for Truman to act swiftly: "Time, Mr. President, is against us, and the situation is desperate, but it is not yet hopeless." Sun also ran through a few well-worn arguments for a U.S. commitment on Taiwan; in closing, he explained that Nix had visited Taiwan for "a few days" and could tell Truman whatever else he needed to know. Sun requested a reply, but Truman decided not to send one. A written reply would have involved Truman much too directly—especially if he eventually decided to support the proposed coup d'état.[65]

Thus, by June 16, 1950, Harry Truman had before him five essential elements upon which to base a decision: Sun's original message indicating his willingness to carry out a coup d'état, Rusk's recommendation that the United States fully support

Sun's coup, Sun's letter urging the President to take action immediately, Chiang's offer through Nix to "do anything the President asked," and Chiang's letter offering to resign if requested to do so.

While Truman contemplated this Byzantine conundrum, the whole situation continued to deteriorate. On June 7, Acheson received a detailed report from Robert Strong, Chargé d'affaires at Taipei, outlining recent developments on Taiwan. The Nationalist Army had built four successive lines of defense. Its soldiers seemed willing to fight, but the quality of its leadership remained problematic. Chiang Kai-shek, Strong warned, had become "more bitter than ever against the U.S." Worse still, the Nationalist government had allowed its expenditures to reach $95,000 a month, and although Chiang hoped to reduce this to $70,000 a month, the regime's remaining $600,000 in gold reserves could not last much longer. Acheson, who together with the ECA had only recently doubled U.S. aid to Taiwan, took his duplicitous aid strategy one step further. Publicly, he continued to rule out any extension of "direct military assistance" for the Nationalists; privately, he sought a second expansion of U.S. economic aid so that the Nationalists could use an even greater proportion of their own funds for the purchase of military hardware. On June 14, Rusk met secretly with the top officials of the ECA and asked them to spend on Taiwan, over the next ninety days, all of the remaining funds from the 1948 China Aid Act. Such a massive economic transfusion, Rusk argued, would stabilize the situation on Taiwan throughout the summer months, and adverse weather conditions would render an invasion unlikely during the fall and winter. After expressing serious concerns about the high level of waste this would entail, the ECA officials agreed to give it their immediate attention.[66]

The Fifth Stage:
June 1950–November 1950

On June 24 (Washington time), North Korea launched an all-out invasion of South Korea. Within hours of the attack, the Departments of State and Defense drew up a series of recommendations, including one to send the U.S. Seventh Fleet into the Formosa Strait to protect Taiwan. Acheson and Rusk had already suggested this same action in conjunction with the proposed coup d'état, but in the absence of a coup d'état, it would only enable Chiang Kai-shek to further consolidate his position. Accordingly, Acheson sought a delay. When Truman gathered the top officials of State and Defense for a meeting at Blair House on June 25, Undersecretary of State James Webb took him aside and explained that Acheson wanted the Seventh Fleet moved toward the Formosa Strait but not into it, at least for the time being. During the meeting itself, Acheson argued that the United States should not tie itself to Chiang Kai-shek but should instead seek a UN settlement of the Taiwan issue at some point in the future. Truman, following Acheson's lead, ordered the Seventh Fleet to steam toward the Formosa Strait. On June 26, Truman again gathered his top officials for a meeting at Blair House. With the magnitude of the North Korean onslaught becoming more evident with each passing hour, Acheson decided that he could no longer accept the risk of a surprise attack on Taiwan. He asked the President to send the Seventh Fleet into the Formosa Strait and to demand the immediate cessation of all Nationalist attacks on the PRC. Truman agreed. He also, however, chose this moment to reveal his secret diplomacy. Through Nix, Chiang had offered to do whatever Truman asked—even to the point of resigning from office—provided that the President would send someone to Taiwan who would "not insult him." Truman now surprised everyone, especially Acheson, by proposing to send General

Douglas MacArthur to replace Chiang. Acheson was not impressed. He cautioned Truman that Chiang might, at the last minute, refuse to resign and "throw the ball game." It might be wiser, Acheson cajoled, to set the whole matter aside until later. The President concurred, although only after declaring that the replacement of Chiang should be the next step.[67]

In the words of his press statement, Truman ordered the Seventh Fleet to "prevent any attack on Formosa," and he called upon the Nationalist regime "to cease all air and naval operations against the mainland." Some in the Pentagon approved of Chiang's air and naval operations; Acheson found them an unacceptable drain on Taiwan's military assets and an unnecessary provocation toward the People's Republic of China. Truman's press statement put an end to both the debate and Chiang's offensive operations. As for the "future status" of Taiwan, that would await "the resolution of security in the Pacific, a peace settlement with Japan, or consideration by the United Nations." All of this came straight out of Rusk's May 30 report, but the most important part of that report—Rusk's proposal for an American-sponsored coup d'état—remained in limbo. In a hastily written "Condensed Check List on China and Formosa," Rusk noted that the United States would maintain the status quo in its relations with Chiang Kai-shek. With Congress now routinely extending the time limits on the various existing aid funds, Rusk estimated that they would suffice "to handle any feasible ECA program in Formosa and Southeast Asia for the next six months." On June 27, Chiang tried once again to hook the United States into closer ties with his regime, and his bait was an offer of 33,000 Nationalist troops to fight in Korea. Truman showed an interest in the bait; Acheson, pointing out the hook, dissuaded him from taking it.[68]

Even the intervention of the U.S. Seventh Fleet did not immediately eliminate the threat to Taiwan. The People's Republic of China, according to the CIA, continued to make preparations for an assault on the island. From July 31 through

August 1, General Douglas MacArthur, in his role as Commander in Chief in the Far East, inspected the defenses on
Taiwan, held talks with Chiang Kai-shek, and lavishly praised
Chiang's leadership—all to the utter consternation of the State
Department and the White House. MacArthur publicly
announced that he had coordinated military planning with the
Nationalists, but, in truth, the U.S. Navy had serious reservations about the ability of its available ships to stop a large and
determined invasion fleet.[69]

Acheson had long insisted that sending new military aid to
Taiwan merely to delay its fall was not worth the associated
risks to U.S. prestige. Yet, conversely, he had also tried to
coax the JCS into a full military commitment, and in that event
he had no objection to military aid. After June 26, the Pentagon approved the desired military commitment, the Nationalists suspended their blockade, and Acheson opened the door
to new military assistance for Taiwan. On July 12, John Stuart
and Dean Rusk requested a review of the military aid issue, as
well as "questions related to the matter of Chinese leadership."
With Acheson and the Pentagon in full agreement, the review
led rapidly to a completely new policy (NSC 37 / 10), which,
in turn, ordered the allocation of "certain military aid to the
Chinese Nationalist Forces." On August 25, Truman notified
Acheson that he had released $14,344,500 for military assis-
tance to Taiwan, with these funds to be drawn from the $75
million China area fund of the 1949 Mutual Defense Assistance Act.[70]

The Chinese Communists, according to U.S. intelligence,
slowly amassed a fleet of 2,636 junks for an invasion of Taiwan, but the CIA reasoned that if the Communists delayed
their invasion past mid-September, weather conditions would
probably force them to postpone it until spring. When mid-
September arrived without an invasion, Acheson saw a win-
dow of opportunity for implementing Rusk's UN strategy. On
September 20, the United States asked the UN General

Assembly to include on its agenda an item entitled "Question of Formosa," and, over Soviet objections, the General Assembly approved the U.S. request. Acheson, laying his UN plans with the help of John Foster Dulles, decided to focus attention on the political desires of the Formosan people, the issue of Formosan autonomy, and the possibility of establishing Formosan neutrality. In his larger strategy, worked out in consultation with Dean Rusk, Acheson hoped that U.S. maneuvers in the UN would prevent a Chinese Communist invasion of Taiwan, line up international support for an American-engineered settlement, help to ameliorate tensions between the United States and the USSR, and buy time for the Nationalists to stabilize the political situation on Taiwan. On September 29, CIA analysts reported that the People's Republic of China had postponed its planned invasion of Taiwan, and on October 25 the PRC launched a massive offensive against UN forces in Korea. Acheson, suddenly finding everything in flux, began to back away from the Rusk-Dulles UN scenario. On November 15, when the Taiwan question came before the UN General Assembly, the United States quietly asked for the matter to be temporarily deferred. The General Assembly unanimously agreed. Acheson initially considered reviving the UN idea at a later time, but before long, he dropped it in favor of simply shoring up the existing Nationalist regime.[71]

While Acheson, Rusk, and Dulles tinkered with plans for choreographing the UN General Assembly, Chiang Kai-shek took full advantage of U.S. naval protection to resume his former pattern of rule by intrigue, corruption, and intimidation. In July, Chiang launched a sweeping campaign to consolidate his power, beginning with a Hitler-like order that all soldiers henceforth swear allegiance to him personally rather than to the state. In September, Robert Strong (recently recalled from Taiwan) reported that Chiang had grown increasingly fearful of the Formosans and Sun Li-jen, since they were "receiving too much American support for his taste." Even Chiang's support within his own party seemed dubious, and as his fears grew, so did his repression. He initiated a ruthless purge, aimed at the most vulnerable of his political enemies. Describing this "reign of terror," Robert Strong wrote, "Criticism of the Government, even in a mild form, is almost out of [the] question; the critic is in dire danger of being arrested as a Communist and disappearing." Chiang also employed "extreme measures" to discourage any private contacts with U.S. officials, but he reserved his most terrifying repression for the army. Political henchmen, according to Strong, arrested some officers on "trumped up charges," while forcing others to spy on their own comrades. Morale plummeted, lines of authority disintegrated, and the resulting confusion seriously degraded the army's combat readiness.[72]

In mid-July, Kenneth Krentz, U.S. Consul General at Taipei, recommended a clandestine system of American support for dissident Nationalist military officers. After holding this plan in abeyance for some time, Acheson and his advisers concluded that it would be too vulnerable to Chiang's omnipresent intelligence network. Nevertheless, the State Department kept open the prospect of implementing it at some point in the future, "with the governing concept being that the personnel under consideration would be contacted only at the eleventh hour."[73]

By the beginning of 1951, Acheson had given up on the whole idea of deposing Chiang. Karl Nix (Truman's businessman turned envoy) suggested in March that Truman invite Chiang to Washington so that Chen Cheng (then Prime Minister) and Sun Li-jen (still Defense Minister) could seize power in Chiang's absence. Sun Li-jen, Nix argued, could then supersede Chen and move Chiang "upstairs" to a position of "great honor" but no authority. By this point, of course, the time for a coup d'état had long passed. Moreover, the Korean War had made it possible for the Truman administration to develop the military means to defend Taiwan. With profound feelings of relief, Truman and Acheson found it no longer necessary to venture into the turbid waters of Chinese politics.[74]

Conclusion

It is by no means an exaggeration to say that throughout this period the fate of Taiwan balanced precariously on the fulcrum of American policy. During the Second World War, the United States pledged to return Taiwan to China, but subsequently the JCS concluded that, given Taiwan's strategic and economic importance, the United States needed to keep it out of Communist hands. Since the Pentagon lacked sufficient forces to accomplish this by military means, Truman and the NSC asked Dean Acheson to attempt it with economic and political means alone. From the outset, Acheson believed that he could safeguard Taiwan only by first wresting it from the grasp of Chiang Kai-shek. Throughout 1949, when Chiang held no formal office, Acheson endeavored to supplant Chiang's behind-the-scenes authority by securing key political appointments for American favorites—particularly Sun Li-jen and K. C. Wu. After a complicated campaign, Acheson finally secured the desired appointments, only to find that Chiang had surreptitiously transferred all real political and military authority to himself. This, coupled with Taiwan's deteriorating military situation, led Acheson to preclude additional military aid in order to both push Chiang toward reform and minimize the damage to U.S. prestige if Taiwan fell to the Communists. When Chiang responded with a transparent imitation of reform, Dean Rusk recommended either forcing him to resign or backing a coup d'état led by Sun Li-jen—with the emphasis on the latter. Acheson took these recommendations to the White House. The President, unwilling to rely entirely upon the State Department, sent his own private emissaries to both Sun and Chiang, and received from Chiang an offer to resign. But Truman delayed making a decision. The outbreak of war in Korea finally forced the JCS to accept a full commitment to protect Taiwan, and this, in turn, rendered a U.S.-backed coup d'état unnecessary. In the final months of 1950, the People's Republic of China abandoned its plans to seize Taiwan, Chiang Kai-shek abandoned even the pretense of reform, and Acheson abandoned his long struggle to eliminate Chiang.

Acheson and his advisers fabricated their Taiwan policy around a prioritized assessment of national interests, an unambiguous core objective, the utilization of available and proportionate means, and an expressed commitment to adapt policy implementation to regional developments. The underlying motivation of Acheson's policy underwent a relatively simple evolution. From early 1949 to May of 1950, Acheson based his policy on a JCS report which defined Taiwan's importance in terms of its strategic location astride Japan's trade routes and its potential as a trading partner for Japan. Then, in late May of 1950, Dean Rusk fielded a revised analysis—deemphasizing Taiwan's trade and attaching greater significance to its strategic location, its psychological importance to Japan, its attractiveness as a place to draw the line against communism, and its potential as a base for covert operations against the People's Republic of China. Acheson, however, never discounted Taiwan's potential trade with Japan. His policy rationale absorbed a potpourri of lesser arguments, but it always hinged primarily on Taiwan's strategic, economic, and psychological importance to Japan. Over the years that followed, Taiwan rapidly emerged as one of Japan's most important Asian trading partners—exactly as Acheson had intended from the outset.

Acheson and the American Cold War with China

DEAN ACHESON NEVER attached much importance to China, and he addressed himself to Chinese issues accordingly. Indeed, his foremost concern in this area was not with China itself, but with the restoration of Sino-Japanese trade, which he saw as yet another means for easing Japan's economic crisis. Beyond that, Acheson and his advisers anticipated that over the course of a few decades the Chinese Communists would drift away from their Soviet mentors and that this, in turn, would lead to improved relations between China and the United States. Acheson's diplomacy in China can be broken down into two distinct stages. During the initial stage, which spanned the first half of 1949, Acheson sought to open an informal dialogue with the Communists. He eventually cut through a poisonous fog of mutual distrust to open secret discussions with Chou En-lai, a ranking member of China's new ruling elite, but the outcome only confirmed his worst suspicions. During the second stage, mid-1949 to late 1950, the positions of both the

U.S. government and the newly formed Communist government, the People's Republic of China, hardened rapidly. At the end of this period, the two nations found themselves not only isolated from one another but fighting each other on the terrible battlefields of the Korean War.

The First Stage:
September 1948–July 1949

In addition to the policy on Taiwan, Dean Acheson adopted two policies for dealing with the Chinese Communists. The first of these evolved from a long report (PPS 39, completed September 7, 1948), which was based on information from the Office of Far Eastern Affairs and written by George Kennan and his Policy Planning Staff (PPS). Describing China's birthrate as "classically Malthusian" and dismissing its resources as "relatively modest," Kennan's planners painted a bleak picture. China, with a population over three times that of the United States, had, in proven reserves, less than half as much iron, a tenth as much coal, and no petroleum. China's iron, its most abundant resource, was strictly "low grade." Worse still, the Chinese economy had absolutely no prospect of finding the capital, markets, and raw materials it needed for industrialization. China's military importance, the policy planners concluded, was likewise unimpressive; for the foreseeable future, China would "more closely resemble a strategic morass than a strategic springboard" for the Soviet Union. Overall, there simply were no compelling economic or strategic reasons for putting a high priority on preserving mainland China from Soviet domination. Kennan and his crew nevertheless outlined a tentative, long-term strategy for achieving that end. In mid-1948, the Soviet-administered Communist Information Bureau, better known as Cominform, strongly denounced Tito's Communist government in Yugoslavia and called for its overthrow.

A few U.S. analysts quickly began to speculate that a similar rift might eventually occur between the Soviet Union and the Chinese Communist Party, and Kennan's staff incorporated this "Asian Titoism" scenario into its report on China. The Soviet Union, the planners argued, would face "a considerable task in seeking to bring the Chinese Communists under its complete control"—especially given the rising tide of Chinese nationalism. Moreover, a flexible U.S. policy might, in the long run, find openings to undermine Sino-Soviet relations.[1]

The State Department forwarded the Policy Planning Staff's report to the National Security Council (NSC), which, in turn, transformed the report into a draft policy statement (NSC 34 / 1). The goal of American policy, the NSC's draft statement specified, was a "unified, stable and independent China, friendly to the U.S." To this end, the United States would seek to prevent China from "becoming an adjunct of Soviet power," and the State Department would maintain its "flexibility," avoiding "irrevocable commitments to any one course of action or to any one faction."[2]

When Dean Acheson assumed office as Secretary of State, on January 21, 1949, he inherited not only the NSC's draft policy statement on China, but also an extremely fluid situation in China itself. The Nationalist (Kuomintang) government, which had ruled China for over two decades, watched impotently as its army retreated before a much smaller Communist force. Chiang Kai-shek, the Nationalist President, resigned on the very day that Acheson took office. Chiang's Vice-President, General Li Tsung-jen, became Acting President not by popular election but by the mandate of the army. Li, quite unlike Chiang, was a gifted strategist. In 1937, he had even administered a brief riposte to the invading Japanese, and he might have achieved more except for Chiang's interference. By 1949, however, in the civil war against the Communists, it was much too late for military strategy—and no one knew this better than Li. He took power, in fact, at the

head of a growing faction which saw a negotiated peace settlement as the last, slim hope for the survival of the Nationalist
Party.[3]

Li wasted no time asking Britain, France, and the United
States to mediate a peace conference, but each in turn refused.
The Soviet Union showed some interest in mediation, provided that Li would accept a three-point accord designed to
eliminate all U.S. influence in China. Li, in desperation, asked
John Leighton Stuart, the American Ambassador, for assistance in working out an accommodation that would satisfy Soviet
demands. Not surprisingly, Stuart declined, and Li, finding no
other choice, opened an unmediated dialogue with the Communists. After three months of discussions, the Communists
produced a list of eight demands—including one which stipulated that all Nationalist forces capitulate before peace talks
could begin, and another which spelled out severe punish-
ments for Chiang Kai-shek and his closest followers. When
the Nationalists rejected these demands, the peace talks fell
apart. The Communists held the esteem of the Chinese people.
Li's regime held a huge expanse of territory, but it shrank with
every passing day. To make matters worse, Chiang Kai-shek
remained the head of the Nationalist Party, and he worked
through well-placed members of his "Whampoa" military clique
to undercut Li's authority over the army. Chiang also managed
to expropriate a large portion of the government's monetary
reserves, roughly $350 million in gold from the Bank of China,
which he smuggled out to Taiwan.[4]

Acheson recognized at once that the crumbling Nationalist
regime could not hold out much longer, and he ordered Kennan's Policy Planning Staff to reexamine the NSC's draft policy statement on China. The PPS complied, and the resulting
draft policy (PPS 39 / 2, completed February 28, 1949) included
a number of clarifications. Acheson, now satisfied, approved
this revised policy without alteration. On March 3, both the
NSC and the President followed suit. Acheson's new policy

(NSC 34 / 2) declared that the Nationalists were losing the war and that the Communists were "deeply suspicious and hostile" toward the United States and could be expected to remain so "for a long time to come." The United States could not alter the circumstances of the Nationalists; it could only work to minimize the hostility of the Communists. More specifically, the new policy indicated that the United States should seek to curtail its military assistance to the Nationalists—unless they began to fight more effectively—and maintain diplomatic contacts with both sides. Acheson's revised policy anticipated that it would take *"twenty to twenty-five years"* (italics added) before China would even begin to draw away from the Soviet Union, but this nevertheless remained a principal objective: "While scrupulously avoiding the appearance of intervention, we should be alert to exploit through political and economic means any rifts between the Chinese Communists and the U.S.S.R., and between the Stalinist and other elements in China . . . ." To avoid "the incubus of interventionists," the State Department would implement its policy through the judicious use of "indigenous Chinese elements" and "appropriate clandestine channels."[5]

Despite the rapidity with which Acheson revised his China policy, he—like Kennan and the PPS—saw no compelling reason to assign a high priority to China. In fact, Acheson excluded China altogether from a list of priorities he drew up before taking office, and China never captured a major share of his attention thereafter. Dean Rusk, Deputy Undersecretary of State in 1949 and Assistant Secretary for Far Eastern Affairs in 1950, later recounted, "Acheson himself, personally, did not give that much attention to China." Max Bishop, Chief of the Office of Northeast Asian Affairs in 1949 and State Department member on the NSC Staff in 1950, rendered a similar appraisal. But what occasioned such ambivalence? Paul Nitze, who rose by stages from Deputy Director of the Office of International Trade to Director of the PPS, subsequently

offered a candid explanation: "If it [China] had had big economic potential, he [Acheson] would have paid more attention
to it, but it didn't have much economic potential." A few statistics told the whole story. U.S. business interests, according
to State Department estimates, had invested only $100–$200
million in China, while the total value of U.S. trade with China
"fluctuated between $100 million and $125 million a year."
China's trade had never accounted for more than 1.9 percent
of all U.S. exports or 3.4 percent of U.S. imports. Thus, even
though the United States had long been a crucial trading partner for China—accounting for 15–25 percent of its imports
and 11–26 percent of its exports—China had no corresponding
significance to the U.S. economy. One pivotal State Department report, "United States Interests in China," cited these
statistical data and concluded, "The loss of the China market
would not be important for American producers as a whole,
although producers of a few commodities . . . might feel the
reduction in market." China exported nothing, the report added,
that was "of predominant importance to the United States,"
and the United States could readily find "alternative suppliers"
for those few commodities which it imported from China.[6]

Yet, while China played only a minor role in American trade,
it played a major role in Japanese trade, and this part of the
equation—like most other matters pertaining to Japanese
recovery—did receive Acheson's full attention. From 1930 to
1938, Sino-Japanese trade averaged $236,848,000 annually and
made up 15.1 percent of Japan's total foreign trade. In 1934,
a fairly typical year, Japan imported 33 percent of its iron ore,
72 percent of its pig iron, and nearly all of its coking coal from
mainland China. During World War II, the total value of Japan's
annual trade with China reached $623,192,000 (34.6 percent
of Japan's total trade), but afterward it plunged to just
$7,200,000. Recognizing the significance of this trade, U.S.
planners quickly began to weigh the prospects for reviving it,
despite the growing probability that China would soon be run

by a Communist regime. On November 3, 1948, almost three months before he became Secretary of State, Acheson received a special report by two analysts in the Economic Cooperation Administration—"United States Policy in China." In it, the ECA's analysts minimized China's direct importance to the United States and emphasized its significance to Japan: "Without the resources of this area [Northern China and Manchuria] *there would be no hope of achieving a viable economy in Japan.* To take only one example of critical importance, the nearest alternative source of coking coal for Japanese blast furnaces is West Virginia." Two months later, the State Department's Office of Intelligence Review (OIR) submitted another report reiterating the same theme: "It has become increasingly clear that Japan is not likely to achieve a self-supporting economy without continued, if not increasing, U.S. aid unless trade with northeast Asia, particularly China and Manchuria, can be restored."[7]

Soon after Acheson took office, he ordered W. Walton Butterworth, Director of the Office of Far Eastern Affairs, to write a definitive policy on Chinese trade. Butterworth, in close consultation with Acheson and various foreign trade specialists, produced a meticulously worded twelve-page policy statement, and Acheson immediately took it to the NSC. On March 3, 1949, the NSC adopted the new policy ("United States Policy regarding Trade with China," NSC 41), and the President approved it that same day. In their new policy, Acheson and Butterworth began by bluntly acknowledging that the United States could not "prevent China from becoming an adjunct of Soviet power" and that the State Department could only seek to choose "the least disadvantageous" course. With similar candor, they also included a statement reflecting Acheson's own attitude toward China: "The direct economic importance of China to the United States is not great. Private American investments in China are small and United States-China trade is of relatively minor significance." This, in keeping with the earlier ECA and OIR reports, left Sino-Japanese trade as the primary U.S. concern: "Trade with China is indirectly of significant importance to the United States in that the achievement of Japanese self-support . . . is to a degree dependent on access to the export surpluses of north China and Manchuria." The complete elimination of Japan's trade with China, Acheson and Butterworth stressed, might raise "the prospect of indefinite support of the Japanese economy by the United States."[8]

As for China itself, Acheson and Butterworth believed that "the subsistence character of the Chinese economy, in combination with China's serious shortages of managerial and technical personnel" would not permit "rapid or large-scale formation of domestic capital." In this circumstance, the United States could either cut off trade to intimidate the Chinese or maintain limited trade relations in the hope of eroding Moscow's influence. The former approach, Acheson and Butterworth concluded, would be unlikely to rally concerted action by America's allies; even if it did, it would not have a significant impact on China's "subsistence" economy. The latter approach, which the new trade policy endorsed, offered the prospect that Western trade could induce the Chinese to resist "political and economic exploitation" by the Soviet Union. "A restoration of mutually beneficial trade relations," Acheson and Butterworth specified, "between China on the one hand and Japan and the Western world on the other, and the progressively increased importance to China of such relations, might bring about serious conflicts between Kremlin and Chinese policy, and thereby tend to produce an independent Chinese Communist regime."[9]

Nonetheless, Acheson firmly opposed any long-term Japanese dependence on trade with the Communists. Dean Rusk and Max Bishop each subsequently remembered Acheson's strong distaste for permitting Japan to trade with the Chinese Communists; Sino-Japanese trade was a two-edged sword which could as easily cut Japan's ties with the U.S. as China's ties with Moscow. Acheson's China trade policy clearly reflected this concern: "Trade between Japan and China should be encouraged on a quid-pro-quo basis, but preponderant dependence on Chinese sources for Japan's food and critical raw material requirements should be avoided, and efforts should be made to develop alternative sources on an economic basis."[10]

In light of Acheson's two new China policies—the general policy and the trade policy—the American Ambassador to China, John Leighton Stuart, requested permission to establish contacts with the Chinese Communists. The Chinese Communist Party, Stuart observed in a March 10 telegram, had "revealed an increasingly anti-American sentiment," which resulted from basic Communist ideology, U.S. assistance to the Nationalists, and a growing "misapprehension" of American intentions. Stuart, who had once been the President of Yenching University, had many former students in the Communist camp, and he expected them to help him promote a dialogue. Acting on Butterworth's advice, Acheson approved Stuart's request on April 6. By that time, Communist forces had moved within striking distance of the capital city, Nanking, forcing the entire Nationalist government to flee. Stuart urged Acheson to maintain the U.S. embassy at Nanking, while Lewis Clark, Minister Counselor of the Embassy in China, recommended moving it to the new Nationalist capital, Canton. Acheson, after consultation with Butterworth and the British Foreign Office, ordered the embassy to stay put. The Communists swept into Nanking on April 24 and clamped tight restrictions on the U.S. embassy. Although Stuart cabled Acheson that he would let the Communists "make the first approach," he quickly initiated talks with Huang Hua—an alumnus of Yenching University, the chief of the Alien Affairs Office of the Nanking Military Control Council, and a protégé of Chou En-lai, one of the most influential members of the Central Committee of the Chinese Communist Party. The discussions with Huang produced only a demand that the United

States immediately cut off all aid to the Nationalists and with-draw diplomatic recognition from their government, but Stuart continued to work toward a broader dialogue.[11]

On May 31, 1949, Michael Keon, an Australian news cor-respondent, passed a message to Colonel David Barrett, the Assistant U.S. Military Attaché in Nanking. The message, which appeared to be from Chou En-lai to the U.S. and British gov-ernments, described a feud within the Chinese Communist Party (CCP) between a pro-Moscow faction, led by Liu Shao-ch'i, and a "realistic" faction, led by Chou. Chou's faction purport-edly hoped for early recognition by the Western powers, fol-lowed by U.S. economic assistance and normalized trade relations. Mao Tse-tung, the Chairman of the CCP's Central Committee and the principal arbiter of the CCP's policies, seemed to be withholding himself from the debate. Both Ambassador Stuart and O. Edmund Clubb, U.S. Consul Gen-eral at Beijing, at once accepted the Keon message as genuine, but Acheson remained suspicious. He ordered Clubb to send an unsigned reply written on plain paper. Clubb complied and instructed Keon to ask his Chinese contact whether either Clubb or Barrett could deliver the message to Chou. To everyone's surprise, Keon's intermediary completely rebuffed the U.S. overture, but Barrett, through his own channels, managed to establish contact with Chou's secretary. Barrett discovered that Chou had become extremely concerned that Keon might soon be interrogated by other Communist authorities. No interro-gation took place, however, and Barrett's clandestine contact with Chou's secretary probably facilitated subsequent U.S. contacts with Chou.[12]

Somewhat discouraged, Stuart began making plans to return to Washington. Then, unexpectedly, his ongoing discussions with Huang Hua produced what Stuart himself described as "almost an invitation" to visit Beijing. In years past, Stuart had always attended the Yenching University commencement exercises in Beijing. His longtime assistant, Philip Fugh, quietly raised with Huang Hua the prospect that Stuart might make this ritual visit before returning to the United States, and Huang, after consulting his superiors, replied that Stuart would be welcome to attend the commencement exercises. On June 30, Stuart asked Acheson for permission to make the trip. This was a "veiled invitation from Mao and Chou," Stuart argued, and if he made the trip, he could both outline U.S. policy to the Communists and "strengthen [the] more liberal anti-Soviet element in [the] CCP." John M. Cabot, Consul General at Shanghai, likewise exhorted Acheson to seize the opportunity, pointing out that a negative reply would risk making the position of Americans in China much more difficult. Butterworth observed that the trip might be feasible if Stuart, on his way to Beijing, could secure the release of American consulate officials being held at Mukden. Acheson, rejecting all of this advice, sent out an unequivocal order on July 1: under no circumstances should Stuart go to Beijing. Somewhat later, Butterworth told Cabot that Acheson based his decision on a strong suspicion that Mao and Chou wanted to lure Stuart to Beijing for the sole purpose of humiliating him. Acheson's caution may have cost him an opportunity to improve relations with the CCP, but it may also have prevented a major diplomatic embarrassment. On June 30, the day *before* Acheson replied to Stuart, Mao Tse-tung published an extremely antagonistic essay—"On the People's Democratic Dictatorship." In it, Mao proclaimed that China did not need American aid, that the United States wanted to "enslave the whole world," and that the CCP had chosen to "lean to one side" in order to "win victory and consolidate it." "Internationally," Mao added, "we belong to the side of the anti-imperialist front headed by the Soviet Union, and so we can turn only to this side for genuine and friendly help, not to the side of the imperialist front."[13]

Yet, even though Acheson eschewed public talks with the CCP, he had no objection to secret ones. "It is my impression," Dean Rusk later recalled, "that Ambassador Stuart did have a talk with Chou En-lai before he left China." A top-secret report—"Two Talks with Mr. Chou En-lai"—subsequently summarized lengthy discussions between a high-ranking U.S. official, probably Stuart, and Chou En-lai. From the outset of these talks, Chou accused the United States of supporting "dictatorial rule" and assisting reactionary elements. In the 1930s, he pointed out, the United States had traded war materials to Japan while it was trying to conquer China, and in the 1940s the United States had sent considerable assistance to the repressive regime of Chiang Kai-shek. The Soviet Union, by comparison, had been the first to establish friendly relations with the Kuomintang of Sun Yat-sen, the first to recognize the Chinese revolution, and the first to send aid to China during its war with Japan. "America's many good points," Chou contended, "pertain to small matters, Soviet Russia's to large." In Chou's view, decades of imperialism had left China dependent on the United States for manufactured goods, while the United States imported little in return from China. America found "no need at all for tung oil, raw silk, pig's bristles, etc.," but China relied heavily on the United States for "petroleum, steel, machinery, cotton, timber, automobiles, paper, photographic supplies, etc." To substantiate his argument, Chou cited numerous statistics, and then, in keeping with Leninist economic theory, he insisted, "The U.S. wants to relieve its [surplus production] crisis and is exporting in great quantity. Its stomach is sick with glut, ours with hunger." The new China, Chou elaborated, would correct this situation by producing much of what it had previously imported—thereby depriving the United States of an important export market. Likewise, China would henceforth "reject unplanned economic surplus material" and base its trade on "the principle of equal advantage." "In conclusion," Chou declared bluntly, "I do not depend upon you, you depend upon me. If you should seek to come in a private capacity, it is possible that you would be able to meet a person in [a] responsible position."[14]

If Chou En-lai's remarks left Acheson pessimistic about relations with the CCP, an astonishingly harsh memorandum from the once conciliatory Stuart confirmed that impression. The United States, Stuart now warned, "should be free from any illusions as to the nature of Chinese Communism." The CCP had become "thoroughly imbued with the Marxist-Leninist doctrines" and sincerely advocated the overthrow of "all capitalist or 'imperialistic' governments." Furthermore, Stuart cautioned, if American policymakers still hoped to make the CCP aware of China's need for U.S. trade, they should remember that the leaders of the CCP would "not hesitate to force the Chinese people to undergo severe privation in order to attain their goal of a socialized China, free from Western influence." Finally, Stuart emphasized that the United States should remain patient, and "should not place undue hope in an early change of CCP policy."[15]

The Second Stage:
July 1949–November 1950

By this time, however, other factors had also begun to play a major role in widening the gulf between the United States and the CCP. In 1948, well before Acheson became Secretary of State, the State Department had decided to leave all of its consulate offices in China open and functioning, even those in Communist-controlled areas. The consulates would continue to serve those U.S. citizens who chose to remain in China, and consular officials would endeavor to open talks with local Communist authorities. According to usual diplomatic custom, even in the absence of American relations with the CCP, the Communists should have temporarily honored the diplomatic status of all U.S. consular officials. But the Communist leadership had little regard for Western customs and, in the absence of formal diplomatic relations, saw no reason to respect the diplomatic immunity of U.S. officials. Consequently, when the CCP decreed that all privately owned radio transmitters be handed over to local authorities, the order included those transmitters operated by the U.S. consulates. The Communists particularly wanted to eliminate the transmitters at the consulate in Mukden, a valued U.S. listening post. When Angus Ward, U.S. Consul General at Mukden, equivocated, local CCP authorities surrounded the consulate, cut off all water and electricity, placed the entire consulate staff under house arrest, and blocked all communication with the outside world. Acheson, who inherited this situation upon taking office in January of 1949, paid scant attention to it until March, when he ordered O. Edmund Clubb, U.S. Consul General at Beijing, to deliver a strongly worded letter of protest to the highest available Communist authority. Clubb made repeated inquiries, but the responsible CCP officials refused even to meet with him.[16]

Unperturbed, Acheson turned the entire problem over to George Kennan, Director of the Policy Planning Staff, and he, in turn, passed it on to John P. Davies, the ranking PPS China expert. Davies thought first of recommending economic sanctions against the CCP, and in a May 2 memorandum he raised this possibility with Merrill C. Gay, Assistant Chief of the Office of Commercial Policy. Gay, unlike Davies, recognized at once that Acheson's China trade policy (NSC 41) held a higher priority than the standoff at Mukden. "Prestige is too slight a thing," Gay told Davies, "to justify a major policy revision, and in any case adoption of an economic warfare line would probably result in prompt expulsion of our people from Communist China rather than recognition of consular status." The whole idea of imposing sanctions might have ended right there, except for a new and more serious incident. John M. Cabot, U.S. Consul General at Shanghai, had so skillfully handled his relations with the local Communist authorities that he had managed to retain in his consulate no fewer than thirty-six of the supposedly outlawed radio transmitters. On July 6, however, Cabot's Vice-Consul, William M. Olive, inadvertently reversed this happy state of affairs. Cabot himself subsequently recounted the incident:

> Olive was a young, very innocent, and not too bright Vice Consul, and he happened to be going down the street one day in his jeep when he was arrested and taken to the police station. Olive protested his consular character and accidentally knocked an ink well off the sergeant's desk, whereupon they grabbed him and beat the hell out of him; threw him in prison and just treated him terribly. He never recovered from it. [17]

The CCP authorities released Olive three days later, but soon thereafter Davies commenced work on a more drastic approach to coercing China's new government—military action. In mid-July, the Communists once more cranked up the level of tension by blocking the departure of Ambassador Stuart. Acheson immediately became concerned, even to the point of keeping Truman regularly informed of the situation. On August 2, the CCP finally allowed Stuart to depart for Washington, but Davies considered this too little and too late. On the twenty-fourth, he delivered his long-awaited report on ways to compel the Chinese Communists "to respect the United States and moderate their behavior." The State Department, Davies asserted, should authorize a full examination of "the concept of coercion through the selective use of air power and having done so make its conclusions known to the National Security Council for further consideration." Stuart—now back in Washington and attached to the Office of Chinese Affairs—promptly argued that any kind of U.S. sanctions would be "largely a wasted gesture," and Raymond B. Fosdick, a consultant to the Office of Far Eastern Affairs, argued even more forcefully that the entire situation in China remained so "confusing" that any decision on sanctions would be premature. [18]

Acheson had for several months been delaying the shutdown of the U.S. consulates in Communist territory, but the founding of the People's Republic of China, announced on October 1, 1949, forced him to act. Through his consular personnel, Acheson officially notified the PRC of the immediate closure of two U.S. consulates and the impending closure of three more—including the consulate at Mukden. In reality, Consul General Angus Ward had been trying to close his consulate and get his staff out of Mukden since May 18, but local authorities had denied him the necessary papers. On October 11, a dispute over wages between Ward and Chi Yu-heng—a Chinese laborer whom Ward had dismissed a few days earlier—escalated into a minor altercation. Chi charged that Ward had beaten him, and Ward countered that it was Chi who had assaulted him. On October 24, the local Public Security Bureau arrested Ward and four members of his staff. Whatever the truth behind this episode, the PRC's propaganda apparatus grossly exaggerated the incident—depicting Ward's alleged crime as an archetypical example of U.S. imperialism. Held in solitary confinement at Pei Pien Men prison, Ward and his staff endured repeated beatings, frigid conditions, and a starvation diet of bread and water. The jailers at Pei Pien Men accepted food and blankets from U.S. officials but passed none of these items on to the prisoners. The prison seldom observed even its own, limited visitation rights. On October 28, Acheson instructed O. Edmund Clubb to contact Chou En-lai or the highest PRC official available and convey the State Department's "greatest concern" over the Ward case. But Clubb found it impossible to meet with anyone in authority. Instead of trying to resolve the issue, local Communist officials allowed thirty-five more laborers to file charges against Ward. On November 2, two high officials of the PRC's Public Security Bureau conducted a full interrogation of the prisoners, who denied the charges against them and complained about severe beatings. Within days, the CIA spirited a transcript of this interrogation out of China and delivered it to the State Department.[19]

By this time, Truman had seen enough. In a meeting with Undersecretary of State James Webb on November 14, 1949, the President ordered the State Department to look into "the possibility of blockading the movements of coal down the coast of China to Shanghai." This move, Truman speculated, might force the PRC to release Ward and his staff. Webb asked Truman how far he was willing to go, and Truman replied that he would not hesitate to sink Chinese ships if that proved necessary. Acheson, alarmed by Truman's anger, gathered his advisers around him and trooped over to the White House on the morning of the seventeenth. Speaking with one voice, they assured the President that working patiently toward the goal of splitting the PRC away from the Soviet Union remained the best course. In a private meeting later that day, Acheson found that Truman still supported the existing China policies, but for additional insurance Acheson personally presented Truman with a follow-up report on the twenty-first. A blockade of Chinese coastal shipping around Shanghai, Acheson maintained, would have little effect, especially since Shanghai already received the bulk of its coal and other supplies by rail. Moreover, a U.S. blockade might be "inconsistent with the principles of Article 33 of the UN Charter" and "might well prove useful to the Communists as a propaganda weapon, both at home and abroad, in support of their argument concerning the imperialistic intentions of the United States." Truman, having already backed away from his blockade idea, now gave it up entirely, and the next day Acheson notified the White House that he had substituted a weaker—but less risky—diplomatic offensive. In a personal message to "the Foreign Ministers of all countries," Acheson exhorted them to launch formal protests against the illegal imprisonment of the U.S. diplomats at Mukden.[20]

On November 21, however, while Acheson was still reeducating the President, Angus Ward and his staff went to trial. The Shenyang Municipal People's Court allowed the Americans no defense counsel, no defense witnesses, and no right to cross-examine the prosecution's witnesses. Finding all five defendants guilty, the court issued them prison sentences which varied from three to six months, and it ordered Ward to pay Chi Yu-heng twenty-one dollars in back wages and hospital expenses. But in the end the court also commuted all of the prison sentences to immediate deportation. While Ward languished in prison, Vice-Consul William N. Stokes took charge of the Mukden consulate. On the day of the trial, Stokes sent a message cautioning Acheson to consider the Angus Ward case in relation to "charges of espionage brought against the Mukden consulate by the Communist authorities in mid-June, 1949." Acheson at once passed this on to Truman. Five days later, local Chinese authorities seized Stokes, forced him to attend a hearing on alleged U.S. espionage activities, and ordered him deported. Finally, on December 10, the PRC allowed the entire staff of the Mukden consulate to leave China. Most of them required urgent medical attention.[21]

All of these incidents—but particularly the treatment of Angus Ward and his staff—significantly affected Acheson's attitude toward granting formal diplomatic recognition to the newly established People's Republic of China. Ward described Shiro Tatsumi, a member of his staff, as having suffered so much that he was "incapable of rational thought or reasonable speech." Ward himself had endured severe beatings and prolonged exposure to cold. After six weeks on bread and water, he had lost twenty-five pounds. Looking back on this period, Dean Rusk reflected, "They [the PRC] not only arrested Angus Ward, they roughed him up pretty badly. So when the Chinese started seeking recognition . . . they did not really seek, and did not do much to prepare the way for, recognition by the United States. They selected us as the dragon, enemy number one." Similarly, Livingston Merchant, Deputy Assistant Secretary for Far Eastern Affairs, later recalled feeling that the PRC "had the same anti-Western attitude as the Russians." In meetings on October 26 and 27, Acheson and his advisers discussed all of this at length, and they concluded that U.S. diplomatic recognition should "not be regarded as a major instrument for showing our interest in the Chinese people or for winning concessions from the Communist regime." At a cabinet meeting on December 22, Acheson solemnly assured Truman that, in the wake of the Mukden incident, he had "adopted [a] firm attitude on [the] Communist regime in China." U.S. diplomats would be "treated respectfully," Acheson declared, or there would be "no point" in recognizing the new Communist government. A week later, Acheson, the National Security Council, and the President approved their first comprehensive policy on Asia (NSC 48 / 1), followed on the thirtieth by a brief amendment (NSC 48 / 2). The latter stated simply that the United States would "continue to recognize the Nationalist Government of China" and would "avoid recognizing the Chinese Communist regime" until it was "clearly in the United States' interest to do so."[22]

Acheson had already initiated a campaign to muster international support for this position. Most nations followed America's lead; a few—most notably India, Pakistan, and Britain—did not. Beginning in September, the State Department repeatedly exhorted the British Foreign Office to defer any decision on the recognition question, but Foreign Minister Ernest Bevin had to weigh solidarity with the United States against Britain's need to safeguard both its sizable investments in China and its profitable lease on Hong Kong. On December 16, 1949, Bevin notified Acheson that his government had decided to extend formal recognition to the PRC, and it did so on January 6, 1950. Soon after Bevin's notification, Sir Oliver Franks, the British Ambassador to the United States, took up the issue with Dean Rusk, Acheson's Deputy Undersecretary. They "speculated," according to Rusk, that if "the Chinese behaved themselves," the United States might eventually join Britain in recognizing the PRC, and if it turned out otherwise, Britain might return to the U.S. position.[23]

In the weeks that followed, Acheson further hardened his attitude toward the PRC. Much earlier, in May of 1949, the State Department had outlined three tentative criteria for diplomatic recognition:

a. *de facto* control of territory and administrative machinery of State, including maintenance of public order;

b. ability and willingness of [the] government to discharge its international obligations; and

c. general acquiescence of [the] people . . . in [the] government in power.

One of China's "international obligations" was a 1901 protocol which allowed each of the nations that suppressed the Boxer Rebellion to establish military barracks in Beijing. On January 6, 1950, the new Communist government proclaimed that it would, within seven days, confiscate all foreign military barracks built under the 1901 protocol. Acheson ordered O. Edmund Clubb, U.S. Consulate General at Beijing, to inform the Chinese that the American barracks building now housed only Clubb's own personal offices and that the United States would willingly surrender another of its properties in Beijing in lieu of the military barracks. The Communists rejected Acheson's offer and seized the barracks. To the Communists, the barracks symbolized China's earlier degradation at the hands of an imperialist power; to Acheson, the barracks symbolized the PRC's general attitude toward its international obligations. Acheson advised Truman that they should no longer accept what was fast becoming a series of humiliations at the hands of the PRC, and Truman agreed. On January 14, Acheson ordered the closing of all remaining U.S. diplomatic facilities in the PRC, a process which extended well into April. In March, as Clubb was completing the final stage of this withdrawal, Acheson asked him to "arrange [an] informal interview with

Chou En-lai or [the] highest other Commie official accessible," but Clubb replied that the Communists had already rendered such contacts impossible.[24]

Acheson, from January forward, essentially shelved the whole question of diplomatic recognition for the PRC. In early February, the Office of Far Eastern Affairs succinctly summarized his policy: "The United States continues to recognize the National Government of China and is giving no serious consideration to recognition of the Communist regime." This approach remained unaltered right up to the outbreak of the Korean War. Indeed, on June 23—the day before the war began (Washington time)—the Office of Far Eastern Affairs reported to the NSC, "The United States continues to recognize the National Government of China and does not have under active consideration recognition of the Communist regime."[25]

In the midst of its campaign for diplomatic recognition, the PRC (with the support of the Soviet Union) launched a corollary effort to replace the Nationalist regime in the UN. This left Acheson with a difficult choice. On one hand, as long as the United States continued to recognize the Nationalist government, it should likewise support that government's position in the UN. The United States also had an interest in preventing the Communists from obtaining China's permanent seat on the UN Security Council. On the other hand, if the PRC eventually managed to seize Taiwan (as the CIA predicted), any full-scale effort to support the Nationalists in the UN would end in an embarrassing defeat for the United States. Acheson selected a middle course. By treating the matter as a procedural question in the UN Security Council, the United States could vote against seating the PRC without exercising its veto. The decision on Chinese representation would then depend on a majority vote of the Security Council—not on the United States alone—and this, in turn, would greatly diminish the risk to U.S. prestige. On January 13, 1950, the Security Council declined to seat the PRC by a vote of six to three, with two abstentions. The Soviet Union, outraged by this result, launched a boycott of the UN. Throughout February and March, Taiwan's strategic position continued to deteriorate, and Acheson became even more concerned about linking U.S. prestige to the survival of the Nationalist regime. On March 22, he instructed Warren R. Austin, the U.S. representative to the UN, to continue to vote against seating the PRC but to stop employing U.S. influence on this issue.[26]

In late June, the outbreak of war in Korea considerably altered the UN equation. Acheson, taking advantage of the Soviet Union's boycott of the UN, swiftly secured a tough UN Security Council response to the crisis. But he accomplished this with only the minimum seven votes required for emergency action, and those seven votes included that of the Nationalist regime. Consequently, Ruth E. Bacon, a State Department UN specialist, recommended a wider effort to keep the PRC from replacing the Nationalist regime in the UN. Dean Rusk, whom Acheson had appointed Assistant Secretary for Far Eastern Affairs in March, threw his support behind Bacon, and Acheson followed suit. Throughout the summer, Acheson, Rusk, and Bacon quietly mobilized U.S. influence. Finally, in a showdown on August 3, they narrowly turned back a Soviet effort to again place the Chinese representation question before the UN Security Council. Rusk, who had once supervised U.S. activities in the UN, followed up this initial victory with an ingenious parliamentary maneuver. Working with the British Foreign Office, he quickly framed a resolution to establish a UN committee on the issue of Chinese representation and postpone all other consideration of the matter indefinitely. The Canadian government agreed to sponsor Rusk's handiwork, and in mid-September, the General Assembly approved it. Rusk expected his parliamentary device to keep the PRC out of the UN for a few months or, at most, a few years; it did so for two decades.[27]

At the same time Acheson was grappling with the diplomatic recognition and UN representation questions, he also commenced a reevaluation of his China trade policy (NSC 41). In September of 1949, when Truman first suggested a review, Acheson replied that none was necessary, but three months later the State Department's battle with the Defense Department over a comprehensive policy for the Far East (NSC 48 / 1 and 48 / 2) forced Acheson's hand. Both the trade policy and the debate it engendered centered on two very separate issues: U.S. trade with the PRC and Japanese trade with the PRC. On the first issue, Acheson and Rusk opted for a major policy revision. Henceforth, according to a key provision in the new comprehensive Asian policy (section 3.F.4 of NSC 48 / 2, approved December 30, 1949), all U.S. trade with the PRC would be carried out on the same basis as trade with "the U.S.S.R. and its European satellites." This restricted such trade to "non-strategic commodities." The new policy further stipulated, "The United States should not extend governmental economic assistance to Communist China or encourage private investment in Communist China." But on the second issue, Japanese trade with the PRC, Acheson saw no need for change. Indeed, two separate studies had vindicated his original approach. First, in September of 1949, a special group of nineteen experts, "The Consultants on the Far East," unanimously agreed that it would serve U.S. interests if China continued its trade with Japan. Second, in December of 1949, a report by the Office of Chinese Affairs insisted that on the question of trade with the PRC, "Japan should be treated as a national entity on a non-discriminatory basis." In the wake of these studies, Acheson and Rusk incorporated into the new comprehensive Asian policy a clear acknowledgment that Japan's economy could not be restored to a self-sustaining basis without "a considerable volume" of Sino-Japanese trade.[28]

Acheson likewise saw no need to change his general policy on China (NSC 34 / 2). The central scenario of this policy— the development of a rift between the USSR and the PRC in "twenty to twenty-five years"—still seemed feasible despite the near-term situation. In testimony before the Senate Committee on Foreign Relations, Acheson clarified his position. First, he wanted to make sure that the PRC did not become "a stooge of Moscow." Second, he wanted to see some other regime replace the PRC because he believed that most Communist regimes tended "to gravitate to Moscow." As for speculation that a Sino-Soviet rift might occur soon, Acheson's advisers gave it short shrift. As early as March of 1949, W. Walton Butterworth, Director of Far Eastern Affairs, told the Senate Committee on Foreign Relations, "I think to count on Titoism in China is slightly premature. Things happen in China with great slowness." This remained the dominant view in the State Department throughout 1949 and 1950. In June of 1950, Walter P. McConaughy, Consul General at Shanghai, told an interdepartmental meeting, "Reports of deviationism among the Chinese Communists on the Titoist model should be discounted. No break between Peiping [Beijing] and Moscow is in the offing." Nevertheless, Acheson and Rusk stepped up U.S. efforts to undermine Sino-Soviet relations. On February 6, 1950, the State Department publicly predicted that the Soviet Union was about to begin "a process of penetration and detachment" with the goal of establishing "control" over "China's northern provinces." Eight days later, the Soviet Union and the People's Republic of China signed a thirty-year Treaty of Friendship, Alliance, and Mutual Assistance. By the terms of this treaty, the PRC received $300 million in Soviet trade credits and the restoration of Chinese control over Port Arthur, Darien, and the Changchun Railway. For its part, the Soviet Union won special investment and trade privileges in China.[29]

The Soviet trade privileges, which somewhat resembled those that the imperialist powers had once enjoyed in China, presented Acheson with an obvious opportunity, and he seized it with both hands. On March 15, in an address before the Commonwealth Club of San Francisco, California, Acheson launched an all-out attack on the leadership of the PRC. "Can the Chinese people," he asked rhetorically, "fail to observe that . . . under the terms of the treaty and agreements recently concluded at Moscow, the U.S.S.R. has special rights in China which represent an infringement of China's sovereignty and which are held by no other foreign power?" In the secret discussions of the previous summer, Chou En-lai had pointed to America's prewar trade with China and defiantly proclaimed, "I do not depend upon you; you depend on me." Now, directing himself far more to Chou En-lai than to his San Francisco audience, Acheson delivered a blistering rejoinder:

> I want to make it entirely clear that we have no desire to thrust this [American] trade upon China, nor is China in a position to extort it from us. In the period 1946–1948 the United States supplied over 50 percent of China's imports and bought approximately a quarter of China's exports. Yet, those same exports from America were less than 5 percent of our total exports and our purchases from China were a mere 2 percent of all we bought abroad. If the present rulers of China wish to believe that we depend on trade with China, we are entirely willing to leave it to the test of experience to prove whether they are right or wrong.[30]

Even while publicly attacking the PRC, however, Acheson continued to defend his permissive policy on Sino-Japanese trade. He still hoped to restore Japan's trade with China as a means of promoting Japanese recovery, and then to supplant that trade as the United States gradually developed noncommunist trading partners for Japan. Acheson told the Senate Committee on Foreign Relations, for example, that any move to cut off Sino-Japanese trade would risk turning Japan into "a pensioner of the United States." "I think at the present time," he added, "Japan has more to offer North China than North China has to offer Japan. That is, in the pull between them the

Japanese position is superior. I doubt whether it will be over a long period of time. At any rate, it is now."[31]

The informal negotiations for establishing trade relations between the PRC and Japan presented surprisingly few problems. Dean Rusk, who supervised these talks, subsequently recalled that the Chinese simply refused to let their bitterness over Japan's wartime atrocities stand in the way of normal trade relations. Likewise, according to Philip Jessup, Acheson's Ambassador-at-Large, the Japanese felt that China was "their natural market." Yet, in reality, the actual restoration of trade required much more than just a mutual willingness to do business. Thirteen years of war and civil war had utterly devastated China's primitive economy. As early as May of 1949, Major General David G. Barr, Director of the U.S. Military Advisory Group in China, called attention to the problem: "There isn't any real exchange of goods in China, because there are no goods in China to exchange at the present time." Acheson soon drew the same conclusion and adjusted his expectations accordingly. In late 1949, he told the Senate Committee on Foreign Relations, "We believe if the Communists want to scrape off some of the small margin of produce there is in China for export, that is all right with us. It is not hurting us at all. It may create problems for them." By May of 1950, China was in the throes of a severe famine and had to cut back its already meager trade with Japan. State Department experts predicted that the famine would last for some time and kill as many as ten million Chinese. The outbreak of the Korean War in June reduced Sino-Japanese trade still further. For 1950 as a whole, the State Department estimated that China accounted for "only 3.3% of Japan's total overseas commerce." Even after the Korean War, Sino-Japanese trade remained small, accounting in 1956 for just 2.6 percent of Japan's imports and 2.7 percent of its exports.[32]

The onset of the Korean War also greatly increased the antipathy between the United States and the PRC. Looking back, Dean Rusk remembered, "We captured a good many prisoners, and prisoner interrogation showed that for several months before the outbreak of the Korean War, they [the leaders of the PRC] had combed the armies of China in the North to find people of Korean ancestry to move from the Chinese armies over into North Korea. And that seemed to us to be clear evidence that the Chinese had been in on the plans all along." In October—on a recommendation from Acheson and Rusk, and with the blessing of the UN—Truman ordered U.S. forces to cross the thirty-eighth parallel and conquer North Korea. The PRC countered by sending its own troops into the war. In a surprise attack launched in late November, the Chinese sent American forces reeling back into South Korea. Casualties were heavy on both sides; among them was the last, faint hope for a renewed dialogue between the United States and China.[33]

Conclusion

Throughout this period, Dean Acheson maintained two separate policies on China (NSC 34 / 2 and NSC 41), neither of which met with much success. The first—anticipating a split between the USSR and the PRC in "twenty to twenty-five years"—called for an ongoing dialogue with the Chinese Communists. Acheson, despite his low opinion of both China and its new government, made at least a limited effort to establish a dialogue. A number of significant episodes punctuated this effort—the aborted Chou demarche, the Yenching commencement invitation, the Olive incident, the Mukden arrests, and the military barracks dispute—but the State Department's talks with Chou En-lai in the summer of 1949 marked the real turning point. Paul Nitze later remembered, "At one point, we thought we had established contact . . . but the Chinese Communists cut it off. They dropped the boom on all negotiation."

When Chou En-lai ended his talks with the United States, he did so on a defiant note: "I do not depend on you; you depend on me." Several months later, Acheson personally and publicly issued his reply: "If the present rulers of China wish to believe that we depend on trade with China, we are entirely willing to leave it to the test of experience to prove whether they are right or wrong." This "test of experience" replaced the quest for dialogue, and it lasted two decades.[34]

Acheson's second policy focused exclusively on trade issues. In it, he and his advisers assigned a low priority to U.S. trade with China and a much higher priority to Japanese trade with China. Acheson hoped first to utilize Sino-Japanese trade as yet another means for addressing Japan's economic crisis and then to supplant this trade by finding new, noncommunist trading partners for Japan. He quite clearly made this scenario his most immediate concern with respect to China. Even after Acheson had abandoned his efforts to establish a dialogue with the Chinese Communist leadership, and even after he had severely curtailed U.S. trade with the PRC, he adamantly refused to consider any change whatsoever in his approach to Sino-Japanese trade. In the end, however, China's economy remained extremely weak, and its trade played only a minor role in Japanese recovery.

Acheson and
the American Commitment
in Vietnam

BY THE CLOSING MONTHS of World War II, the United States had developed a heightened awareness of southern Asia's economic and strategic importance. Accordingly, State Department planners began to align their policies with Asian nationalism and to expand U.S. influence in this region. Thailand, already an independent nation, immediately set a pro-American course. After the United States granted independence to the Philippines in 1946, the latter remained close to its longtime mentor. Britain withdrew from India and Burma between 1947 and 1949, and the Dutch left Indonesia in 1950. The new nations thus produced—Pakistan, India, Burma, and Indonesia—all proved, to one extent or another, amenable to American influence. Malaysia and Singapore, two of Britain's most profitable colonies, did not achieve full independence until the late 1950s, but, even so, they essentially maintained a pro-Western orientation.[1]

The general success of American diplomacy in Southeast

Asia owed much to the judicious application of economic leverage. To develop their economies, Thailand, Pakistan, and the Philippines required U.S. economic assistance and Western capital investment. By utilizing America's economic power, as well as various preexisting cultural and diplomatic ties, the State Department swiftly solidified its influence in all three nations. Burma and India likewise nurtured at least favorable relations with the United States and sought economic assistance in return. Dutch Indonesia presented a more formidable problem, since the Dutch were loath to part with its valuable resources, but American pressure eventually produced an independent Indonesia and American aid stabilized it. Nonetheless, there remained one area in southern Asia which resisted America's wealth, power, and influence—French Indochina.[2]

America's postwar policy toward Indochina passed through three distinct stages. In the initial stage, August 1945 through June 1947, the United States acknowledged France's right to reclaim its overseas empire, and a strong communist movement, the Vietminh, stood up against the return of French authority to Indochina. Dean Acheson, then Undersecretary of State, supervised U.S. efforts to promote a peaceful settlement, but he secured only a few promises from France that it would continue to seek a negotiated solution. Over the course of the second stage, July 1947 through January 1949, the United States watched quietly from a distance while the French government abandoned all discussions with the Vietminh and laid plans to divide Indochina into three states—Laos, Cambodia, and Vietnam. In Vietnam, the French launched a sweeping military campaign and began putting together a puppet regime. During the third stage, January 1949 through December 1950, Dean Acheson again took charge of U.S. diplomacy toward Indochina, this time as Secretary of State, and, through a series of difficult decisions, he made the United States a virtual partner in France's policies. Initially, Acheson framed his approach to Southeast Asia around American and European economic interests; by late 1949, however, the need to revive Japan's regional trade became a primary consideration. In the end, Acheson's policies and decisions produced an economic aid program for most of Southeast Asia, a military aid program for the French-backed regime in Vietnam, and a burgeoning U.S. commitment to a war he had originally tried to prevent.

The First Stage:
August 1945–June 1947

France first established a strong presence in Southeast Asia during the mid-1800s, and by 1893 its armies had conquered all of Cambodia, Vietnam, and Laos. To rule these vast territories—collectively named French Indochina—the French government spawned a colonial bureaucracy so corrupt, exploitative, and bloated that it embarrassed even its political supporters. Nevertheless, the French Foreign Ministry achieved most of its economic objectives. Indochina became a reliable supplier of rice, rubber, and other raw materials, as well as a captive market for France's manufactured goods. Aside from lining its own pockets, the French colonial bureaucracy proved particularly adept at expanding agricultural production in southern Vietnam and creating there a "rice bowl" of considerable commercial importance. In the wake of France's defeat in 1940, the Vichy government in unoccupied France inherited Indochina and ceded actual authority over it to Japan. Indochina's new rulers initially operated behind a façade of local French administration, but on March 9, 1945, the Japanese Army seized direct control.[3]

As the vulnerability of the French regime in Indochina became apparent, indigenous opposition to it coalesced around a single individual, a man of extraordinary energy and charisma—Ho Chi Minh. In 1941, Ho shrewdly recast his Indochina Communist Party into the *Viet Nam Doc Lap Dong Minh* (Vietnamese Independence League), a broad political coalition better known as the Vietminh. Ho, with help from the U.S. Office of Strategic Services, also organized a small guerrilla campaign against the Japanese. The Vietminh Army became operational too late to have much impact on the war, but on August 20, 1945, just days before the war ended, it seized the city of Hanoi, in northern Vietnam, and established there the Provisional Government of Vietnam. France, now under a provisional government of its own, that of Charles de Gaulle, rejected this fait accompli out of hand. After five long years of defeat and humiliation, the French intended to restore both their prestige in Europe and their empire abroad. A battalion of British Commonwealth troops and a company of French regulars reestablished French control in the city of Saigon, in southern Vietnam, on August 12, and General Jean Leclerc (commander of the French forces which liberated Paris in 1944) arrived with 40,000 French reinforcements shortly thereafter. Leclerc, facing a Vietminh Army of 30,000 men, at once employed France's classic colonial strategy—the *tache d'huile* (oil slick tactic)—which had proven effective in campaigns from the Far East to North Africa. By stages, Leclerc's forces worked their way outward (like oil slicks) from carefully selected strategic centers. But the Vietminh Army, mustering volunteers to the rallying cry *doc-lap* (independence), grew faster than Leclerc expected. By late 1946, the Vietminh could field over 60,000 troops. Moreover, the leader of these forces, General Vo Nguyen Giap, found an effective answer to Leclerc's *tache d'huile*. "The blitzkrieg," Giap projected, "will transform itself into a war of long duration. Thus, the enemy will be caught in a dilemma: he has to drag out the war in order to win it and does not possess, on the other hand, the psychological and political means to fight a long drawn out war . . . ."[4]

This growing conflict took American policymakers by surprise. President Franklin D. Roosevelt, who despised colonialism in general and French colonialism in particular, originally hoped to replace all of the colonial regimes in Southeast Asia with trusteeships. These trusteeships, FDR imagined, could be modeled after the American tutelage of democracy in the Philippines, but few outside the United States shared his vision. The British—offended by Roosevelt's apparent effrontery and condescension—reacted with unrestrained indignation to the whole idea of breaking up their empire, and many U.S. policymakers rushed to their defense. Both England and France, FDR's advisers cautioned, suffered horrendous devastation during the war, and the further loss of their colonies might seriously diminish their prospects for economic recovery. Roosevelt pondered the issue for some time, and at the Yalta conference, in February of 1945, he succumbed to British pressure. On April 3, Secretary of State Edward R. Stettinius issued a formal statement which restricted FDR's trusteeship plan to "territories taken from the enemy" and to those additional areas which the colonial powers themselves agreed to relinquish. Roosevelt died nine days later. His successor, Harry S. Truman, chose James F. Byrnes to be his Secretary of State and Dean Acheson to be his Undersecretary of State. Together, Truman, Byrnes, and Acheson decided to maintain most of Roosevelt's existing policies, including his revised approach to trusteeship. In June, however, the State Department declared that even though the United States recognized "French sovereignty over Indochina," it still favored "a policy which would allow colonial peoples an opportunity to prepare themselves for increased participation in their own government with eventual self-government as the goal."[5]

This immediately touched off an acrimonious debate within the State Department. The Office of Far Eastern Affairs argued vehemently that the United States should support Asian nationalism and oppose French colonialism. The much more powerful Office of European Affairs pointed to France's pivotal role in U.S. plans for Europe and insisted that the State Department could not afford to alienate French policymakers.

Some analysts in European Affairs also contended that France would rapidly reestablish its control over Indochina with or without U.S. approval. In August, Byrnes, Acheson, and John Carter Vincent, Director of the Office of Far Eastern Affairs, opted for a rough compromise. The State Department would acknowledge "French sovereignty over Indochina," predicated on the assumption that the "French claim to have the support of the population of Indochina" would be "borne out by future events." Acheson reaffirmed this approach in a secret memorandum in early October, and on the twenty-fifth, Vincent issued a public statement which reiterated the U.S. decision not to question Dutch, British, or French sovereignty over their former empires. With respect to Indochina, Byrnes, Acheson, and Vincent offered tacit U.S. support for the reintroduction of French forces, but they reserved the right to reconsider that support if the people of Indochina rejected French rule.[6]

Ho Chi Minh, undeterred by U.S. posturing, swiftly transformed his provisional regime into a permanent government—the Democratic Republic of Vietnam (DRV). American analysts found it difficult to keep abreast of Ho's maneuvers, or even those of the French Foreign Ministry. In early February of 1946, reports filtered in that the French High Commissioner for Indochina, Admiral Thierry d'Argenlieu, had organized a "conciliatory and moderate faction" within the colonial administration, while Leclerc headed an opposing faction that was "intransigent and uncompromising." Then, a third element in France's hydra-headed colonial bureaucracy—Jean Sainteny, the commissioner for the Tonkin region of Vietnam—suddenly opened negotiations with the Communists. On March 6, Sainteny and Ho signed an agreement by which France recognized the DRV "as a free state and as a member of both the Indochinese Federation and the French Union, with its own government, army, and finances." The two sides also entered into a binding commitment to spell out the details of their new arrangement in future negotiations.[7]

But Paris had already begun to move in a different direction. Jean Monnet—a noted economist selected by the French government to modernize both France's domestic economy and its colonial administration—assigned considerable economic importance to French interests in Indochina. In keeping with Monnet's assessment, d'Argenlieu first publicly attacked Sainteny's March 6 agreement and then, on May 30, undercut it entirely by creating a new splinter state—the Cochinchinese Republic. This "republic," of course, had a French-sponsored, anticommunist government and included within its borders virtually all of Indochina's "rice bowl region." Furthermore, d'Argenlieu and his political allies quickly committed France to a policy of dividing all of Indochina into five separate states—Laos, Cambodia, Annam, Tonkin, and Cochinchina—each of which would belong to a "French Union." Guided by Jean Monnet's economic analysis, d'Argenlieu included in his planning numerous measures designed to safeguard French interests in Cochinchina. Ho Chi Minh, still hoping to revive negotiations, journeyed to Paris in late March, but his entreaties fell on deaf ears. From then until the early fall of 1946, the French Foreign Ministry generated a steady stream of proposals based on d'Argenlieu's federation approach, none of which even came close to granting the level of independence sought by Ho and his government.[8]

Byrnes, Acheson, and Vincent kept track of these French machinations with their fingers crossed. On the one hand, they were apprehensive about a protracted war in Indochina and implored the French to make meaningful concessions in the pursuit of peace. On the other hand, they consistently distanced the United States from Ho Chi Minh, ignoring his repeated appeals for U.S. support. Byrnes, who spent much of his time traveling abroad, shifted an ever-increasing share of his authority over policy implementation to Acheson—particularly with respect to secondary issues like Indochina. Acheson subsequently recalled, ". . . toward the end of '45, I was

Undersecretary, and I suddenly found myself carrying on arbitration between the French who were in Indochina and the Siamese." Because of his extensive knowledge of French affairs (and despite a general lack of interest in Southeast Asia), Acheson soon accepted, along with Vincent, most of the responsibility for the day-to-day implementation of U.S. policy in Indochina.[9]

To Acheson's dismay, he found that the prospects for negotiations were dismal, while localized military confrontations appeared to be escalating. In December, Byrnes and Acheson dispatched Abbot Moffat, Chief of the Office of Philippine and Southeast Asian Affairs, on a fact-finding mission to Indochina. Acheson, who wrote Moffat's instructions, insisted that Ho Chi Minh should be regarded as "an agent of international communism," and he emphasized that the "least desirable eventuality would be [the] establishment of [a] Communist-dominated, Moscow-oriented Indochina." As for France, Acheson expressed a firm conviction that the French Foreign Ministry would eventually move in the right direction. France, he explained, had offered clear assurances that it would later resume negotiations and base them on both the March 6 accords and a closely related modus vivendi which the two sides signed on September 15. The French government, Acheson asserted, would "resort to forceful measures only on [a] restricted scale in case [of] flagrant violation [of the] agreements [on] Vietnam." As proof, Acheson cited two recent developments. First, the Foreign Ministry had promised to replace Admiral d'Argenlieu, now regarded by the United States as an unyielding conservative. Second, Paris had specifically acknowledged that Leclerc's grand design for the reconquest of Indochina ran "counter to French public opinion" and was "probably beyond French military resources." Moffat, following Acheson's instructions, met privately with Ho Chi Minh and a long list of French colonial officials, but he could find no fertile ground for compromise.[10]

On December 19, after a bewildering flurry of peace over-
tures and military provocations from both sides, the Vietminh
launched a surprise attack on French garrisons throughout
Vietnam. Full-scale warfare ensued, and on the twenty-third,
Acheson held an urgent meeting with the French Ambassador,
Henri Bonnet. The Undersecretary of State began by advising
Bonnet that the United States was "deeply concerned by the
outbreak of hostilities," and then he edged into a carefully
worded offer of assistance: "While we have no wish to offer
to mediate under the present conditions, we do want the French
Government to know that we are ready and willing to do any-
thing which it might consider helpful in the circumstances."
Acheson's offer held out the prospect of using the State
Department's good offices to bring both sides to the bargaining
table, but it ruled out the possibility of American mediation
once the peace talks convened. Adding a bit of subtle pressure,
Acheson wondered aloud whether the French would attempt
to reconquer Indochina, "a step that the British had found unwise
to attempt in Burma." Bonnet replied that the newly elected
Socialist government of Premier Léon Blum (which replaced
the provisional regime of Charles de Gaulle) would allow limited self-government for the states of Indochina, but only if
they remained within the French Union. As soon as the French
Army could restore order, Bonnet promised, France would
resume negotiations on the basis of the March 6, 1946, accords
and at some point thereafter France would "implement the far-
reaching concessions" of that agreement.[11]

Acheson, putting his faith in Bonnet, decided against any
expansion of his December 23 offer. He considered but rejected
the idea of offering direct U.S. mediation, and in a memorandum to the U.S. embassy in England, he enumerated three
reasons for this decision. First, Premier Blum had recently dispatched Marius Moutet, Minister for Overseas France, on a
special mission to Indochina. Prudence dictated that the United
States await the results. Second, the State Department needed

"clarification" of both the "French line [regarding] Indochina"
and the "confusion" in France's overall political system. U.S.
intelligence had already proved faulty with respect to
d'Argenlieu's intentions in February, and there were indica-
tions that the French government would soon be voted out of
office. Third, Acheson believed that an unequivocal U.S. offer
to mediate negotiations would probably be "resentfully rejected
by the French." All three of these arguments proved sound.
On January 8, 1947, the Blum government respectfully declined
"Mr. Acheson's offer of 'good offices,' " while thanking
Acheson personally for his "understanding attitude." The United
States, the Foreign Ministry signaled, could do nothing to
facilitate a resumption of negotiations; the French government
would "handle the situation single-handedly."[12]

As Acheson anticipated, the situation continued to evolve.
In January of 1947, a weak coalition government under Premier Paul Ramadier replaced that of Léon Blum, and, at the
same time, George C. Marshall took over the U.S. State
Department. Marshall at once made it clear that he intended to
rely heavily on Acheson, who agreed to stay on as Undersecretary for six more months, and he readily accepted Acheson's
approach to Indochina. Together, Marshall, Acheson, and
Vincent organized a new overture to the Ramadier government—modeled on the overture to the Blum government—and
Marshall ordered Jefferson Caffery, U.S. Ambassador to France,
to deliver it. Caffery's instructions included most of Acheson's earlier arguments, followed by the specific details of the
overture itself. The Ambassador would begin by indicating that
the U.S. "fully recognized France's sovereign position" in
Indochina, and only then would he offer "appropriate" U.S.
assistance to find a "solution for [the] Indochinese problem."
Caffery would also remind the French Foreign Ministry that
colonial empires were "rapidly becoming a thing of the past"
and that the United States considered Ho Chi Minh an agent
of the Kremlin. Above all, the State Department stressed, Caf-

fery should make it absolutely clear that the United States wanted
to facilitate negotiations, not dictate a solution.[13]

Caffery delivered the new initiative to French Foreign Minister Georges Bidault on February 6, 1947, but once again the
French declined the State Department's assistance. Leclerc's
tache d'huile had finally begun to reap dividends, giving the
new Ramadier government reason to believe that it could impose
a French solution in Indochina by force. Over a period of several months, the French Army first cleared the areas around
Hanoi, Haiphong, Hué, and other major cities, and then cut
Vietnam in two with a well-planned pincer movement. In January of 1947, Leclerc estimated that he would need 500,000
men to end the war quickly. Thereafter, however, he supplemented his basic *tache d'huile* with Operation Lea, a strategy
designed to win the war with only modest reinforcements.
Leclerc's new plan called for an all-out effort to capture Ho
Chi Minh or, failing this, to destroy the bulk of the regular
Vietminh forces. By mid-February, the French Army claimed
to have killed 8,000–10,000 of the enemy. Ramadier and
Bidault, much impressed, asked Leclerc to replace d'Argenlieu
as High Commissioner, but on the advice of his mentor, Charles
de Gaulle, Leclerc declined. In his stead, the French cabinet
gave the job to Emile Bollaert, a compromise candidate with
useful political connections but no colonial experience. After
announcing the Bollaert appointment at a press conference on
March 7, Premier Ramadier declared that his government still
intended to create a federation of independent states in Indochina under the banner of a French Union. Although Ramadier
softened some aspects of France's earlier position, he insisted
that France should retain its economic privileges in Cochinchina, as well as absolute control over the military and foreign
policies of the new Indochinese states.[14]

From March 4 through April 8, 1947, while Marshall was
attending the Moscow conference, Acheson served as Acting
Secretary of State. Impatient with French policy, he directed

Ambassador Caffery to determine what would be required to promote a resumption of negotiations, "[in] view of [the] French refusal [to] acknowledge any Vietnamese appeals." Caffery held a discreet discussion with Philippe Baudet, Director of the Foreign Ministry's Asiatic Division, and then reported that Bollaert, the new High Commissioner, would carry with him to Indochina some limited discretionary powers to talk to officials of Ho Chi Minh's DRV. Renewed negotiations might be possible, according to Baudet, if the DRV broadened its base and expelled the extremists from its ranks. In fact, as Acheson well knew, Ho Chi Minh had begun moving in the opposite direction and had only recently purged most of the moderates from his National Assembly. Baudet, nevertheless, pointed to the appointment of moderate Hoang Minh Giam, the DRV's new Foreign Minister, as evidence that French demands were not entirely unrealistic. Acheson clearly wanted more from France, but the Hoang appointment portended a greater change than he expected. On April 25, shortly after Bollaert arrived in Saigon, Hoang greeted him with a bold proposal for "the immediate cessation of hostilities and opening of negotiations." After three weeks of intense deliberation, the Ramadier government dispatched Paul Mus, Bollaert's chief economic adviser, with a list of conditions that the DRV would have to meet before France would agree to resume negotiations. Ho Chi Minh, in a meeting with Mus on May 12, angrily refused to consider any preconditions.[15]

Although policy analysts in Paris and Washington still thought that a negotiated settlement could be achieved, their hopes now began to dim. The French Foreign Ministry groped desperately for a formula that would simultaneously protect its economic interests and restore its talks with the DRV. But given the Foreign Ministry's distrust for Ho Chi Minh, no such formula was possible. France's internal politics likewise militated against a diplomatic solution. The French people, like their government, opposed any settlement which went beyond the existing

French Union concept. As time passed, France tapered off even its token efforts to revive negotiations, and after the United States announced the Truman Doctrine, the Foreign Ministry justified its actions by pointing to Ho Chi Minh's links with Moscow. Finally, in June of 1947, the Foreign Ministry further stiffened its negotiating posture, thereby eliminating any remaining prospects for a diplomatic solution.[16]

The Second Stage:
July 1947–January 1949

The State Department accepted France's policy shift with hardly a murmur. Acheson, as previously scheduled, left the State Department at the end of June, and no one else felt much inclined to press the French on their handling of Indochina. In early July, the Foreign Ministry sent Washington new evidence to confirm its assessment of Ho Chi Minh: eight Soviet agents, led by a man known as Karkov, had begun to reorganize and retrain the Vietminh Army. The State Department—more convinced than ever that it could neither endorse French colonialism nor trust the Vietminh—maintained an awkward neutrality. On the one side, U.S. policymakers ruled out direct assistance for the French war effort, even to the point of making it illegal for American ships to carry military supplies to Indochina. On the other side, the United States provided $1.9 billion in unrestricted economic assistance to France between July 1945 and July 1948. Whether the State Department liked it or not, U.S. aid fueled not only an astonishing French economic recovery but also the steadily intensifying war in Indochina. The chronic instability of the French Fourth Republic (which would have nineteen governments in the twelve years of its existence) only compounded the problem. Between 1946 and 1956, the French Communist Party received over 25 percent of the votes in almost every election, and the State

Department's Office of European Affairs believed that heavy
U.S. pressure on the Indochina issue would cause an unfavor-
able political outcome in France itself. Measured against
France's role in the economic recovery and military security
of Europe, the fate of Indochina seemed a minor concern to
many U.S. policymakers.[17]

For the remainder of 1947 and all of 1948, France concen-
trated on effecting a military solution to the Indochina war,
but neither Leclerc's long-standing *tache d'huile* strategy nor
his more recent Operation Lea achieved decisive results. Leclerc
could seize territory, but he could seldom hold it; he could
defeat the DRV's military units, but he could seldom destroy
them. Consequently, with Leclerc's strong support, the French
Foreign Ministry slowly began to evolve a supplementary
political strategy. Despite earlier assurances to Acheson that
France would not install a puppet regime, the Foreign Ministry
initiated secret negotiations to develop an "alternative nationalist movement" around Annam's former Emperor, Bao Dai.
Even so, the French seized upon, rather than invented, the
"Bao Dai solution." Bao Dai had been gathering political support for some time, and as early as May 21, 1947, Charles S.
Reed, U.S. Consul in Saigon, advised the State Department
that there were two "main contenders" for power in Vietnam—
the Vietminh, led by Ho Chi Minh, and the National Union
Front, led by Bao Dai. Unfortunately for the French, Ho Chi
Minh boasted widespread political appeal, while Bao Dai found
support only in Annam, where he had held token authority as
Emperor before World War II. Worse still, Bao Dai was a man
of limited abilities who had never endorsed the idea of a French
Union. The DRV, after briefly considering the French Union
concept, had adopted a constitution which excluded any mention of it, and Bao Dai based his demands on those of the
DRV. This left the French with only one hope: that Bao Dai,
being weaker than Ho Chi Minh, would prove more pliable as
well.[18]

As the war escalated, the political situation began to clarify. The Laotians and Cambodians—who detested the Vietnamese as much as they did the French—decided that they needed France's support to prevent the DRV from seizing their border territories. On November 25 and 27, 1947, Laos and Cambodia joined the French Union, rendering complete control of their foreign policies to France. In southern Vietnam, Bao Dai drew closer to Nguyen Van Xuan, the President of Cochinchina—raising the prospect of a united anticommunist movement. In northern Vietnam, Ho Chi Minh consolidated his power, purged the remaining noncommunist elements from his government, and stepped up military operations inside Cochinchina and Annam. Everywhere, lines were being drawn. Nevertheless, on September 10, 1947, Bollaert, the French High Commissioner, issued another appeal for a resumption of negotiations. Ho Chi Minh made no reply. The French government then launched a furious effort to construct a new, pro-French regime based in southern Vietnam, and in the first Ha Long Bay agreement, signed on December 7, Bao Dai offered his conditional support. To the outside world, the Foreign Ministry defiantly announced that since the DRV had ignored its most recent overture, France had every right to negotiate with other nationalist elements. Further discussions with Bao Dai and Nguyen Van Xuan quickly produced a more definitive political accord—the second Ha Long Bay agreement—which instituted a pro-French "Provisional Government of Vietnam" under the leadership of Nguyen Van Xuan.[19]

Signed on June 5, 1948 by Bao Dai, Nguyen Van Xuan, and representatives from every region of Vietnam, the second Ha Long Bay agreement consisted of three parts. In the first part, France recognized the independence of Vietnam, "to whom falls hereafter the task of freely realizing its unity." The second part enumerated certain economic and political privileges to be retained by France, including a stipulation that the new regime "give priority to French advisors and technicians for the needs of its internal administration and its economy." Taken together, these concessions gave France effective control over Vietnam's economy. The third part of the agreement called for additional negotiations to outline the cultural, diplomatic, military, economic, financial, and technical aspects of Vietnam's role within the French Union. Not surprisingly, the ink had hardly dried on this accord when Ho Chi Minh delivered a vitriolic counterattack. "The French authorities," he proclaimed, "have now taken the step of setting up a puppet government which is prepared to commit every treason against the Vietnamese people. The Government of the Democratic Republic of Vietnam reserves the right to judge these traitors in conformity with the legal code of the Vietnam state."[20]

The U.S. State Department reacted more slowly, but in September, Ambassador Jefferson Caffery urged the French Foreign Ministry to waste no time in unifying the new Vietnamese regime and granting it the autonomy promised in the two Ha Long Bay agreements. Hinting vaguely at a future American commitment, he also indicated that the United States might be willing to consider assistance for Indochina through the Economic Cooperation Administration (ECA) if the French could make "real progress" toward reaching a "non-communist solution in Indochina based on [the] cooperation of [the] true nationalists of that country." In January of 1949, however, Undersecretary of State Robert A. Lovett further qualified the American position. Through Caffery, he notified the French that although the United States wanted them to come to terms with Bao Dai, the State Department could not "irretrievably commit the U.S. to [the] support of a native government which by failing to develop appeal among [the] Vietnamese might become virtually a puppet government separated from the people and existing only by the presence of French military forces."[21]

In order to implement the Ha Long Bay agreements, the Foreign Ministry needed three things: Bao Dai would have to accept a direct role in the provisional government; the people of Cochinchina would have to ratify reunification with the newly formed Vietnamese state; and the French Assembly would have to approve the whole process. While a host of French diplomats and politicians grappled with these problems, France's military campaign slowed almost to a halt. General Jean de Lattre de Tassigny, who assumed command following the untimely death of General Leclerc, gradually scaled down his offensive operations. At the outset of 1949, the U.S. consulate in Saigon reported that the French Army in Vietnam—described as 100,000 troops led by "decidedly second rate" commanders—had been completely "pinned down" by a Vietminh Army of approximately 75,000 men. A subsequent estimate put the actual Vietminh strength at 168,000 troops, which, if true, meant that the situation was even worse than either U.S. or French planners realized.[22]

The Third Stage: January 1949–December 1950

When Dean Acheson assumed office as Secretary of State on January 21, 1949, he faced a situation in Indochina very different from the one he had encountered as Undersecretary. Two years earlier, the French Foreign Ministry had discounted prospects for a military solution, disclaimed any plans for a puppet regime, and offered solemn assurances that France would continue to seek a negotiated settlement. By 1949, however, the French had endorsed a military solution, laid the groundwork for a puppet government, and forsworn further negotiations with the Democratic Republic of Vietnam. Surveying these developments in a telegram to the U.S. embassy in Paris on February 25, Acheson gave vent to bitter feelings of betrayal. "Over the past three years," he declared, "[the] French have shown no impressively sincere intention or desire [to] make

[the] concessions which seem necessary [to] solve [the] Indo-china question." The State Department, Acheson added, could not tell if the Bao Dai "formula" had merit or amounted to just "another device to obtain delay," but unless proof was "adduced to offset [the] record of the past three years," the United States would remain "far from inclined [to] give public approval [to] any arrangements with Bao Dai." With acid-dipped pen, the new Secretary also reminded the staff of the Paris embassy—including Ambassador Caffery—that just two years earlier the French themselves had expressed serious reservations concerning "Bao Dai's capacities and abilities." Nevertheless, Acheson reserved the right to review both his position on Bao Dai and the larger question of providing direct U.S. economic assistance to Indochina.[23]

Prodded by Acheson's angry skepticism from without, and by diminishing support for the Indochina war from within, the French Foreign Ministry lurched into action. On March 8, 1949, Vincent Auriol, President of the French Union, exchanged diplomatic letters at the Elysée Palace with Bao Dai. In these "Elysée agreements," Bao Dai vowed to take a direct role in the new government of Vietnam in exchange for important concessions on that government's autonomy in domestic affairs. The French National Assembly then created a limited-franchise territorial assembly in Cochinchina, which, in turn, ratified the reattachment of Cochinchina to Vietnam. Finally, on May 21, the National Assembly officially recognized Vietnamese reunification and formally authorized further negotiations to bring Vietnam into the French Union.[24]

As French diplomacy regained its momentum, Acheson came under heavy pressure from his advisers to reevaluate what they now dubbed the Bao Dai solution. Ambassador Caffery advised Acheson in mid-March that a clandestine informant in the Bao Dai camp had indicated that the former Emperor was generally satisfied with the French concessions. Caffery also counseled that Bao Dai represented the "only foreseeable opportunity for

[an] anti-Communist solution [in] Indochina" and that Acheson should therefore review the Elysée agreements with a "view to [the] possibility of extending to the Bao Dai solution as a calculated risk, moral and perhaps some economic support." Not to do so, Caffery asserted, would "constitute a negative rather than a neutral factor." On March 25, Theodore C. Achilles, Chief of the Office of Western European Affairs, set forth a simple equation in support of Caffery: "While we obviously do not wish to get ourselves involved in a repetition of the painful Chiang Kai-shek situation, we must realize that the only alternative to a Bao Dai regime is one led by [the] Communist Ho Chi Minh." Yet, few of the State Department's Asia specialists accepted this view. Charles Reed—former Consul General in Saigon and the newly appointed Chief of the Office of Philippine and Southeast Asian Affairs—argued that given Bao Dai's "very dubious chances of succeeding," the United States should refrain from following France down what might turn out to be "a dead-end alley."[25]

Acheson hesitated before the precipice. On May 2, he instructed the American consulate in Saigon to guard first against any "premature endorsement or *de facto* recognition" of the new regime and, second, against any impression that the United States might oppose France's Bao Dai formula. George M. Abbott, the new U.S. Consul General in Saigon, immediately asked for clarification. Since the State Department did not want a communist state in Southeast Asia, and since only the United States had the resources to impose a purely military solution there, Abbott reasoned that Acheson should swiftly throw America's influence behind the new French policy. "Our support will not insure Bao Dai['s] success," the Consul General acknowledged, "but the lack of it will probably make certain his failure." Abbott also enumerated four measures by which the United States could improve the chances of the new regime: "immediate and continued pressure" on the French at the highest level for rapid implementation of the March 8 agreements, a statement of "sympathy" from the State Department, consultation on the issue with Britain and India looking to parallel early recognition, and exploration of prospects for economic aid to Indochina through enhanced ECA assistance to France. Caffery at once declared himself squarely behind Abbott, and he "expressly" concurred with Abbott's request for "immediate and continued pressure" on the French government with respect to the expeditious implementation of the March 8 agreements.[26]

On May 10, 1949, Acheson reluctantly set aside his reservations and enunciated conditional U.S. support for the Bao Dai solution. In a telegram to Abbott, he began by confirming that he wanted the Bao Dai "experiment" to succeed, and then, in words clearly borrowed from Caffery and Achilles, he added, "Since [there] appears [to] be no other alternative to establishing [a] Commie pattern Vietnam, [the] Department considers no efforts should be spared by France, other Western powers, and non-Commie Asian nations to assure [that the] experiment [has] the best chance [of] success." Why did Acheson reverse himself on this issue within the space of a few months? Dean Rusk, Deputy Undersecretary of State, later remembered that Acheson lacked expertise on, as well as interest in, Southeast Asia, and this left him heavily dependent on his advisers with respect to Indochina. The documentary evidence points in the same direction. Hence, when Acheson found a majority of his advisers in agreement, he ignored his own instincts, abandoned the position he had taken on February 25, and swallowed whole the views of Caffery, Achilles, and Abbott. Nevertheless, in his clarification to Abbott, Acheson warned that if Bao Dai failed to quickly earn popular support, a "government created [in] Indochina analogous [to the] Kuomintang [in China] would be foredoomed [to] failure."[27]

In the wake of these developments, policymakers from the Office of Western European Affairs, the Office of Philippine and Southeast Asian Affairs, and the Policy Planning Staff came together on May 17 to hammer out a common approach. The European specialists kicked off the debate by proclaiming that there was "no chance whatsoever of the French making any concessions" beyond those contained in their March 8, 1949, agreements with Bao Dai. This, of course, effectively precluded putting heavier pressure on France, as espoused by the Asian specialists. After a brief debate, the two sides reached a consensus that "the U.S. should not put itself in a forward position in the Indochina problem since there appeared to be nothing we could do to alter the very discouraging prospects, and that we should endeavor to 'collectivize' our approach to the situation." To facilitate further policy development, the planners also stipulated that the Office of Western European Affairs try to secure a complete version of the March 8 agreements and that the department as a whole endeavor to establish a common approach to the Vietnam question with Britain, India, and the Philippines.[28]

At Acheson's request, and under his direct supervision, George Kennan's Policy Planning Staff (PPS) spent nearly two months producing a comprehensive study on Southeast Asia. In its final report—"United States Policy toward Southeast Asia" (PPS-51, completed May 19, 1949)—the PPS began with the observation that Southeast Asia had earlier been the world's major source of rubber, tin, quinine, copra, and hard fiber. In addition, the region had exported substantial quantities of food, "principally for nearby Asiatic countries," and had provided a market for the "imperial powers." In the present circumstances, however, Southeast Asia confronted the State Department with an insoluble dilemma. On the one hand, "the attainment of U.S. objectives with respect to Japanese, Indian, and Western European self-support" would "require continued emphasis at least over the near term, on production of foodstuffs and raw materials in this area." On the other hand, most of Southeast Asia had become essentially nonproductive. Burma, "the rice granary of the Far East," had plunged into a chaotic civil war and exported "only a fraction of its normal surplus." Indonesia, which likewise suffered from serious political unrest, had become a "net drain" on the economy of Holland, as had Indochina on the economy of France. Overall, the PPS predicted that, for the foreseeable future, the entire region would be unable to make any significant contribution to U.S. plans for global economic recovery:

> The fact that fully half of SEA [Southeast Asia] is convulsed in political turmoil makes early progress toward the achievement of these [U.S.] long-term [trade] goals impossible. Furthermore, so long as conditions remain unsettled in SEA, the area can make . . . only limited contributions to ERP [Europe Recovery Program] countries' self-support, to the solution of India's food problem, or to the orientation of Japan's trade southward in search of survival. . . . *Only when a political settlement has been achieved, will gradual progress toward a rationalization of [the] Southeast Asian economy become possible* [italics added].[29]

The Policy Planning Staff believed that, even though the Soviet Union would gain economically if it could dominate Southeast Asia, Soviet planners were far more interested in denying the region to the United States. The Soviet leadership, Kennan and his staff asserted, was particularly aware of the economic and strategic importance of Indonesia and the Philippines. Soviet domination of these areas would directly threaten Australia, India, and Japan. This, in turn, rendered the communist insurgencies in Indochina and Indonesia a principal concern, but the PPS explicitly rejected three obvious policy alternatives: "full support of Dutch and French imperialism," "unlimited support of militant nationalism," and "evasion of the problem." The United States, the PPS recommended, "should discreetly but strongly press the Dutch and French to accommodate themselves to SEA [Southeast Asian] nationalism." The United States should also urge Britain, India, Pakistan, Australia, and the Philippines to put pressure on Holland and France. Finally, Kennan and his crew forecast that unless France abandoned its "niggardly" attitude and granted meaningful independence to the Bao Dai regime, the Vietminh would soon control most of Indochina.[30]

Kennan—according to his deputy, Paul Nitze—sometimes irritated Acheson by insisting that each of his PPS reports be treated "as a chalice." But the report on Southeast Asia marked an exception. Kennan asked Acheson to utilize his study only as "broad guidance to Departmental thinking on the subject and as a strategic concept from which tactical planning by operational offices should flow." Although this eliminated the need for formal NSC approval, it severely undermined the authority of the PPS's recommendations. Nonetheless, W. Walton Butterworth, Director of the Office of Far Eastern Affairs, seized upon the PPS study as justification for circumventing the authority of the Office of Western European Affairs. Having at last secured a complete text of the Bao Dai–Auriol agreements of March 8, 1949, Butterworth penned a "frank" U.S. response. He began with a simple premise: ". . . one of the strongest motivating forces behind nationalist movements among dependent peoples is resentment of the imputation of inferiority implicit in a subordinate status." Then, on the basis of this premise, Butterworth argued that unless the French government agreed to terms that were compatible with "Vietnamese national pride," a majority of the Vietnamese people would continue to support Ho Chi Minh and his Democratic Republic of Vietnam. Just in case the Foreign Ministry missed the point, Butterworth reiterated it through several pages of scalding prose; at one point, he warned the French, "The United States Government believes that the Vietnamese will willingly accept a partnership with France only if the equality of Vietnam is recognized and if . . . the sovereignty of Vietnam is acknowledged." This, of course, implicitly condemned the whole concept of a French Union and, with it, the main thrust of France's policies in Indochina.[31]

After nearly four years, the United States finally stood poised to challenge France's fundamental approach to Vietnam. On June 6, 1949, Butterworth forwarded his blunt missive to David K. E. Bruce, the new U.S. Ambassador to France, along with instructions that Bruce personally deliver it to the Foreign Ministry. Butterworth could scarcely have selected a less likely candidate to play messenger boy. Shocked by the tone as well as the substance of Butterworth's epistle, Bruce held it in abeyance for several days, pending Acheson's arrival in Paris for the 1949 foreign ministers' conference. In effect, Bruce stood alone against the combined authority of the Policy Planning Staff and the Director of Far Eastern Affairs, but he was not overmatched. Few men were as close to Acheson as David Bruce. Later, in 1952, Acheson made Bruce his Undersecretary, and in his memoirs Acheson would describe Bruce as the finest Ambassador to France since Benjamin Franklin.[32]

In a long and gritty discussion with Acheson, Bruce explained that while Butterworth's memorandum accurately reflected the situation in Indochina, it failed to consider the circumstances in Paris. The French government, he elaborated, had made substantial progress with the March 8 agreements, and more recently, on June 4, it had successfully reattached Cochinchina to the rest of Vietnam. Since several key members of the French government were already "battered and bruised" from these two struggles, Bruce insisted, Butterworth's "unrealistic document" would only "impede rather than encourage" further movement. Moreover, Bruce contended, Butterworth's demands for additional French concessions would entail a complete renegotiation of the March 8 agreements, and this would be impossible both diplomatically and politically. On the diplomatic front, Bruce maintained, the Foreign Ministry could not grant full independence to Vietnam without setting a precedent that would dominate France's future negotiations with its other territories—particularly Tunisia and Morocco. France could not afford to see its empire evaporate in the space of a few years. On the political front, the French public clearly opposed any further concessions in Vietnam and would not support a government that thought otherwise. Acheson—caught between Butterworth's well-reasoned arguments and Bruce's cogent rebuttal—devised an ostensible compromise, which in reality favored Bruce. Instead of delivering Butterworth's potentially explosive communiqué, Acheson instructed Bruce to orally apprise the French of Butterworth's principal concerns. Bruce should insist on nothing, but he should "urge the adoption of a liberal interpretation and loyal implementation of the agreements already reached and a similarly generous attitude in the negotiations still to be conducted." The ambassador happily delivered Acheson's toothless message, thereby ending the Kennan-Butterworth drive to put heavier pressure on France.[33]

Acheson selected this course neither because he deemed additional French concessions unnecessary nor because he thought the question could wait; he simply allowed a trusted friend to convince him that such concessions were unattainable. In truth, they were unattainable, and Acheson, in taking Bruce's advice, only bowed to reality. The historian Herbert Tint, an authority on French foreign policy, later observed, "It is important to recognize that French economic dependence on the United States did not bring with it political dependence in any significant way." This was particularly true with respect to France's colonial policies. Although the Marshall Plan provided the French with desperately needed short-term assistance, France's empire—which had previously accounted for 25 percent of its foreign trade—seemed essential to long-term economic development. As far back as 1945, when France first embraced the French Union concept, it decided to retain its colonies by granting their peoples the constitutional rights of citizenship. If the Foreign Ministry deviated from this formula by granting full independence to Vietnam, it would set a governing precedent for future negotiations with Algeria, Tunisia, Morocco, Madagascar, Martinique, Guadeloupe, and West Africa. France could not compromise in one part of its empire without bringing down the whole fragile edifice. Moreover, anything that diminished the empire would simultaneously threaten France's own tenuous political stability. Since the constitution of 1795, France had considered its colonies to be an integral part of the republic, and, in the eyes of most Frenchmen, the empire remained an indispensable symbol of France's status as a great power. The loss of even one colony would constitute an intolerable admission of decline and would risk incalculable political consequences.[34]

Following the Butterworth initiative, Acheson resigned himself to what he subsequently called "the limits on the extent to which one may successfully coerce an ally." Taken together, his decision in May to support the Bao Dai solution and his decision in June not to increase U.S. pressure on France marked a decisive turning point. He wrote much later, "I decided . . . that having put our hand to the plow, we would not look back." Two important reports seemed to confirm Acheson's May and June decisions. The first, issued in early October by the Central Intelligence Agency, included an early version of what would later be called the "domino theory." The war in Indochina, the CIA warned, had become an extremely serious drain on the French economy, but if the Communists eventually won, "then Burma, Thailand, and Malaya would undoubtedly turn to communism"—and Indonesia might follow as well. The CIA's analysts listed three policy options: a greatly expanded military aid program to support the French Army in Indochina, a renewed effort to persuade France to grant full independence to the Bao Dai regime, and a broad acceptance of France's existing policies. The analysts also pointed out three potential pitfalls: military aid for France might put the United States on the wrong side of Asian nationalism; France probably would not grant full independence to the Bao Dai regime; and Bao

Dai himself was unpopular and "untrustworthy." The second report on Indochina came from "the Consultants on the Far East"—an ad hoc collection of academic and State Department experts which Acheson assembled to advise him on Asian policy issues. The consultants observed that there was considerable danger that the "Bao Dai experiment" would fail, and they recommended that, if it did, Acheson should seek some sort of UN solution. Above all, the consultants warned, the United States should avoid any "arrangements which might bring the Communists into control of Vietnam."[35]

During the second half of 1949, Southeast Asia's economic potential gradually began to exert a larger influence on Acheson's policies. In 1938, the region accounted for 10.3 percent of all world trade. (In comparison, Japan accounted for only 5.4 percent.) Europe had cornered most of this trade, but Japan had aggressively expanded its share, and by the beginning of World War II, Southeast Asia, taken as a whole, provided 15.9 percent of Japan's imports and received 18.6 percent of its exports. But the war left much of the region in utter devastation, and its trade recovered very slowly. Early in 1948, for example, Acheson told a congressional committee that although Southeast Asia had once absorbed nearly a billion dollars worth of European exports annually, it now accounted for "practically none." In addressing this problem, State Department planners divided into two schools. One school, composed largely of analysts in the Office of European Affairs, wanted to see Southeast Asia resume its prewar trade patterns. The other school, a militant faction within the Office of Far Eastern Affairs, hoped to expedite Japan's recovery by increasing its trade in Southeast Asia. Paul Hoffman, Director of the Economic Cooperation Administration, immediately weighed in on the side of European Affairs, and Acheson did the same. But the debate continued. In mid-1949, George Kennan came out solidly in favor of enlarging Japan's share of Southeast Asia's trade. A few months later, Acheson asked

Dean Rusk, his Deputy Undersecretary of State, to assume a
larger role in Asian policy, and Rusk, who had served in
Southeast Asia during World War II, promptly added his voice
to Kennan's. Finally, Europe experienced a phenomenal
recovery in 1949, while Japan's economy barely inched upward.
By year's end, Acheson had largely reversed his position on
Southeast Asian trade, and in December he quietly authorized
an Asian economic-commercial conference (held in Tokyo five
months later) to promote the expansion of Japanese trade in
the Far East—especially Southeast Asia.[36]

Once the State Department commenced work on expanding
Japan's trade in Southeast Asia, Indochina's role in that trade
came into sharper focus. Japan had long imported 30 percent
of its food, principally from Korea and Taiwan, both of which
were part of its prewar empire. From 1936 to 1940, Korea had
exported an average of 1,183,697 tons of rice annually,
accounting for two-thirds of Japan's rice imports. By comparison, Indochina had exported an average of 1,116,499 tons of
rice annually, Burma 2,267,870 tons, and Thailand 1,460,218
tons. All three, however, had traded primarily with Europe
and India, not with Japan. After World War II—when Japan
became heavily dependent on distant and expensive American
food—Acheson found himself waging a desperate struggle to
revive the agricultural exports of Korea and Taiwan. Together
with his advisers, he also briefly explored the idea of trying to
revive Burma's rice exports, but he paid little heed to Indochina's potential. Indochina seemed neither susceptible to U.S.
control nor likely to make a rapid recovery. The French colony's rubber production came to just 45,000 tons in 1948,
against a prewar average of over 100,000 tons. Its annual rice
exports stood at a meager 11 percent of their antebellum level
in 1946 and then rose to just 13 percent in 1950. Indeed, at the
onset of 1950, Indochina faced a sobering annual trade deficit
of $85 million. Nevertheless, when Acheson's campaign to
revive Korea's exports bogged down and Burma plunged into

an intractable civil war, Dean Rusk suggested an effort to restore Indochina's rice exports, with a very substantial portion to be earmarked for Japan. Acheson, believing it easier to build fertilizer plants in Korea than to end the war in Indochina, accepted Rusk's plan reluctantly and with modest expectations. Early in 1950, he told a Senate committee that he hoped to increase Indochina's rice yield by only 15–20 percent. U.S. economic assistance actually accomplished far more, and over the next two years Indochina's rice exports rose to 33 percent of their prewar level. At first, Vietnam, with its much vaunted rice bowl region, seemed to be sharing in this modest recovery, but U.S. experts soon determined that virtually all of Vietnam's rice exports consisted of Cambodian rice shipped through Vietnamese ports. Taken as a whole, Indochina's foreign trade never fully recovered, and in Acheson's calculations it remained a tertiary consideration behind U.S. relations with France and Indochina's strategic location.[37]

In the closing weeks of 1949, Acheson mobilized all of his influence to shape the Truman administration's first comprehensive policy on the Far East (NSC 48 / 1 and NSC 48 / 2), and he incorporated into it his newly formed views on Southeast Asia. The Soviet Union, the policy proclaimed, had commenced a drive to "acquire Southeast Asia's resources and communication lines, and to deny them to us." Should this effort succeed, the United States would suffer "a major political rout" which would be "felt throughout the world, especially in the Middle East and in a then critically exposed Australia." Moreover, in a watershed statement, Acheson acknowledged explicitly (and for the first time) that reestablishing Japan's prewar trade with Korea and Taiwan would not be enough; the United States would have to facilitate a large-scale expansion of Japanese trade in Southeast Asia.

> Japan can only maintain its present living standard on a self-supporting basis if it is able to secure a greater proportion of its

needed food and raw material (principally cotton) imports from the Asiatic area, in which its natural markets lie, rather than from the U.S., in which its export market is small. *In view of the desirability of avoiding preponderant dependence on Chinese sources, and the limited availability of supplies from pre-war sources in Korea and Formosa, this will require a considerable increase in Southern Asiatic food and raw material exports* [italics added].

This marked the final expansion of Acheson's campaign to rebuild Japan's regional trade network. In 1947, his campaign focused on Korea; in early 1949, he enlarged it to include Taiwan and China; now he had drawn in all of the nations of Southeast Asia as well.[38]

On January 29, 1950, the French National Assembly approved legislation granting autonomy within the French Union to the state of Vietnam, a new entity which encompassed the former states of Tonkin, Annam, and Cochinchina. The Soviet Union and the People's Republic of China responded the next day by recognizing the Democratic Republic of Vietnam as the only legitimate Vietnamese government, and Acheson parried this Soviet move with a public statement denouncing the DRV as a Soviet puppet regime. France then formally ratified, on February 2, the creation of the governments of Vietnam, Laos, and Cambodia, and before the day was out, Acheson personally pressed Truman to grant all three new nations immediate diplomatic recognition. Although the CIA held "a gloomier view" with respect to Vietnam, Acheson elaborated, it supported his recommendations. Acheson also left Truman with a memorandum which estimated French troop strength in Indochina at 130,000, against a Vietminh strength of only 75,000. In truth, the most recent intelligence reports indicated that the Vietminh Army had just thrown at least 100,000 troops into an all-out offensive. Truman's cabinet voted unanimously for recognition on the third, and the President accepted their rec-

ommendation. Four days later, the United States officially recognized the new French-backed governments in Vietnam,
Cambodia, and Laos.[39]

The French Ambassador, Henri Bonnet, acting on instructions from Paris, met with Acheson on February 16 and pleaded
for three kinds of support: direct U.S. military aid for the new
nations of Indochina, a guarantee of Anglo-American support
in the event that the People's Republic of China intervened in
Vietnam, and an effective U.S. economic assistance program
for the whole region. Acheson and his advisers were generally
sympathetic. In a report on Asia in late 1949, Philip Jessup,
Acheson's Ambassador-at-Large, described Southeast Asia as
"weak and vulnerable" and in urgent need of U.S. aid. Paul
Nitze, who took over the Policy Planning Staff from Kennan
on January 1, 1950, swiftly issued a report on Soviet intentions which singled out Southeast Asia (particularly Indochina) as "a primary area of Soviet-Communist action." On
February 1 (more than two weeks before Bonnet requested
additional U.S. assistance), a State Department study, "Military Aid for Indochina," confirmed that the United States would
have to send aid to Vietnam, Laos, and Cambodia. On the
basis of these opinions, as well as the CIA's October 1948
report and the Indochina section of the recently approved NSC
policy on the Far East (NSC 48 / 1 and NSC 48 / 2), Acheson
ordered the formulation of a specific policy statement on Indochina. His advisers completed it on February 27. The new policy (NSC 64, approved April 24, 1950) centered primarily on
the views expressed earlier by the CIA: if Indochina fell to
"communist expansion," Thailand and Burma would fall as
well, and the rest of Southeast Asia would be left "in grave
hazard." The Departments of State and Defense should therefore "prepare as a matter of priority a program of all practicable measures designed to protect United States security interests
in Indochina."[40]

"All practicable measures" seemed to imply positive responses to all three of France's requests on Indochina, beginning with military aid. On March 9, 1950, Acheson asked Truman in person to allocate a portion of the Mutual Defense Assistance Program to Thailand and Indochina. The President agreed. Dean Rusk then formally requested a full military assessment. In a report forwarded to Acheson on April 14, the Joint Chiefs of Staff asserted that Southeast Asia was of "critical strategic importance to the United States." Taken as a whole, JCS planners observed, the region produced important strategic materials, stood at a crossroads of trade and communications, provided raw materials and food for Japan, and could, if captured by communist elements, provide raw materials for the Soviet Union and food for the People's Republic of China. The Pentagon's planners acknowledged that, according to CIA estimates, the situation in Southeast Asia had already deteriorated considerably, but they contended that a heavy dose of economic assistance would probably reverse this deterioration and shift the initiative to the United States. Acheson and his advisers at first suggested $15 million in military aid for Indochina; later, with the JCS in support, they raised this to $20 million. Truman, on the advice of his Budget Director, approved the full amount but only released it in stages. On May 1, he authorized the transfer of an initial $13 million package, consisting of $10 million for Indochina and $3 million for Indonesia. The JCS, eager to herald the new U.S. commitment, sent two of its ships—the USS *Stickell* and the USS *Anderson*—to show the flag in Saigon harbor. Local Vietminh forces welcomed them with a well-timed mortar barrage, and although both ships emerged unscathed, American servicemen received their first taste of combat in Vietnam.[41]

With only a preliminary plan for aid to Indochina in hand, Acheson flew off to London for the fourth conference of the North Atlantic Treaty Organization (NATO). He left behind Dean Rusk, now Assistant Secretary of State for Far Eastern Affairs, with orders to finish up a comprehensive aid plan for all of Southeast Asia. En route, Acheson stopped off in Paris for discussions with Robert Schuman, the French Foreign Minister. Schuman bluntly declared that France would accept U.S. plans for German rearmament only if the French Army could maintain its countervailing strength in Europe, and this, in turn, would require full U.S. support in Indochina. Expecting to mollify the Frenchman, Acheson announced that the United States would provide roughly $20 million worth of economic and military assistance to Indochina by the end of the fiscal year. But Schuman was not satisfied. He moved directly to the second of the requests his government had made earlier through Henri Bonnet: France wanted a guarantee that if the newly formed People's Republic of China invaded Indochina, the United States and Britain would then enter the conflict on the side of France. Acheson made no commitment. When the NATO conference opened in London a few days later, Acheson, Schuman, and Ernest Bevin, the British Foreign Minister, set up a special committee to examine Schuman's demands. Paul Nitze and Frank Nash, representing the United States, persuaded the committee to recommend a purely defensive three-nation response to any Chinese aggression in Southeast Asia, and the ministers forwarded this concept to their governments. When the conference finally ended, on May 18, Acheson indulged himself with a leisurely return passage on the ocean liner *Britannia,* while Nitze hurried back for an urgent consultation with the Joint Chiefs of Staff. The JCS, much to Nitze's chagrin, at once rejected any form of military guarantee for Indochina, and even after Britain and France signaled their approval, the JCS remained adamantly opposed. The JCS did not reverse itself until two years later, and even then it pledged only an air and naval response if the PRC intervened directly in Vietnam.[42]

When Acheson arrived back in Washington at the end of May, Rusk handed him a tentative military aid plan, which called for spending $39.5 million in Southeast Asia and $21 million of that in Indochina. During the first six months of 1950, Acheson and Rusk also developed a comprehensive economic assistance program for Southeast Asia. Acheson assigned this matter a high priority in his first policy statement on the region (NSC 64), but he knew that it would be difficult to line up the necessary political support. In late January of 1950, congressional Republicans, weary of an endless series of foreign aid appropriations, temporarily blocked Acheson's Korean aid plan and signaled their skepticism about any additional recovery programs in Asia. The Republicans seemed particularly dubious about large-scale assistance for Southeast Asia. Then, as always, there were two standard responses to this kind of obstacle—a high-level commission or a special diplomatic mission—either of which could manufacture documentary justification for the desired level of expenditure. The Departments of State and Defense each selected the second option, but in light of the ongoing feud between Acheson and Secretary of Defense Louis Johnson, each department sent out its own mission. The Pentagon's team—headed by Robert West, Deputy Secretary of the Army, and Stanley Andrews, Director of the Office of Foreign Agricultural Relations in the Department of Agriculture—got out of the starting blocks first. Like a few other missions before it, the Andrews-West mission centered its investigation around Japan's desperate need for low-cost food and raw materials. If American intervention could resolve Southeast Asia's military conflicts and rebuild its economy, the army team speculated, the region's exports might eventually provide as much as two-thirds of the food and raw materials that Japan needed to revive its economy. To this end, West and Andrews reasoned that the United States should extend economic assistance and work to facilitate a rapid increase in trade between Japan and Southeast Asia.[43]

Acheson and his subordinates took a bit more time to get their mission off the mark, but this only reflected the meticulousness of their planning. To head the mission, they selected

R. Allen Griffin, who was both an Acheson supporter and a prominent Republican. Griffin understood his role clearly. "I think that this whole mission that became known as the Griffin mission," he later recounted, "was set up to show to the Republicans in Congress that we were going to do something about Southeast Asia. I think that's all it was." Between February 27 and April 22, the Griffin Mission visited Tokyo, Saigon, Singapore, Kuala Lumpur, Rangoon, Bangkok, and Djakarta, but it focused most of its attention on Vietnam. State Department officers guided the Griffin team through every stop. Robert Hoey, the State Department's Officer in Charge of Indochinese Affairs, met the mission in Saigon, and after its departure he cabled his superiors, "I worked practically 24 hours a day with the Mission and did much of the reporting for it." Griffin, in a telegram dated March 18, told Acheson that the situation in Vietnam did not "justify defeatism" but did "justify [the] effective application of US aid." A large portion of the population, he asserted, consisted of "fence sitters" who could be won over by U.S. aid, and, even without that aid, the French Army had already begun to turn the tide. To no one's surprise, Griffin's final report gave Acheson precisely what he wanted. It recommended spending $66,093,000 for economic assistance in Southeast Asia over the next fifteen months, including $23,500,000 for Indochina, $4,500,000 for Malaya and Singapore, $12,228,000 for Burma, $11,420,000 for Thailand, and $14,445,000 for Indonesia. The opening days of the Korean War presented Acheson with the perfect opportunity to sell this plan to the President. On June 26, at the second Blair House meeting, Acheson recommended that the United States immediately increase its assistance to Indochina and send "a strong military mission" to Vietnam. Truman agreed, and Acheson quickly secured the approval of Congress as well. By June of 1951, the Economic Cooperation Administration had doled out $49,722,000 worth of economic assistance in Southeast Asia, including $7,973,000 to Indonesia,

$8,876,000 to Thailand, $10,400,000 to Burma, and $22,473,000 to Indochina.[44]

As soon as Acheson was certain that his economic assistance program for Southeast Asia would be approved, he again turned his attentions to the military aid question. Rusk had completed a tentative military aid plan for the region in late May, but the Korean War rendered it obsolete. To develop a new and larger plan, the Departments of State and Defense set up a joint fact-finding mission led by John F. Melby, a State Department expert on Southeast Asia, and Graves B. Erskine, a Marine Corps general. Melby later recounted that although "the real focus was on Indochina," the mission spent most of July and part of August touring all of Southeast Asia for the sake of appearances. Melby and Erskine carried explicit instructions to report only on ways to implement an expanded military aid program in Indochina; once there, however, Melby defiantly concluded that the United States was "making a terrible mistake." In a ten-page telegram to Acheson, he pleaded, "Please take this up with the President again; ask him to review his decision to help the French; it is not going to work." Donald R. Heath—the State Department's Minister to Vietnam, Laos, and Cambodia—at once denigrated Melby's arguments in a long telegram of his own. Joining the debate, George Kennan, now only a policy adviser, counseled Acheson to abandon Indochina, neutralize Japan, allow China to enter the UN, and accept the eventual Soviet domination of Korea. Dean Rusk, taking the opposite view, not only disparaged Kennan's recommendations but even engaged in discussions with Henri Bonnet, the French Ambassador, on prospects for committing U.S. air power in Vietnam. None of this, however, made much of an impression on Acheson. Having already decided "not to look back," he neither reevaluated the U.S. commitment in Indochina nor acceded to French requests for American air support. On August 7, the Melby-Erskine Mission dutifully delivered its recipe for expanded military assistance. Congress, as Acheson expected, took the Melby-Erskine Mission's "findings" at face value and appropriated $303 million in new military assistance for the Far East. Much of this would be allocated to Vietnam, and by year's end, total U.S. assistance for Vietnam, economic and military, reached $133 million.[45]

In its April 14 report—developed at the request of Dean Rusk—the JCS had recommended the establishment of both a committee to coordinate all assistance to Southeast Asia and a military advisory group to facilitate the utilization of military aid in Indochina. The resulting Southeast Asia Aid Policy Committee held its first meeting on July 13, 1950, and before the meeting ended, Rusk, the State Department member, took upon himself the responsibility for ensuring that U.S. military aid arrived in Southeast Asia "at the required pace." On June 26, at the second Blair House meeting, Acheson had persuaded Truman to send a "strong military mission" to Vietnam. Accordingly, the JCS developed the U.S. Military Advisory Group for Indochina. Its initial contingent—thirty-five American military officers—arrived in Vietnam on August 2, 1950. But despite U.S. aid and advisers, the military situation continued to deteriorate. To counter the anti-French and anti-imperialism sentiments which fueled the Vietminh movement, Acheson struck a deal with the French government in the fall of 1950: the French would create a Vietnamese army, and the United States would pay most of the cost and provide nearly all of the equipment. Thus, the closing months of 1950 saw American military advisers arriving in Vietnam, the Pentagon financing a new Vietnamese army, and the ECA distributing U.S. economic assistance to much of Southeast Asia.[46]

The Korean War stalled Acheson's plans to rebuild Japanese trade with Korea and deflated the last remaining hopes for reviving Japanese trade with China. Acheson and Rusk, therefore, attached an ever increasing importance to the expansion of Japanese trade in Southeast Asia. In early 1952, a new

200 CONTROLLING THE WAVES

summary of U.S. policy in the region declared that the loss of Southeast Asia's "three rice surplus countries"—Indochina, Thailand, and Burma—would "create real difficulties for the continued maintenance of a Western oriented Japan," and that the loss of Southeast Asia as a whole would put Japan in serious jeopardy. This, in turn, completed the transformation of Acheson's policy toward Vietnam. The political and economic situation in France receded as a rationale for the steadily escalating U.S. commitment in Vietnam, and Vietnam's role as the strategic cornerstone of Southeast Asia (the domino theory) took center stage. In effect, the U.S. commitment in Vietnam became one of the principal elements of Acheson's larger plans for the reconstruction of Japan's Asian trade system.[47]

Conclusion

Dean Acheson played the leading role in U.S. policy on Indochina during two critical periods: his tenure as Undersecretary of State, 1945–47, and his tenure as Secretary of State, 1949–53. As Undersecretary, Acheson both purposefully encouraged and inadvertently hindered progress toward a negotiated settlement. On one side, he organized two separate State Department offers to facilitate a resumption of negotiations between France and the Democratic Republic of Vietnam. On the other side, his disdain for Ho Chi Minh severely limited U.S. pressure on France. Ultimately, Acheson's hopes for a negotiated settlement came to naught, but, given the instability and recalcitrance of the French government, it is unlikely that any other American policies or actions would have achieved a different result.

As Secretary of State, Acheson initially distrusted the French government and disdained any U.S. involvement in its Bao Dai experiment. By stages, however, he reversed himself. In May of 1949, Acheson accepted the majority view of his advisers and extended U.S. diplomatic support to the Bao Dai regime. A month later, he allowed Ambassador Bruce to dissuade him from pressing France for a more liberal policy on Vietnam. By year's end, with Japan's economy barely inching toward a postwar recovery, Acheson began to place new emphasis on Southeast Asia's potential role in Japanese trade, and on Vietnam's role in regional security. During the spring and summer of 1950, Acheson orchestrated the development of substantial assistance programs for Southeast Asia in general and Vietnam in particular. Finally, in 1951–52, the Korean War blocked the revival of Japan's trade with Korea and China, sharply increased Japan's need for Southeast Asian trade, and completed the transformation of America's Vietnam commitment into a major element in Acheson's plans for the reconstruction of Japan's Asian trade network.

Toward the middle of this long process, Acheson could have opted to maintain U.S. neutrality in Indochina, but once he abandoned that neutrality, he lacked the means to significantly influence French policy. Hence, in a larger sense, Acheson had only two alternatives—to do nothing or to support a French policy on French terms. In his memoirs, he explained, "So while we may have tried to muddle through and were certainly not successful, I could not think then or later of a better course. One can suggest, perhaps, doing nothing. That might have had merit, but . . . it had its demerits, too." In the final analysis, Indochina was so important to France, and the security of Southeast Asia was so important to both Japan and Europe, that Acheson could not accept the risk of doing nothing. Yet, when Acheson chose to do something rather than nothing— when he chose to support a French policy on French terms— he put the United States directly in line to inherit a French war.[48]

CHAPTER SEVEN

Acheson and
the New Co-Prosperity
Sphere

FROM START TO FINISH, Dean Acheson's primary concern in the Far East was the reconstruction of Japan. Max Bishop, his first Chief of Northeast Asian Affairs, described Japan as the only nation in Asia with any "real strategic importance." John Allison, Acheson's second Chief of Northeast Asian Affairs, described Japan as "the real prize in Asia." Acheson therefore worked to secure Japan's economic and political future by developing a U.S.-sponsored recovery program, revising Japan's reparations obligations, replacing MacArthur's economic advisory staff, negotiating a peace treaty, and rebuilding Japan's Asian trade. To one extent or another, he succeeded in each of these areas, but the last was by far the most important.[1]

There was nothing inevitable about America's postwar campaign to rebuild Japan's Asian trade. The United States could have set out to create a new economic order in the Far East, and indeed, at the end of World War II, many American planners wanted to dole out Japan's machine tools as reparations, destroy its powerful family-owned corporations, and dissolve its foreign trade system. Moreover, a number of other paradigms were also available, and had someone other than Acheson been orchestrating U.S. policy, the results might have been quite different. George Kennan, for example, wanted to neutralize Japan, accept Soviet domination of Korea, seize Taiwan, allow the People's Republic of China into the UN, and abandon all of Indochina. But, as the preceding chapters have demonstrated, the pivotal decisions on U.S. policy in the Far East fell to Dean Acheson, and he pursued a long series of policies which were designed to reconstruct Japan's prewar regional trade system. As to whether Acheson's primary objective was global economic recovery or the containment of communism, Paul Nitze, one of his closest advisers, has offered this insight: "They were viewed as being one and the same thing."[2]

In 1941, Japan's newly extended empire—which its propaganda ministry dubbed the Greater East Asia Co-Prosperity Sphere—included Korea, Taiwan, Indochina, and much of China; in the immediate postwar era, Acheson focused his attentions on these same four areas. He sought to rebuild South Korea because it could provide Japan with essential food and markets, and because it had considerable psychological importance to the Japanese people. He went to great lengths to keep Taiwan out of Communist hands, because it dominated Japan's trade routes and because it, too, was economically and psychologically important to the Japanese. He sought to expand Japan's trade with the People's Republic of China, albeit only as a temporary measure, because Japan needed China's raw materials. And although Acheson initially involved the United States in Indochina as a means of supporting a war-weakened France, his subsequent decisions to maintain and expand that involvement owed much to Japan's need for Southeast Asian trade. The net result of Acheson's policies was a new and revised version of the Greater East Asia Co-Prosperity Sphere—one in which Japan recovered its regional economic preeminence but exchanged its failed militarism for American tutelage, protection, and domination. This new Co-Prosperity Sphere blocked the spread of communism in Asia, facilitated Japanese economic recovery, and accelerated the expansion of American trade throughout the Far East. Japan's foreign trade reached its prewar average in 1959, doubled that level by 1964, and continued to grow rapidly in the decades that followed. America's Asian trade, led by a robust trade with Japan, increased at a similar pace, and in the late 1980s U.S. trade with Asia surpassed even U.S. trade with Europe. This, in turn, helped create an unprecedented era of economic growth and prosperity. But the new Co-Prosperity Sphere came at a heavy price, and the Korean War was only the down payment.[3]

In 1952, Dwight D. Eisenhower ran for the presidency on the Republican ticket. Earlier, Eisenhower had led the Pentagon's drive to withdraw U.S. troops from Korea, but now, in the heat of the political season, he disingenuously blamed Acheson for having invited North Korean aggression. Eisenhower won the election, made John Foster Dulles his Secretary of State, and brought the Korean War to an end. Dulles adjusted, but did not substantially change, Acheson's core policies on Japan, South Korea, Taiwan, the People's Republic of China, and Vietnam. On Taiwan, Sun Li-jen hatched yet another conspiracy. Chiang Kai-shek arrested Sun in 1955, and K. C. Wu, the other "American favorite," fled to safety in the United States. Sun did not emerge from prison until 1988, and Wu lived out his life in exile. (Most documents pertaining to the U.S. role in these events remain classified.) The French finally bowed out of Vietnam in 1954, leaving it divided into North and South Vietnam, and the United States assumed the full burden of supporting South Vietnam.[4]

John F. Kennedy, a Democrat who began his career in the Truman years, succeeded Eisenhower in 1961 and appointed Dean Rusk to be his Secretary of State. Paul Nitze served first as the head of Kennedy's preelection committee on national defense and then as Assistant Secretary of Defense for International Security Affairs. Acheson served as an occasional but highly regarded adviser. Rusk, like Dulles (his old friend), maintained the momentum of Acheson's original policies in the Far East. In 1950, Acheson and Rusk had forged a policy which sent 35 U.S. military advisers to Vietnam; by the end of 1962, the number had risen to 10,700. But South Vietnam's French-made government, headed by President Ngo Dinh Diem, was repressive, corrupt, and unpopular. In a scenario reminiscent of the earlier Sun Li-jen intrigues, Kennedy and Rusk supported a military coup d'état which eliminated Diem and increased U.S. control over both South Vietnam and its war. Kennedy developed serious doubts about the situation in Vietnam, but he never discussed them with Rusk. Lyndon B. Johnson, who succeeded to the presidency after Kennedy's assassination, kept Rusk on as Secretary of State and brought U.S. forces directly into the Vietnam War. By early 1968, the United States had 535,000 troops in Vietnam, but growing casualty lists and a surprise North Vietnamese offensive (the Tet offensive) demolished Johnson's political support. Some of Johnson's top policymakers, including Rusk, began to recommend a negotiated solution. On March 15, 1968, Dean Acheson met with Johnson over lunch and counseled him that the war could no longer be won. A follow-up gathering of elder statesmen and senior advisers, including Acheson, produced the same advice. Johnson announced on March 31 that he would seek a negotiated settlement in Vietnam and that he would not run for reelection. The last U.S. troops left Vietnam in 1973. Two years later, the North Vietnamese Army won the war and completed the reunification of Vietnam.[5]

Even then, the full price of Acheson's paradigm had not yet been paid. Acheson and his advisers had confidently assumed that the United States could and should "control every wave in the Pacific Ocean" and that their reformed version of Japan's

Co-Prosperity Sphere would indefinitely serve this end. The Japanese economy, however, eventually began to outperform that of its overburdened protector and benefactor. Ironically, beginning in the 1980s, Japan rose up to challenge the American trade dominance upon which all of Acheson's planning was predicated.[6]

✝ Notes

Foreign Relations   U.S. Department of State, *Foreign Relations of the United States* (cited by year, volume, and pages)
GPO   U.S. Government Printing Office
HSTL   Harry S. Truman Library, Independence, Missouri
Nat. Arch.   National Archives, Washington, D.C.

CHAPTER ONE: Dean Acheson

1. Gaddis Smith, "Acheson, Dean Gooderham," in *The Harry S. Truman Encyclopedia,* ed. Richard S. Kirkendall (Boston: G. K. Hall, 1989), pp. 1–2; David S. McLellan, *Dean Acheson* (New York: Dodd, Mead, 1976), pp. 15–29.

2. McLellan, *Dean Acheson,* pp. 15–29; Dean Acheson, *Sketches from Life of Men I Have Known* (New York: Harper, 1956), p. 213; interview with Dean Rusk, Athens, Ga., April 11, 1988 (hereafter cited as Rusk interview with author); David McCullough, *Truman* (New York: Simon & Schuster, 1992), pp. 752 and 755; interview with Lucius D. Battle, Washington, D.C., May 30, 1990 (hereafter cited as Battle interview with author).

3. Rusk interview with author; interview with Max Bishop, Ailey, Ga., April 12, 1988 (hereafter cited as Bishop interview with author); telephone interview with Max Bishop, Ailey, Ga., April 10, 1992. Lucius Battle, Acheson's personal assistant, and Paul Nitze, the Director of his Policy Planning Staff, repeatedly emphasized that Acheson had an exceptional mind. Battle interview with author; interview with Paul H. Nitze, Washington, D.C., July 25, 1989 (hereafter cited as Nitze interview with author).

4. McLellan, *Dean Acheson,* p. 54; Rusk interview with author.

5. Bishop interview with author; telephone interview with Max Bishop,

Ailey, Ga., April 11, 1992; Rusk interview with author; Battle interview with author.

6. Acheson used a code to designate those documents which he did and did not write, approve, or read. Documents which Acheson did not actually handle, but which nevertheless bear his name or signature, were labeled D.A.L.D.B. on the reverse side. When Acheson traveled, he received most communications through "telach" and sent most communications through "achtel," both of which were secured systems. Any message which went through one of these systems was written, approved, or received by Acheson, unless otherwise marked. Any document which Acheson wrote himself, except for the most formal kinds of statements, always contained a personal pronoun, either singular or plural, somewhere within its text. There was a strict rule that only Acheson could use the first person in any form in a document bearing his signature. This code has helped to make it possible for the present work to distinguish accurately between Acheson's own role and that of his advisers. Battle interview with author. Dean Acheson's involvement with Asian issues varied according to the circumstances. He was fairly active in Far Eastern policy in 1947, not too active in January–February of 1949, very active from March of 1949 to March of 1950, and progressively less active after March 28, 1950. Acheson's relatively high level of involvement in Asian issues during 1949 and early 1950 was partly the result of staffing problems. In late 1947, when John Carter Vincent resigned his post as Director of Far Eastern Affairs, Acheson, who was not then in the State Department, asked Secretary of State George C. Marshall to give the job to W. Walton Butterworth—even though Butterworth twice refused it on the grounds that he knew almost nothing about the Far East. Butterworth, describing himself as "the first of a long line of expendable Directors of Far Eastern Affairs," finally took the job. He struggled against extreme difficulties to uphold Acheson's views and muddle through. When Acheson returned in 1949, he kept his old friend on, but Butterworth never managed to get his office well in hand. Acheson therefore became far more involved in Far Eastern Affairs than he might have otherwise. The transfer of Max Bishop to Far Eastern Affairs helped for a while, but the leadership of the National Security Council (NSC) and the President wanted Bishop on the NSC staff. Acheson obliged. He approved a series of special councils, committees, and working groups to supplement Butterworth's advice on Far Eastern issues, but these accomplished little. Undersecretary James Webb was not an expert on foreign policy; Paul Nitze and others sometimes cut him out of the decision-making process. Consequently, Acheson asked Dean Rusk, then Webb's assistant, to quietly assume a larger role in the formulation of Asian policies. Acheson, however, still found himself heavily involved with Far Eastern

issues. In early 1950, he even considered creating a second ambassador-at-large to address Asian questions and help Butterworth. On March 28, 1950, Acheson finally replaced Butterworth with Rusk. Rusk immediately provided much stronger leadership for the Office of Far Eastern Affairs and became the dominant voice on Asian matters. By May of 1950, Acheson had largely reverted to the role of final arbiter, leaving most of the details of Asian policy to Rusk. W. Walton Butterworth, oral history interview with Richard D. McKenzie and Theodore S. Wilson, Princeton, N.J., July 6, 1971, HSTL, pp. 53–54; Bishop interview with author; Nitze interview with author; Rusk interview with author.

CHAPTER TWO: Acheson and
the American Reconstruction of Japan

1. U.S. Department of State, *Occupation of Japan* (Washington: GPO, 1946), pp. 2–11 and 73–82. For more detailed accounts of the wartime evolution of occupation policy, see those of Akira Iriye and Marlene J. Mayo. Iriye's account, however, incorrectly describes SWNCC 150 / 2 as the initial occupation policy. Harry S. Truman never approved SWNCC 150 / 2; he approved instead SWNCC 150 / 4, a quite different policy statement. Akira Iriye, "Continuities in U.S.-Japanese Relations, 1941–1949," in *The Origins of the Cold War in Asia,* ed. Yonosuke Nagai and Akira Iriye (New York: Columbia Univ. Press, 1977), pp. 378–407; Marlene J. Mayo, "American Wartime Planning for Occupied Japan," in *Americans as Proconsuls,* ed. Robert Wolfe (Carbondale: Southern Illinois Univ. Press, 1984), pp. 37–51.

2. William J. Sebald with Russell Brines, *With MacArthur in Japan* (New York: Norton, 1965), p. 48; Jerome B. Cohen, *Japan's Postwar Economy* (Bloomington: Indiana Univ. Press, 1958), pp. 15, 123, 125, and 126; interview with Max Bishop, April 12, 1988, Ailey, Ga. (hereafter cited as Bishop interview with author); U.S. Department of War, "United States Strategic Bombing Survey, Japan's Struggle to End the War," July 1, 1946, HSTL, Papers of George M. Elsey, Box 71, Japanese Surrender Aug. 1945 File (hereafter cited as U.S. Department of War, "Strategic Bombing Survey"); Jerome B. Cohen, *Japan's Economy in War and Reconstruction* (Minneapolis: Univ. of Minnesota, 1949), p. 494.

3. Congress, House, Subcommittee of the Committee on Appropriations, *First Deficiency Appropriations Bill for 1947: Hearings before the Subcommittee of the Committee on Appropriations on H.R. 2849,* 80th Cong., 1st sess., 1947, pp. 702, 725, 729, 746–47, 846, and 849; Tatsuro Uchino,

Japan's Postwar Economy (Tokyo: Kodansha International, 1983), pp. 42 and 254. Cohen, *Japan's Postwar Economy,* p. 11; telephone interview with Max Bishop, April 11, 1992, Ailey, Ga.; U.S. Department of War, "Strategic Bombing Survey"; U.S. Department of State, *Occupation of Japan,* p. 40. On March 20, 1947, George Atcheson, the State Department Political Adviser in Japan, spoke of "extreme protein food shortages in Japan." George Atcheson to George C. Marshall, March 18, 1947, *Foreign Relations,* 1947, vol. 6, pp. 190–91.

4. Dean Acheson, *Present at the Creation* (New York: Norton, 1969), pp. 16–27, 36–38, 87–91, and 119–20. Dean Rusk—Dean Acheson's Deputy Undersecretary and later his Director of Far Eastern Affairs—subsequently recounted that Acheson had a good working knowledge of the economics of Japan's old empire but knew very little about the rest of the Far East. Interview with Dean Rusk, April 11, 1988, Athens, Ga. (hereafter cited as Rusk interview with author); Waldo Heinrichs, *Threshold of War* (New York: Oxford Univ. Press, 1988), pp. 70, 141, 177–79, and 246–47; Jonathan G. Utley, *Going to War with Japan, 1937–1941* (Knoxville: Univ. of Tennessee Press, 1985), pp. 152–57, 172, and 180.

5. Interview with Paul H. Nitze, Washington, D.C., July 25, 1989 (hereafter cited as Nitze interview with author); Paul Nitze, oral history interview with Richard D. McKinzie, Arlington, Va., June 11 and 17 and Aug. 4, 5, and 6, 1975, HSTL (hereafter cited as Nitze, HSTL Oral History), pp. 146–50.

6. Nitze's first concern was to discern which nations were most in need of U.S. aid, and this became a priority in the resulting SWNCC study. In the end, Nitze's five-billion-dollars-per-year estimate proved quite close to the mark. Nitze interview with author; Acheson to Robert P. Patterson, March 5, 1947, *Foreign Relations,* 1947, vol. 3, pp. 197–98; editorial notes 3 and 4, ibid., pp. 198–99; Report of the "Ad Hoc" Committee, April 21, 1947, ibid., pp. 204–20; SWNCC 360, April 21, 1947, ibid., vol. 1, pp. 725–34; Acheson, *Present at the Creation,* pp. 226–34.

7. Nitze interview with author; Nitze, HSTL Oral History, p. 148; Paul Nitze, *From Hiroshima to Glasnost* (New York: Grove Weidenfeld, 1989), p. 52; Acheson, "The Requirements of Reconstruction," *Department of State Bulletin* 16 (May 18, 1947): 991–92. A few years later, when Acheson was Secretary of State, he told his personal assistant, Lucius Battle, the full story of his Cleveland speech. According to Battle, Acheson intended the Cleveland speech to initiate the Marshall Plan debate, and when it received insufficient attention, he spared no effort in generating greater press coverage for Secretary of State Marshall's speech. Interview with Lucius D. Battle, Washington, D.C., May 30, 1990 (hereafter cited as Battle interview with

author). Paul Hoffman likewise believed that Acheson was central to the early development of the Marshall Plan. Paul G. Hoffman, oral history interview with Philip C. Brooks, New York, Oct. 25, 1964, HSTL, pp. 25–26. David Bruce, who much later served as Acheson's Undersecretary, attributed the origins of the Marshall Plan to Truman, Marshall, Acheson, and William Clayton. David K. E. Bruce, oral history interview with Jerry N. Hess, Washington, D.C., March 1, 1972, HSTL (hereafter cited as Bruce, HSTL Oral History), p. 8.

8. Nitze interview with author; William S. Borden, *The Pacific Alliance* (Madison: Univ of Wisconsin Press, 1984), p. 68; Saburo Okita, *The Rehabilitation of Japan's Economy and Asia* (Tokyo: Public Information and Cultural Affairs Bureau, 1956), p. 6.

9. Nitze interview with author; Policy Planning Staff, PPS 1, May 23, 1947, U.S. Department of State, *The State Department Policy Planning Staff Papers*, 3 vols. (New York: Garland, 1983), 1:3–11; Battle interview with author.

10. Charles E. Saltzman to the State-War-Navy Coordinating Committee, Oct. 9, 1947, *Foreign Relations*, 1947, vol. 6, pp. 302–4. Congress attached the $165 million Japanese recovery package to the newly approved Economic Recovery for Occupied Areas Program. Michael Schaller, *The American Occupation of Japan* (New York: Oxford Univ. Press, 1985), pp. 92, 110, and 113–14; Borden, *Pacific Alliance*, p. 75.

11. Nitze interview with author; U.S. Department of War, "Strategic Bombing Survey"; Peter Lowe, *The Origins of the Korean War* (New York: Longman, 1986), p. 74. Max Bishop's recommendations may have strengthened Nitze's hand. Max Bishop to Marshall, Feb. 13, 1947, *Foreign Relations*, 1947, vol. 6, pp. 356–57; Marshall to Bishop, Feb. 28, 1947, ibid., pp. 365–66. The historian William S. Borden's view that the United States was "not greatly concerned" about the Japanese economy in 1946 is essentially correct, although the State Department began to take more notice toward the end of that year. Borden, *Pacific Alliance*, p. 67. To a large extent, the State Department was slow to appreciate Asian problems because it was organizationally structured to focus on Europe much more than on other areas, and on political problems much more than on economic ones. Lucius Battle, who later served as Acheson's personal assistant, vigorously opposed this organizational structure when it was set up, but to no avail. When Acheson became Secretary of State, he restructured the department in ways which put greater emphasis on both economics and the Far East. Battle interview with author.

12. "Report by the State-War-Navy Coordinating Subcommittee for the Far East" (SWNCC 236 / 10 and footnotes), April 25, 1946, *Foreign Rela-*

tions, 1946, vol. 8, pp. 493–504; Acheson to Certain Chiefs of Mission, Dec. 6, 1946, ibid., pp. 598–99; Atcheson to Harry S. Truman, Jan. 5, 1947, ibid., 1947, vol. 6, pp. 157–60. Initially, the State Department thought in terms of transferring up to 30 percent of Japan's industrial assets as reparations. Bishop to Marshall, Feb. 19, 1947, ibid., pp. 359–60.

13. John H. Hilldring to Frank R. McCoy, March 24, 1947, *Foreign Relations,* 1947, vol. 6, p. 374; JCS to Douglas MacArthur, April 4, 1947, ibid., pp. 376–80. Curiously enough, the committee which formulated the initial U.S. approach to Japanese reparations did not even include a member from the Department of the Army; it did include members from the Departments of State, Commerce, Agriculture, and Treasury, and the State Department member, R. W. Whitman, chaired the committee. Meetings of the Committee on Development of Japanese and Korean Trade, Nat. Arch., Record Group 353, Department of State, Box 9, Lot 122, 2 A.16—Occupied Areas Affairs-Advisory Committee on Development of Japanese and Korean Trade File, Obtained through the Freedom of Information Act; Ernest A. Gross to Saltzman, Dec. 27, 1948, *Foreign Relations,* 1948, vol. 6, pp. 1068–70; W. Walton Butterworth to Acheson, Jan. 27, 1949, ibid., 1949, vol. 7, pp. 633–37. Although the U.S. government developed no further proposals on reparations until 1949, it continued to study the issue. The State Department based its early proposals at least partly on a study which Edwin Pauley, Special Ambassador on Reparations, completed in April of 1946. Pauley recommended that Japan should be forced to forfeit industrial material valued at 990,033,000 yen and primary war facilities valued at 1,475,887,000 yen. In March of 1948, the Department of the Army authorized a study by Overseas Consultants, under the supervision of Clifford Strike, and it recommended lowering the figure for industrial material to 172,269,000 yen. Undersecretary of the Army William H. Draper then led a mission to Japan in early 1948, and its report, released on April 26, 1948, suggested that reparations consist of industrial material valued at only 102,247,000 yen and war facilities valued at 500,000,000 yen; this represented one-tenth of Pauley's original figure for industrial material and one-third of his figure for war facilities. Under the U.S.-imposed interim reparations plan, Japan shipped 41,309 metric tons of material to China, the Dutch Indies, the Philippines, and Great Britain by June 30, 1948. Hugh Borton, one of the State Department's leading experts on Japan, published all of these figures in 1949. Hugh Borton, "Japan," in *The Encyclopedia Americana Annual, 1949.*

14. Cohen, *Japan's Economy in War and Reconstruction,* p. 495; Acheson to William J. Sebald, Feb. 24, 1949, *Foreign Relations,* 1949, vol. 7, pp. 666–67. The cited figures on U.S. assistance are from the Japanese government and include some types of aid not always calculated in U.S.

figures. Japanese Ministry of Foreign Affairs, *Economic Rehabilitation and Foreign Commerce of Japan* (Tokyo: Bureau of Public Information and Cultural Affairs, 1953), p. 13. Japan's population reached 79,990,000 in late 1948, and it would grow to 84 million by mid-1950. Borton, "Japan"; Chitoshi Yanaga, "Japan," in *The Encyclopedia Americana Annual, 1951*.

15. Gross to Saltzman, Dec. 27, 1948, *Foreign Relations*, 1948, vol. 6, pp. 1068–70; Jack B. Tate to Acheson, Jan. 27, 1949, ibid., 1949, vol. 7, pp. 631–33; Butterworth to Acheson, Jan. 27, 1949, ibid., pp. 633–34; Memorandum by Acheson, Feb. 1, 1949, ibid., pp. 640–42; Bishop, Memorandum of Conversation (with MacArthur and Sebald), Feb. 16, 1949, pp. 655–58; Bishop to Butterworth, Feb. 18, 1949, ibid., pp. 659–62; Acheson to Certain Diplomatic Offices, April 27, 1949, pp. 716–17; Robert A. Lovett to Kenneth Royall with enclosure of "Long Army Proposal on Japanese Reparations for Incorporation in NSC 13 / 1," Oct. 28, 1948, ibid., 1948, vol. 6, pp. 1035–40; Bishop to Butterworth, Dec. 17, 1948, ibid., pp. 1064–66.

16. Bishop believed that the United States, "with political courage and diplomatic skill," could persuade most of the member nations of the Far Eastern Commission to accept an end to reparations—particularly since earlier U.S. moves had already provided a "conditioning process." Bishop to Butterworth, Dec. 17, 1948, *Foreign Relations*, 1948, vol. 6, pp. 1064–66; Bishop to Butterworth, Jan. 6, 1949, ibid., 1949, vol. 7, pp. 608–9; Butterworth to Acheson, Jan. 27, 1949, ibid., pp. 633–39; Bishop interview with author; Bishop, Memorandum of Conversation (with MacArthur and Sebald), Feb. 16, 1949, ibid., pp. 655–58; Bishop to Butterworth, Feb. 18, 1949, ibid., pp. 659–62. Nitze summed up his views in a memorandum and sent it to Butterworth, Saltzman, Gross, George F. Kennan, and Willard L. Thorp. Paul Nitze to Willard L. Thorp (and editorial note 1), Jan. 7, 1949, *Foreign Relations*, 1949, vol. 7, pp. 609–14; Saltzman to Acheson, Jan. 27, 1949, ibid., pp. 639–40; "Memorandum Prepared for the Secretary of State" (and note 1), Feb. 15, 1949, ibid., pp. 650–55; Acheson to Certain Diplomatic Offices, Feb. 19, 1949, ibid., p. 664; NSC 13 / 3, May 6, 1949, ibid., pp. 730–36. On May 12, MacArthur received notification that the interim reparations directive had been rescinded but that transfers already processed under that directive could proceed. JCS to MacArthur, May 12, 1949, ibid., pp. 744–46; Robert A. Feary, *The Occupation of Japan* (New York: Macmillan, 1950), p. 145; Cohen, *Japan's Postwar Economy*, p. 165. Japan's final reparations settlements included one with Burma in 1954 for $200 million, one with the Philippines in 1956 for $800 million, and one with Indonesia in 1957 for $393 million, plus $400 million in loans. Borden, *Pacific Alliance*, p. 204.

17. Bishop interview with author; telephone interview with Max Bishop,

April 12, 1991, Ailey, Ga. In early 1947, Bishop also served as the U.S. representative on, and the chairman pro tempore of, the Allied Council for Japan. Bishop, "Meeting of General MacArthur with Members of the Allied Council for Japan," Feb. 7, 1947, *Foreign Relations, 1947*, vol. 6, pp. 177–79; Note explaining memorandum to Richard B. Russell from the Office of the President, Aug. 7, 1947, HSTL, Papers of Harry S. Truman, Official Files; Richmond B. Keech to Truman, Dec. 9, 1947, ibid.; Niles W. Bond, oral history interview with Richard D. McKinzie, Washington, D.C., Dec. 28, 1973, HSTL (hereafter cited as Bond, HSTL Oral History), pp. 52–54; Atcheson to Truman, Jan. 5, 1947, *Foreign Relations, 1947*, vol. 6, pp. 157–60; Raymond L. Harrison, The Results of the Survey on Food and Fertilizer of the Joint War-Agriculture-State Department Mission to Japan and Korea, Feb. 15, 1947, Nat. Arch., Record Group 59, Department of State, Office of Northeast Asian Affairs, 894.5018 / 2-2647, Memo 883 File; Harrison, The Results of the Survey on Food and Fertilizer of the Joint War-State-Agriculture Department Mission to Korea and Japan, Feb. 15, 1947, Nat. Arch., Record Group 331, Department of Defense, Modern Military Records, SCAP Public Health and Welfare Section, Administrative Division, Administrative Subject File, 1945–1951. Only one of the five known copies of the Harrison Mission's preliminary report has survived, and the mission's final report does not seem to have survived at all. Harrison's congressional testimony suggests that the final report may have been even more alarming than the preliminary report. U.S. Congress, House, Committee on Appropriations, *First Deficiency Appropriation Bill for 1947*, pp. 702, 725, 729, 746–47, 846, and 849. Harrison, a university-trained expert in agriculture and economics, was an army officer, but he was permanently attached to—and taking his orders from—the Department of Agriculture. He also reported directly to the State Department's Office of Economic Affairs. Before heading the Harrison Mission in early 1947, Harrison made a series of trips to the Far East in 1946. His reports to the State Department reaffirmed Nitze's handiwork in the U.S. Strategic Bombing Survey and probably strengthened Nitze's hand in urging Acheson to move quickly on Japan's economic crisis. In the first of these reports, dated March 18, 1946, Harrison said that although the headquarters of the Supreme Commander for Allied Powers (SCAP) was providing a ration "already 20% below [the] recognized subsistence level," this ration would soon be reduced to "the lowest possible level," and he added that SCAP might not be able to maintain even this "lowest" level. Harrison to William Clayton, March 18, 1946, Nat. Arch., Record Group 16, Office of the Secretary of Agriculture, General Correspondence, 1906–75, Box 1946, Foods File.

18. Acheson to Patterson, April 14, 1947, *Foreign Relations, 1947*, vol. 6, pp. 200–201; Nitze interview with author.

19. Howard B. Schonberger, "Zaibatsu Dissolution and the American Restoration of Japan," *Bulletin of Concerned Asian Scholars* 5 (Sept. 1973): 16; U.S. Department of State, *Occupation of Japan,* pp. 41–43; Acheson, *Present at the Creation,* p. 126.

20. Nitze interview with author; Nitze, *Hiroshima to Glasnost,* xxi–xxii and 11–12; Schaller, *American Occupation of Japan,* p. 85.

21. Nitze interview with author; NSC 13 / 2, Oct. 7, 1948, *Foreign Relations,* 1948, vol. 6, pp. 857–62; Schaller, *American Occupation of Japan,* p. 127; Statement of the United States, "Economic Stabilization in Japan," Dec. 10, 1948, *Foreign Relations,* 1948, vol. 6, pp. 1059–60 and 1060 n. 2. Butterworth, Director of the Office of Far Eastern Affairs, later commented, "The impulse to send Joe Dodge, and to correct the inflationary situation in Japan, came really from the State Department, strongly backed by the Federal Reserve, and later by the Treasury. The Pentagon was quite happy with the inflation. . . . Everybody was operating in this never-never land." Nitze told the present author that he agreed with Butterworth's recollection on this question. W. Walton Butterworth, oral history interview with Richard D. McKinzie and Theodore S. Wilson, Princeton, N.J., July 6, 1971, HSTL (hereafter cited as Butterworth, HSTL Oral History), pp. 60–61. Draper himself said upon taking office that he "knew nothing of Japan." Howard Schonberger, "U.S. Policy in Post-War Japan: Retreat from Liberalism," *Science & Society* 46 (Spring 1982): 41; Dick K. Nanto, "The Dodge Line: A Re-evaluation," in *The Occupation of Japan: Economic Policy and Reform,* ed. Lawrence H. Redford (Norfolk: MacArthur Memorial, 1980), pp. 46–47. For further details on the roles of Kennan, Draper, and James V. Forrestal, see Schaller, *American Occupation of Japan,* pp. 78–87, 111–17, and 123–29, and Theodore Cohen, *Remaking Japan* (New York: Free Press, 1987), pp. 366–428.

22. Acheson, Memorandum of Conversation with Royall and William H. Draper, Jan. 26, 1949, HSTL, Papers of Dean Acheson, Box 64, Jan. 1949 Conversations File; Butterworth, HSTL Oral History, pp. 60–62; Bishop interview with author.

23. NSC 13 / 2, Oct. 7, 1948, *Foreign Relations,* 1948, vol. 6, pp. 858–62; Bishop interview with author; Bishop, Memorandum of Conversation with MacArthur and Sebald, Feb. 16, 1949, *Foreign Relations,* 1949, vol. 7, pp. 655–58. There was a strong anti-MacArthur sentiment in some quarters of the State Department, which resulted in part from an old rivalry between Marshall and MacArthur. Telephone interview with Max Bishop, April 12, 1991, Ailey, Ga. Like MacArthur, Bishop felt that Acheson paid far more attention to Japan than Marshall ever did. Telephone interview with Max Bishop, June 20, 1992, Ailey, Ga.

24. Bishop interview with author; Bishop, Memorandum of Conversation

with MacArthur and Sebald, Feb. 16, 1949, *Foreign Relations,* 1949, vol.
7, pp. 655–58; Bishop to Butterworth, Feb. 18, 1949, ibid., pp. 659–62;
Butterworth, HSTL Oral History, pp. 60–62; Acheson, Memorandum of
Conversation with Royall and Draper, Jan. 26, 1949, HSTL, Papers of Dean
Acheson, Box 64, Jan. 1949 Conversations File. American business interests, including the "Japan lobby," complained bitterly that U.S. policies
were damaging American as well as Japanese business interests, but they
blamed this more on Truman than on MacArthur. Dennis McEvoy, president
of the American Chamber of Commerce in Japan, even laid all of the blame
on the "Washington bosses." "U.S. Business Accuses Occupation in Japan,"
New York Times, 17 March 1949, p. L13. Max Bishop, a University of
Chicago trained expert on Japan, ignored the Japan lobby and focused instead
on the psychological impact of U.S. policies on the Japanese people. The
Japan lobby benefited from some policy revisions but played no significant
role in policy formulation. Telephone interview with Max Bishop, April 12,
1991, Ailey, Ga.

25. Bishop interview with author; Butterworth to Acheson, April 15, 1949,
Foreign Relations, 1949, vol. 7, pp. 708–9; NSC 13 / 3, May 6, 1949,
ibid., pp. 730–36; Cloyce K. Huston to Acheson, May 10, 1949, ibid., pp.
740–43; T. A. Bisson, "Japan," in *The Encyclopedia Americana Annual,
1950.* The Japanese government inherited and, to a limited extent, continued
MacArthur's *zaibatsu* dissolution program until 1951, when Japan loosened
its antimonopoly laws and allowed the *zaibatsu* to evolve into the present-
day *keiretsu.* Uchino, *Japan's Postwar Economy,* p. 42.

26. Nitze interview with author; Jerome Cohen, *Japan's Postwar Economy,* pp. 15 and 110; Theodore Cohen, *Remaking Japan,* pp. 429–42; Nanto,
"Dodge Line," pp. 44–83. The Central Intelligence Agency (CIA) reported
that the Democratic Liberal Party, headed by the conservative Prime Minister Shigeru Yoshida, had a sufficient majority in the Japanese Diet to "permit 'steam roller' passage" of its legislation, and the CIA expected this to
improve Japan's chances for recovery. The Japanese Communist Party received
10 percent of the votes in a January 1949 election, but the CIA thought that
this figure could be cut in half by an improvement in economic conditions.
CIA, Sept. 20, 1949, HSTL, Records of NSC, Box 2, NSC / CIA Intelligence Memorandums Dec. 1948–Dec. 1949 File. With Japan's limited
recovery, U.S. aid dropped to $361,000,000 in 1950 and stayed close to that
level in 1951. Japanese Ministry of Foreign Affairs, *Economic Rehabilitation and Foreign Commerce of Japan,* p. 13. For more-detailed evaluations
of Dodge's policies, see Borden, *Pacific Alliance,* pp. 92–102. Japan's iron
and steel production had fully recovered by late 1949. Some figures cited
are from a mid-1950 State Department "white paper" on the Japanese economy. Yanaga, "Japan."

27. Bishop interview with author; Rusk interview with author; Ruth E. Bacon to John Carter Vincent, "Working Group on Japan Treaty, Notes of Meeting of Friday, October 25, 1946," *Foreign Relations,* 1946, vol. 8, pp. 348–49; Memorandum of conversation by John M. Allison, March 24, 1947, ibid., 1947, vol. 6, p. 457; Allison, Memorandum of Conversation (with Alfred Sterling), March 20, 1947, ibid., pp. 449–50; Vincent, "Preparatory Conference on a Japanese Peace Treaty," May 12, 1947, ibid., p. 458; Hugh Borton to John H. Hilldring, May 20, 1947, ibid., pp. 459–60; Spruille Braden to Acheson, June 17, 1947, ibid., pp. 463–64; Borton, Memorandum of Conversation (large meeting), July 8, 1947, ibid., pp. 467–69.

28. Lovett to Atcheson, Aug. 13, 1947, *Foreign Relations,* 1947, vol. 6, pp. 489–91; Embassy of the Soviet Union to the Department of State, Aug. 29, 1947, ibid., pp. 509–11; Borton, Memorandum of Conversation (large meeting), July 1, 1947, ibid., pp. 467–69; Bishop interview with author; telephone interview with Max Bishop, April 12, 1991, Ailey, Ga.; Bishop to James K. Penfield, Aug. 14, 1947, ibid., pp. 492–94; Borton to Charles E. Bohlen, Aug. 6, 1947, ibid., pp. 478–79; John P. Davies to George F. Kennan, Aug. 11, 1947, ibid., pp. 485–86; Kennan, "PPS 10," Oct. 14, 1947, ibid., pp. 537–43; Marshall, Memorandum of Conversation with H. V. Evatt, John F. Dulles, and Bohlen, Oct. 28, 1947, ibid., pp. 551–54; Butterworth, Memorandum, Nov. 18, 1947, ibid., pp. 569–72; NSC 13 / 2, Oct. 7, 1948, ibid., pp. 858–62. PPS 28 / 2 made, according to its cover statement, "comparatively minor" revisions to PPS 10, but it emphasized even more strongly Kennan's view that negotiations to achieve a peace treaty should be postponed. PPS, PPS 28 / 2, May 26, 1948, U.S. Department of State, *State Department Policy Planning Staff Papers,* 2:175–243.

29. Bishop interview with author; Rusk interview with author; J. W. Dower, *Empire and Aftermath* (Cambridge: Council on East Asian Studies, 1979), pp. 318–29; Bishop, Memorandum of Conversation with MacArthur and Sebald, Feb. 16, 1949, *Foreign Relations,* 1949, vol. 7, pp. 655–58; Bishop to Butterworth, Feb. 18, 1949, ibid., pp. 659–62. In the spring of 1949, the Soviet Union suggested that a Japanese peace treaty should be negotiated by the Council of Foreign Ministers—a forum that would maximize Soviet influence—but Acheson blocked this move. U.S. Congress, Senate, Committee on Foreign Relations, *Reviews of the World Situation, 1949–1950: Hearings Held in Executive Session before the Committee on Foreign Relations,* 81st Cong., 1st and 2d sess., 1974, p. 102.

30. NSC 13 / 2, Oct. 7, 1948, *Foreign Relations,* 1948, vol. 6, p. 858; NSC 13 / 3, May 6, 1949, ibid., 1949, vol. 7, p. 730; John B. Howard, Memorandum of Conversation (large meeting), "Japanese Peace Treaty," Dec. 15, 1949, HSTL, Papers of Dean Acheson, Box 64, Dec. 1949 Con-

versations File; JCS to Louis A. Johnson, Dec. 22, 1949, *Foreign Relations,* 1949, vol. 7, pp. 922–23; JCS, "Strategic Evaluation of United States Security Needs in Japan," June 9, 1949, ibid., pp. 774–77. Sebald also sounded out MacArthur on the possibility that Dodge might become the General's civilian deputy, but MacArthur was not receptive. Sebald to Butterworth, July 26, 1949, *Foreign Relations,* 1949, vol. 7, pp. 808–12; Sebald to Acheson, Aug. 20, 1949, ibid., pp. 830–40; Marshall Green, Memorandum of Conversation (large meeting), Sept. 9, 1949, ibid., pp. 853–56; Charles W. Yost, "Discussion of Far Eastern Affairs in Preparation for Conversations with Mr. Bevin," Sept. 13, 1949, Nat. Arch., Record Group 59, Department of State, Office of Chinese Affairs, Box 14, U.S. Policy toward China and the Far East File; Acheson, Memorandum of Conversation (large meeting), Sept. 13, 1949, *Foreign Relations,* 1949, vol. 7, pp. 858–59; Butterworth to Acheson, Nov. 30, 1949, ibid., pp. 907–8; Butterworth, Memorandum of Conversation with Sir Oliver Franks, Dec. 24, 1949, HSTL, Papers of Dean Acheson, Box 64, Dec. 1949 Conversations File. On Sept. 30, Kennan's Policy Planning Staff issued a long report which rejected many of the Pentagon's conclusions. PPS, "Department of State Comments on Current Strategic Evaluation of U.S. Security Needs in Japan (NSC 49)," Sept. 30, 1949, U.S. Department of State, *State Department Policy Planning Staff Papers,* 3:183–86. On Oct. 12, 1949, Acheson told the Senate Committee on Foreign Relations, "We believe very strongly in the State Department that it is desirable to have a treaty with Japan as soon as possible, and in that view we coincide entirely with the views of General MacArthur." U.S. Congress, Senate, Committee on Foreign Relations, *Reviews of the World Situation,* p. 102. Lucius Battle, Acheson's personal assistant, later remembered that Acheson initially focused on European questions—like the Berlin airlift—and that the Japanese issues "popped up with enormous force later." The documentary evidence, however, shows that Acheson immediately became involved in most aspects of U.S. policy on Japan, putting off only the treaty issue until it "popped up with enormous force." Battle interview with author.

31. Bishop interview with author; Schaller, *American Occupation of Japan,* p. 170; Charlton Ogburn, "Decisions Reached by Consensus at the Meetings with the Secretary and the Consultants on the Far East," Nov. 2, 1949, Nat. Arch., Record Group 59, Department of State, Office of Chinese Affairs, Box 14, U.S. Policy toward China and the Far East File. In a meeting on Dec. 15, 1949, Undersecretary of the Army Tracy S. Voorhees warned Acheson and his advisers to desist immediately from circumventing the Pentagon's channels and discussing the treaty issue directly with MacArthur. Howard, Memorandum of Conversation (large meeting), HSTL, Papers of

Dean Acheson, Box 64, Dec. 1949 Conversations File. Voorhees probably found out about the discussions with MacArthur because State Department messages to and from Japan went through military channels. Early in 1950, Acheson established direct coded communications with his personnel in Japan, without securing permission from the Pentagon or MacArthur. Bond, HSTL Oral History, pp. 52–54; Johnson to Acheson, Dec. 23, 1949, *Foreign Relations,* 1949, vol. 7, p. 922; JCS to Johnson, Dec. 22, 1949, ibid., pp. 922–26; Maxwell M. Hamilton, Memorandum of Conversation (large meeting), Dec. 24, 1949, ibid., pp. 924–26.

32. Acheson to Oliver Franks, Dec. 24, 1949, *Foreign Relations,* 1949, vol. 7, pp. 927–29; NSC 48, Dec. 23, 1949, U.S. Department of Defense, *United States–Vietnam Relations, 1945–1967* (Washington, D.C.: GPO, 1971), 8:239–42; NSC 48 / 2, Dec. 30, 1949, *Foreign Relations,* 1949, vol. 7, pp. 1215–20; Acheson, Memorandum of Conversation with Truman, Feb. 20, 1950, HSTL, Papers of Dean Acheson, Box 64B, Feb. 1950 Conversations File.

33. When John Foster Dulles later became Secretary of State under President Dwight D. Eisenhower, he rewarded Carl W. McCardle with the post of Assistant Secretary for Public Affairs. Battle interview with author. Battle was unclear about where he and Acheson were when they received Webb's telegram, but Acheson's appointment book indicates that his only trip in March was to San Francisco on the fourteenth to the sixteenth. Acheson Appointment Book, HSTL, Papers of Dean Acheson, Box 45, Appointment File.

34. The historian Ronald Prussen, on the basis of available evidence, laid the foundations for the erroneous but often repeated notion that Arthur Vandenberg's letter effected the Dulles appointment. Acheson appointed John Sherman Cooper, another Republican, to be an adviser well before the Dulles appointment. Ronald W. Prussen, *John Foster Dulles* (New York: Free Press, 1982), pp. 434–37; Arthur Vandenberg to Acheson, March 31, 1950, HSTL, Acheson Papers, Box 65, March 1950 Conversations File; Acheson, Memorandum of Conversation with Truman, April 4, 1950, HSTL, Papers of Dean Acheson, Box 65, April 1950 Conversations File; Acheson to Truman, April 5, 1950, ibid. Truman later told Acheson that the people in the State Department did not "understand politics," but that if they did, they would also understand why Dulles's earlier attacks could be overlooked. Rusk interview with author. John Allison had replaced Bishop as Director of Northeast Asian Affairs. John M. Allison, *Ambassador from the Prairie; or, Allison Wonderland* (Boston: Houghton Mifflin, 1973), pp. 122–23; Acheson, Memorandum of Conversation with Dulles, April 5, 1950, HSTL, Papers of Dean Acheson, Box 65, April 1950 Conversations File. Acheson initially

220   NOTES

assigned Dulles the title of Consultant, but then, at the insistence of Dulles
himself, Acheson changed this to "Top Consultant." Acheson, Memorandum of Conversation with Dulles, April 6, 1950, ibid.

35. On April 3, 1950, Philip C. Jessup, Ambassador-at-Large, returned
from a fact-finding trip and reported, regarding the treaty question, "MacArthur
supports the [State] Department's line." Ogburn, Memorandum of Conversation (large meeting), April 3, 1950, *Foreign Relations,* 1950, vol. 6, pp.
68–73; Acheson, *Present at the Creation,* pp. 539–40; Howard, Memorandum of Conversation (large meeting), April 24, 1950, HSTL, Papers of
Dean Acheson, Box 65, April 1950 Conversations File.

36. Acheson, *Present at the Creation,* pp. 540–42; Rusk interview with
author. In mid-1950, Shigeru Yoshida, the Japanese Prime Minister, told
Dulles that he would oppose any rearmament for Japan, but the Korean War
helped Dulles to change Yoshida's mind. Yamamoto Mitksuru, "The Cold
War and U.S.-Japan Economic Cooperation," in *The Origins of the Cold
War In Asia,* ed. Yonosuke Nagai and Akira Iriye (New York: Columbia
Univ. Press, 1977), p. 409. Both Acheson and MacArthur revised their positions to support a modest Japanese rearmament, and by November of 1950
MacArthur had persuaded the Japanese government to build an internal security
force of 75,000 men. This compromise satisfied the Pentagon. U.S. Congress, Senate, Committee on Foreign Relations, *Reviews of the World Situation,* p. 392. Dulles to Acheson, July 27, 1950, *Foreign Relations,* 1950,
vol. 6, pp. 1259–62; Unsigned Memorandum Prepared in the Department
of State, "Japanese Peace Treaty," Aug. 14, 1950, ibid., pp. 1273–75; Philip
C. Jessup to Acheson with Enclosed Memorandum from Omar N. Bradley
to Johnson, Aug. 22, 1950, ibid., pp. 1278–82; The final peace treaty did
include a reparations clause, Article 14, but it was very weak. John F. Melby,
oral history interview with Robert Accinelli, Ontario, Can., Nov. 7, 14, 21,
and 28, 1986, HSTL, pp. 225–26; George F. Kennan, "Japanese Security
and American Policy," *Foreign Affairs* 43 (Oct. 1964): 14–15.

37. Battle interview with author.

38. Rusk interview with author; Acheson, *Present at the Creation,* pp.
542–44; Chae-Jin Lee and Hideo Sato, *U.S. Policy toward Japan and Korea*
(New York: Praeger, 1982), p. 18. To settle the question of Japanese relations with the two governments claiming to represent China, Prime Minister
Shigeru Yoshida delivered a letter to the United States on December 24,
1951, stating that Japan would normalize relations with the Nationalist government and abstain from any bilateral agreements with the People's Republic of China. Acheson, *Present at the Creation,* pp. 603–5. In addition to
helping the United States develop a peace treaty and secure international
approval for it, Britain signed an agreement with Japan in 1949 which was

expected to significantly increase trade between the two island nations. The British anticipated that 80 percent of their purchases under this agreement would come from Japan's depressed cotton industry. Roger Buckley, *Occupation Diplomacy* (New York: Cambridge Univ. Press, 1982), p. 170. The mutual security treaty the United States signed with Japan in 1951 gave way to a revised security treaty on Feb. 28, 1952, and this in turn gave way to another treaty in 1960. Kennan, "Japanese Security and American Policy," p. 15; Borden, *Pacific Alliance*, pp. 203–4.

39. Cohen, *Japan's Economy in War and Reconstruction*, p. 494; Borden, *Pacific Alliance*, p. 68; Saburo Okita, *Rehabilitation of Japan's Economy and Asia* (Tokyo: Public Information and Cultural Affairs Bureau, 1956), pp. 10–11.

CHAPTER THREE: Acheson and
the American Commitment in Korea

1. Dean Rusk to author, March 17, 1987. Rusk, then an army colonel, and Colonel Charles Bonesteel chose the thirty-eighth parallel in a brief meeting, using only an improvised map and operating without any detailed knowledge of the country. Interview with Dean Rusk, Athens, Ga., April 11, 1988 (hereafter cited as Rusk interview with author); U.S. Department of State, *The Record on Korean Unification: 1943–1960* (Washington, D.C.: GPO, 1960), pp. 3–5; U.S. Congress, House, Committee on International Relations, *United States Policy in the Far East: Selected Executive Sessions of the Committee on International Relations: Hearings on the Far East Portion of the Mutual Defense Assistance Act of 1950*, 8 vols., 81st Cong., 1st and 2d sess., 1976, 8:417. Over 750,000 Japanese had lived in Korea and administered every aspect of its government and economy when it was part of the Japanese Empire. U.S. Congress, Senate, Committee on Foreign Relations, *Economic Assistance to China and Korea, 1949–1950: Hearings Held in Executive Session before the Committee on Foreign Relations on S. 1063, S. 2319, and S. 2845*, 81st Cong., 1st and 2d sess., 1974, p. 126. General John Hodges, who was in charge of the U.S. occupation of Korea, did not possess appropriate skills for this assignment, but when the State Department requested that he be replaced, Army Chief of Staff Dwight D. Eisenhower blocked the request. Dwight D. Eisenhower to George C. Marshall, Dec. 3, 1947, *Foreign Relations*, 1947, vol. . 6, pp. 869–70; Charles Saltzman to Marshall, Dec. 4, 1947, ibid., p. 869; Marshall to Eisenhower, Dec. 4, 1947, ibid., p. 868. For the decision-making process on Korea up to 1946, see Carl Berger, *The Korea Knot* (Philadelphia: Univ. of Pennsyl-

vania Press, 1957), pp. 1–61. For additional details on the origins of the trusteeship concept, see Bruce Cumings, *The Origins of the Korean War,* vol. 1 (Princeton: Princeton Univ. Press, 1981), pp. 104–5, 109, 120, and 123–24. For an interpretation which emphasizes the roles of ideology and American politics in the development of U.S. policy toward Korea, see William Stueck, Jr., *The Road to Confrontation* (Chapel Hill: Univ. of North Carolina, 1981). Departing slightly from Stueck's theme, the historian James Matray developed the thesis that U.S. policy on Korea emanated from "ideological and diplomatic reasons rather than military or strategic factors." See James I. Matray, *The Reluctant Crusade* (Honolulu: Univ. of Hawaii Press, 1985), p. 115.

2. John Carter Vincent to Marshall, Jan. 27, 1947, *Foreign Relations, 1947,* vol. 6, p. 601; James Forrestal, *The Forrestal Diaries,* ed. Walter Millis (New York: Viking, 1951), pp. 241–42; Marshall to Douglas MacArthur, Feb. 7, 1947, *Foreign Relations,* 1947, vol. 6, pp. 605–6.

3. Joseph Marion Jones, *The Fifteen Weeks* (New York: Harcourt, Brace & World, 1955), pp. 111–14; Dean Acheson, "U.S. Objectives in Policy toward Korea," *Department of State Bulletin* 15 (Sept. 8, 1946): 462; Raymond L. Harrison, The Results of the Survey on Food and Fertilizer of the Joint War-Agriculture-State Department Mission to Japan and Korea, Feb. 15, 1947, Nat. Arch. Record Group 59, Department of State, Office of Northeast Asian Affairs, Lot 894.5018/2-2647, Memorandum 883 File; Harrison, The Results of the Survey on Food and Fertilizer of the Joint War-State-Agriculture Department Mission to Korea and Japan, Feb. 15, 1947, Nat. Arch., Modern Military Records, Record Group 331, Supreme Commander Allied Powers, Public Health and Welfare Section, Administrative Division, Administrative Subject 1945–51 File; Special Inter-Departmental Committee on Korea to Marshall, Feb. 25, 1947, *Foreign Relations,* 1947, vol. 6, pp. 608–16. In a memorandum to the Secretary of War, Acheson cited the Harrison Report as evidence of "increasing difficulties with respect to the internal economic and financial structure of Japan." Acheson to Robert B. Patterson, April 14, 1947, ibid., pp. 200–201. Acheson also set up the Advisory Committee on Development of Japanese and Korean Trade, which included representatives from the Departments of State, Commerce, Agriculture, and Treasury. Chaired by R. W. Whitman, the State Department member, this committee began work on May 14, 1947, and thereafter played a significant role in facilitating the restoration of Korean and Japanese trade. Meetings of the Committee on Development of Japanese and Korean Trade, Nat. Arch., Record Group 353, Department of State, Box 9, Lot 122, 2 A.16—Occupied Areas Affairs-Advisory Committee on Development of Japanese and Korean Trade File, obtained through the Freedom of Infor-

mation Act. Even before the Harrison Mission, U.S. officials understood the situation in Japan. The U.S. Strategic Bombing Survey reported in July of 1946, "The [Japanese] people will have to get along on an absolute minimum of rice and salt required for subsistence, considering . . . the appearance of starvation conditions in the isolated sections of the nation. It is apparent that the food situation will become further aggravated this year." This survey cited reduced food imports from Korea (rice) and Manchuria (soybeans) as a major factor. Paul Nitze, the Vice-Chairman of the Strategic Bombing Survey Committee, wrote most of the report's economic analysis in 1946 and then served as one of Acheson's key advisers in 1947. U.S. Department of War, "United States Strategic Bombing Survey, Japan's Struggle to End the War," July 1, 1946, HSTL, Papers of George M. Elsey, Box 71, Japanese Surrender Aug. 1945 File, pp. vii–viii; interview with Paul H. Nitze, Washington, D.C., July 25, 1989 (hereafter cited as Nitze interview with author).

4. Special Interdepartmental Committee on Korea to Marshall, Feb. 25, 1947, *Foreign Relations,* 1947, vol. 6, pp. 608–16. For the full text, see Special Interdepartmental Committee on Korea, "Memorandum for the Secretary of State and the Secretary of War, Feb. 25, 1947, Nat. Arch., Microfilm LM 80. Reel 5, 895.01/2-2547 File; Michael Schaller, *The American Occupation of Japan* (New York: Oxford Univ. Press, 1985), p. 91. John Carter Vincent's $50 million proposal correlated to the U.S. Army's request for a small aid supplement to repair Korea's railroads and facilitate the U.S. occupation, which ran counter to Acheson's approach. When Vincent resigned several months later, Acheson persuaded Marshall to make W. Walton Butterworth the new Director of Far Eastern Affairs. Butterworth, whose principal qualifications were his administrative skills and his loyalty to Acheson, protested first to Acheson and then to Marshall that the job required someone with more expertise on the Far East. Marshall appointed him anyway. W. Walton Butterworth, oral history interview with Richard D. McKinzie and Theodore A. Wilson, Princeton, N.J., July 6, 1971, HSTL, pp. 52–54.

5. David S. McLellan, *Dean Acheson* (New York: Dodd, Mead, 1976), pp. 110–20; Acheson, "U.S. Objectives in Policy toward Korea," 462; Acheson, "U.S. Policy in Korea," 670; Special Interdepartmental Committee on Korea to Marshall, Feb. 25, 1947, *Foreign Relations,* 1947, vol. 6, pp. 608–16. Marshall gave Acheson wide authority to develop his economic aid plans not only because he was preoccupied with the Moscow conference but also because he was still learning his job. To Robert A. Lovett, Acheson's replacement, Marshall confided, "Frankly, I don't understand half of this business going on." Robert A. Lovett, Interview with Richard D. McKinzie and Theodore A. Wilson, New York, July 7, 1971, HSTL, p. 10.

6. Robert J. Donovan, *Conflict and Crisis* (New York: Norton, 1977), pp. 279–83; Harry S. Truman, "Recommendations on Greece and Turkey," *Department of State Bulletin* 16 (March 23, 1947): 536; U.S. Congress, Senate, Committee on Foreign Relations, *Legislative Origins of the Truman Doctrine: Hearings before the Committee on Foreign Relations in Executive Session on S. 938,* 80th Cong., 1st sess., 1973, pp. 21–22. The terms of the Supreme Allied Agreement signed at the end of World War II fixed low levels of production for Japan's postwar industry in order to prevent future rearmament. These terms considerably exacerbated Japan's economic difficulties, but the Soviet Union refused to alter them. Paul Nitze cites this refusal as "a contributing factor" in Acheson's decision to confront the Soviets and develop the Truman Doctrine. Paul Nitze, *From Hiroshima to Glasnost* (New York: Grove Weidenfeld, 1989), pp. 49–50. On Nitze's advice, Acheson ultimately decided to simply ignore the Supreme Allied Agreement's limitations on Japanese industrial production and move ahead with rebuilding Japanese industry. Nitze interview with author.

7. Forrestal, *Forrestal Diaries,* p. 265; Acheson to Patterson, March 28, 1947, *Foreign Relations,* 1947, vol. 6, pp. 621–23; Patterson to Acheson, April 4, 1947, ibid., pp. 625–28; Marshall to Acheson, April 2, 1947, ibid., pp. 623–25; Acheson to Marshall, April 5, 1947, ibid., pp. 628–30.

8. Nitze interview with author; Paul Nitze, oral history interview with Richard D. McKinzie, Arlington, Va., June 11 and 17 and Aug. 4, 5, and 6, 1975, HSTL, pp. 146–50. SWNCC 360, written by an ad hoc subcommittee of the State-War-Navy Coordinating Committee, listed Korea as fourth among nations urgently in need of U.S. aid—behind Greece, Turkey, and Iran. SWNCC 360, April 21, 1947, *Foreign Relations,* 1947, vol. 1, pp. 725–34. SWNCC 360 also called for an American-sponsored program to increase Japanese trade in the Far East. Schaller, *American Occupation of Japan,* p. 91. Another list in SWNCC 360/1—which combined "urgency of need" with "importance to U.S. security"—placed Korea far below the priority it held in SWNCC 360. Nevertheless, Acheson continued to press forward with his plans for Korea. SWNCC 360/1, May 12, 1947, *Foreign Relations,* 1949, vol. 1, pp. 734–50. Acheson's aid plans for Greece and Turkey faced resistance similar to that which met his aid plans for Korea. Walter LaFeber, "American Policy-Makers, Public Opinion, and the Outbreak of the Cold War, 1945–1950," in *The Origins of the Cold War in Asia,* ed. Yonosuke Nagai and Akira Iriye (New York: Columbia Univ. Press, 1977), pp. 53–54; Nitze, *Hiroshima to Glasnost,* p. 52; Dean Acheson, "The Requirements of Reconstruction," *Department of State Bulletin* 16 (May 18, 1947): 991–92; interview with Lucius D. Battle, Washington, D.C., May 30, 1990 (hereafter cited as Battle interview with author). Paul Hoffman likewise stated

that Acheson was a central figure in the development of the Marshall Plan. Paul G. Hoffman, oral history interview with Philip C. Brooks, New York, N.Y., Oct. 25, 1964, HSTL, pp. 25–26. David Bruce, who much later served as Acheson's Undersecretary, attributed the origins of the Marshall Plan to Truman, Marshall, Acheson, and William Clayton. David K. E. Bruce, oral history interview with Jerry N. Hess, Washington, D.C., March 1, 1972, HSTL (hereafter cited as Bruce, HSTL Oral History), p. 8.

    9. Waldo Heinrichs, *Threshold of War* (New York: Oxford Univ. Press, 1988), pp. 70, 141, 177–79, and 246–47; Jonathan G. Utley, *Going to War with Japan, 1937–1941* (Knoxville: Univ. of Tennessee Press, 1985), pp. 152–57, 172, and 180. According to Dean Rusk, Acheson understood the economic relationships of Northeast Asia (from his work in 1941), but he knew very little about the rest of the Far East. This led Acheson to focus primarily on Japan's old empire (especially Korea and Formosa) in his efforts to restore Japan's postwar trade. Rusk interview with author; U.S. Congress, House, Subcommittee of the Committee on Appropriations, *First Deficiency Appropriations Bill for 1947: Hearings before the Subcommittee of the Committee on Appropriations on H.R. 2849*, 80th Cong., 1st sess., 1947, pp. 702, 725, 729, 746–47, 846, and 849. Not only was 900 calories a day a starvation level, but Acheson himself believed that even 2,000 calories a day would soon promote epidemic levels of "tuberculosis and diseases of that sort." U.S. Congress, House, Committee on Foreign Affairs, *United States Foreign Policy for a Post-War Recovery Program: Hearings before the Committee on Foreign Affairs on H.R. 4840 and H.R. 4570*, 80th Cong., 1st and 2d sess., 1948, p. 717. U.S. planners estimated that during 1946 they would have to provide 1,200,000 tons of grain to maintain a Japanese diet of 900 calories per day. Actual shipments, however, came to just 700,000 tons, including 528,000 tons of wheat. Somehow, the Japanese managed to avoid mass starvation, but their food supply situation remained critical until 1949. Tatsuro Uchino, *Japan's Postwar Economy* (Tokyo: Kodansha International, 1983), pp. 42 and 254. It is clear that Acheson read the Harrison Mission's report, because he used it as the basis for a subsequent memorandum. Acheson to Patterson, April 14, 1947, *Foreign Relations, 1947*, vol. 6, pp. 200–201.

    10. U.S. House, Subcommittee of the Committee on Appropriations, *First Deficiency Appropriations Bill for 1947*, pp. 747 and 849. The rice production figures cited are converted from metric tons, and the figures for 1938 are cited because those for 1937 and 1939–45 were affected by the conversion of fertilizer production to munitions production. Jerome B. Cohen, *Japan's Economy in War and Reconstruction* (Minneapolis: Univ. of Minnesota Press, 1949), p. 369; U.S. Department of Agriculture, *Agricultural Statistics, 1948*

(Washington, D.C.: GPO, 1949), pp. 23, 38, and 32 n. 6; Saltzman to
Marshall through Lovett, Sept. 7, 1948, *Foreign Relations*, 1948, vol. 6,
pp. 1292–97.

11. U.S. House, Subcommittee of the Committee on Appropriations, *First
Deficiency Appropriations Bill for 1947*, pp. 703, 770–71, 844, and 855;
Cohen, *Japan's Economy in War and Reconstruction*, p. 494; U.S. Congress, House, Committee on Foreign Affairs, *Korean Aid: Hearings before
the Committee on Foreign Affairs on H.R. 5330*, 80th Cong., 1st sess.,
1949, pp. 15–16; U.S. Congress, House, Committee on International Relations, *United States Policy in the Far East*, pp. 357 and 922.

12. U.S. Congress, Senate, Committee on Foreign Relations, *Executive
Sessions of the Committee on Foreign Relations, 1947–1948*, 2 vols., 80th
Cong., 1st and 2d sess., 1976, 1:53–55; Saltzman to Marshall, Sept. 7,
1948, *Foreign Relations*, 1948, vol. 6, pp. 1292–97.

13. Nitze interview with author. The political seduction of Senator Arthur
Vandenberg included some rather saccharine flattery; in one letter to the
Senator, Acheson wrote, "Your leadership in the battle for the Recovery
Program has been and is superb. Each move and each speech you make
seems to me the perfect one. I marvel at how you maintain your good humor,
your strength, and your zest for the fray." Acheson to Arthur H. Vandenberg, March 3, 1948, in David S. McLellan and David C. Acheson, eds.,
Among Friends (New York: Dodd, Mead, 1980), p. 67; Acheson to John
Hilldring, June 27, 1947, Nat. Arch., Record Group 59, Department of
State, Office of Northeast Asian Affairs, Lot 740.00119, control (Korea)/6-
2747 File; Saltzman to Marshall, Sept. 7, 1948, *Foreign Relations*, 1948,
vol. 6, pp. 1292–97, Acheson to "Jim" [Webb], Aug. 1950, HSTL, Papers
of Dean Acheson, Box 65, Conversations File. Truman was of little help to
Acheson on this matter. When asked about the Korean aid package at four
news conferences, Truman either denied knowledge of the details or declined
comment. *Public Papers of the Presidents of the United States: Harry S.
Truman* (Washington, D.C.: GPO, 1963), pp. 191, 240, 247, and 282. Senator Arthur Vandenberg's response clearly did not indicate opposition to the
Korean aid plan; it was simply an assessment of the mood of the Congress.
Vandenberg also, for example, insisted that Acheson should not introduce
the Marshall Plan during that session, although he later supported it. McLellan,
Dean Acheson, p. 132. Another interdepartmental committee, dominated by
the State Department, put together a public relations campaign to promote
Acheson's Korean aid package. The committee even wrote a presidential
speech to sell the public on the Korean aid bill; it reiterated Acheson's earlier
rhetoric, but Truman never delivered it. H. W. Moseley, W. A. Schulgen,
and V. L. Lowrance, "Public Information Program on the Korean Grant-

Aid Program," approved by the State-War-Navy Coordinating Committee on June 4, 1947, Nat. Arch., Microfilm, LM 80, Reel 4, 895.01/3-346 File.

14. John M. Allison to Marshall and n. 41, undated, *Foreign Relations, 1947*, vol. 6, pp. 713–14; Allison to Marshall, July 29, 1947, ibid., pp. 734–35. The three members of the ad hoc committee on Korea were John Allison (State Department), Captain H. R. Hummer (Navy), and Colonel Trevor Nevitt Dupuy. Dupuy later remembered, "The Army position (with which—as I recall—State generally agreed) was that we should reduce our commitment in Korea as soon as possible." Trevor Nevitt Dupuy to author, Aug. 14, 1989; SWNCC 176/30, *Foreign Relations, 1947*, vol. 6, pp. 738–41.

15. U.S. Department of Defense, JCS, JCS 1483/44, Nat. Arch., Modern Military Records Division, Record Group 218, JCS 1483/44, CCS 383.21 Korea (3-19-45), sec. 13, Enclosure B, p. 372. John Muccio, the Ambassador to Korea, later recalled that two men led the campaign to get the United States out of Korea in 1947—General Douglas MacArthur, Commander in Chief in the Far East, and General Dwight Eisenhower, Army Chief of Staff and unofficial chairman of the JCS. (Omar Bradley became the first official chairman in early 1948.) John J. Muccio, oral history interview with Richard D. McKinzie, Washington, D.C., Feb. 10 and 18, 1971, HSTL, p. 8. Paul Nitze, Director of the State Department PPS, later remembered, "General Eisenhower was the person who signed the JCS opinions which took an adamant opinion on the necessity for withdrawing our forces from Korea." Nitze, HSTL Oral History, p. 261; Clay Blair, *The Forgotten War* (New York: Times Books, 1987), pp. 40–41; Lovett to Embassy in the Soviet Union, Aug. 26, 1947, *Foreign Relations, 1947*, vol. 6, pp. 771–74; Jacobs to Marshall, Sept. 8, 1947, ibid., pp. 783; U.S. Congress, House, Committee on Foreign Affairs, *Background Information on Korea, Report of the Committee on Foreign Relations Pursuant to H.R. 206*, 81st Cong., 2d sess., 1950, p. 10; State-Army-Navy-Air Force Coordinating Committee to the JCS, Sept. 12, 1947, *Foreign Relations, 1947*, vol. 6, p. 789; James F. Schnabel and Robert J. Watson, *The History of the Joint Chiefs of Staff*, 5 vols. (Wilmington, Del.: Michael Glazier, 1979), 3:13–14; U.S. Department of Defense, JCS, JCS 1483/44, Nat. Arch., Modern Military Records Division, Record Group 218, JCS 1483/44, CCS 383.21 Korea (3-19-45), sec. 13, Appendix A, p. 368; Forrestal to Marshall, Sept. 26, 1947, *Foreign Relations, 1947*, vol. 6, pp. 817–18; Schaller, *American Occupation of Japan*, p. 56; Jacobs to Marshall, Sept. 30, 1947, *Foreign Relations, 1947*, vol. 6, p. 819.

16. Donovan, *Conflict and Crisis*, pp. 282 and 288; George Kennan to W. Walton Butterworth, Sept. 24, 1947, *Foreign Relations, 1947*, vol. 6,

p. 814; Nitze interview with author. The differences of opinion between Acheson and Kennan on Asian policy might not have been apparent in early 1947, since, according to Kennan, they never discussed matters of Asian policy "in substance." Kennan to author, June 13, 1990.

17. Butterworth to Lovett, Oct. 1, 1947, *Foreign Relations,* 1947, vol. 6, pp. 820–21; Report by the Policy Planning Staff, ibid., vol. 1, p. 776.

18. State-Army-Navy-Air Force Coordinating Committee (SANACC), SANACC 176/35, Jan. 14, 1948, Nat. Arch., Modern Military Records Division, Record Group 218, enclosure to JCS 1483/44, CCS 383.21 (3-19-45), sec. 14, Appendix A, p. 259; Memorandum of Conversation, General Charles G. Helmick with John Z. Williams, Feb. 4, 1948, *Foreign Relations,* 1948, vol. 6, p. 1092; U.S. Department of State, *Korean Unification,* pp. 8–9; Niles W. Bond, oral history interview with Richard D. McKinzie, Washington, D.C., Dec. 28, 1973, HSTL (hereafter cited as Bond, HSTL, Oral History), pp. 26 and 29.

19. Butterworth to Marshall, March 4, 1948, *Foreign Relations,* 1948, vol. 6, pp. 1137–39; W. G. Labor to SANACC, Feb. 21, 1948, Nat. Arch., Modern Military Records Division, Record Group 218, Enclosure to JCS 1483/50, CCS 383.21 Korea (3-19-45), sec. 15, pp. 2–3; NSC, NSC 8, April 2, 1948, *Foreign Relations,* 1948, vol. 6, pp. 1164–69.

20. NSC 8, April 2, 1948, *Foreign Relations,* 1948, vol. 6, pp. 1164–69. The President approved NSC 8, even though it went against his own early instincts to safeguard southern Korea, because George Marshall backed the new policy. Max Bishop, the Director of Northeast Asian Affairs, subsequently recalled, "Of course, Marshall was the darling of President Truman. In President Truman's eyes, Marshall was just one step short of Saint Peter. He could do no wrong; he was right on everything." Interview with Max Bishop, Ailey, Ga., April 12, 1988 (hereafter cited as Bishop interview with author). Even after the adoption of NSC 8, Butterworth continued his campaign to slow down the U.S. military withdrawal from Korea. Niles Bond, Assistant Director of Northeast Asian Affairs, later remembered, "This process went on; the military trying to pull out and the State Department saying, 'No you can't do it, yet.' During this time there was a gradual withdrawal, as I say, from 50,000 [troops] down to about 8,000." Bond, HSTL Oral History, pp. 29–32.

21. U.S. Congress, House, Committee on Foreign Affairs, *Korean Aid,* pp. 5–6; Jacobs to Marshall, May 29, 1948, *Foreign Relations,* 1948, vol. 6, pp. 1207–09; Marshall to Royall, June 23, 1948, ibid., pp. 1224–25; Royall to Marshall, June 23, 1948, ibid., pp. 1225–26; Truman to Marshall, Aug. 25, 1948, ibid., p. 1288; U.S. Congress, House, Committee on Foreign Affairs, *Background Information on Korea,* p. 32.

22. Saltzman to Marshall through Lovett, Sept. 7, 1948, *Foreign Relations, 1948*, vol. 6, pp. 1292–97; NSC 8, April 2, 1948, ibid., pp. 1164–69; editorial note, ibid., p. 1297. Marshall's strict order to keep the full three-year plan secret grew out of his desire to avoid committing American prestige by revealing a long-term commitment to Korea; John Foster Dulles, then temporarily attached to the U.S. delegation to the UN, first suggested this approach. Marshall to Hoffman, Sept. 17, 1948, *Foreign Relations, 1948*, vol. 6, pp. 1303–5; editorial note, ibid., vol. 8, pp. 1296–97. Harry Truman initially asked Acheson to run the ECA, but Acheson declined and recommended Paul Hoffman. Acheson hoped this move would consolidate the support of Senator Arthur Vandenberg. Truman appointed Hoffman; Vandenberg expressed his delight; and Hoffman thereafter supported most of Acheson's policies. McLellan, *Dean Acheson*, p. 136; Hoffman, HSTL Oral History, pp. 1–5.

23. Memorandum by Butterworth, Aug. 17, 1948, *Foreign Relations, 1948*, vol. 6, p. 1277. Bishop later recalled that Syngman Rhee was "a damn poor administrator" and that "the people around him were corrupt." Bishop interview with author; Muccio to Marshall, Oct. 28, 1948, *Foreign Relations, 1948*, vol. 6, pp. 1317–18; Lovett to Marshall, Nov. 5, 1948, ibid., p. 1319; Saltzman to Wedemeyer, Nov. 9, 1948, ibid., pp. 1324–25; Draper to Saltzman, Dec. 22, 1948, ibid., pp. 1341–42; U.S. Department of State, *Korean Unification*, p. 11; U.S. Congress, Senate, Committee on Armed Services and Committee on Foreign Relations, *Military Situation in the Far East: Hearings before the Committee on Armed Services and the Committee on Foreign Relations: An Inquiry into the Military Situation and the Facts surrounding the Relief of General of the Army Douglas MacArthur from His Assignments in That Area*, 3 pts., 81st Cong., 2d sess., 1951, pt. 3, p. 373.

24. Dean Acheson, *Present at the Creation* (New York: Norton, 1969), p. 249.

25. Bishop interview with author; Bishop to Butterworth, Dec. 17, 1948, *Foreign Relations, 1948*, vol. 6, pp. 1337–40. Before Max Bishop took over Northeast Asian Affairs, he served as the State Department's representative on the staff of the National Security Council, and in that capacity he tried unsuccessfully to persuade both Marshall and the NSC to review NSC 8. Marshall therefore actually delayed this decision much longer than just one month. Max Bishop to author, Dec. 1, 1987. The author asked Lucius Battle, Acheson's personal assistant, if Marshall delayed the decision to request a review of NSC 8 in order to first consult with Acheson. Battle replied that he did not become Acheson's assistant until just after this period, but he added that he could not imagine Marshall making such a decision without first discussing it with Acheson—especially since the decision came

just four days before Acheson took office. The fact that Acheson discussed other matters with State Department officials well before he officially took office points to the same conclusion. Battle interview with author. Furthermore, job transitions in the State Department seldom took place instantaneously on an official date. For example, when Nitze took over the Policy Planning Staff and when Rusk took over Far Eastern Affairs, each did so gradually in the weeks preceding their official appointment. This, too, suggests that Marshall had probably begun consulting with Acheson by the time of the decision to ask for a review of NSC 8. Nitze interview with author; Rusk interview with author.

26. Bond, HSTL Oral History, p. 34; Bishop interview with author; U.S. Department of State, "Policy Statement: Korea," Jan. 31, 1949, Nat. Arch., Record Group 59, Department of State, Office of Northeast Asian Affairs, Lot 711.95/1-31490 File. NSC 8/2 was the fifth policy on Korea in two years. The Interdepartmental Committee on Korea framed the first policy with its report of February 25, 1947; it called for a "positive program" to rebuild Korea. An ad hoc subcommittee of the State-War-Navy Coordinating Committee (SWNCC) pulled back from this commitment in the second policy, SWNCC 176/30, approved August 4, 1947. The State-Army-Navy-Air Force Coordinating Committee (SANACC) replaced SWNCC and approved a third policy, SANACC 176/35, on January 14, 1948. This policy moved toward abandoning Korea. The NSC replaced SWNCC and approved the fourth policy, NSC 8, on April 2, 1948. NSC 8 specified that the United States would create a government in South Korea as a means of abandoning Korea gracefully. NSC 8/2, the fifth policy, replaced NSC 8 on March 23, 1949, and it reverted to the original concept of rebuilding South Korea with U.S. economic assistance. NCS 8/2, March 22, 1949, *Foreign Relations, 1949*, vol. 7, pp. 969–78. Paul Nitze opposed the military withdrawal from Korea, but Truman decided to proceed with it. Nitze interview with author. Dean Rusk later remembered, "I, myself, personally joined that State Department in opposing the total [military] withdrawal from Korea but that point of view was overridden by President Truman." Dean Rusk to author, April 10, 1989. According to Lucius Battle, however, "Acheson did nothing to oppose withdrawal [of U.S. troops from Korea] on schedule." Lucius Battle to author, Aug. 14, 1989.

27. Rusk interview with author; Nitze interview with author.

28. NSC 8, April 2, 1948, *Foreign Relations, 1948*, vol. 6, pp. 1164–69; Stueck, *Road to Confrontation*, p. 99; Schnabel and Watson, *History of the Joint Chiefs of Staff*, 3:18 and 22–23; NSC 8/2, March 22, 1949, *Foreign Relations, 1949*, vol. 7, pp. 969–78; U.S. Congress, House, Committee on Foreign Affairs, *Korean Aid*, pp. 12–13; James F. Schnabel, *Policy*

and Direction: The First Year, vol. 3 of *U.S. Army in the Korean War* (Washington, D.C.: Office of the Chief of Military History, U.S. Army, 1972), p. 32; Rusk interview with author. The infant South Korean Navy needed fast patrol boats to thwart the North Korean infiltration tactics, and Nitze succeeded in persuading the Pentagon to include these boats in the military aid package for Korea. Nitze interview with author. A report on U.S. military aid policy stated, "Token military assistance should be planned for Korea for fiscal 1950 . . . . The whole problem is under review . . . and it may be determined that Korea should be placed in the category of countries receiving limited rather than token assistance." Unattributed, untitled, and undated report on military aid to China, the Philippines, Korea, Siam, and Indonesia, Nat. Arch., Record Group 59, Department of State, Office of Chinese Affairs, Box 15, 400.5001, China Aid Program 1949 File.

29. Forrestal, *Forrestal Diaries,* p. 265; Harry Temple, "Deaf Captains: Intelligence, Policy, and the Origins of the Korean War," *International Studies Notes* 8 (1981–82): 21; Schnabel and Watson, *History of the Joint Chiefs of Staff,* 3:27. Apparently, the State Department was unaware that some intelligence analysts expected a North Korean invasion of South Korea after the last U.S. troops were withdrawn. Rusk interview with author; Bishop interview with author; Battle interview with author.

30. Louis Johnson served as Chairman of the Democratic National Committee and raised money for Truman's 1948 election campaign, which resulted in Truman's decision to make Johnson his Secretary of Defense. Bruce, HSTL Oral History, p. 21. Johnson severely limited Acheson's knowledge of the Pentagon's aid policies by insisting that all communications between State and Defense go through him. Rusk considered Johnson "almost a disaster as Secretary of Defense." Rusk interview with author. Max Bishop echoed Rusk's opinion of Johnson. Bishop interview with author. Battle agreed with Rusk and Bishop. Battle interview with author. Acheson thought that Johnson was mentally ill, and Omar Bradley characterized him in similar terms: "Unwittingly, Truman replaced one mental case [James Forrestal] with another [Louis Johnson]." Blair, *Forgotten War,* p. 17; U.S. Congress, House, Committee on International Relations, *United States Policy in the Far East,* pp. 12, 140, 351–52, 357, 392, and 420–21; U.S. Congress, House, Committee on Foreign Affairs, *Korean Aid,* pp. 15–20.

31. U.S. Congress, House, Committee on Foreign Affairs, *Korean Aid,* pp. 115–17; U.S. Congress, House, Committee on International Relations, *United States Policy in the Far East,* pp. 13, 17, 32–34, 70, 101–2, 238, and 248.

32. U.S. Congress, Senate, Committee on Foreign Relations, *Economic Assistance to China and Korea,* pp. 16, 134–37, 174, 176, and 190–91.

Dr. Edgar Johnson, the administrator of the ECA's program in Korea, testified that, before World War II, Japan accounted for roughly 80 percent of Korea's foreign trade; he expected this to "level off" at 65 percent in the postwar years. Ibid., p. 162.

33. Kennan to Marshall, March 14, 1948, *Foreign Relations,* 1948, vol. 1, p. 534; "MacArthur Pledges Defense of Japan," *New York Times,* March 2, 1949, p. 22; Schnabel, *Policy and Direction,* pp. 49–51; Robert Blum, *Drawing the Line* (New York: Norton, 1982), pp. 168 and 171–72; NSC 48/2, Dec. 30, 1949, *Foreign Relations,* 1949, vol. 7, p. 1215; Schaller, *American Occupation of Japan,* pp. 202–4; NSC 48, Dec. 23, 1949, in U.S. Department of Defense, *United States–Vietnam Relations, 1945–1967* (Washington, D.C.: GPO, 1971), 8:241–43 and 255–57.

34. Acheson, *Present at the Creation,* p. 354; Dean Acheson, "Crisis in Asia—An Examination of U.S. Policy," *Department of State Bulletin* 22 (Jan. 23, 1950): 116. Acheson worked with Rusk and others on several drafts of the Press Club speech, but in the end he pushed these aside and delivered the speech from a few notes which he wrote himself. Despite his low regard for the UN, Acheson adopted months before the Press Club speech Rusk's concept of going first to the UN in any major crisis. Rusk interview with author; Acheson to the Embassy in Korea, Dec. 14, 1949, *Foreign Relations,* 1949, vol. 7, p. 1108; U.S. Congress, Senate, Committee on Foreign Relations, *Reviews of the World Situation, 1949–1950: Hearings Held in Executive Session before the Committee on Foreign Relations,* 81st Cong., 1st and 2d sess., 1974, p. 191.

35. U.S. Congress, House, Committee on Foreign Affairs, *Background Information on Korea,* pp. 71–72; U.S. Congress, Senate, Committee on Foreign Relations, *Reviews of the World Situation,* p. 103; U.S. Department of State, *Hearings on American Foreign Policy, 1950–1955,* 2 vols. (Washington, D.C.: GPO, 1957), 2:2527; U.S. Congress, House, Committee on International Relations, *United States Policy in the Far East,* pp. 17, 407, 421, and 441–43. Acheson worked closely with Truman to secure passage of the Korean aid bill both before and after its January 1950 defeat, and Truman gave the bill his full support. Acheson, "White House Help on the Korean Bill," July 7, 1949, HSTL, Papers of Dean Acheson, Box 64, July 1949 Conversations File; Acheson, "Conversations with the President, Korean Aid Bill," July 14, 1949, ibid.; Acheson, "Meeting with the President, Korean Legislation," Oct. 14, 1949, ibid., Oct.–Nov. Conversations File; Acheson, "Memorandum of Conversation with the President," Jan. 23, 1950, ibid., Box 64B, Jan. 1950 Conversations File; Acheson, "Memorandum of Conversation with the President," Jan. 26, 1950, ibid. After the initial defeat of his Korean aid bill, Acheson immediately set up a meeting with Senator

Arthur Vandenberg, who then helped Acheson plan the legislative strategy that ultimately prevailed. Acheson, "Substance of Conversation with Senator Vandenberg," Jan. 21, 1950, ibid.

36. U.S. Congress, Senate, Committee on Foreign Relations, *Reviews of the World Situation,* pp. 135, 152, and 256; Jim Impoco, "Motherhood and the Future of Japan," *U.S. News & World Report,* Dec. 24, 1990, pp. 56–57; U.S. Congress, House, Committee on Foreign Affairs, *Korean Aid,* p. 116; U.S. Congress, House, Subcommittee of the Committee on Appropriations, *First Deficiency Appropriations Bill for 1947,* p. 845; Uchino, *Japan's Postwar Recovery,* p. 42. Another set of Japanese figures, which combines U.S. aid for relief, reconstruction, and other items, puts total U.S. expenditures at $404 million in 1947, $461 million in 1948, and $535 million in 1949. Japanese Ministry of Foreign Affairs, *Economic Rehabilitation and Foreign Commerce of Japan* (Tokyo: Bureau of Public Information and Cultural Affairs, 1953), p. 13.

37. Rusk interview with author. In March of 1949, the Policy Planning Staff said in a major report, "Burma, the rice granary of the Far East, is able to export only a fraction of its normal food surplus because of widespread internal political disorder. These and comparable conditions endanger Indian and Japanese economic self-support because of their inability to obtain needed foodstuffs from Asiatic sources." PPS, PPS-51, May 19, 1949, U.S. Department of State, *The State Department Policy Planning Staff Papers,* 3 vols. (New York: Garland, 1983), 3:34; Cohen, *Japan's Economy in War and Reconstruction,* p. 369 and see note 10; U.S. Department of Agriculture, *Agricultural Statistics, 1948,* p. 32; Bishop interview with author; U.S. Congress, Senate, Committee on Foreign Relations, *Economic Assistance to China and Korea,* p. 135. On January 10, 1950, Acheson explained his policy on Japan to the Senate Committee on Foreign Relations: "I think what we will have to do is to both [Congress and the State Department] use the funds we expend in the Far East in such a way that we can get double benefits from them." By subsidizing Japan's trading partners, Acheson believed, the United States could help both them and Japan. U.S. Congress, Senate, Committee on Foreign Relations, *Reviews of the World Situation,* p. 135. In 1935—according to Japanese figures—Asia had accounted for 63.6 percent of Japan's exports, of which 6.6 percent went to Taiwan, 17 percent to Korea, 17.5 percent to China, and 18.6 percent to Southeast Asia. In that same year, Asia accounted for 51.1 percent of Japan's imports—9.6 percent from Taiwan, 10.7 percent from China, 14.9 percent from Korea, and 15.9 percent from Southeast Asia. The diversion of Japanese nitrate production from fertilizer to munitions reduced Korean rice exports in 1935, but it is safe to say that Korea accounted for less than one-third of Japan's

annual Asian trade. (Japanese figures for 1950, as cited by Jerome Cohen, neither include trade with Korea paid for by U.S. aid nor consider that the Korean War shortened the trading period to six months. Figures for 1955 and 1956 reflect only the devastation brought on by the Korean War.) Jerome B. Cohen, *Japan's Postwar Economy* (Bloomington: Indiana Univ. Press, 1958), pp. 119–20.

38. Muccio to Acheson, April 4, 1950, *Foreign Relations, 1950,* vol. 7, pp. 44–45; Edward S. Mason et al., *The Economic and Social Modernization of Korea* (Cambridge: Harvard Univ. Press, 1980), pp. 169 and 223; U.S. Congress, House, Committee on Foreign Affairs, *Background Information on Korea,* p. 71; U.S. Department of State, *Korean Unification,* p. 14. The State Department now anticipated a much more protracted Korean recovery, partly because Acheson's original plan had been reduced from $600 million in 1947 to $320 million in 1950. However, Korea had already made considerable progress, and some earlier U.S. aid allocated for simple relief assistance had, in fact, been used for economic rehabilitation. Economic assistance for Korea amounted to $6 million in 1946, $93 million in 1947, $113 million in 1948, and $148 million in 1949. U.S. Congress, House, Committee on International Relations, *United States Policy in the Far East,* pp. 351 and 447. Dr. Edgar Johnson, who administered the Economic Cooperation Administration's program in South Korea, believed that improved political stability in Korea would lead to substantial American and Japanese private investment and a much more rapid economic recovery, but neither the ECA nor the State Department included private investment in its projections. "Japanese investment [in Korea] on an annual basis," Johnson noted, "amounted to about $46 million a year." U.S. Congress, Senate, Committee on Foreign Relations, *Economic Assistance to China and Korea,* pp. 134 and 146. UN statistics do not accurately reflect South Korea's trade with Japan, because the United States actually paid for much of this trade at both ends with foreign aid credits. The two nations finally signed an agreement for direct trade—without the U.S. middleman—just before the Korean War began. According to Dean Rusk, the talks leading to direct trade were difficult and protracted because of strong Korean hostility toward Japan. The Koreans, Rusk recalled, had many grievances against the Japanese, not the least of which was Japan's wartime practice of impressing Korean women to serve as prostitutes for the Japanese Army. Rusk interview with author; Cohen, *Japan's Postwar Economy,* pp. 119–20.

39. Schnabel and Watson, *History of the Joint Chiefs of Staff,* 3:28; David Rees, *Korea* (New York: St. Martin's Press, 1964), p. 16; James E. Webb to author, March 17, 1986.

40. Rees, *Korea,* p. 16; Matthew B. Ridgway, *The Korean War* (Garden

City, N.Y.: Doubleday, 1967), p. 15; Schnabel and Watson, *History of the Joint Chiefs of Staff*, 3:24 and 42–43; U.S. Congress, Senate, Committee on Foreign Relations, *Executive Sessions of the Committee on Foreign Relations*, 2:421.

41. Ridgway, *Korean War*, p. 29; Muccio to Acheson, May 23, 1950, *Foreign Relations*, 1950, vol. 7, pp. 86–88; Battle interview with author. Dean Rusk became Acheson's Assistant Secretary for Far Eastern Affairs in March of 1950 and quickly used his personal contacts in the Pentagon to figure out that South Korea could not resist a North Korean invasion. Rusk related this to the House Committee on International Relations on June 20, 1950, just four days before the outbreak of war in Korea. Rusk interview with author; U.S. Congress, House, Committee on International Relations, *United States Policy in the Far East*, p. 464.

42. U.S. Congress, Senate, Committee on Foreign Relations, *Economic Assistance to China and Korea*, p. 176; "World Policy and Bipartisanship: An Interview with Senator Tom Connally," *U.S. News & World Report*, May 5, 1950, p. 30.

43. F. A. Godfrey, "Crisis in Korea," in *War in Peace*, ed. Sir Robert Thompson (New York: Harmony Books, 1981), p. 42; Larry Davis, *Mig Alley* (Warren: Squadron/Signal, 1978), p. 3; Merle Miller, *Plain Speaking* (New York: Berkley, 1973), pp. 288–94; Harry S. Truman, *Memoirs: Years of Trial and Hope* (Garden City, N.Y.: Doubleday, 1956), pp. 332–33. Rusk later recalled that the immediate discussions focused primarily on how, rather than whether, to mobilize a military response. Rusk interview with author. Lucius Battle, Acheson's personal assistant, echoed Rusk's recollection and added that General Douglas MacArthur was slow to call the North Korean attack a full-scale invasion, thereby complicating the military issues. Battle interview with author. The documentary evidence that North Korea launched a premeditated attack with Soviet and Chinese support is considerable. See Matthew B. Ridgway, "Special Report of the Commanding General," *Department of State Bulletin* 24 (May 21, 1951): 828–32; U.S. Department of State, *North Korea: A Case Study in the Techniques of Takeover* (Washington, D.C.: GPO, 1961), pp. 2–9 and 109–16; U.S. Department of State, *Conflict in Korea* (Washington, D.C.: GPO, 1951), pp. 28–36. Nikita Khrushchev, an aide to Stalin during this period, recalled that Kim Il Sung sought and received the approval from both Stalin and Mao Tse-tung while planning his attack. Nikita Khrushchev, *Khrushchev Remembers* (Boston: Little, Brown, 1970) pp. 367–73. Pawel Monat, a Polish defector, wrote a firsthand account which correlates well with that of Khrushchev. Pawel Monat, "Russians in Korea: Hidden Bosses," *Life*, June 27, 1960, pp. 76–101. U.S. planners immediately concluded that the intri-

cate strategic planning and enormous logistical stockpiles required for an invasion of such magnitude could have resulted only from months of close cooperation between North Korea and the Soviet Union. Within a few months, the United States also found evidence of Chinese complicity. The People's Republic of China, according to Dean Rusk, combed its army for soldiers of Korean origin and transferred them to the North Korean Army just before the war. The U.S. Army captured and interrogated some of these soldiers and then apprised Rusk of Chinese involvement in North Korean planning. Rusk interview with author. The historian Bruce Cumings contends that the Soviet Union sent North Korea primarily second-class arms; as evidence for this, he cites the fact that the Soviets provided neither Stalin (JS III) tanks nor 152-mm howitzers. In reality, however, both the Stalin tank and the 152-mm howitzer were far too heavy for Korea's roads, bridges, and terrain, and both would have been more of a liability than an asset in fast-paced offensive operations. The Soviet Union had available in the Far East enormous quantities of obsolete pre–World War II tanks, guns, and small arms. Instead of sending these to North Korea, Stalin sent his best small arms (even the new SKS rifle), his best medium artillery (much of it self-propelled), and his finest medium tanks (the legendary T-34/85, against which South Korea's ancient 37-mm and 57-mm antitank guns were virtually useless). Many of these tanks and guns were captured by U.S. forces, and several are still on display at the Aberdeen Proving Grounds, in Maryland. Bruce Cumings, *The Origins of the Korean War,* vol. 2 (Princeton: Princeton Univ. Press, 1990), pp. 446; Simon Dunstan, *Armor of the Korean War, 1950–1953* (London: Osprey, 1982), pp. 3–5, 14, and 35; Nigel Thomas and Peter Abbott, *The Korean War* (London: Osprey, 1986), pp. 25 and 37–38; Jim Mesko, *Armor in Korea* (Carrollton, Tex.: Squadron/Signal, 1984), pp. 3–7; Acheson, *Present at the Creation,* pp. 402–5.

44. Rosemary Foot, *The Wrong War* (Ithaca: Cornell Univ. Press, 1985), p. 60; Allison to Nitze, July 24, 1950, *Foreign Relations,* 1950, vol. 7, pp. 458–61; James E. Webb to author, March 17, 1986; Rusk interview with author. The "dagger" concept, while quite old in Japan, was probably injected into the State Department's rhetoric in 1949 by Max Bishop, who worked closely with Webb and Rusk. Bishop interview with author.

45. Acheson, *Present at the Creation,* pp. 405–6.

46. Ibid.; Truman, *Memoirs: Years of Hope and Trial,* pp. 333–34; Rusk interview with author; James Webb to John Snyder, April 25, 1975, HSTL, Papers of James E. Webb.

47. Webb to Snyder, April 25, 1975, HSTL, Papers of James E. Webb; Truman, *Memoirs: Years of Hope and Trial,* pp. 334–36; Acheson, *Present at the Creation,* p. 412. Bradley resisted sending troops to Korea even more

forcefully in private. Niles Bond later recounted, "Oddly enough, the one who argued most strongly against going to help the Koreans in any way was Omar Bradley. He was adamant on this, that there were no American military interests there." Bond, HSTL Oral History, p. 44; Philip Jessup, Memorandum of Conversation (large meeting), June 25, 1950, HSTL, Papers of Dean Acheson, Box 65, June 1950 Conversations File.

48. Philip Jessup, Memorandum of Conversation (large meeting), June 26, 1950, HSTL, Papers of Dean Acheson, Box 65, June 1950 Conversations File; Philip Jessup, "Notes on the Meeting in Cabinet Room at the White House," June 27, 1950, ibid.; Philip Jessup, Memorandum of Conversation (large meeting), June 28, 1950, ibid. Beverly Smith, a well-known journalist, interviewed many of the participants of these meetings and preserved an invaluable record. Beverly Smith, "The White House Story: Why We Went to War in Korea," *Saturday Evening Post,* Nov. 10, 1951, pp. 22, 23, 76, 77, 78, 82, and 90. For an in-depth analysis of the meeting on June 25, 1950, see Glenn Paige, *1950: Truman's Decision* (New York: Chelsea House, 1970), pp. 70–75.

49. U.S. Congress, House, Subcommittee of the Committee on Appropriations, *First Deficiency Appropriations Bill for 1947,* p. 855; Bishop to Butterworth, Dec. 17, 1948, *Foreign Relations,* 1948, vol. 6, pp. 1337–38; U.S. Congress, Senate, Committee on Foreign Relations, *Economic Assistance to China and Korea,* p. 134; Allison to Nitze, July 24, 1950, *Foreign Relations,* 1950, vol. 7, pp. 458–61.

50. Schaller, *American Occupation of Japan,* p. 296; Mason, *Modernization of Korea,* pp. 223–27.

CHAPTER FOUR: Acheson and
the American Commitment on Taiwan

1. NSC 34/1, Jan. 11, 1949, *Foreign Relations,* 1949, vol. 9, pp. 474–75; NSC 37/2, Feb. 3, 1949, ibid., pp. 281–82; NSC 41, Feb. 28, 1949, ibid., pp. 826–34.

2. NSC 37/1, Jan. 19, 1949, *Foreign Relations,* 1949, vol. 9, pp. 270–75.

3. NSC 37, Dec. 1, 1948, *Foreign Relations,* 1949, vol. 9, pp. 261–62; U.S. Department of Agriculture, *Agricultural Statistics, 1948* (Washington, D.C.: GPO, 1949), pp. 23, 38, and 32 n. 6; Neil H. Jacoby, *U.S. Aid to Taiwan* (New York: Praeger, 1966), p. 79; NSC 37, Dec. 1, 1948, *Foreign Relations,* 1949, vol. 9, pp. 261–62; Toshiyuki Mizoguchi, "Foreign Trade in Taiwan and Korea under Japanese Rule," *Hitotsubashi Journal of*

Economics 14 (Feb. 1974): 38–39; Jerome B. Cohen, *Japan's Postwar Economy* (Bloomington: Indiana Univ. Press, 1958), pp. 119–20; Joseph W. Ballantine, *Formosa* (Washington, D.C.: Brookings Institution, 1952), p. 113; interview with Dean Rusk, Athens, Ga., April 11, 1988 (hereafter cited as Rusk interview with author); Robert A. Lovett to Harry S. Truman, Jan. 14, 1949, *Foreign Relations,* 1949, vol. 9, pp. 265–67.

4. Max Bishop expressed his opinions on Taiwan orally rather than in writing, as he did his opinions on Korea, because Taiwan was outside of the purview of his office. Interview with Max Bishop, Ailey, Ga., April 12, 1988 (hereafter cited as Bishop interview with author).

5. CIA, "Review of the World Situation," Dec. 16, 1948, HSTL, President's Secretary's Files, Box 250, Situation Summary File; "Intelligence Memorandum No. 111," Jan. 3, 1949, HSTL, Records of the National Security Council, Box 2, NSC/CIA Intelligence Memorandums Dec. 1948–Dec. 1949 File. In June of 1949, the State Department and the Economic Cooperation Administration began to develop a barter exchange program so that Japan could trade manufactured goods for Taiwan's sugar, but they had to overcome an initial lack of interest on the part of the American occupation authorities in Japan. Livingston T. Merchant, Memorandum of Conversation (large meeting, presided over by Acheson), June 29, 1949, HSTL, Papers of Dean Acheson, Box 64, May–June Conversations File; Lovett to Truman, Jan. 14, 1949, *Foreign Relations,* 1949, vol. 9, pp. 265–67; Note by John P. Davies, Jan. 14, 1949, Nat. Arch., Record Group 59, Department of State, Office of Chinese Affairs, Box 13, China 1949 File.

6. John M. Cabot to Dean Acheson, Jan. 28, 1949, *Foreign Relations,* 1949, vol. 8, pp. 91–92.

7. NSC 37/1, Jan. 19, 1949, *Foreign Relations,* 1949, vol. 9, pp. 270–75. A report by the State Department's Office of Intelligence Review established as early as November 1948 that economic assistance would be essential to keep Taiwan out of Communist hands. Office of Intelligence Review, "Prospects in Formosa, November 1948," and cover letter by W. Walton Butterworth to Dean Rusk, Sept. 7, 1949, Nat. Arch., Record Group 59, Department of State, Office of Chinese Affairs, Box 15, Lot 360 File. Actually, U.S. contacts with Taiwanese leaders had three goals: to prevent Communist infiltration of the Taiwanese independence movement, to increase U.S. leverage for reform with Chinese leaders, and to supply an alternative if the United States withdrew support for whatever Chinese regime developed on Taiwan. "China: Taiwan (Formosa)," Jan. 28, 1949, Nat. Arch., Record Group 59, Department of State, Office of Chinese Affairs, Box 14, Lot 306.001 File.

8. NSC 37/2, Feb. 3, 1949, *Foreign Relations,* 1949, vol. 9, pp. 281–

82; NSC 37/3, Feb. 11, 1949, ibid., pp. 284–86; NSC 37/5, March 1, 1949, ibid., pp. 290–92; Merchant to Butterworth, May 24, 1949, ibid., p. 337.

9. NSC 37/4, Feb. 18, 1949, *Foreign Relations,* 1949, vol. 9, pp. 288–89; Philip D. Sprouse to Acheson, Feb. 18, 1949, Nat. Arch., Record Group 59, Department of State, Office of Chinese Affairs, Box 14, Lot 306.001 File; NSC 37/5, March 1, 1949, *Foreign Relations,* 1949, vol. 9, pp. 290–92. In a telegram discussing NSC 37/2, Acheson stressed that "with [the] orientation [of Taiwan's] trade toward Japan" the U.S. economic program for Taiwan "should produce a viable Formosan economy." Taiwan's trade with Japan remained central in Acheson's thinking. Acheson to Kenneth C. Krentz, March 2, 1949, *Foreign Relations,* 1949, vol. 9, pp. 293–94; NSC 37/5, March 1, 1949, ibid., pp. 290–92; Acheson, "Statement by the Secretary of State at the 35th Meeting of the National Security Council," March 1, 1949, HSTL, President's Secretary's Files, Box 205, NSC Meeting No. 35 File. After the approval of NSC 37/5, U.S. policy on Taiwan consisted of NSC 37/2 and NSC 37/5 together. John L. Stuart, "Review of NSC Policies Respecting China in Light of the President's Statement of June 27, 1950," July 12, 1950, Nat. Arch., Record Group 59, Department of State, Office of Chinese Affairs, Box 17, Lot 306.0015 File; Merchant to Butterworth, May 29, 1949, *Foreign Relations,* 1949, vol. 9, p. 337.

10. The China Aid Act was signed into law on April 3, 1948. Butterworth to Stuart and enclosed "Legislative History of the China Aid Program," April 7, 1949, Nat. Arch., Record Group 59, Department of State, Office of Chinese Affairs, Box 14, 030.001, Ambassador Stuart File. Since the unobligated balance of the economic aid fund for China came to $104 million on February 15, 1950, more than half of the total fund must have remained available in March of 1949. ECA, "Summary Statement and Program Requirements for the Period February 16, 1950–June 30, 1951," HSTL, Papers of Clark Clifford, Box 2, Economic Cooperation Administration China Aid Program File. James Webb probably had to handle the Taiwan aid issue during the first few weeks after Acheson became Secretary of State, because Acheson initially focused most of his attention on Europe. According to Acheson's personal assistant, Lucius Battle, the new Secretary of State placed a low priority on China and Taiwan in the first few months of 1949. Interview with Lucius D. Battle, May 30, 1990, Washington, D.C. (hereafter cited as Battle interview with author); Rusk interview with author; Lovett to Truman, Jan. 14, 1949, *Foreign Relations,* 1949, vol. 9, p. 267; James E. Webb to Paul G. Hoffman, Jan. 31, 1949, ibid., p. 278; Stuart to Acheson, March 23, 1949, ibid., p. 302; Acheson to Stuart, March 24, 1949, ibid., p. 304; Edgar to Acheson, April 6, 1949, ibid., pp. 308–9.

11. Donald D. Edgar to Acheson, March 6, 1949, *Foreign Relations,*

1949, vol. 9, p. 297; Edgar to Acheson, March 9, 1949, ibid., pp. 298–99; Stuart to Acheson, March 23, 1949, ibid., p. 302; Acheson to Stuart, March 24, 1949, ibid., p. 304; R. Allen Griffin to Harlan Cleveland, April 14, 1949, ibid., p. 319; Edgar to Acheson, May 4, 1949, ibid., pp. 324–26.

12. NSC 22/3, Feb. 2, 1949, *Foreign Relations,* 1949, vol. 9, pp. 479–80; Editorial note on NSC Meeting, ibid., pp. 482–83; Marshall S. Carter, Memorandum on Off the Record Meeting, Feb. 7, 1950, Nat. Arch., Record Group 59, Department of State, Office of Chinese Affairs, Box 15, 500.3, Aid to China—General and Economic Cooperation Administration—File; William Stueck, *The Road to Confrontation* (Chapel Hill: Univ. of North Carolina Press, 1981), pp. 116–17; Gaddis Smith, *Dean Acheson,* vol. 15 of *American Secretaries of State and Their Diplomacy,* ed. Samuel Flagg Bemis and Robert H. Ferrell (New York: Cooper Square, 1972), pp. 110–11; Acheson to Truman, March 10, 1949, HSTL, President's Secretary's Files, Box 173, China 1949 File.

13. Acheson, Memorandum of Conversation with the President, Feb. 14, 1949, HSTL, Papers of Dean Acheson, Box 64, Jan.–Feb. 1949 Conversations File; Smith, *Dean Acheson,* pp. 112–14; Dean Acheson, *Present at the Creation* (New York: Norton, 1969), p. 306.

14. David S. McLellan, *Dean Acheson* (New York: Dodd, Mead, 1976), pp. 188–89; "50 Senators Back Bill to Aid China," *New York Times,* March 11, 1949, p. 13; Acheson to Connally, March 15, 1949, *Foreign Relations,* 1949, vol. 9, pp. 607–9 and 607n; U.S. Congress, Senate, Committee on Foreign Relations, *Economic Assistance to China and Korea, 1949–1950: Hearings Held in Executive Session before the Committee on Foreign Relations on S. 1063, S. 2319, and S. 2845,* 81st Cong., 1st and 2d sess., 1974, p. 3. The China Aid Act was due to expire on April 3, 1949, and the ECA wanted to both extend this date and ask Congress to appropriate the $63 million left unappropriated in 1948. The additional $63 million, some ECA officials contended, could be used as a carrot to induce reform on Taiwan. W. Walton Butterworth, Acheson's Director of Far Eastern Affairs, eventually convinced both Acheson and the ECA that they could not possibly justify an additional $63 million to Congress. The 1948 China Aid Act reserved $60 million for industrial development, and since the industrial development fund went untapped, it made up the bulk of the $70 million that remained in 1949. From this $60 million fund, Acheson expected to actually spend only $17 million for industrial development on Taiwan, and he would spend that only if he could reach an agreement with Chinese leaders on the island. He also anticipated using an unspecified sum from the funds of the Joint Commission for Rural Reconstruction (part of the unallocated $10 million) to continue efforts to increase Taiwanese agricultural production. In 1948, Sec-

retary of State George Marshall had utilized the China Aid Act to win Republican support for the Marshall Plan. Now, by simply extending this same measure, Acheson not only supplanted the McCarran bill but smoothed the way for his own European assistance package for fiscal year 1950. Office of Far Eastern Affairs, "United States Economic Aid to China," Jan. 14, 1949, *Foreign Relations*, 1949, vol. 9, pp. 599–601; Memorandum by W. Walton Butterworth, undated, ibid., pp. 601–6; Hoffman to Lovett, Jan. 19, 1949, ibid., p. 270; Stuart to Acheson, March 23, 1949, ibid., p. 302; Acheson to Stuart, March 24, 1949, ibid., p. 304; Edgar to Acheson, April 6, 1949, ibid., pp. 308–9; editorial note, ibid., p. 610. The figures for the unexpended China aid funds given by Gaddis Smith ($54 million), David McLellan ($54 million), and June Grasso ($275 million) are all incorrect. Likewise Grasso's figure for the anticipated expenditures on Taiwan ($14,125,000) is incorrect, since this represents an early projection rather than the final figure. Smith, *Dean Acheson*, p. 114; McLellan, *Dean Acheson*, p. 189; June M. Grasso, *Truman's Two-China Policy, 1948–1950* (New York: M. E. Sharpe, 1987), p. 40.

15. Memorandum of Conversation by Fayett J. Flexer, Dec. 7, 1948, *Foreign Relations*, 1949, vol. 9, p. 263 (written in 1948, this is nevertheless included in the 1949 volume); Stuart to Acheson, Feb. 18, 1949, ibid., vol. 8, pp. 135–36; NSC 37/5, March 1, 1949, ibid., vol. 9, pp. 290–92. In December of 1948, Chiang Kai-shek's wife journeyed to Washington in an effort to win more U.S. aid for the Nationalist regime. The effort failed, and Chiang resigned a few weeks later. The U.S. Central Intelligence Agency, apparently using sources within Chiang's inner circle, kept abreast of these developments and even predicted Chiang's resignation weeks before it occurred. George C. Marshall, Memorandum of Conversation with Madame Chiang, Dec. 3, 1948, HSTL, President's Secretary's Files, Box 173, China 1948 File; R. H. Hillenkoetter, Memorandum on Madame Chiang Kai-shek, Dec. 15, 1948, ibid.; R. H. Hillenkoetter, Memorandum on Generalissimo Chiang Kai-shek, Dec. 28, 1949, ibid. Li Tsung-jen had been elected Vice-President in April of 1948, despite opposition from Chiang Kai-shek. Upon becoming Acting President, Li found that Chiang had retained control of the monetary reserves and the military stockpiles. Li immediately tried to negotiate a settlement with the Communists, but they demanded something close to unconditional surrender. Although Li spent ten years in the United States (in college and graduate school) and married an American-born Chinese, he spoke little English and did not maintain particularly close ties to U.S. officials. "Biographical Sketch of LI Tsung-jen (pronounced LEE Zong-ren), Acting President of the Republic of China," undated, HSTL, President's Secretary's Files, Box 173, China File.

16. Merchant to Butterworth, May 24, 1949, *Foreign Relations,* 1949, vol. 9, p. 337; Edgar to Acheson, March 6, 1949, ibid., p. 297; Acheson to Sidney W. Souers, April 8, 1949, ibid., p. 310; Acheson to Edgar for Merchant, March 8, 1949, ibid., p. 297; Acheson to Stuart, March 11, 1949, ibid., p. 299; Stuart to Acheson, March 14, 1949, ibid., pp. 299–300.

17. Barbara W. Tuchman, *Stilwell and the American Experience in China, 1911–1945* (New York: Bantam Books, 1970), pp. 41, 361, 364, 369, 384, 421, 502–3, 536–37, 554, 566–68, 575, 579, and 659; Memorandum by James Webb, Nov. 14, 1949, *Foreign Relations,* 1949, vol. 9, pp. 582–88; Raymond P. Ludden, Sept. 1–2, 1948, ibid., 1948, vol. 7, pp. 446–47; Stuart to George C. Marshall, May 11, 1947, ibid., 1947, vol. 7, pp. 117–18; Stuart to Marshall, June 20, 1947, ibid., p. 192; note 91, ibid., 1948, vol. 7, p. 446.

18. Stuart to Acheson, Feb. 16, 1949, *Foreign Relations,* 1949, vol. 8, p. 134; Stuart to Acheson, March 14, 1949, ibid., vol. 9, p. 300; Acheson to Souers, April 8, 1949, ibid., pp. 310–11.

19. Lewis Clark to Acheson, April 27, 1949, *Foreign Relations,* 1949, vol. 8, pp. 282–83; Merchant to Butterworth, May 24, 1949, ibid., vol. 9, pp. 337–38; Edgar to Acheson, May 10, 1949, ibid., p. 330; Stuart to Acheson, March 14, 1949, ibid., p. 300; Edgar to Acheson, March 19, 1949, ibid., pp. 300–301; Edgar to Acheson, May 18, 1949, ibid., pp. 334–35. Chiang stood ready to use force to prevent the replacement of Chen Cheng, if that became necessary. Edgar to Acheson, May 11, 1949, ibid., p. 331.

20. Edgar (from Merchant) to Acheson, April 6, 1949, *Foreign Relations,* 1949, vol. 9, pp. 308–9; Edgar (from Merchant) to Acheson, April 9, 1949, ibid., p. 311; Stuart to Acheson, April 10, 1949, ibid., p. 312; Clark to Acheson, April 27, 1949, vol. 8, p. 282; Edgar (from Merchant) to Acheson, May 4, 1949, ibid., vol. 9, pp. 324–26. Merchant also proposed another alternative policy, which included the development of a $60 million aid plan for Taiwan in exchange for U.S. bases on the island, the appointment of Sun Li-jen to be Supreme Commander of all Chinese forces on the island, and various U.S.-sponsored economic reforms. This alternative proposal never received serious consideration. Edgar (from Merchant) to Acheson, May 4, 1949, ibid., pp. 326–27.

21. Acheson to Edgar (for Merchant) May 9, 1949, *Foreign Relations,* 1949, vol. 9, pp. 329–30; Edgar (from Merchant) to Acheson, May 13, 1949, ibid., pp. 332–33; Sprouse, "China: Taiwan (Formosa)," May 12, 1949, Nat. Arch., Record Group 59, Department of State, Office of Chinese Affairs, Box 14, Lot 306.001 File; Merchant to Butterworth, May 24, 1949, *Foreign Relations,* 1949, vol. 9, pp. 337–41. In the late spring and early summer of 1949, Chiang tried to promote a Far Eastern version of NATO— an alliance which would include Taiwan, Korea, the Philippines, the United

States, and other nations—but Acheson quickly made it clear that he was not interested. Nancy Bernkopf Tucker, *Patterns in the Dust* (New York: Columbia Univ. Press, 1983), pp. 72–73.

22. Merchant to Butterworth, May 24, 1949, *Foreign Relations,* 1949, vol. 9, p. 337; Butterworth to Rusk, June 9, 1949, ibid., pp. 346–50.

23. Acheson, Memorandum of Conversation (large meeting), June 29, 1949, HSTL, Papers of Dean Acheson, Box 64, May–June Conversations File.

24. PPS-53 also called for making use of Sun Li-jen in the process of occupying Taiwan. PPS, PPS-53, July 7, 1949, U.S. Department of State, *The State Department Policy Planning Staff Papers,* 3 vols. (New York: Garland, 1983), 3:63–74. PPS-53 may have evolved from Bishop's ideas, since he once served on the PPS. Bishop interview with author.

25. Acheson to Clark, May 18, 1949, *Foreign Relations,* 1949, vol. 9, pp. 336–37; Edgar to Acheson, May 17, 1949, ibid., p. 334; Edgar to Acheson, May 11, 1949, ibid., p. 331; Clark to Acheson, July 1, 1949, ibid., vol. 8, pp. 403–5.

26. Edgar to Acheson, May 17, 1949, *Foreign Relations,* 1949, vol. 9, p. 333; Edgar to Acheson, June 24, 1949, ibid., p. 354; U.S. Congress, House, Committee on International Relations, *United States Policy in the Far East: Selected Executive Sessions of the House Committee on International Relations: Hearings on the Far East Portion of the Mutual Defense Assistance Act of 1950,* 8 vols., 81st Cong., 1st and 2d sess., 1976, 7:500; Memorandum of Conversation by Butterworth (large meeting), 1949, Dec. 23, 1949, *Foreign Relations,* 1949, vol. 9, pp. 456 57.

27. Edgar to Acheson, June 3, 1949, *Foreign Relations,* 1949, vol. 9, pp. 344–45; John J. MacDonald to Acheson, July 23, 1949, ibid., pp. 364–65; Edwin W. Martin, *Divided Counsel* (Lexington: Univ. Press of Kentucky, 1986), p. 94; MacDonald to Acheson, Aug. 11, 1949, ibid., vol. 8, pp. 483–84; Stuart to Acheson, Nov. 6, 1949, ibid., vol. 9, pp. 412–13; MacDonald to Acheson, Sept. 15, 1949, ibid., pp. 390–91; Memorandum of Conversation by Fulton Freeman, Sept. 16, 1949, ibid., pp. 718–21. The State Department had actually been aware of Li Tsung-jen's deteriorating finances since May of 1949, and Acheson had discussed the matter with Li's emissary in July. Nanking Embassy to Department of the Army, May 27, 1949, Nat. Arch., Record Group 59, Department of State, Office of Chinese Affairs, Box 15, Lot 500.3 File; Acheson, Memorandum of Conversation with Kan Chieh-hou and V. K. Wellington Koo, July 1, 1949, HSTL, Papers of Dean Acheson, Box 64, July 1949 Conversations File. For more details, see unattributed, untitled, and undated report, HSTL, Papers of John W. Snyder, Box 129, Personal Correspondence 1947 "E" File.

28. Rusk interview with author; Acheson to Philip C. Jessup, July 18,

1949, Nat. Arch., Record Group 59, Department of State, Office of Chinese Affairs, Box 14, 306.0011, U.S. Policy toward Communist China File.

29. Butterworth to Rusk, Sept. 23, 1949, Nat. Arch., Record Group 59, Department of State, Office of Chinese Affairs, Box 14, 306, U.S. Policy toward China and the Far East File. NSC 37/6 and NSC 37/7 remain classified, but several critical passages from them are cited in NSC 37/8. NSC 37/ 8, Oct. 6, 1949, *Foreign Relations*, 1949, vol. 9, pp. 392–97.

30. "Discussion of Far Eastern Affairs in Preparation for Conversations with Mr. Bevin," Sept. 13, 1949, Nat. Arch., Record Group 59, Department of State, Office of Chinese Affairs, Box 14, 306, U.S. Policy toward China and the Far East File. According to a subsequent memorandum, NSC 37 / 8 was treated as a report rather than a new policy, and this may explain why it appears to have been implemented without formal approval. Memorandum by W. W. Stuart, March 29, 1950, ibid., Box 17, 306.13, NSC 37 / 8 File. Rusk interview with author. The special working group ruled out military action for two reasons—the Pentagon's lack of forces and the contention of a substantial clique within the Office of Far Eastern Affairs that military intervention on Taiwan would handicap American efforts to "exploit Chinese irredentist sentiment with respect to Soviet actions in Manchuria, Mongolia, and Sinkiang." NSC 37/8, Oct. 6, 1949, *Foreign Relations*, 1949, vol. 9, pp. 392–97; Walter Wilds to Jessup, Sept. 16, 1949, Nat. Arch., Record Group 59, Department of State, Office of Chinese Affairs, Box 16, 306.0015, NSC Reports File; Butterworth to Rusk, Sept. 23, 1949, ibid., Box 14, 306, U.S. Policy toward China and the Far East File. Acheson later testified that there were "two studies, in September and October," both of which "indicated the imminence and danger" of the fall of Taiwan. Both studies also indicated that it "would occur probably in the year 1950." U.S. Congress, Senate, Committee on Armed Services and Committee on Foreign Relations, *Military Situation in the Far East: Hearings before the Committee on Armed Services and the Committee on Foreign Relations: An Inquiry into the Military Situation and the Facts Surrounding the Relief of General of the Army Douglas MacArthur from His Assignments in That Area*, 3 pts., 81st Cong., 2d sess., 1951, pt. 3, p. 1672. In late 1949, State Department officials indicated to Ernest Bevin, the British Foreign Minister, that "no practical steps could be taken to prevent Formosa falling into Communist hands, and that such a development was in fact inevitable." Office of Far Eastern Affairs, "Formosa," Dec. 6, 1949, HSTL, Papers of Dean Acheson, Box 64, Dec. 1949 Conversations File.

31. MacDonald's instructions also told him to inform Sun Li-jen of the approach to Chiang. Butterworth to Acheson, Oct. 27, 1949, Nat. Arch., Record Group 59, Department of State, Office of Chinese Affairs, Box 14,

306, U.S. Policy toward China and the Far East File; Acheson to Robert C. Strong, Oct. 28, 1949, *Foreign Relations,* 1949, vol. 9, p. 401; Acheson to MacDonald, Oct. 28, 1949, ibid., pp. 401–2; MacDonald to Acheson, Oct. 31, 1949, ibid., pp. 403–4; Acheson to MacDonald, Nov. 1, 1949, ibid., pp. 404–5; MacDonald to Acheson, Nov. 3, 1949, ibid., pp. 405–6; MacDonald to Acheson, Nov. 3, 1949, ibid., pp. 406–7; Strong to Acheson, Nov. 4, 1949, ibid., pp. 407–8; MacDonald to Acheson, Nov. 5, 1949, ibid., pp. 408–11.

32. Stuart Memorandum of Conversation, Nov. 6, 1949, *Foreign Relations,* 1949, vol. 9, pp. 412–14; MacDonald to Acheson, Nov. 11, 1949, ibid., pp. 422–23; MacDonald to Acheson, Nov. 14, 1949, ibid., pp. 423–25; Freeman, Memorandum of Conversation (large meeting), Nov. 15, 1949, ibid., vol. 8, pp. 597–99; Acheson to MacDonald, Nov. 18, 1949, ibid., vol. 9, pp. 428–29; Martin, *Divided Counsel,* p. 95; MacDonald to Acheson, Dec. 7, 1949, *Foreign Relations,* 1949, vol. 9, p. 441; Edgar to Acheson, Dec. 14, ibid., pp. 445–46; Edgar to Acheson, Dec. 16, 1949, ibid., p. 446. The State Department also drew up a plan for U.S. reaction in the event that Taiwan fell to the Chinese Communists. Merchant to Butterworth, Dec. 1, 1949, Nat. Arch., Record Group 59, Department of State, Office of Chinese Affairs, Box 14, 306.001, U.S. Policy toward Taiwan File.

33. Office of the Military Attaché, Taipei, Formosa to U.S. Army (CSGID), Jan. 3, 1950, Nat. Arch., Record Group 59, Department of State, Office of Chinese Affairs, Box 18, Lot 56D151 File; Strong to Sprouse, May 11, 1950, ibid.; Strong to Acheson, Dec. 15, 1949, *Foreign Relations,* 1949, vol. 8, pp. 629–30; Acheson to Edgar, Dec. 19, 1949, ibid., vol. 9, pp. 446–47.

34. Acheson to Koo, Jan. 13, 1950, *Foreign Relations,* 1950, vol. 6, pp. 277–78; Memorandum of Conversation by Butterworth (large meeting), Dec. 23, 1949, ibid., 1949, vol. 9, p. 456; K. C. Wu to Sprouse, Dec. 30, 1949, ibid., p. 470; Strong to Acheson, Dec. 31, 1949, ibid., p. 471.

35. NSC 48, in U.S. Department of Defense, *United States–Vietnam Relations, 1945–1967* (Washington, D.C.: GPO, 1971), 8:245; Acheson to Edgar, Dec. 19, 1949, *Foreign Relations,* 1949, vol. 9, pp. 446–47; Edgar to Acheson, Dec. 23, 1949, ibid., pp. 451–55.

36. "Decision Reached by Consensus at the Meeting with the Secretary and the Consultants on the Far East," Nov. 2, 1949, Nat. Arch., Record Group 59, Department of State, Office of Chinese Affairs, Box 14, 306, U.S. Policy toward China and the Far East File; NSC 37/9, Dec. 27, 1949, *Foreign Relations,* 1949, vol. 9, pp. 460–61; Louis F. Johnson to Acheson, Jan. 11, 1950, Nat. Arch., Record Group 59, Department of State, Office of Chinese Affairs, Box 15, 400.5001, China Aid Program 1949 File; NSC

48, in U.S. Department of Defense, *United States–Vietnam Relations, 1945–1967,* 8:244–46; Butterworth to Acheson, Oct. 21, 1949, Nat. Arch., Record Group 59, Department of State, Office of Chinese Affairs, Box 15, 500.3, Aid to China File; U.S. Congress, House, Committee on International Relations, *United States Policy in the Far East,* 7:455–59; Butterworth to Acheson, Dec. 28, 1949, *Foreign Relations,* 1949, vol. 9, pp. 461–63. The military aid plan resulted from a study completed by the Joint Chiefs of Staff in October of 1949. Acheson and Butterworth also objected that this plan would create an irredentist issue for the Soviet Union to exploit in China. Memorandum of Conversation by Acheson (large meeting), Dec. 29, 1949, *Foreign Relations,* 1949, vol. 9, pp. 463–67. Discussions between Undersecretary of the Army Tracy Voorhees and Douglas MacArthur probably increased the Pentagon's concern over the strategic value of Taiwan's airfields, but the Joint Chiefs of Staff already believed that any delay in the fall of Taiwan would give the United States time to build up Southeast Asia's defenses against increased communist infiltration supported by the People's Republic of China. Robert M. Blum, *Drawing the Line* (New York: Norton, 1982), pp. 160–77. For a more exhaustive legislative history of the $75 million China area fund (section 303 of the 1949 Mutual Defense Assistance Act), see Stueck, *Road to Confrontation,* pp. 128–31. Another portion of this aid fund paid for clandestine operations in Taiwan and China. Michael Schaller, *The American Occupation of Japan* (New York: Oxford Univ. Press, 1985), pp. 242–45. NSC 48/2 included a specific confirmation of Acheson's existing Taiwan policy: "The United States should continue the policy set forth in NSC 37/2 and 37/5 of attempting to deny Formosa and the Pescadores to the Chinese Communists through diplomatic and economic means . . . ." NSC 48/2, Dec. 30, 1949, *Foreign Relations,* 1949, vol. 7, pp. 1215–20. Although NSC 48 and NSC 48/2 included other material on Taiwan, the State Department clearly considered the above-cited reaffirmation of the existing policy to be the central element with respect to Taiwan. W. W. Stuart and O. E. Clubb, "Review of NSC Policies Respecting China in the Light of the President's Statement of June 27," July 14, 1950, Nat. Arch., Record Group 59, Department of State, Office of Chinese Affairs, Box 17, 306.0015 File.

37. Smith, *Dean Acheson,* pp. 115–21. For Acheson's letter of transmittal, see U.S. Department of State, *United States Relations with China* (Washington, D.C.: GPO, 1949), pp. III–XVII.

38. Butterworth to George Kennan, Jan. 3, 1950, and enclosed copy of "Agenda for the Meeting with the Secretary, 4 p.m., January 3, 1950," which is addressed to Rusk, Nat. Arch., Record Group 59, Department of State, Office of Chinese Affairs, Box 17, 306.0015, NSC Reports—General

File. The press statement said, "The United States has no desire to obtain special rights or privileges or to establish bases on Formosa at this time." Truman deleted the phrase "or to detach Formosa from China" and added the words "at this time" at the insistence of Omar Bradley—who believed that, in case of war, the United States might need bases on Taiwan. Lucius D. Battle, "Meeting with the President," Jan. 5, 1950, Nat. Arch., Record Group 59, Department of State, Office of Chinese Affairs, Box 16, 306.11, U.S. Policy toward Nationalist China File; Battle, Memorandum of Conversation with Sidney Souers, Jan. 5, 1950, HSTL, Acheson Papers, Box 64B, Jan. 1950 Conversations File; Acheson, Memorandum of Conversation with John Kee, Jan. 4, 1949, ibid.; Acheson, "Extemporaneous Remarks," *Department of State Bulletin* 22 (Jan. 16, 1950): 79–81; Acheson, Memorandum of Conversation with William F. Knowland and H. Alexander Smith, Jan. 5, 1950, HSTL, Papers of Dean Acheson, Box 64B, Jan. 1950 Conversations File. Actually, nearly $5 million worth of military aid from the old program would continue to be delivered, which made Truman's speech look like an exercise in duplicity to the Chinese Communists. This largely negated any beneficial effect on U.S. relations with the Chinese Communists. Butterworth to Webb, Jan. 11, 1950, Nat. Arch., Record Group 59, Department of State, Office of Chinese Affairs, Box 15, 400.5001, China Aid Program 1949 File; Rusk, Memorandum of Conversation (large meeting), Jan. 2, 1950, *Foreign Relations, 1950,* vol. 6, pp. 256–57. Acheson publicly credited Truman with bringing to his attention the fact that the Potsdam Conference (which Truman attended) reiterated the Cairo conference decision on Taiwan, but, in reality, this connection had long since been elaborated in a number of reports, including one by the State Department Legal Adviser, Adrian S. Fisher. Adrian S. Fisher to Butterworth, Jan. 4, 1950, Nat. Arch., Record Group 59, Department of State, Office of Chinese Affairs, Box 15, Lot 56D151 File. Tom Connally helped Acheson set up the January 5 meeting with the Senate committee, and that same day Acheson also met privately with the ranking Republican on the House Committee on Foreign Affairs, Charles Eaton. Blum, *Drawing the Line,* pp. 179–80.

39. Acheson, "Extemporaneous Remarks," 79–81; Acheson, "Crisis in Asia—An Examination of U.S. Policy," *State Department Bulletin* 22 (Jan. 23, 1950): 111–18; Blum, *Drawing the Line,* pp. 182–83.

40. Acheson, "Meeting with the President," Jan. 19, 1950, HSTL, Papers of Dean Acheson, Box 64A, Jan. 1950 Conversations File; U.S. Congress, Senate, Committee on Foreign Relations, *Economic Assistance to China and Korea,* pp. 193–200 and 223–27; Blum, *Drawing the Line,* pp. 186–87. Although Acheson tended to round off the figures, the ECA actually anticipated that $104 million would remain unexpended in the China aid fund as

of Feb. 15, 1950. Of this, the ECA proposed to spend $28,170,000 on Taiwan over the ensuing eighteen months. Since the ECA set down these figures before the defeat of the 1949 Korean aid bill, they did not constitute a compromise to secure China bloc support for the Korean aid bill. Rather, Acheson's part in this compromise consisted of curtailing his proposal for expanding the coverage of the China aid fund to the greater "China area," abandoning his effort to extend the aid program for eighteen months, and scaling down his Korean aid package. ECA, "China Aid Program," Jan. 19, 1950, HSTL, Papers of Clark Clifford, Subject File, Box 2, ECA China Aid Program File.

41. The Nationalists had 300 combat aircraft and 200 transports, nearly all of which had been received from the United States during and after World War II. These aircraft were superior to anything the Chinese Communists had, but their crews were poorly trained and organized. The U.S. advisers who had earlier helped to train the Nationalist Air Force reported that it was of "questionable value." Office of Chinese Affairs, "Status of Forces and Equipment on Formosa," undated, Nat. Arch., Record Group 59, Department of State, Office of Chinese Affairs, Box 18, Records of the Office of Chinese Affairs File. Acheson received at about this time an impressive list of military equipment sent to Taiwan under the 1948 China Aid Act. Among the items listed were 500 armored cars, 194 tanks, 160 aircraft, and enormous quantities of small arms—enough in all to equip a very powerful mechanized force. U.S. Department of State, "List of Military Material Procured or Being Procured for the Chinese Government," Estimated as of Nov. 1, 1949, HSTL, Papers of Dean Acheson, Box 64, Dec. 1949 Conversations File.

42. Interview with Paul H. Nitze, Washington, D.C., July 25, 1989 (hereafter cited as Nitze interview with author).

43. Ibid.; Kennan to author, June 13, 1990. Nitze also recommended in his proposed "two-China policy" that Acheson ask Tom Dewey to be the U.S. Ambassador to Taiwan. As instructed, Nitze burned every copy of this draft policy except one, which he kept in his own safe for some time. Nitze to author, Feb. 12, 1992. Like Nitze, at least one China analyst also concluded that having three separate policies on China and Taiwan had created serious difficulties. Office of Chinese Affairs, untitled three-page document headed "Top Secret" and containing items numbered 1–6, dated only 1950, Nat. Arch., Record Group 59, Department of State, Office of Chinese Affairs, Box 18, Lot 56D151 File.

44. Jack K. McFall, Memorandum of Conversation with Acheson and Smith, Nov. 30, 1949, HSTL, Papers of Dean Acheson, Box 64, Oct.–Nov. 1949 Conversations File; Acheson, "Meeting with the President," Oct. 17,

1949, ibid.; Charlton Ogburn, Memorandum of Conversation (large meeting), April 3, 1950, *Foreign Relations,* 1950, vol. 6, pp. 68–76. On March 29, Jessup told the Senate Committee on Foreign Relations that he believed K. C. Wu to be "a good man" doing "a good job," but he added that Chiang and his cronies would not give Wu a "free hand" to implement more substantial reforms. Thus, Jessup—like others before him—clearly concluded that if Sun Li-jen and K. C. Wu received sufficient authority, the situation on Taiwan would improve rapidly. U.S. Congress, Senate, Committee on Foreign Relations, *Reviews of the World Situation; 1949–1950: Hearings Held in Executive Session before the Committee on Foreign Relations,* 81st Cong., 1st and 2d sess., 1974, pp. 271–72. Max Bishop, formerly Acheson's Director of Northeast Asian Affairs, served throughout 1950 as his representative on the National Security Council Staff. Bishop therefore had full knowledge of both Acheson's intentions and his policies during this period, and he later stated categorically that Acheson never wanted to abandon Taiwan. Bishop interview with author.

45. CIA, Memorandum, Jan. 4, 1950, HSTL, President's Secretary's Files, Box 250, CIA Intelligence Memorandums 1950–52 File; CIA, Review of the World Situation, Jan. 18, 1950, ibid., CIA Intelligence Reports File.

46. Walter McConaughy to Acheson, Feb. 1, 1950, *Foreign Relations,* 1950, vol. 6, pp. 302–4; Merchant to Sprouse, "Formosa," Feb. 1, 1950, Nat. Arch., Record Group 59, Department of State, Office of Chinese Affairs, Box 18, Lot 56D151 File; Sprouse to Merchant, Feb. 15, 1950, ibid.; Memorandum beginning with subsection titled, "Substance," undated, ibid., Formosa and Hainan Islands Jan.–July File. In the absence of a consensus of opinion, the U.S. policy on Taiwan (NSC 37/2 and NSC 37/5) remained unchanged, and Sprouse's views dominated all explanations for the State Department's rejection of further military aid for Taiwan. Charlton Ogburn, "U.S. Policies toward the Far East," March 29, 1950, Nat. Arch., Record Group 59, Department of State, Office of Southeast Asian and Philippine Affairs, Box 5, Philippines and Southeast Asia, 1949, U.S. Policy File, pp. 1–2.

47. Stuart, untitled memorandum, March 16, 1950, Nat. Arch., Record Group 59, Department of State, Office of Chinese Affairs, Box 18, Formosa and Hainan Islands Jan.–July File.

48. W. Walton Butterworth, oral history interview with Richard D. McKenzie and Theodore S. Wilson, Princeton, N.J., July 6, 1971, HSTL, pp. 53–54; footnote 1, *Foreign Relations,* 1950, vol. 1, p. 314; Rusk interview with author; Bishop interview with author; Nitze interview with author.

49. Thomas J. Schoenbaum, *Waging Peace and War* (New York: Simon & Schuster, 1988), pp. 31–32 and 42–43; Rusk interview with author;

Acheson, *Present at the Creation,* p. 369; *New York Times,* April 23, 1950, p. 29. In a letter to Harry Truman dated July 14, 1961, Acheson wrote, "I don't remember a case where you stopped to think of the effect on your fortunes—or the party's for that matter—of a decision in foreign policy." David McCullough, *Truman* (New York: Simon & Schuster, 1992), p. 980; "Notes on the President's Meeting with James Webb," March 26, 1950, HSTL, President's Secretary's Files, Box 159, Secretary of State Subject File.

50. Rusk interview with author. Major General James Burns was the Special Assistant to the Secretary of Defense for Foreign Military Affairs and Assistance. Burns to Rusk, May 29, 1950, *Foreign Relations,* 1950, vol. 6, p. 346; Schoenbaum, *Waging Peace and War,* p. 207. Max Bishop echoed Rusk's assessment of Louis Johnson. Bishop interview with author. In late March, Undersecretary of State James Webb took up Johnson's outrageous behavior with Truman, who thereafter put pressure on Johnson to mend his ways. "Notes on the President's Meeting with James Webb," March 26, 1950, HSTL, President's Secretary's Files, Box 159, Secretary of State Subject File.

51. Even after the outbreak of war in Korea, it required a sustained effort to win approval for NSC 68. First, Acheson secured the support of each member of the Joint Chiefs of Staff; second, he used this support to force Secretary of Defense Johnson to fall in line; and finally, with everything in order, Acheson won Truman over to the new policy. Paul H. Nitze, oral history interview with Richard D. McKenzie, Arlington, Va., June 11 and 17, and Aug. 4, 5, and 6, 1975, HSTL, pp. 244–46; Strong to Acheson (Telegram No. 342), March 2, 1950, HSTL, President's Secretary's Files; Strong to Acheson (Telegram No. 343), March 2, 1950, HSTL, President's Secretary's Files, Box 173, China 1950–51 File. Acheson also orchestrated a meeting between Truman and Li Tsung-jen on March 2 and recommended that in this meeting Truman "remain completely non-committal." Acheson to Truman and enclosed "Biographical Sketch of Li Tsung-jen"), March 1, 1950, ibid. After March 1, 1950, Chiang personally held the positions of Chief of the Nationalist (Kuomintang) Party, President of the Nationalist Government, and Commander in Chief of the Nationalist Army. In theory, Chiang's authority over the army ran through the Executive Yuan to Sun Li-jen to the Army Chief of Staff to the field commanders, but in reality Chiang often exercised his authority directly through the Army Chief of Staff, circumventing Sun Li-jen. Joseph W. Ballantine, *Taiwan* (Washington, D.C.: Brookings Institution, 1952), pp. 98–99.

52. Rusk passed the CIA's assessments and the Pentagon's recommendations on to Acheson without written comment, but he often avoided writ-

ing down his opinions, preferring instead to deliver them orally and only to Acheson. Rusk to Acheson, April 17, 1950, *Foreign Relations, 1950*, vol. 6, p. 330; Strong to Acheson and note 1, April 27, 1950, ibid., pp. 335–39; CIA, "Review of the World Situation," April 19, 1950, HSTL, President's Secretary's Files, Box 250, CIA Intelligence Reports File; Rusk to Acheson, April 26, 1950, *Foreign Relations, 1950*, vol. 6, pp. 333–35; Strong to Acheson and note 1, May 17, 1950, ibid., pp. 340–42.

53. The Nationalists had already received numerous medium tanks, but no heavy tanks or jet aircraft. Acheson to Johnson, March 7, 1950, *Foreign Relations, 1950*, vol. 6, pp. 316–17. Johnson acceded to Acheson's instructions. Johnson to Acheson, May 6, 1950, *Foreign Relations, 1950*, vol. 6, p. 339; Burns to Rusk, May 29, 1950, ibid., pp. 346–47; U.S. Congress, House, Committee on International Relations, *United States Policy in the Far East*, 8:492–95.

54. Jessup, Memorandum of Conversation, Jan. 16, 1950, *Foreign Relations, 1950*, vol. 6, pp. 280–83; W. W. Stuart, Untitled Report on "a United States cultivated *coup d'état* in Formosa," Feb. 20, 1950, Nat. Arch., Record Group 59, Department of State, Office of Chinese Affairs, Box 18, Lot 56D151, Folder TS (1950) #2P Formosa and Hainan Islands Jan.–July, Tab 14.

55. Krentz to Nitze, Merchant, and Rusk, March 9, 1950, Nat. Arch., Record Group 59, Department of State, Office of Chinese Affairs, Box 18, Lot 56D151, 7S (1950)-350.3006 Sun Li-jen File, Tab 63. Some of Dean Rusk's friends initially thought he was indecisive on the Taiwan issue, and he himself admitted to being "deeply impressed" with its "complications and difficulties." Schoenbaum, *Waging Peace and War*, p. 206; U.S. Congress, House, Committee on International Relations, *United States Policy in the Far East*, 8:492.

56. Nitze also suggested a more aggressive attitude toward the People's Republic of China: "Because, so far as we know, no Chinese have come forward with an ideology which can counter Communism, we would have to seek out and work out with selected Chinese a synthetic ideology appealing to the Chinese people. As we did this, we would have to experiment with the disoriented and nebulous resistance elements in China and Formosa, seeking through a process of elimination a reliable organization which could function as an effective instrument of revolution in Communist China." Paul H. Nitze, "Hypothetical Development of the Formosan Situation," May 3, 1950, Nat. Arch., Record Group 59, Department of State, Decimal Files, Box 4195, 793.00/5-350, 1950–54 File.

57. No fewer than nine officials initialed Strong's report, indicating very broad interest in, and knowledge of, Sun's plan. Strong to Sprouse, May

11, 1950, Nat. Arch., Record Group 59, Department of State, Office of Chinese Affairs, Box 18, Lot 56D151 File; Sprouse to Rusk and enclosed report entitled "Formosa Alternatives," May 11, 1950, ibid., Formosa and Hainan Islands Jan.–July File; Memorandum by John Foster Dulles (to Rusk and Nitze), May 18, 1950, *Foreign Relations,* 1950, vol. 1, pp. 314–16.

58. Fisher Howe to W. Park Armstrong, May 31, 1950, *Foreign Relations,* 1950, vol. 6, pp. 347–48. Rusk also included in his final draft to Acheson a verbatim copy of the memorandum Dulles sent him on May 18, 1950. In June, Rusk produced a slightly better organized version of his report, but it contained no significant changes. Draft of Memorandum by Rusk to Acheson, May 30, 1950, ibid., pp. 349–51; Rusk to Acheson, "U.S. Policy toward Formosa," May 30, 1950, Nat. Arch., Record Group 59, Department of State, Office of Chinese Affairs, Box 18, Office of Chinese Affairs 1945–50 File. During World War II, Max Bishop had served in a State Department post in the Far East at the same time when Rusk was there as an army colonel. The two met in India and became friends. Later, in 1949, Acheson instructed Rusk, then his Deputy Undersecretary, to become more involved in Far Eastern Affairs. To help Rusk with this additional responsibility, Acheson made Bishop the Assistant to the Deputy Undersecretary. Bishop's views on the psychological importance of Taiwan may have influenced those of Rusk. Bishop interview with author; Rusk interview with author.

59. Rusk to Acheson, May 30, 1950, "U.S. Policy toward Formosa," Nat. Arch., Record Group 59, Department of State, Office of Chinese Affairs, Box 18, Office of Chinese Affairs 1945–50 File. Fisher Howe, the State Department's Deputy Special Assistant for Intelligence, described in a contemporary memorandum how Rusk thought the United States could force Chiang to resign if Acheson selected that option: "The Gimo [Chiang Kai-shek] would be approached, probably by Dulles in the course of his trip to Japan on June 15, with the word that (a) the fall of Formosa in the present circumstances was inevitable, (b) the US would do nothing to assist [the] Gimo in preventing this, (c) the only course open to the Gimo to prevent the bloodshed of his people was to request UN trusteeship. The US would be prepared to back such a move for trusteeship and would ready the fleet to prevent any armed attack on Formosa while the move for trusteeship was pending." Rusk probably outlined only his first option to Howe, in keeping with his usual "need-to-know" approach to secrecy. Howe to Armstrong, May 31, 1950, *Foreign Relations,* 1950, vol. 6, pp. 347–49.

60. Rusk submitted with his report a proposed ultimatum to Chiang for use with his first option. He also included proposed statements to the press and to the UN that could be used with the UN strategy, and this in turn could

be implemented in conjunction with either of the options for getting rid of Chiang. Rusk to Acheson, May 30, 1950, "U.S. Policy toward Formosa," Nat. Arch., Record Group 59, Department of State, Office of Chinese Affairs, Box 18, Office of Chinese Affairs 1945–50 File. In response to a query from Rusk, the government of the Philippines made it clear that Chiang would not be welcome there if he was forced to flee Taiwan. Editorial note 2, *Foreign Relations,* 1950, vol. 6, p. 346.

61. Howe indicated that Rusk hoped to discuss his Taiwan memorandum with Acheson on May 31, and Acheson's files show that Rusk did meet privately with Acheson on that date. Howe to Armstrong, May 31, 1950, *Foreign Relations,* 1950, vol. 6, pp. 347–49; Listing for May 31, 1950, Appointments File, HSTL, Papers of Dean Acheson; Schoenbaum, *Waging Peace and War,* p. 209; Agenda for June 1, 1950, President's Appointment File, HSTL, President's Secretary's Files. Acheson found the situation so serious at this point that he authorized the gradual reduction of U.S. personnel on Taiwan to facilitate total withdrawal in the event that a Communist invasion made this necessary. Acheson to Embassy in China, May 26, 1950, *Foreign Relations,* 1950, vol. 6, pp. 344–56.

62. For more on the 1944 plot, based on Dorn's own account, see Michael Schaller, *The U.S. Crusade in China, 1938–1945* (New York: Columbia Univ. Press, 1979), pp. 151–53. In Dec. 1985, the Presidio Army Museum displayed an exhibit titled "Behind Enemy Lines—OSS Detachment 101." Eric Saul, the curator of this exhibit, told the reporter Bill Boldenweck, that Stilwell "set Detachment 101 the task of taking Chiang out of the picture." "They worked at it for two months," Saul explained, "but the effort came to nothing and was dropped." Bill Boldenweck, "Well-kept War Secret Gets Its Due," *Chicago Tribune,* 20 Dec. 1985, p. A41; Schoenbaum, *Waging Peace and War,* pp. 84, 89, and 106. When questioned by the author, Rusk denied any knowledge of the 1944 assassination plan and repeatedly declined to discuss the 1950 plan for a coup d'état. Otherwise quite congenial and helpful, Rusk freely discussed all other issues. Rusk interview with author. Telephone interviews with Dean Rusk, to Athens, Ga., July 16 and Nov. 30, 1988.

63. Albert Chow had a long relationship with Truman, and he occasionally delivered his information in person. On one such visit, Chow brought with him a close friend—Mrs. W. F. Doon. Mrs. Doon, who was Chinese and pregnant, sat in the President's chair and silently wished for a boy. She subsequently gave birth to a boy, credited his gender to the chair, and named him Truman. When apprised of this amusing turn of events, the President approved of the name but cautioned Chow that his chair could not always guarantee "the desired effect." Truman, it seems, did not want to find a bevy

of pregnant Chinese women queuing up at his office door. Albert K. Chow to Harry H. Vaughn, Jan. 4, 1947, HSTL, Papers of Harry S. Truman, General File, Box 442, Albert Chow File; Chow to Truman, Dec. 27, 1949, ibid.; Truman to Chow, Dec. 31, 1949, ibid.; Ross [first name unknown] to Acheson, March 9, 1950, ibid.; Chow to Truman and enclosed report, Feb. 3, 1950, HSTL, President's Secretary's Files, Box 173, Foreign Affairs—China 1950–52 File; Chow to Truman, July 5, 1950, ibid.; Chiang Kai-shek to Truman, May 23, 1950, HSTL, Official File, Box 633, 1950–53 File.

64. Karl W. V. Nix to Truman, Feb. 25, 1949, HSTL, Papers of Harry S. Truman, General File, Box 1768, Karl W. V. Nix File. Truman tried unsuccessfully to get Nix appointed to the Philippine Survey Commission. Memorandum by William M. Boyle, June 30, 1950, ibid. Nix also asked Truman to appoint him to the rank of Brigadier General in the U.S. Army Intelligence Reserve, but there is no evidence that Truman took this seriously. Nix to Bess Truman, March 19, 1951, ibid.; Nix to Truman with enclosed memoranda, March 4, 1951, "Reorganization of the Chinese Nationalist Government," ibid., p. 2; Jessup, Memorandum of Conversation (large meeting), June 26, 1950, *Foreign Relations,* 1950, vol. 7, pp. 178–80.

65. Truman dispatched Nix to Taiwan before receiving Rusk's full plan, which may indicate that Acheson discussed its general content with Truman in March, April, or early May. In his letter of May 23, 1950, Sun Li-jen alluded to "the strategic importance of Taiwan," depicted the suffering of the Chinese people under Communist rule, and then added,

> Taiwan must also be held as a source of encouragement to those who are revolting against the rule of the Communists by waging guerrilla warfare behind their lines. It will give them the satisfaction of knowing that they are not engaged in a hopeless task, and the hope that someday they will be able to work in conjunction with an outside force that will unseat their oppressors. Taiwan must be held then as a base from which, when the time comes, a counter attack on the mainland will be launched. As long as Taiwan stands the Communists will have to keep a large part of their troops within the boundaries of mainland China, and we may be reasonably sure that as soon as Taiwan falls, the Communists will let loose their troops on Indo-China, Burma, the Philippines, and the other countries of Southeast Asia.

After choosing not to respond to Sun's letter, Truman labeled it accordingly on June 20, but his secretary did not file the letter until June 26, the day he ordered the Seventh Fleet into the Formosa Strait. Sun Li-jen to Truman, May 23, 1950, HSTL, Harry S. Truman Papers, Official File, Box 633, 1950–53 File. Interestingly enough, Truman's other unofficial envoy, Albert

Chow, was on Taiwan at the same time that Nix was there, and he returned with a letter to Truman from Chiang Kai-shek which had the same date as the letter to Truman from Sun Li-jen carried by Nix. Chiang Kai-shek to Truman (carried by Albert Chow), May 23, 1950, ibid.

66. Strong estimated the strength of the Nationalist Army at 410,000 men. Whether this represented an actual increase over the CIA's original estimate or simply an alternative figure is unclear. Strong to Acheson, June 7, 1950, *Foreign Relations, 1950,* vol. 6, pp. 359–60; "U.S. Defense Chiefs Back from Orient," June 25, 1950, *New York Times,* p. 18; Schaller, *American Occupation of Japan,* pp. 264–65. The CIA indicated that although Mao Tse-tung avoided any public commitments to invade Taiwan during 1950, this remained a high probability. Memorandum on "Mao Tse-tung's Speech to the Chinese Communist Party Central Committee," June 19, 1950, HSTL, President's Secretary's Files, Box 250, CIA Intelligence Memorandums 1950–52 File.

67. Memorandum of Conversation by Jessup (large meeting), June 25, 1950, *Foreign Relations, 1950,* vol. 7, pp. 157–83; Jessup, Memorandum of Conversation (large meeting), June 26, 1950, ibid., pp. 178–83; Webb to John Snyder, April 25, 1975, HSTL, Papers of James E. Webb.

68. Editorial note, *Foreign Relations, 1950,* vol. 6, p. 367; Johnson to Acheson, April 14, 1950, ibid., pp. 780–84; Rusk, "Condensed Check List on China and Formosa," June 29, 1950, Nat. Arch., Record Group 59, Department of State, Office of Chinese Affairs, Box 17, 306.001, U.S. Policy toward China File; Acheson, *Present at the Creation,* p. 412. Rusk later had a conversation with a high Nationalist official who claimed that he was the one who had first proposed to Chiang Kai-shek the idea of offering Nationalist troops for the war in Korea. This unnamed official told Rusk that Chiang made the offer only after being assured that it would be turned down by the United States. Schoenbaum, *Waging Peace and War,* p. 213.

69. CIA, "Situation Summary," July 20, 1950, HSTL, Papers of Harry S. Truman, President's Secretary's Files, Box 250, CIA Situation Summary File; Stueck, *Road to Confrontation,* pp. 210–11; Acheson to Johnson, July 31, 1950, *Foreign Relations, 1950,* vol. 6, pp. 402–4.

70. The British remained concerned that U.S. weapons sent to Taiwan might be turned against Hong Kong if Taiwan fell, but the Joint Chiefs of Staff had secretly decided to write off Hong Kong if it were attacked. At this time, O. Edmund Clubb took over the Office of Chinese Affairs. Stuart and Clubb to Rusk and Merchant, "Review of NSC Policies Respecting China in the Light of the President's Statement of June 27," Nat. Arch., Record Group 59, Department of State, Office of Chinese Affairs, Box 17, Lot 306.0015 File; JCS to Johnson, July 27, 1950, *Foreign Relations, 1950,*

vol. 6, pp. 391–94; Johnson to Acheson, July 29, 1950, ibid., p. 401; Acheson to Johnson, July 31, 1950, ibid., pp. 402–4; NSC 37 / 10 received approval from the President on July 27, 1950, at the sixty-second meeting of the NSC, but with some revisions indicated. The NSC staff completed the revised version on August 3, 1950. NSC 37 / 10, Aug. 3, 1950, ibid., pp. 413–14 and 414 n. 4; Memorandum by Richard E. Johnson, Dec. 7, 1950, ibid., pp. 591–96; Acheson to Embassy in the United Kingdom, Aug. 13, 1950, pp. 431–33. MacArthur wanted to base U.S. Air Force squadrons on Taiwan, but the Joint Chiefs of Staff blocked this idea. JCS to Douglas MacArthur, Aug. 14, 1950, ibid., p. 439.

71. Editorial note, *Foreign Relations, 1950,* vol. 6, p. 515; Acheson to the Embassy in the United Kingdom, July 28, 1950, ibid., pp. 396–98; Acheson to the U.S. Mission at the United Nations, Sept. 8, 1950, ibid., pp. 492–93; CIA, "Situation Summary," Sept. 8, 1950, HSTL, Papers of Harry S. Truman, President's Secretary's Files, Box 250, CIA Situation Summary File; John M. Allison, Memorandum of Conversation with Acheson, John Foster Dulles, Lucius Battle, and John Allison, Oct. 23, 1950, HSTL, Papers of Dean Acheson, Box 65, Oct. 1950 Conversations File; Anonymous, "M / C on Formosa" (notes on the meeting of Acheson, Dulles, Battle, and Allison), Oct. 23, 1950, ibid., Box 167, Conversations on China File; Clubb, Memorandum of Conversation by Clubb with Rusk and Koo, Sept. 19, 1950, *Foreign Relations, 1950,* vol. 6, pp. 510–13; CIA, "Situation Summary," Sept. 29, 1950, HSTL, Papers of Harry S. Truman, President's Secretary's File, Box 250, CIA Situation Summary File; Acheson to Marshall, Dec. 4, 1950, *Foreign Relations, 1950,* vol. 6, pp. 587–88. In October, the State Department expected aid to Taiwan for the current fiscal year to reach $45–$50 million. Memorandum of Conversation by Robert N. Magill (large meeting), Oct. 11, 1950, ibid., pp. 524–25. In December, Acheson notified the Defense Department that he had deferred UN action on Taiwan, that he wanted the Joint Chiefs of Staff to again review Taiwan's strategic importance, and that he would soon request a full-scale NSC review of the existing Taiwan policy. Acheson to Marshall, Dec. 4, 1950, ibid., pp. 587–88.

72. Assistant Military Attaché in Taipei to the Department of Defense, July 29, 1950, Nat. Arch., Record Group 59, Department of State, Office of Chinese Affairs, Box 18, Lot 56D151 File; Strong to Clubb, Sept. 6, 1950, *Foreign Relations, 1950,* vol. 6, pp. 485–88.

73. Merchant to Krentz, Nov. 22, 1950, Nat. Arch., Record Group 59, Department of State, Office of Chinese Affairs, Box 17, 306001, U.S. Policy toward China File.

74. Nix to Truman and enclosed Memorandum entitled "Reorganization

of the Chinese Nationalist Government," March 4, 1951, HSTL, Papers of
Harry S. Truman, General File, Box 1768, Karl W. V. Nix File.

CHAPTER FIVE: Acheson and
the American Cold War with China

1. Proven coal reserves in 1948 stood at 2,800 billion metric tons in the
United States, against only 284 billion metric tons in China. In iron ore, the
United States had 10.5 billion metric tons; China, only 4.6 billion metric
tons. Estimates of China's population varied from 300 million to 600 million, with 450 million being accepted by the PPS. PPS, PPS-39, "United
States Policy toward China," Sept. 7, 1948, U.S. Department of State, *The
State Department Policy Planning Staff Papers,* 3 vols. (New York: Garland, 1983), 2:412–46. The historian June Grasso has emphasized a different report—"Problems of Domestic and Foreign Policy Confronting the
Chinese Communists," completed on July 28, 1948, by the State Department's Office of Intelligence Research—but this report never became policy.
The official policy, NSC 34 / 1, grew out of PPS 39—which was quite different from the report Grasso discusses—and, indeed, much of NSC 34 / 1
is identical to PPS 39. See June M. Grasso, *Truman's Two-China Policy*
(New York: M. E. Sharpe, 1987), pp. 59–60. The PPS also wrote another
report in November, PPS 39 / 1, but this only updated certain background
information, without revising the conclusions of the original report. PPS,
PPS 39 / 1, Nov. 24, 1948, U.S. Department of State, *State Department
Policy Planning Staff Papers,* 2:447–51.

2. NSC 34 / 1, Jan. 11, 1949, *Foreign Relations,* 1949, vol. 9, pp. 474–
75.

3. William Green and Gordon Swanborough, "The Zero Precursor," *Air
Enthusiast* 19 (Aug.–Nov. 1982): 37; John Leighton Stuart to Acheson,
Dec. 1, 1948, *Foreign Relations,* 1948, vol. 7, pp. 625–27.

4. Nancy Bernkopf Tucker, *Patterns in the Dust* (New York: Columbia
Univ. Press, 1983), pp. 60–66; Stuart to Acheson, Dec. 21, 1948, *Foreign
Relations,* 1948, vol. 7, pp. 674–77; Stuart to Acheson, Jan. 21, 1949,
ibid., 1949, vol. 8, pp. 65–66; Stuart to Acheson, Jan. 26, 1949, ibid., p.
86; John M. Cabot to Acheson, Jan. 28, 1949, ibid., pp. 91–92.

5. PPS, PPS-39 / 2, Feb. 25, 1949, U.S. Department of State, *State
Department Policy Planning Staff Papers,* 3:25–28; Paragraph 18 of NSC
34 / 2 remains classified, but it is available in PPS 39 / 2, which is identical
to NSC 34 / 2. NSC 34 / 2, Feb. 28, 1949, *Foreign Relations,* 1949, vol. 9,
pp. 491–95; James S. Lay to the NSC, March 3, 1949, ibid., p. 499.

6. Gaddis Smith, *Dean Acheson,* vol. 15 of *American Secretaries of State and Their Diplomacy,* ed. Samuel Flagg Bemis and Robert H. Ferrell (New York: Cooper Square, 1972), p. 108. Dean Rusk remembered that Acheson generally preferred to be led on policy toward the Chinese Communists, rather than to take the lead himself. Interview with Dean Rusk, Athens, Ga., April 11, 1988 (hereafter cited as Rusk interview with author); interview with Max Bishop, Ailey, Ga., April 12, 1988 (hereafter cited as Bishop interview with author); interview with Paul Nitze, Washington, D.C., July 25, 1989 (hereafter cited as Nitze interview with author); Office of Far Eastern Affairs, "United States Interests in China," dated only 1949, HSTL, Papers of Harry S. Truman, President's Secretary's Files, Box 173, China 1949 File.

7. Department of State Office of Intelligence Research, "Japan's Expanding Trade with Communist China," IR 7445, March 21, 1957, Nat. Arch., Record Group 59, Department of State, OSS / State Department Intelligence and Research Reports, Box 59, 1945–49 File. Edwin M. Martin, Acting Chief of the Office of Occupied Areas Economic Affairs, and Robert A. Feary, attached to the Office of Northeast Asian Affairs, had each pointed out the importance of Sino-Japanese trade. Nancy Bernkopf Tucker, "American Policy toward Sino-Japanese Trade in the Postwar Years: Politics and Prosperity," *Diplomatic History* 8 (Summer 1984): 185–87 and 198; "Joe" to Dean Acheson with enclosed report, "United States Policy in China," Nov. 3, 1948, HSTL, Papers of Dean Acheson, Box 27, China 1948–49 File. Japanese figures for 1935 show that China accounted for 10.7 percent of Japan's imports and for 17.5 percent of its exports. Jerome B. Cohen, *Japan's Postwar Economy* (Bloomington: Indiana Univ. Press, 1958), pp. 119–20.

8. W. Walton Butterworth to Carlisle H. Humelsine, "Papers for NSC on Policy regarding Trade with China," Feb. 16, 1949, Nat. Arch., Record Group 59, Department of State, Office of Chinese Affairs, Box 15, 500.004, U.S. Policy toward China File; NSC 41 (with note by Sidney Souers), Feb. 28, 1949, *Foreign Relations,* 1949, vol. 9, pp. 826–34; Sidney Souers to NSC, March 3, 1949, ibid., p. 834; Rusk interview with author; Bishop interview with author.

9. NSC 41, Feb. 28, 1949, *Foreign Relations,* 1949, vol. 9, pp. 826–34. Nitze likewise felt that China's economic potential was negligible, and this may have helped to confirm Acheson's opinion. Nitze interview with author.

10. NSC 41, Feb. 28, 1949, *Foreign Relations,* 1949, vol. 9, pp. 826–34. The ECA also withdrew U.S. assistance to Communist-occupied areas and curtailed aid to those areas likely soon to be occupied by Communist

forces. Roger D. Lapham to Paul Hoffman, March 9, 1949, ibid., pp. 626–30.

11. Stuart to Acheson, March 10, 1949, *Foreign Relations,* 1949, vol. 8, pp. 173–77; Stuart to Acheson, May 11, 1949, in *The Forgotten Ambassador: The Reports of John Leighton Stuart, 1946–1949,* ed. Kenneth W. Rea and John C. Brewer (Boulder, Colo.: Westview, 1981) (hereafter cited as Rea and Brewer, *Stuart Reports*), pp. 322–23 and 319n; Stuart to Acheson, Jan. 26, 1949, *Foreign Relations,* 1949, vol. 8, pp. 667–68; Acheson to Stuart, April 12, 1949, ibid., p. 679; Butterworth to Acheson, April 14, 1949, Nat. Arch., Record Group 59, Department of State, Office of Chinese Affairs, Box 14, 030.001, Ambassador Stuart File; Lewis Clark to Acheson, April 15, 1949, ibid., Box 14, Status of the Ambassador and Embassy in China File; Acheson to Stuart, April 6, 1949, *Foreign Relations,* 1949, vol. 8, pp. 230–31; Stuart to Acheson, May 3, 1949, ibid., vol. 9, pp. 14–15; Stuart to Acheson, May 14, 1949, ibid., vol. 8, pp. 745–47; Stuart to Acheson, June 8, 1949, ibid., pp. 752–53; Edwin W. Martin, *Divided Counsel* (Lexington: Univ. Press of Kentucky, 1986), pp. 27–31.

12. O. Edmund Clubb to Acheson, June 1, 1949, *Foreign Relations,* 1949, vol. 8, pp. 357–60; Stuart to Acheson, June 30, 1949, ibid., pp. 766–67; Acheson to Stuart, July 1, 1949, ibid., p. 769; Office of the Military Attaché, Nanking, to Department of the Army, Nat. Arch., Record Group 59, Department of State, Office of Chinese Affairs, Box 14, 030.001, Ambassador Stuart File.

13. John Leighton Stuart, *Fifty Years in China* (New York: Random House, 1954), pp. 247–48; Stuart to Acheson, June 30, 1949, *Foreign Relations,* 1949, vol. 8, pp. 766–67; Davies to Kennan, June 30, 1949, ibid., pp. 768–69; Acheson to Stuart, July 1, 1949, ibid., p. 769. John Cabot thought that Acheson's decision on the Stuart invitation resulted from domestic politics; Louis Clark thought it resulted from a lack of confidence in Stuart. Two important facts, however, support Butterworth's account against Cabot's and Clark's. First, NSC 34 / 2—approved by Truman—specified the need for a clandestine rather than a public approach to relations with the Chinese Communists, because a public approach would risk serious international complications. Butterworth's account simply shows Acheson complying with official policy, as Acheson almost invariably did. Second, Acheson made this decision in consultation with Butterworth, and not with either Cabot or Clark. John M. Cabot, oral history interview with Richard D. McKinzie, Manchester, Mass., July 18, 1973, HSTL (hereafter cited as Cabot, HSTL Oral History), pp. 83–84; Mao Tse-tung, *Selected Works of Mao Tse-tung* (Beijing: Foreign Languages Press, 1961), pp. 414–17. Acheson undoubtedly took Mao Tse-tung's essay at face value, since Stuart told him that it was

"an unprecedentedly clear exposition of just where [the] top leadership of [the] CCP stands." Stuart to Acheson, July 6, 1949, *Foreign Relations, 1949*, vol. 8, pp. 405–7.

14. Dean Rusk to author, Feb. 1, 1991. Four other elements tend to indicate that Stuart was the man who conducted these talks with Chou En-lai and that he did so in July. First, the summary of the talks with Chou En-lai alludes to the prospect of a visit to Beijing, and only Stuart contemplated such a visit. Second, Stuart apprised Acheson of the keen disappointment felt by Mao Tse-tung and Chou En-lai over Stuart's failure to accept their back-channel invitation to Beijing. Third, although Stuart usually communicated with Washington almost every day, none of his communications for the period July 19–Aug. 2 have survived. These communications probably discussed the talks with Chou, and someone probably destroyed them before the Republicans took office in 1953. Fourth, Stuart, and only Stuart, received an exemption from the usual baggage search when he left China, as well as special permission to leave with all of his confidential documents. This seems reminiscent of the special treatment Chou provided for Michael Keon after the Chou demarche. "Two Talks with Mr. Chou En-lai," undated, Nat. Arch., Record Group 59, Department of State, Office of Chinese Affairs, Box 16, 320.2057, British-Sino-U.S. Relations and Japan File; Carlisle H. Humelsine to Philip D. Sprouse, Aug. 1, 1949, ibid., Box 14, 300, China General Status of Ambassador and Embassy at Nanking File; Stuart to Acheson, July 14, 1949, Rea and Brewer, *Stuart Reports,* pp. 337–38; Stuart to Acheson, July 18, 1949, *Foreign Relations,* 1949, vol. 8, p. 791.

15. Stuart, "Notes on a Future American China Policy," July 14, 1949, Nat. Arch., Record Group 59, Department of State, Office of Chinese Affairs, Box 14, U.S. Policy toward China and the Far East File; Bishop interview with author.

16. Ward to Acheson, Dec. 11, 1949, *Foreign Relations,* 1949, vol. 8, pp. 1047–50; Acheson to Clubb, March 2, 1949, ibid., pp. 943–44; Clubb to Acheson, March 8, 1949, ibid., pp. 944–45; Clubb to Acheson, March 18, 1949, ibid., p. 946.

17. Merrill C. Gay to John P. Davies, May 11, 1949, Nat. Arch., Record Group 59, Department of State, Office of Chinese Affairs, 306.0015, 1949 NSC 41 File; Cabot to Acheson, July 7, 1949, *Foreign Relations,* 1949, vol. 8, pp. 1202–5; Cabot to Acheson, July 8, 1949, ibid., p. 1207; Cabot to Acheson, July 8, 1949, ibid., pp. 1208–9; Cabot to Acheson, July 9, 1949, ibid., pp. 1212–13; Cabot, HSTL Oral History, pp. 77–79.

18. Cabot to Acheson, July 9, 1949, *Foreign Relations,* 1949, vol. 8, pp. 1220–22; Humelsine to Sprouse, Aug. 1, 1949, Nat. Arch., Record Group 59, Department of State, Office of Chinese Affairs, Box 14, China—

General Status of Ambassador and Embassy at Nanking File; Acheson, Memorandum of Conversation with Harry S. Truman, July 18, 1949, *Foreign Relations,* 1949, vol. 8, p. 793. Stuart considered visiting the Nationalist leadership at Canton, but Butterworth advised Acheson against this on the grounds that it would prejudice Stuart's ability to return later to a Communist-dominated China, and Acheson accepted Butterworth's advice. Butterworth to Acheson, "Ambassador Stuart's Projected Trip to Canton," July 18, 1949, Nat. Arch., Record Group 59, Department of State, Office of Chinese Affairs, Box 14, 030.001, Ambassador Stuart File; Memorandum by Davies, Aug. 24, 1949, *Foreign Relations,* 1949, vol. 9, pp. 536–40. Davies actually sent an initial copy of his memorandum to Sprouse on August 21, 1949. Memorandum by Davies, Aug. 21, 1949, Nat. Arch., Record Group 59, Department of State, Office of Chinese Affairs, Box 16, 350.1001, 1949 Communists in China File; Raymond B. Fosdick to Philip C. Jessup, "Some Notes on an Approach to China," Aug. 29, 1949, ibid., Box 14, 306, U.S. Policy toward China and the Far East File. Cabot, who was suffering from "stomach trouble," left China with Stuart on August 2, 1949. Cabot, HSTL Oral History, pp. 88–89.

19. Ward to Acheson, Dec. 11, 1949, *Foreign Relations,* 1949, vol. 8, pp. 1047–50; Clubb to Acheson, Oct. 2, 1949, ibid., vol. 9, pp. 93–94; Acheson to Certain Diplomatic and Consular Offices, Oct. 13, 1949, ibid., vol. 8, p. 1323; Acheson to Clubb, Oct. 14, 1949, ibid., p. 982; Acheson to Clubb, Sept. 23, 1949, ibid., pp. 979–80; Clubb to Acheson, Oct. 26, 1949, ibid., pp. 984–85; Clubb to Acheson, Oct. 27, 1949, ibid., pp. 986–87; Clubb to Acheson, Oct. 27, 1949, ibid., p. 987; Acheson to Clubb, Oct. 28, 1949, ibid., pp. 988–89; Clubb to Acheson, Nov. 4, 1949, ibid., vol. 8, pp. 1000–1002; Clubb to Acheson, Nov. 28, 1949, ibid., vol. 8, pp. 1026–28; R. H. Hillenkoetter (Director of the CIA), "Consul General Angus Ward," received Oct. 18, 1949, Nat. Arch., Record Group 59, Department of State, Office of Chinese Affairs, Box 14, 306.001, American Foreign Policy toward Formosa File; Rusk interview with author.

20. James E. Webb, "Meeting with the President, Monday, November 14," Nov. 14, 1949, Nat. Arch., Record Group 59, Department of State, Office of Chinese Affairs, Box 14, 123.002, Ward Case—Mukden 1949–50 File; Acheson, Memorandum of Conversation with Truman, Nov. 17, 1949, HSTL Papers of Dean Acheson, Box 64, Oct.–Nov. 1949 Conversations File; Acheson to Truman (with cover letter to file clerk William Hopkins), Nov. 21, 1949, HSTL, President's Secretary's Files, Box 173, China 1949 File; Acheson, Memorandum of Conversation with the President, Nov. 21, 1949, HSTL, Papers of Dean Acheson, Box 64, Oct.–Nov. Conversations File. The Joint Chiefs of Staff drew up a report on the situation in

China, in which they recommended against a naval blockade or any other military action. Although this report was dated November 18, Acheson received it on the twenty-first, and Truman must have received it after Acheson had already dissuaded him from taking military action. Omar Bradley to Louis Johnson, Nov. 18, 1949, *Foreign Relations,* 1949, vol. 8, pp. 1011–13 and 1011 n. 65.

21. Ward to Acheson, Dec. 11, 1949, *Foreign Relations,* 1949, vol. 8, pp. 1047–50; Clubb to Acheson, Nov. 27, 1949, ibid., pp. 1023–24; Clubb to Acheson, Nov. 23, 1949, ibid., p. 1020; Clubb to Acheson, Nov. 28, 1949, ibid., pp. 1026–28; Acheson to Truman, "Recent Developments in the Mukden Case," Nov. 21, 1949, HSTL, President's Secretary's Files, Box 173, China 1949 File; Clubb to Acheson, Nov. 21, 1949, *Foreign Relations,* 1949, vol. 8, p. 1021; Clubb to Acheson, Dec. 1, 1949, ibid., p. 1029. For a detailed account of the charges of spying leveled against the U.S. consulate at Mukden, see Clubb to Acheson, Dec. 3, 1949, ibid., pp. 1035–37; and Clubb to Acheson, December 3, 1949, ibid., pp. 1037–38; Clubb to Acheson, Dec. 6, 1949, ibid., p. 1042; Alfred T. Wellborn to Acheson, Dec. 15, 1949, ibid., pp. 1050–51. After the trial of Angus Ward, James Webb ordered Clubb to deliver a letter of protest to Chou En-lai, which Clubb did without significant results. Webb to Clubb, Nov. 26, 1949, ibid., p. 1022; Clubb to Acheson, Nov. 28, 1949, ibid., p. 1024.

22. Clubb to Acheson, Nov. 28, 1949, *Foreign Relations,* 1949, vol. 8, pp. 1026–28. Ward felt that his treatment might have marked an effort by "pro-Moscow elements in the CCP" to "drive a wedge between the United States and sympathetic elements in the CCP." Wellborn to Acheson, Dec. 10, 1949, ibid., pp. 1044–46. When asked if Acheson took a wait-and-see attitude toward diplomatic recognition for the PRC, Max Bishop replied, "I wouldn't say it was a wait-and-see attitude; it was a conscious decision not to recognize them, and to recognize that they were an inimically antagonistic force in Asia. It wasn't a wait-and-see attitude; I'm sure of it!" Bishop interview with author. Rusk later recalled, "When Mao Tse-tung and his colleagues came to power, they selected the United States as enemy number one. They tried to erase all traces of one hundred years of good relations between the Chinese people and the American people. They, for example, charged that the great Beijing Union Medical College that had been built by the Rockefeller Foundation was simply a device for Americans to practice vivisection on Chinese. That was the leading medical facility in all of Asia at the time." Rusk interview with author; Livingston T. Merchant, oral history interview with Richard D. McKinzie, Washington, D.C., May 27, 1975, HSTL, pp. 36–37; Charlton Ogburn, Jr., Memorandum on "Decisions Reached by Consensus at the Meetings with the Secretary and the Meetings

with the Secretary and the Consultants on the Far East," Nov. 2, 1949, *Foreign Relations,* 1949, vol. 9, pp. 160–61; Matthew Connelly, "Notes from Cabinet Meeting," Dec. 22, 1949, HSTL, Papers of Matthew Connelly, Cabinet Notes Files, Box 1, Jan. 3–Dec. 30, 1949, File; NSC 48 / 2, Dec. 30, 1949, *Foreign Relations,* 1949, vol. 7, pp. 1215–20. Also in early December, Philip Jessup, Ambassador-at-Large, began planning his fourteen-nation tour of the Far East (December 15, 1949–March 15, 1950), and Jessup raised the possibility of stopping in Beijing for "exploratory conversations with Mao Tze tung." Butterworth, Sprouse, and Jessup discussed the idea and decided against it. Butterworth to Sprouse, Dec. 10, 1949, Nat. Arch., Record Group 59, Department of State, Office of Chinese Affairs, Box 14, 030.002, Ambassador Jessup's Trip File; note 1, *Foreign Relations,* 1950, vol. 6, p. 11.

23. Butterworth, Memorandum of Conversation (large meeting), Sept. 9, 1949, Nat. Arch., Record Group 59, Department of State, Office of Chinese Affairs, Box 17, 306.0011, U.S. Policy toward Communist China File; Acheson, Memorandum of Conversation (large meeting), Sept. 13, 1949, *Foreign Relations,* 1949, vol. 9, pp. 81–85; Acheson, Memorandum of Conversation (large meeting), Sept. 17, 1949, ibid., pp. 88–91; British Embassy to the Department of State, Nov. 1, 1949, ibid., pp. 151–54; British Embassy to the Department of State, Nov. 28, 1949, ibid., pp. 200–201; Acheson, Memorandum of Conversation with Sir Oliver Franks and Butterworth, Dec. 8, 1949, ibid., pp. 219–20; British Embassy to the Department of State, "Personal Message from Mr. Bevin to Mr. Acheson," Dec. 16, 1949, ibid., pp. 225–26; Sprouse, Memorandum of Conversation with J. F. Ford, Dec. 24, 1949, ibid., p. 242; Rusk interview with author.

24. Acheson to Stuart, May 13, 1949, *Foreign Relations,* 1949, vol. 9, pp. 21–23; Martin, *Divided Counsel,* pp. 106–12. The State Department apprised the National Security Council that since the U.S. ownership of the barracks building had been approved not only in the 1901 protocol but also in the Sino-American treaty of 1943, "the U.S. position was legally and morally unassailable." The State Department also, however, wanted to try to maintain contact with "all elements" in China to the extent that this remained possible. W. W. Stuart to James S. Lay, Jr., undated, Nat. Arch., Record Group 59, Department of State, Office of Chinese Affairs, Box 17, 306.0015, NSC Reports File; Acheson to Clubb, March 22, 1950, *Foreign Relations,* 1950, vol. 6, pp. 321–22; Rusk to Acheson, April 14, 1950, ibid., pp. 327–28; Rusk to Acheson, April 17, 1950, ibid., pp. 328–29.

25. Windsor G. Hackler (the executive staff officer of the Office of Far Eastern Affairs) to Sprouse, Feb. 3, 1950, Nat. Arch., Record Group 59, Department of State, Office of Chinese Affairs, Box 17, 306.0015, NSC

Papers File; Hackler to Fulton Freeman, June 23, 1950, ibid. On May 2, a group of thirty-five senators, headed by Senator Pat McCarran, sent a letter to Truman requesting him to make it clear that the United States did not intend to recognize the PRC, but by this time Acheson had long since dropped the idea of granting diplomatic recognition to the PRC. Pat McCarran et al., to Truman, May 2, 1950, HSTL, Official Files, Box 633, 1950–51 (150) File. Since no inconsistency existed between the dominant Republican view on this issue and Acheson's current policy, Dean Rusk (then Assistant Secretary for Far Eastern Affairs) recommended on June 9 that Acheson include in his bipartisan foreign policy "an interim policy" of not granting diplomatic recognition to the PRC. Rusk to Acheson, "Bi-partisan Policy on China-Formosa Problems," June 9, 1950, Nat. Arch., Record Group 59, Department of State, Office of Chinese Affairs, Box 17, 306.001, American Foreign Policy toward Formosa File. Rusk later recalled that the Korean War laid the recognition question to rest, but the documentary evidence suggests that Acheson never gave it any serious consideration after January. Rusk interview with author.

26. David S. McLellan, *Dean Acheson* (New York: Dodd, Mead, 1976), pp. 216–17; Warren R. Austin to Acheson, Nov. 20, 1949, *Foreign Relations,* 1949, vol. 9, p. 195; Ruth E. Bacon to Merchant, Dec. 30, 1949, ibid., pp. 258–60; Grasso, *Truman's Two-China Policy,* pp. 142–55. One summary described U.S. policy on China's UN seat as accepting "the majority decisions in [the] UN organs on [the] seating of [the] Chinese Communists." Ogburn to Rusk, March 29, 1950, Nat. Arch., Record Group 59, Department of State, Office of Southeast Asian and Philippine Affairs, Box 5, Southeast Asia 1949 U.S. Policy File; Acheson to Warren R. Austin, March 22, 1950, *Foreign Relations,* 1950, vol. 2, p. 243.

27. Rusk interview with author; Rusk to author, Feb. 1, 1991; Thomas J. Schoenbaum, *Waging Peace and War* (New York: Simon & Schuster, 1988), p. 205; Grasso, *Truman's Two-China Policy,* pp. 156–63; Ruth E. Bacon to Fulton Freeman, June 29, 1950, *Foreign Relations,* 1950, vol. 2, pp. 246–47. G. Hayden Raynor also recommended a policy change, but Rusk cited only Bacon's report. G. Hayden Raynor to George W. Perkins, June 29, 1950, *Foreign Relations,* 1950, vol. 2, p. 245. In a report prepared at the onset of the Korean War, Rusk wrote, ". . . it is recommended that we not only continue to support [Nationalist] Chinese representation in the U.N. but that we exert pressure on key countries such as [the] UK, France and Ecuador affirmatively to side with us on this issue." With the United States blocking any PRC invasion of Taiwan, a closer alignment with the Chinese Nationalists in the UN entailed less risk to American prestige than it had previously. Rusk, "Condensed Checklist on China and Formosa,"

June 29, 1950, Nat. Arch., Record Group 59, Department of State, Office of Chinese Affairs, Box 17, 306.001, U.S. Policy toward China File.

28. Acheson, "Discussion with the President, Item 2, NSC Document No. 41 on Trade with China," Sept. 16, 1949, HSTL, Papers of Dean Acheson, Box 64, Aug.–Sept. 1949 Conversations File; Webb to Charles W. Sawyer, Oct. 4, 1949, *Foreign Relations,* 1949, vol. 9, pp. 878–80; Acheson to Sidney Souers, Nov. 4, 1949, ibid., pp. 890–96; H. S. Foster, "Nineteen Statements from Far East Specialists: Summary of Recommendations," Sept. 30, 1949, Nat. Arch., Record Group 59, Department of State, Office of Chinese Affairs, Box 14, 030.002, Ambassador Jessup's Trip File; Office of Chinese Affairs, "Memorandum for Major General [John A.] Magruder," Dec. 19, 1949, ibid., Box 18, Formosa and Hainan Islands Jan.–July File; NSC 48, U.S. Department of Defense, *United States–Vietnam Relations, 1945–1967* (Washington, D.C.: GPO, 1971), 8:263; NSC 48 / 2, Dec. 30, 1949, *Foreign Relations,* 1949, vol. 7, pp. 1215–20. Technically, NSC 41 was "superseded by section 3.F.(4) of NSC 48 / 2," but NSC 41 was not immediately declared void, and its analysis section—particularly with respect to the desirability of Sino-Japanese trade—continued to carry some weight. O. E. Clubb to W. W. Stuart, "Review of NSC Policies Respecting China in the Light of the President's Statement of June 27," July 12, 1949, Nat. Arch., Record Group 59, Department of State, Office of Chinese Affairs, Box 17, 306.0015 NSC 48 File. Dissatisfied with what had become a patchwork policy (parts of NSC 41 and section 3.F.(4) of NSC 48 / 2), the Defense Department initiated an effort in March of 1950 to write a completely new policy statement. Like their State Department counterparts, Pentagon planners concluded that economic factors would have to be the basis of U.S. policy toward the PRC. They also confirmed that the direct importance of China's trade to the United States was "not great," and that China's trade was "indirectly important to the United States for the achievement of Japanese self-support and independence." The resulting discussions between State and Defense accomplished little, and when the question surfaced again in October, the State Department recommended that the National Security Council "formally void NSC 41, thereby leaving NSC 48 / 2 as the only NSC policy dealing with U.S. policy regarding trade with China." This suggestion ultimately resolved the question. Sprouse to Butterworth, "Defense Redraft of NSC 41" with enclosed copy, March 27, 1950, ibid., Box 17, 306.13, NSC 41 File; Merchant to Philip C. Jessup, "Review of NSC 41," Oct. 31, 1950, ibid., Box 17, 306.0015, NSC 48 File; Department of State, "Memorandum for James C. Lay, Jr.," undated, ibid., Box 17, 306.0015 / 48, NSC 48 File.

29. NSC 34 / 2, Feb. 28, 1949, *Foreign Relations,* 1949, vol. 9, pp. 491–95. Paragraph 18 of NSC 34 / 2 remains classified but is available in

PPS 39 / 2, which is identical to NSC 34 / 2. PPS, PPS-39 / 2, Feb. 25, 1949, U.S. Department of State, *State Department Policy Planning Staff Papers*, 3:25–28. Acheson told the senators, "What we are concerned with in China are two great things. The first one is that whoever runs China, even if the devil himself runs China, if he is an independent devil [*sic*]. That is infinitely better than if he is a stooge of Moscow or [if] China comes under Russia. . . . The second thing is, if we can have somebody other than the Communists running China, we would like that, because Communists try to gravitate to Moscow. Those are our objectives." U.S. Congress, Senate, Committee on Foreign Relations, *Reviews of the World Situation, 1949–1950: Hearings Held in Executive Session before the Committee on Foreign Relations*, 81st Cong., 1st and 2d sess., 1974, pp. 272–73; U.S. Congress, Senate, Committee on Foreign Relations, *Economic Assistance to China and Korea, 1949–1950: Hearings Held in Executive Session before the Committee on Foreign Relations on S. 1063, S. 2319, and S. 2845*, 81st Cong., 1st and 2d sess., 1974, p. 34; Charlton Ogburn, "Remarks on the Situation in China by Consul General McConaughy at the Inter-Departmental Meeting on the Far East," June 2, 1950, *Foreign Relations*, 1950, vol. 6, pp. 352–54; U.S. Department of State, "Soviet Penetration in Northern Areas of China," *Department of State Bulletin* 22 (Feb. 6, 1950): 218–19; Acheson to Embassy in France, Feb. 11, 1950, *Foreign Relations*, 1950, vol. 6, pp. 308–11; editorial note, ibid., pp. 311–12. Merchant rendered the most succinct analysis of Acheson's policy toward the PRC: "Our objective, of course, is to destroy the basis for a durable alliance between the Soviet Union and China." Merchant to Rusk, Nov. 27, 1950, ibid., pp. 581–83.

30. Acheson, "United States Policy toward Asia," *Department of State Bulletin* 22 (March 27, 1950): 469–70; Anonymous (probably Stuart), "Two Talks with Mr. Chou En-lai," undated, Nat. Arch., Record Group 59, Department of State, Office of Chinese Affairs, Box 16, 320.2057, British-Sino-U.S. Relations and Japan File.

31. NSC 41, Feb. 28, 1949, *Foreign Relations*, 1949, vol. 9, pp. 826–34; Rusk interview with author; Bishop interview with author; U.S. Congress, Senate, Committee on Foreign Relations, *Reviews of the World Situation*, p. 135.

32. Rusk interview with author; U.S. Congress, Senate, Committee on Foreign Relations, *Reviews of the World Situation*, pp. 98, 278, and 300. A month after General David G. Barr made his observation, Dr. Edgar D. J. Johnson, Director of the Korean Division of the Economic Cooperation Administration, testified on Korea's trade with Japan, and he noted, "Obviously there would be greater prosperity if the trade relations in the entire Mongolian basin could be restored, but it would be unrealistic to count on that in

any projections." U.S. Congress, Senate, Committee on Foreign Relations, *Economic Assistance to China and Korea,* pp. 83 and 135. The total value of Japan's trade with the PRC for all of 1950, exports and imports, came to just $59,200,000. Department of State, Office of Intelligence Review, Division of Research for Far East, "Intelligence Report IR 7445," March 21, 1957, Nat. Arch., Record Group 59, Department of State, Office of Chinese Affairs, Box 59, Confidential Decimal 1945–49 File; Cohen, *Japan's Postwar Economy,* pp. 119–20.

33. Rusk interview with author.

34. Nitze interview with author; Anonymous (probably Stuart), "Two Talks with Mr. Chou En-lai," undated, Nat. Arch., Record Group 59, Department of State, Office of Chinese Affairs, Box 16, 320.2057, British-Sino-U.S. Relations and Japan File; Acheson, "United States Policy toward Asia," 469–70.

CHAPTER SIX: Acheson and
the American Commitment in Vietnam

1. Paul M. Kattenburg, *The Vietnam Trauma in American Foreign Policy, 1945–1975* (New Brunswick, N.J.: Transaction, 1980), p. 9.

2. Ibid., pp. 7–10; PPS, PPS-51, May 19, 1949, U.S. Department of State, *The State Department Policy Planning Staff Papers,* 3 vols. (New York: Garland, 1983), 3:33–57. Although Indonesia did not receive its independence from Holland until December 27, 1949, the major part of the U.S. effort which brought this about took place earlier, when Acheson was not in the State Department. Acheson, who knew little about either the complex situation in Indonesia or the problems of the Philippines, generally delegated U.S. policy on both of these to his subordinates. For additional details on U.S. diplomatic maneuvers with respect to Indonesia, see Michael Schaller, *The American Occupation of Japan* (New York: Oxford Univ. Press, 1985), pp. 155–57.

3. Edward Doyle, Samuel Lipsman, and the editors of Boston Publishing Company, *Setting the Stage* (Boston: Boston Publishing, 1981), pp. 32 and 100–114; S. L. Mayer, "Indo-China and the French," in *History of the Second World War,* ed. Barrie Pitt (London: BPC Publishing, 1966), p. 3370; Lloyd C. Gardner, *Approaching Vietnam* (New York: Norton, 1968), p. 51.

4. Mayer, "Indo-China and the French," pp. 3370–71; James Pinckney Harrison, *The Endless War* (New York: Free Press, 1982), p. 115; Lauran Paine, *Viet-Nam* (London: R. Hale, 1965), pp. 49–50; Edward R. Drach-

man, *United States Policy toward Vietnam, 1940–1945* (Rutherford, N.J.: Fairleigh Dickinson Univ. Press, 1970), pp. 147–49; Peter A. Poole, *The United States and Indochina, from FDR to Nixon* (Hinsdale: Dryden Press, 1973), pp. 13–14.

5. Gardner, *Approaching Vietnam*, pp. 54–55; George C. Herring, *America's Longest War* (New York: John Wiley, 1979), p. 4; U.S. Department of Defense, *United States–Vietnam Relations, 1944–1967*, 12 vols. (Washington, D.C.: GPO, 1971), 1:A-1-A-2 and 8:16. Gary Hess cites an Office of Strategic Services report dated April 2, 1945, as evidence for what he describes as a Truman administration shift away from Franklin Roosevelt's anticolonial policy in Southeast Asia; in fact, both this report and the policy shift preceded Roosevelt's death. Gary R. Hess, *The United States' Emergence as a Southeast Asian Power, 1940–1950* (New York: Columbia Univ. Press, 1987), pp. 180–84.

6. Interview with Max Bishop, April 12, 1988 (hereafter cited as Bishop interview with author); Acheson to Walter S. Robertson, Oct. 5, 1945, *Foreign Relations, 1945*, vol. 6, p. 313; Hess, *United States' Emergence*, pp. 180–84; John Carter Vincent, "The Post-War Period in the Far East," *Department of State Bulletin* 13 (Oct. 21, 1945): 646.

7. On February 28, 1946, France concluded a treaty with the Chinese Nationalist government, which agreed to recognize French sovereignty in Indochina and remove all Chinese forces from the region. Mayer, "Indo-China and the French," p. 3373; James F. Byrnes to Jefferson Caffery, Feb. 4, 1946, *Foreign Relations, 1946*, vol. 8, p. 23; U.S. Department of Defense, *United States–Vietnam Relations*, 1:A-3 and A-39.

8. Guy De Carmoy, *The Foreign Policies of France, 1944–1968* (Chicago: Univ. of Chicago Press, 1970), pp. 134–35; Michael Dawson Stephens, "South Vietnam: New American Frontier," *Contemporary Review* 204 (Dec. 1963): 306; Kattenburg, *Vietnam Trauma*, pp. 8–9; Bernard Newman, *Background to Viet-Nam* (New York: Roy, 1965), pp. 119–20; Herring, *America's Longest War*, pp. 4–5.

9. George C. Herring, "The Truman Administration and the Restoration of French Sovereignty in Indochina," *Diplomatic History* 1 (Spring 1977): 97; Interview with Dean Rusk, Athens, Ga., 11 April 1988 (hereafter cited as Rusk interview with author). Acheson privately reconfirmed U.S. policy on Indochina on October 5, 1945, two weeks before John Carter Vincent did so publicly. Acheson to Robertson, Oct. 5, 1945, *Foreign Relations, 1945*, vol. 6, p. 313; Acheson to Certain Diplomatic and Consular Officers, May 1, 1946, ibid., 1946, vol. 8, p. 39; Acheson to Certain Diplomatic and Consular Officers, May 13, 1946, ibid., p. 41; Acheson to Certain Diplomatic and Consular Officers, May 14, 1946, ibid., p. 42; Acheson to Charles

S. Reed, Oct. 9, 1946, ibid., p. 61; Acheson to Reed, Dec. 5, 1946, ibid., pp. 67–69; Acheson to Reed for Abbot Low Moffat, Dec. 5, 1946, ibid., pp. 67–69.

10. Acheson to Reed for Moffat, Dec. 5, 1946, *Foreign Relations*, 1946, vol. 8, pp. 67–69; U.S. Department of Defense, *United States–Vietnam Relations*, 1:A-30–A-31 and 8:17–20.

11. U.S. Department of Defense, *United States–Vietnam Relations*, 1:A-39 and 8:93–94.

12. Ibid., 8:95 and 1:A-34; Allan W. Cameron, ed., *Viet-Nam Crisis*, 2 vols. (Ithaca: Cornell Univ. Press, 1971), 1:75.

13. De Carmoy, *Foreign Policies of France*, p. 137; U.S. Department of Defense, *United States–Vietnam Relations*, 1:A-45–A-46.

14. Jefferson Caffery to George C. Marshall, Feb. 6, 1947, *Foreign Relations*, 1947, vol. 6, p. 69; Caffery to Marshall, Feb. 8, 1947, ibid., p. 71; Caffery to Marshall, Feb. 16, 1947, ibid., pp. 73–74; Mayer, "Indo-China and the French," p. 3371; Caffery to Marshall, March 7, 1947, *Foreign Relations*, 1947, vol. 6, pp. 78–80; Caffery to Marshall, March 6, 1947, ibid., pp. 77–78; De Carmoy, *Foreign Policies of France*, pp. 137 and 140; Cameron, *Viet-Nam Crisis*, 1:101. Despite a limited clarification of the political situation in France and a slightly improved understanding of French policy on Indochina, the State Department's picture of events remained somewhat confused in March. A mysterious forgery that purported to be a peace overture from Ho Chi Minh and persistent false rumors of Ho's death contributed to this confusion. Acheson to Embassy in France, March 24, 1947, *Foreign Relations*, 1947, vol. 6, p. 81; Caffery to Marshall, March 27, 1947, ibid., pp. 81–82.

15. Note 43, *Foreign Relations*, 1947, vol. 6, p. 67; Acheson to the Embassy in France, March 24, 1947, ibid., p. 81; Caffery to Marshall, March 27, 1947, ibid., pp. 81–82; James L. O'Sullivan to Marshall, May 7, 1947, ibid., pp. 94–95; Bernard B. Fall, *The Two Viet-Nams* (New York: Praeger, 1964), p. 131; Cameron, *Viet-Nam Crisis*, 1:101; Reed to Marshall, May 7, 1947, *Foreign Relations*, 1947, vol. 6, p. 93; note 92, ibid., p. 93.

16. Marshall to the Embassy in France, May 13, 1947, *Foreign Relations*, 1947, vol. 6, pp. 95–96; Reed to Marshall, May 23, 1947, ibid., p. 100; Edwin F. Stanton to Marshall, June 13, 1947, ibid., pp. 102–3; Acheson to the Consulate at Hanoi, April 4, 1947, ibid., p. 85; Reed to Marshall, June 24, 1947, ibid., pp. 106–7.

17. U.S. Department of Defense, *United States–Vietnam Relations*, 1:A-1–A-4; U.S. Congress, Senate, Committee on Foreign Relations, *The United States and Vietnam: 1944–1947* (Washington, D.C.: GPO, 1972), pp. 11–

14 and 18–19; Herring, *America's Longest War,* pp. 7–8; Poole, *United States and Indochina,* pp. 16–17; Hess, *United States' Emergence,* pp. 162–63; David Schoenbrun, *As France Goes* (New York: Harper, 1957), p. 89; Gordon A. Craig, *Europe since 1815* (New York: Holt, Rinehart and Winston, 1961), p. 774. There is some evidence that Moscow also took a Europe-first approach and that Soviet aspirations for the French Communist Party initially made Stalin reluctant to send strong assistance to Ho Chi Minh's struggling movement. Ho Chi Minh may have likewise anticipated that the French Communist Party would soon secure political control of the French government. Both the United States and the USSR initially tended to exaggerate the strength of the French Communist Party. Mayer, "Indochina and the French," pp. 3371–73.

18. Caffery to Marshall, March 27, 1947, *Foreign Relations,* 1947, vol. 6, pp. 81–82; Caffery to Marshall, April 11, 1947, ibid., pp. 86–87; Reed to Marshall, May 2, 1947, ibid., p. 89; Reed to Marshall, May 21, 1947, ibid., p. 99; Cameron, *Viet-Nam Crisis,* 1:102, 113–14, and 116–17; De Carmoy, *Foreign Policies of France,* p. 136; Mayer, "Indo-China and the French," p. 3373.

19. Mayer, "Indo-China and the French," p. 3373; Cameron, *Viet-Nam Crisis,* 1:102–3, 109–12, and 117; U.S. Department of Defense, *United States–Vietnam Relations,* 1:A-39, A-40, and A-47. Under the influence of his advisers, Bao Dai subsequently renounced the first Ha Long Bay agreement, but it nevertheless served to bring Bao Dai into serious negotiations. De Carmoy, *Foreign Policies of France,* p. 139.

20. Cameron, *Viet-Nam Crisis,* 1:117 and 118.

21. U.S. Department of Defense, *United States–Vietnam Relations,* 1:A-34; Robert A. Lovett to Embassy in France, Jan. 17, 1949, *Foreign Relations,* 1949, vol. 7, pt. 1, pp. 4–5.

22. Cameron, *Viet-Nam Crisis,* 1:103; De Carmoy, *Foreign Policies of France,* p. 138; Kattenburg, *Vietnam Trauma,* p. 11; American Consulate to Acheson, Feb. 12, 1949, U.S. Department of Defense, *United States–Vietnam Relations,* 8:159 and 180–81; Harrison, *Endless War,* p. 115.

23. Acheson to Embassy in France, Feb. 25, 1949, *Foreign Relations,* 1949, vol. 7, pt. 1, p. 8.

24. Cameron, *Viet-Nam Crisis,* 1:103–4 and 120–28; De Carmoy, *Foreign Policies of France,* pp. 139–40.

25. Caffery to Acheson, March 16, 1949, *Foreign Relations,* 1949, vol. 7, pt. 1, pp. 12–14; Gareth Porter, ed., *Vietnam: The Definitive Documentation of Human Decisions,* 2 vols. (New York: Earl M. Coleman, 1979), 1:195; Hess, *United States' Emergence,* p. 323.

26. George M. Abbott to Acheson, May 6, 1949, *Foreign Relations,*

1949, vol. 7, pt. 1, pp. 22–23; Caffery to Acheson, May 7, 1949, ibid., p. 23.

27. Acheson to Abbott, May 7, 1949, *Foreign Relations,* 1949, vol. 7, pt. 1, pp. 23–25; Rusk interview with author.

28. Memorandum of Conversation by Charlton Ogburn, Jr. (large meeting), May 17, 1949, *Foreign Relations,* 1949, vol. 7, pt. 1, p. 27.

29. PPS, PPS-51, March 29, 1949, U.S. Department of State, *State Department Policy Planning Staff Papers,* 3:33–35 and 49–50.

30. Ibid., 3:39–40, 43, and 52–53. Three close advisers—Dean Rusk, Deputy Undersecretary of State; Max Bishop, Chief of Northeast Asian Affairs; and Paul Nitze, Deputy Director of the Policy Planning Staff—all subsequently described Acheson as having little interest in Southeast Asia during 1949. Acheson's lack of interest—together with Southeast Asia's stalled economic recovery and ongoing political turmoil—precluded a more aggressive U.S. policy in the region. Rusk interview with author; Bishop interview with author; interview with Paul Nitze, Washington, D.C., 25 July 1989 (hereafter cited as Nitze interview with author).

31. Nitze interview with author; Kennan to Acheson, May 19, 1949, U.S. Department of State, *State Department Policy Planning Staff Papers,* 3:32; James E. Webb to the Embassy in France, June 6, 1949, *Foreign Relations,* 1949, vol. 7, pt. 1, pp. 38–45. Michael Schaller notes that Acheson sent copies of PPS-51 to the National Security Council and U.S. diplomatic posts in July of 1949 only as a source of information. Schaller asserts that Acheson did this in lieu of submitting PPS-51 to the NSC for approval because of "confusion" within the State Department. In reality, there was no confusion, and Acheson used PPS-51 exactly as Kennan himself recommended in the cover letter. Schaller, *American Occupation of Japan,* p. 163.

32. Webb to the Embassy in France, June 6, 1949, *Foreign Relations,* 1949, vol. 9, pt. 1, pp. 38–39; June 6, 1949; oral history interview with David K. E. Bruce, Washington, D.C., 1 March 1972, by Jerry N. Hess, HSTL, pp. 1, 8, and 14; Dean Acheson, *Present at the Creation* (New York: Norton, 1969), p. 294; Lucius Battle, "Schedule for Loading, Departure and Arrival of the Special Flight of the Independence to Paris on May 20," May 18, 1949, HSTL, Papers of Dean Acheson, Box 64, May–June 1949 File.

33. David Bruce to Acheson, June 13, 1949; *Foreign Relations,* 1949, vol. 7, pt. 1, pp. 45–46; Bruce to Acheson, June 2, 1949, ibid., pp. 36–38.

34. Herbert Tint, *French Foreign Policy since the Second World War* (London: Weidenfeld and Nicolson, 1972), p. 18; Dorothy Pickles, *French Politics* (New York: Royal Institute of International Affairs, 1953), pp. 149–52 and 163.

35. Acheson, *Present at the Creation,* pp. 273–74; French Embassy to

Acheson with enclosed Vietnamese Constitution, Aug. 31, 1949, HSTL, Official Files, Box 771, 203F File. The CIA also rejected the idea of a negotiated solution. CIA, "Intelligence Memorandum No. 231," Oct. 7, 1949, HSTL, Records of NSC, Box 2, NSC / CIA Intelligence Memorandums Dec. 1948–Dec. 1949 File; Charlton Ogburn, "Decisions Reached by Consensus at the Meetings with the Secretary and the Consultants on the Far East," Nov. 2, 1949, Nat. Arch., Record Group 59, Box 14, U.S. Policy toward China and the Far East File. An earlier CIA assessment concluded that, of the nations of Southern Asia, only Indochina and Burma were actually threatened by communist forces "too strong for decisive counter-action." CIA, "Intelligence Memorandum No. 209," Sept. 20, 1949, HSTL, Records of NSC, Box 2, NSC / CIA Intelligence Memorandums Dec. 1948–Dec. 1949 File. Various Pacific Pact schemes surfaced in 1949–51, but Acheson refused to consider them seriously. David W. Mabon, "Elusive Agreements: The Pacific Pact Proposals of 1949–1951," *Pacific Historical Review* 57 (May 1988): 147–77.

36. For comparison, one may note that, in 1938, all the nations of Southeast Asia accounted for 15.9 percent of Japan's imports and received 18.6 percent of its exports, while Korea, a single state, accounted for 14.9 percent of Japan's imports and 17.0 percent of its exports. Not surprisingly, Acheson focused on rebuilding Korea, where the United States could control events, long before he even considered rebuilding the strife-torn nations of Southeast Asia. Jerome B. Cohen, *Japan's Postwar Economy* (Bloomington: Indiana Univ. Press, 1958), pp. 119–20. Japanese figures for 1934–36 show that Southeast Asia accounted for 19 percent of Japan's exports and 17 percent of its imports. Saburo Okita, *The Rehabilitation of Japan's Economy and Asia* (Tokyo: Public Information and Cultural Affairs Bureau, 1956), pp. 7 and 11; Howard Schonberger, "U.S. Policy in Post-War Japan: Retreat from Liberalism," *Science & Society* 46 (Spring 1982): 51; U.S. Congress, House, Committee on Foreign Affairs, *United States Foreign Policy for a Post-War Recovery Program: Hearings for a Post-War Recovery Program,* 80th Cong., 1st sess., 1948, p. 739. Rusk, who had served in Southeast Asia during World War II, knew the region reasonably well, and he quickly took the lead on developing U.S. policy in this area. Rusk interview with author; Acheson to William J. Sebald, Dec. 22, 1949, *Foreign Relations, 1949,* vol. 7, p. 921. At the Asian economic conference in April, the United States addressed the problem of economic nationalism in a preliminary effort to eliminate trade barriers, and that same month Acheson tentatively approved a plan by John Allison to tie U.S. aid for Southeast Asia to the purchase of goods from Japan. Leon Hollerman, "The Formation of International Economic Policy during the Occupation of Japan," in *The Occupation of Japan,*

ed. Lawrence H. Redford (Norfolk: MacArthur Memorial, 1980), p. 281. U.S. planners began to argue in earnest about Southeast Asia's trade in late 1948, but these early discussions produced little beyond an Economic Cooperation Administration grant to help the Dutch East Indies trade its cotton to Japan. Schaller, *American Occupation of Japan,* pp. 146–47. Bishop, who first advocated greater regional integration of Asian trade in 1945, probably provided the impetus for it in 1949. Max Bishop to E. R. Stettinius, Feb. 17, 1945, Nat. Arch., Record Group 59, Department of State, Office of Philippine and Southeast Asian Affairs, Box 5, Integration in Southeast Asia File. Bishop interview with author. In April of 1950, John Foster Dulles, a Republican foreign policy specialist, joined the State Department, and he too lined up with Rusk on the question of expanding Japanese trade in Southeast Asia. Roger Buckley, *Occupation Diplomacy* (New York: Cambridge Univ. Press, 1982), p. 172.

37. State Department to American Consulate in Saigon, Indochina, Feb. 12, 1949, U.S. Department of Defense, *United States–Vietnam Relations,* 8:182. Burma and Thailand continued to send the bulk of their surplus rice to India, although Thailand opened a growing trade with Japan. By 1950, Thailand slightly exceeded its prewar exports, but Burma, racked by civil war, managed to reach only 40 percent of its prewar levels. This created a serious food shortage in India. Japan's prewar rice imports averaged 2,061,198 tons annually, of which all but 297,368 tons came from Korea and Taiwan. The United States also exported rice before the war, and Japan once bought California's entire rice crop. Because rice has a greater nutritional value per volume than wheat, and because transportation costs from the United States to Japan were high, feeding a given number of Japanese with U.S.-grown wheat could cost several times as much as feeding them with Asian-grown rice. Nearby Korea provided rice to Japan at the lowest transportation cost. U.S. Department of Agriculture, *Agricultural Statistics, 1948* (Washington, D.C.: GPO, 1949), p. 38; U.S. Department of Agriculture, *Agricultural Statistics, 1952* (Washington, D.C.: GPO, 1952), p. 30; State Department Working Group (not named), "Military Aid for Indochina," Feb. 1, 1950, *Foreign Relations,* 1950, vol. 6, pp. 711–13; Rusk interview with author; U.S. Congress, Senate, Committee on Foreign Relations, *Economic Assistance to China and Korea, 1949–1950: Hearings Held in Executive Session before the Committee on Foreign Relations on S. 1063, S. 2319, and S. 2845,* 81st Cong., 1st and 2d sess., 1974, p. 195; C. J. Shohan to William Gibson and Robert E. Hoey, May 7, 1951, Nat. Arch., Record Group 59, Department of State, Office of Philippine and Southeast Asian Affairs, Box 7, Indochina 1948–51 File. When Livingston Merchant, Deputy Assistant Secretary for Far Eastern Affairs, reported on Indochina's importance, he

made no mention whatsoever of its trade with Japan, and this was indicative of early expectations for Indochina's trade. Livingston T. Merchant to Butterworth, March 7, 1950, *Foreign Relations,* 1950, vol. 6, p. 750. In a report summarizing his tour of the Far East, Philip C. Jessup, Ambassador-at-Large, listed six potential food suppliers in the Far East—"Korea, the Philippines, Indochina, Thailand, Burma, and Pakistan." Memorandum of Conversation by Ogburn, (summary of a large meeting), April 3, 1950, ibid., pp. 68–72.

38. NSC 48, Dec. 23, 1949, U.S. Department of Defense, *United States–Vietnam Relations,* 8:248 and 258. In an addendum to NSC 48, the State Department specified that the United States should continue to try to "bring home the urgency of removing the barriers to the obtaining by Bao Dai or other non-Communist leaders of the support of a substantial proportion of the Vietnamese people." NSC 48 / 2, Dec. 30, 1949, *Foreign Relations,* 1949, vol. 7, pp. 1215–20.

39. U.S. Department of Defense, *United States–Vietnam Relations,* 1:A-7–A-8. As early as September 1949, Walton Butterworth and Philip Jessup advised Acheson to quickly recognize the Bao Dai regime. Charles W. Yost, "Discussion of Far Eastern Affairs in Preparation for Conversations with Mr. Bevin" (large meeting), Sept. 13, 1949, Nat. Arch., Record Group 59, Department of State, Office of Chinese Affairs, Box 14, U.S. Policy toward China and the Far East File; Acheson, Memorandum of Conversation with Truman, Feb. 2, 1950, HSTL, Papers of Dean Acheson, Box 64B, Feb. 1950 Conversations File; Acheson to Truman, Feb. 2, 1949, *Foreign Relations,* 1950, vol. 6, pp. 716–17. The Vietminh remained on the offensive throughout 1950, prompting a French change of command at year's end. The offensive ended in early 1951. Archimedes L. A. Patti, *Why Vietnam?* (Berkeley: Univ. of California Press, 1980), p. 408; Acheson, Memorandum of Conversation (large meeting), Feb. 3, 1950, HSTL, Papers of Dean Acheson, Box 64B, Feb. 1950 Conversations File; George M. Abbott to Acheson, Jan. 31, 1950, *Foreign Relations,* 1950, vol. 6, pp. 707–9; Office of Far Eastern Affairs, "U.S. Recognizes Viet Nam, Laos, and Cambodia," released to the press on Feb. 7, 1950, *Department of State Bulletin* 22 (Feb. 20, 1950): 291. Acheson also took his guarded optimism to Congress, telling a Senate committee on Jan. 24, 1950, "In Indochina the situation has improved a great deal, of course, in the last year." U.S. Congress, Senate, Committee on Foreign Relations, *Economic Assistance to China and Korea,* p. 216.

40. Bonnet thought that Anglo-American support in the UN might suffice in the event of Chinese intervention in Indochina, but in subsequent discussions neither Acheson nor Nitze pursued a UN formula. Merchant, Memorandum of Conversation with Acheson, Henri Bonnet, and Jean Daridan,

Feb. 16, 1950, *Foreign Relations,* 1950, vol. 6, pp. 730–33; Acheson, Memorandum of Conversation with Truman, March 9, 1950, HSTL, Papers of Dean Acheson, Box 64B, March 1950 Conversations File; Paul Nitze, "Recent Soviet Moves," Feb. 8, 1950, *Foreign Relations,* 1950, vol. 1, pp. 145–47; State Department Working Group (not named), "Military Aid for Indochina," Feb. 1, 1950, *Foreign Relations,* 1950, vol. 6, pp. 711–13; NSC 64, Feb. 27, 1950, ibid., pp. 744–47.

41. Acheson, Memorandum of Conversation with Truman, March 9, 1950, HSTL, Papers of Dean Acheson, Box 64B, March 1950 Conversations File; Rusk to James H. Burns, March 7, 1950, *Foreign Relations,* 1950, vol. 6, p. 752; Louis Johnson to Acheson, April 14, 1950, ibid., pp. 780–84; Truman to Acheson, May 1, 1950, ibid., p. 791; Merchant to Acheson, March 7, 1950, ibid., pp. 749–51; Edmund A. Gullion to Acheson, March 19, 1950, ibid., p. 765.

42. Merchant to Acheson, March 7, 1950, *Foreign Relations,* 1950, vol. 6, pp. 749–50; Acheson Appointment Book, HSTL, Papers of Dean Acheson, Box 45, Appointment File; Nitze interview with author; Paul Nitze, oral history interview with Richard D. McKinzie, Arlington, Va., June 11 and 17, and Aug. 4, 5, and 6, 1975, HSTL (hereafter cited as Nitze, HSTL Oral History), pp. 301–2. Before leaving Paris, Acheson issued a press statement announcing U.S. aid to the new states of Indochina. William S. Lacy to Rusk, May 22, 1950, *Foreign Relations,* 1950, vol. 6, pp. 94–96; Acheson, Press Statement, May 8, 1950, contained in editorial note, ibid., p. 812; Schaller, *American Occupation of Japan,* pp. 242–43; Herring, *America's Longest War,* p. 21.

43. R. Allen Griffin, oral history interview with James R. Fuchs, Pebble Beach, Calif., Feb. 15, 1974, HSTL (hereafter cited as Griffin, HSTL Oral History), pp. 51–52; Schaller, *American Occupation of Japan,* pp. 223–24 and 243.

44. Acheson, Memorandum of Conversation with Truman, Feb. 20, 1950, HSTL, Papers of Dean Acheson, Box 64B, Feb. Conversations File; James E. Webb, Cross Reference Sheet, Feb. 27, 1950, HSTL, Official Files, Box 771, 203F File. Griffin also recalled, "We were used by Mr. Truman's men, and so forth, to make a better picture for the Democrats before the Republicans in Congress. . . ." Griffin, HSTL Oral History, pp. 52–53 and 71–72; Robert Hoey to the State Department, March 18, 1950, Nat. Arch., Record Group 59, Department of State, Office of Philippine and Southeast Asian Affairs, Box 7, Indochina File; Gullion to Acheson, March 18, 1950, *Foreign Relations,* 1950, vol. 6, pp. 762–63; Windsor G. Hackler, "Record of an Interdepartmental Meeting on the Far East at the State Department," May 11, 1950, ibid., pp. 87–91. Although the Defense Department urged

the Griffin Mission to reiterate the arguments for increasing Japan's trade in Southeast Asia, the mission made no formal recommendations on this subject. The initial funding for aid to Southeast Asia came from the 1950 extension of the 1948 China Aid Act. Samuel P. Hayes, *The Beginning of American Aid to Southeast Asia* (Lexington, Mass.: Heath Lexington, 1971), pp. 15, 22, 36, 44, 48–49, and 71–72. The Griffin Mission urged an immediate response to the "deplorable health conditions" in Vietnam, and Truman quickly allocated $750,000 from the Mutual Defense Assistance Program for this purpose. Gullion to Acheson, March 18, 1950, *Foreign Relations,* 1950, vol. 6, pp. 762–63; Philip Jessup, Memorandum of Conversation (large meeting), June 26, 1950, HSTL, Papers of Dean Acheson, Box 65, June 1950 Conversations File.

45. Editorial note, *Foreign Relations,* 1950, vol. 6, p. 836. Melby was particularly dismayed to find that not a single U.S. official in Saigon spoke Vietnamese. John F. Melby, oral history interview with Robert Accinelli, Ontario, Can., Nov. 7, 14, 21, and 28, 1986, HSTL, pp. 212–13 and 216–18; George F. Kennan to Acheson, Aug. 23, 1950, HSTL, Papers of Dean Acheson, Box 65, Aug. 1950 Conversations File; Acheson, Memorandum of Conversation with Bonnet, Aug. 23, 1950, ibid.; Rusk interview with author. Rusk hoped to administer both the military and the economic assistance to Vietnam in a way that would "recognize our interest in the nationalism of the Vietnamese, themselves." U.S. Congress, House, Committee on International Relations, *United States Policy in the Far East: Selected Executive Sessions of the House Committee on International Relations: Hearings on the Far East Portion of the Mutual Defense Assistance Act of 1950,* 8 vols., 81st Cong., 1st and 2d sess., 1976, 8:489; Acheson, *Present at the Creation,* pp. 673–75; Herring, *America's Longest War,* p. 16.

46. Johnson to Acheson, April 14, 1950, *Foreign Relations,* 1950, vol. 6, pp. 780–84; Samuel T. Parelman, Minutes of the First Meeting of the Southeast Asia Aid Policy Committee, July 13, 1950, ibid., pp. 117–19; Patti, *Why Vietnam?* p. 460.

47. The 1952 policy summary also noted that Soviet domination of Southeast Asia would give the Soviet Union and its allies "an economic advantage of far greater importance to them than the loss of the area may be to the free world." This was a new consideration which had not been given much attention in 1950. Charles C. Stelle, "Draft Indochina Section of NSC Paper," March 27, 1952, *Foreign Relations,* 1952–54, vol. 13, pp. 82–83.

48. Acheson, *Present at the Creation,* p. 673.

CHAPTER SEVEN: Acheson and
the New Co-Prosperity Sphere

1. Telephone interview with Max Bishop, Ailey, Ga., April 11, 1992; John Allison to Nitze, July 24, 1950, *Foreign Relations,* 1950, vol. 7, pp. 458–61.

2. Interview with Paul H. Nitze, Washington, D.C., July 25, 1989. Any notion that Acheson's primary motivation was a deep concern for the people of Asia would be ill founded. Dean Rusk recalled that Acheson "did not give much of a damn about the little red-yellow-black people in various parts of the world." Edwin W. Martin, an analyst in the Office of Far Eastern Affairs, recounted, "I've heard him [Acheson] make remarks about the people of Southeast Asia that I wouldn't want to repeat." Interview with Dean Rusk, Athens, Ga., April 11, 1988 (hereafter cited as Rusk interview with author); Edwin W. Martin, Oral History Interview with Richard D. McKinzie, Washington, D.C., June 3, 1975, HSTL, p. 114.

3. Tatsuro Uchino, *Japan's Postwar Economy* (Tokyo: Kodansha International, 1983), p. 84.

4. Clay Blair, *The Forgotten War* (New York: Times Books, 1987), pp. 40–41; Telephone interview with Max Bishop, Ailey, Ga., April 11, 1992.

5. Thomas J. Schoenbaum, *Waging Peace and War* (New York: Simon & Schuster, 1988), pp. 390–405 and 468–79. Nitze went on to serve in high-level positions in the administrations of Lyndon B. Johnson and Ronald Reagan.

6. Rusk interview with author.

ᵉ Bibliography

BOOKS AND ARTICLES

Acheson, Dean. *Post-War Foreign Policy—Second Phase: The Woodrow Wilson Award for Distinguished Service to Dean Gooderham Acheson.* Stamford, Conn.: Overbrook, 1953.
————. *Present at the Creation.* New York: Norton, 1969.
————. *Sketches from Life of Men I Have Known.* New York: Harper, 1956.
Allen, G. C. *Japan's Economic Recovery.* New York: Oxford Univ. Press, 1958.
————. *A Short Economic History of Modern Japan.* New York: St. Martin's Press, 1972.
Allen, Richard C. *Korea's Syngman Rhee.* Rutland, Vt.: Charles E. Tuttle, 1960.
Allison, John M. *Ambassador from the Prairie; or, Allison Wonderland.* Boston: Houghton Mifflin, 1973.
Almond, Gabriel A. *The American People and Foreign Policy.* New York: Praeger, 1950.
Ambrose, Stephen E. *Eisenhower.* New York: Simon & Schuster, 1983.
————. *Rise to Globalism: American Foreign Policy, 1938–1970.* Baltimore: Penguin, 1972.

Amter, Joseph A. *Vietnam Verdict: A Citizen's History*. New York: Continuum, 1982.

Arkes, Hadley. *Bureaucracy, the Marshall Plan, and the National Interest*. Princeton: Princeton Univ. Press, 1972.

Aron, Raymond. *France Steadfast and Changing: The Fourth to the Fifth Republic*. Cambridge: Harvard Univ. Press, 1960.

Aron, Raymond. *The Imperial Republic: The United States and the World, 1945–1973*. Translated by Frank Jellinek. Englewood Cliffs, N.J.: Prentice-Hall, 1974.

Asada, Sadao. "Recent Works on the American Occupation of Japan: The State of the Art." *Japanese Journal of American Studies* 1 (1981): 175–91.

Bachrack, Stanley D. *The Committee of One Million: "China Lobby" Politics, 1953–1971*. New York: Columbia Univ. Press, 1976.

Baerwald, Hans H. *The Purge of Japanese Leaders under the Occupation*. Berkeley: Univ. of California Press, 1959.

Baldwin, Frank, ed. *Without Parallel: The American-Korean Relationship since 1945*. New York: Random House, 1973.

Ballantine, Joseph W. *Formosa: A Problem for United States Foreign Policy*. Washington, D.C.: Brookings Institution, 1952.

Barber, Joseph, ed. *American Policy toward China: A Report on the Views of Leading Citizens in Twenty-three Cities*. New York: Council on Foreign Relations, 1950.

Barnds, William J., ed. *The Two Koreas in East Asian Affairs*. New York: New York Univ. Press, 1976.

Barnet, Richard. *The Alliance: America-Europe-Japan—Makers of the Postwar World*. New York: Simon & Schuster, 1983.

———. *Intervention and Revolution: The United States in the Third World*. New York: World Publishing, 1968.

Barnett, A. Doak. *China on the Eve of Communist Takeover*. New York: Praeger, 1963.

Beal, John Robinson. *Marshall in China*. Garden City, N.Y.: Doubleday, 1970.

Bell, Coral. "Korea and the Balance of Power." *Political Quarterly* 25 (Jan.–March 1954): 17–29.

Beloff, Max. *Soviet Policy in the Far East, 1944–1951*. London: Oxford Univ. Press, 1953.

Berger, Carl. *The Korea Knot: A Political-Military History*. Philadelphia: Univ. of Pennsylvania Press, 1957.

Bernstein, Barton J. "The Week We Went to War: American Intervention in the Korean Civil War," *Foreign Service Journal* 54 (Jan. 1977): 6–9 and 33–35.

————, ed. *Politics and Policies of the Truman Administration*. Chicago: Quadrangle, 1970.

Bisson, T. A. "Japan." In *The Encyclopedia Americana Annual, 1950.*

————. *Zaibatsu Dissolution in Japan*. Berkeley: Univ. of California Press, 1954.

Blair, Clay. *The Forgotten War: America in Korea, 1950–1953*. New York: Times Books, 1987.

Bloomfield, Lincoln. *The United Nations and U.S. Foreign Policy: A New Look at the National Interest*. Boston: Little, Brown, 1967.

Blum, Robert M. *Drawing the Line: The Origin of American Containment Policy in East Asia*. New York: Norton, 1982.

Bohlen, Charles E. *The Transformation of American Foreign Policy*. New York: Norton, 1969.

————. *Witness to History, 1929–1969*. New York: Norton, 1973.

Boldenweck, Bill. "Well-kept War Secret Gets Its Due," *Chicago Tribune*, Dec. 20, 1985, p. A41.

Borden, William S. *The Pacific Alliance: United States Foreign Economic Policy and Japanese Trade Recovery, 1947–1955*. Madison: Univ. of Wisconsin Press, 1984.

Borg, Dorothy, and Waldo Heinrichs, eds. *Uncertain Years: Chinese American Relations, 1947–1959*. New York: Columbia Univ. Press, 1980.

Borton, Hugh. "Japan." In *The Encyclopedia Americana Annual, 1949.*

Bourne, Kenneth, and Donald Cameron Watt, eds. *Records of the Joint Chiefs of Staff: Meetings of the Joint Chiefs of Staff (8 reels) and Far East (14 reels)*. Frederick, Md.: Univ. Publications of America, 1989. Microfilm.

Brown, Weldon Amzy. *Prelude to Disaster: The American Role in Vietnam, 1940–1963*. Port Washington, N.Y.: Kennikat, 1975.

Buckley, Jerry. "Motherhood and the Future of Japan." *U.S. News & World Report*, Dec. 24, 1990, pp. 56–57.

Buckley, Roger. *Occupation Diplomacy: Britain, the United States, and Japan, 1945–1952*. New York: Cambridge Univ. Press, 1982.

Buhite, Russell D. "Major Interests: American Policy toward China, Taiwan, and Korea, 1945–1950." *Pacific Historical Review* 47 (Aug. 1978): 425–51.

Bundy, McGeorge, ed. *The Pattern of Responsibility*. Boston: Houghton Mifflin, 1952.

Burchett, Wilfred G. *The Furtive War: The United States in Vietnam and Laos*. New York: International Publishers, 1963.

Burns, Richard Dean. *The Wars in Vietnam, Cambodia, and Laos, 1945–1982*. Santa Barbara, Calif.: ABC-Clio Information Services, 1983.

Buttinger, Joseph. *Vietnam: A Dragon Embattled.* 2 vols. New York: Praeger, 1967.

Cameron, Allan W., ed. *Viet-Nam Crisis: A Documentary History.* 2 vols. Ithaca: Cornell Univ. Press, 1971.

Cardi, Ronald James. "The G.O.P. and the Korean War." *Pacific Historical Review* 37 (Nov. 1968): 423–43.

———. *The Korean War and American Politics: The Republican Party as a Case Study.* Philadelphia: Univ. of Pennsylvania Press, 1968.

Chaffee, Wilbur. "Two Hypotheses of Sino-Soviet Relations as Concerns the Instigation of the Korean War." *Journal of Korean Affairs* 6, nos. 3–4: (Oct. 1976–Jan. 1977): 1–13.

Chennault, Claire Lee. *Way of a Fighter: The Memoirs of Claire Lee Chennault.* New York: Putnam's, 1949.

Chiang Kai-shek. *China's Destiny and Chinese Economic Theory.* Edited and translated by Philip J. Jaffe. New York: Roy, 1947.

Cho, Soon Sung. *Korea in World Politics, 1940–1950: An Evolution of American Responsibility.* Los Angeles: Univ. of California Press, 1967.

Clubb, O. Edmund. *China and Russia: The Great Game.* New York: Columbia Univ. Press, 1971.

———. *The Witness and I.* New York: Columbia Univ. Press, 1974.

Cochran, Bert. *Harry Truman and the Crisis Presidency.* New York: Funk & Wagnalls, 1973.

Chochrane, Willard W. *The World Food Problem.* New York: Crowell, 1969.

Cohen, Jerome B. *Japan's Economy in War and Reconstruction.* Minneapolis: Univ. of Minnesota Press, 1949.

———. *Japan's Postwar Economy.* Bloomington: Indiana Univ. Press, 1958.

Cohen, Mortimer T. *From Prologue to Epilogue in Vietnam.* New York: Retriever Bookshop, 1979.

Cohen, Theodore. *Remaking Japan: The American Occupation as New Deal.* New York: Free Press, 1987.

Cohen, Warren J. "Ambassador Philip D. Sprouse on the Question of Recognition of the People's Republic of China in 1949 and 1950." *Diplomatic History* 2 (Spring 1978): 213–17.

———. *America's Response to China: A Short History of Sino-Americans Relations.* New York: John Wiley, 1971.

———. "The Development of Chinese Communist Attitudes toward the United States." *Orbis* 2 (Summer 1967): 551–69.

Collins, J. Lawton. *War in Peacetime: The History and Lessons of Korea.* Boston: Houghton Mifflin, 1969.

Connally, Tom. *My Name Is Tom Connally.* New York: Crowell, 1954.

Cooper, Chester L. *The Lost Crusade: America in Vietnam.* New York: Dodd, Mead, 1970.

Crabb, Cecil V., Jr. *Bipartisan Foreign Policy: Myth or Reality?* White Plains, N.Y.: Row, Peterson, 1957.

Craig, Gordon A. *Europe since 1815.* New York: Holt, Rinehart and Winston, 1961.

Crofts, Alfred. "The Start of the Korean War Reconsidered." *Rocky Mountain Social Science Journal* 7 (April 1970): 109–17.

Cumings, Bruce. "The Origins and Development of the Northeast Asian Political Economy: Industrial Sectors, Product Cycles, and Political Consequences." *International Organization* 38 (Winter 1984): 1–40.

———. *The Origins of the Korean War: Liberation & Emergence of Separate Regimes, 1945–1947.* Princeton: Princeton Univ. Press, 1981.

———. *The Origins of the Korean War: The Roaring of the Cataract, 1947–1950.* Prinecton: Princeton Univ. Press, 1990.

———, ed. *Child of Conflict: The Korean-American Relationship, 1943–1953.* Seattle: Univ. of Washington Press, 1983.

Curry, George. *James F. Byrnes.* Vol. 14 of *American Secretaries of State and Their Diplomacy,* ed. Samuel Flagg Bemis and Robert H. Ferrell. New York: Cooper Square, 1972.

Curtis, Gerald L., and Sung-joo Han, eds. *The U.S.–South Korean Alliance: Evolving Patterns of Security Relations.* Toronto: Lexington Books, 1983.

Dallin, David J. *Soviet Russia and the Far East.* New Haven: Yale Univ. Press, 1949.

Davies, John Paton, Jr. *Dragon by the Tail: American, British, Japanese, and Russian Encounters with China and One Another.* New York: Norton, 1972.

Daniels, Jonathan. *The Man of Independence.* Philadelphia: Lippincott, 1950.

Davis, Larry. *Mig Alley.* Warren, Mich.: Squadron / Signal, 1978.

De Carmoy, Guy. *The Foreign Policies of France, 1944–1968.* Chicago: Univ. of Chicago Press, 1970.

Denison, Edward Fulton. *How Japan's Economy Grew So Fast: The Sources of Power Expansion.* Washington, D.C.: Brookings Institution, 1976.

Detzer, David. *Thunder of the Captains: The Short Summer in 1950.* New York: Crowell, 1977.

DeWeerd, H. A. "Lessons of the Korean War." *Yale Review* 40 (Summer 1951): 592–603.

———. "Strategic Surprise in the Korean War." *Orbis* 6 (Fall 1962): 435–52.

Dietrich, Ethel B. *Far East Trade of the United States.* New York: Institute of Pacific Relations, 1940.

Dingman, Roger. "The Diplomacy of Dependency." *Journal of Southeast Asian Studies* 17 (Sept. 1986): 307–21.

————. "Strategic Planning and the Policy Process: American Plans for War in East Asia, 1945–1950." *Naval War College Review* 32 (Nov.– Dec. 1979): 4–21.

Dobbs, Charles M. *The Unwanted Symbol: American Foreign Policy, the Cold War, and Korea, 1945–1950.* Kent, Ohio: Kent State Univ. Press, 1981.

Doenecke, Justus D. *Not to the Swift: The Old Isolationists in the Cold War Era.* Lewisburg, Penn.: Bucknell Univ. Press, 1979.

Donovan, Robert J. *Conflict and Crisis: The Presidency of Harry S. Truman, 1945–1948.* New York: Norton, 1977.

————. *Nemesis: Truman and Johnson in the Coils of War in Asia.* New York: St. Martin's Merek, 1984.

————. *Tumultuous Years: The Presidency of Harry S. Truman, 1949– 1953.* New York: Norton, 1982.

Douglass, Bruce, and Ross Terrill, eds. *China and Ourselves: Explorations and Revisions by a New Generation.* Boston: Beacon, 1969.

Dower, John W. *Empire and Aftermath: Yoshida Shigeru and the Japanese Experience, 1878–1954.* Cambridge: Harvard Univ. Press, 1979.

Dower, John W. "Occupied Japan as History and Occupation History as Politics." *Journal of Asian Studies* 34 (1975): 485–504.

Doyle, Edward, Samuel Lipsman, and the editors of Boston Publishing Company. *Setting the Stage.* Boston: Boston Publishing, 1981.

Drachman, Edward R. *United States Policy toward Vietnam, 1940–1945.* Rutherford, N.J.: Fairleigh Dickinson Univ. Press, 1970.

Druks, Herbert. *Harry S. Truman and the Russians, 1945–1953.* New York: Robert Speller and Sons, 1966.

Dubin, Wilbert B. "The Poltical Evolution of the Pyongyang Government." *Pacific Affairs* 23 (Dec. 1950): 381–92.

Dull, Paul S. "South Korean Constitution." *Far Eastern Survey* 17 (Sept. 8, 1948): 205–7.

Dulles, Foster Rhea. *American Policy toward Communist China: The Historical Record, 1949–1969.* New York: Crowell, 1972.

Dulles, John Foster. *War or Peace?* New York: Macmillan, 1950.

Duncanson, Dennis J. *Government and Revolution in Vietnam.* London: Oxford Univ. Press, 1968.

Dunn, William Brothers. *American Policy and Vietnamese Nationalism, 1950– 54.* Chicago: Univ. of Chicago Press, 1960.

Dunstan, Simon. *Armor of the Korean War, 1950–1953.* London: Osprey, 1982.

Fall, Bernard B. *Street without Joy.* New York: Schocken, 1961.

————. *The Two Viet-Nams: A Political and Military Analysis.* New York: Praeger, 1964.

Farnsworth, David N. *The Senate Committee on Foreign Relations.* Urbana: Univ. of Illinois Press, 1961.

Feary, Robert A. *The Occupation of Japan: Second Phase, 1948–50.* New York: Macmillan, 1950.

Fehrenbach, T. R. *This Kind of War: A Study in Unpreparedness.* New York: Macmillan, 1963.

Feis, Herbert. *Contest over Japan.* New York: Norton, 1967.

Feraru, Arthur N. "Public Opinion Polls on China." *Far Eastern Survey* 20 (July 12, 1950): 130–32.

Ferrell, Robert H. *The Eisenhower Diaries.* New York: Norton, 1981.

————. *George Marshall.* Vol. 15 of *American Secretaries of State and Their Diplomacy,* ed. Samuel Flagg Bemis and Robert H. Ferrell. New York: Cooper Square, 1972.

————, ed. *Off the Record: The Private Papers of Harry S. Truman.* Middlesex, Eng.: Penguin, 1985.

Fetzer, James Alan. "Senator Vandenberg and the American Commitment to China." *Historian* 36 (Feb. 1974): 283–303.

"50 Senators Back Bill to Aid China." *New York Times,* March 11, 1949, p. 13.

Foot, Rosemary. *The Wrong War: American Policy and the Dimensions of the Korean Conflict, 1950–1953.* Cornell Univ. Press, 1985.

Forrestal, James. *The Forrestal Diaries.* Edited by Walter Millis. New York: Viking, 1951.

Freeland, Richard M. *The Truman Doctrine and the Origins of McCarthyism: Foreign Policy, Domestic Politics, and Internal Security, 1946–1948.* New York: Knopf, 1971.

Friedman, Edward, and Mark Selden, eds. *America's Asia: Dissenting Essays on Asian-American Relations.* New York: Pantheon Books, 1971.

Fukui, Harushiro. "Economic Planning in Postwar Japan: A Case Study in Policy Making." *Asian Survey* 12 (April 1972): 327–49.

Furniss, Edgar S., Jr. *France, Troubled Ally.* New York: Harper, 1960.

Gaddis, John Lewis. "Containment: A Reassessment." *Foreign Affairs* 55 (July 1977): 873–86.

————. *The United States and the Origins of the Cold War, 1941–1947.* New York: Columbia Univ. Press, 1972.

————. "Was the Truman Doctrine a Real Turning Point?" *Foreign Affairs* 52 (Jan. 1974): 386–402.

Gardner, Lloyd C. *Approaching Vietnam: From World War II through Dienbienphu, 1941–1954.* New York: Norton, 1968.

————, ed. *The Korean War*. New York: Quadrangle, 1972.

Gati, Charles, ed. *Caging the Bear: Containment and the Cold War*. New York: Bobbs-Merrill, 1974.

Gerson, Louis L. *John Foster Dulles*. Vol. 17 of *American Secretaries of State and Their Diplomacy,* ed. Samuel Flagg Bemis and Robert H. Ferrell. New York: Cooper Square, 1972.

Gettleman, Marvin E. *Vietnam: History, Documents and Opinions on a Major World Crisis*. Greenwich, Conn.: Fawcett, 1965.

Gittings, John. *The World and China, 1922–1972*. New York: Harper & Row, 1974.

Godfrey, F. A. "Crisis in Korea." In *War in Peace,* ed. Sir Robert Thompson. New York: Harmony, 1981.

Goguel, François. *France under the Fourth Republic*. Ithaca: Cornell Univ. Press, 1952.

Goldman, Eric F. "The President, the People, and the Power to Make War." *American Heritage* 21 (April 1970): 28–35.

Goldsmith, Raymond W. *The Financial Development of Japan, 1868–1977*. New Haven: Yale Univ. Press, 1983.

Goodman, Grant Kohn. *The American Occupation of Japan: A Retrospective View*. Lawrence: Univ. of Kansas Press, 1968.

Goodrich, Leland. *Korea: A Study of U.S. Policy in the United Nations*. New York: Council on Foreign Relations, 1956.

Gordenker, Leon. *The United Nations and the Peaceful Unification of Korea: The Politics of Field Operations, 1947–1950*. The Hague: Martinus Nijhoff, 1959.

Gosnell, Harold F. *Truman's Crises: A Political Biography of Harry S. Truman*. Westport, Conn.: Greewood, 1980.

Goulden, Joseph C. *Korea: The Untold Story of the War*. New York: Times Books, 1982.

Graebner, Norman A. *The Age of Global Power: The United States since 1939*. New York: John Wiley, 1979.

————. *Cold War Diplomacy: American Foreign Policy, 1945–1975*. Princeton: Van Nostrand, 1962.

————. "Global Containment: The Truman Years." *Current History* 57 (Aug. 1969): 77–83.

————. *Ideas and Diplomacy: Readings in the Intellectual Tradition of American Foreign Policy*. New York: Oxford Univ. Press, 1964.

————. *The New Isolationism: A Study in Politics and Foreign Policy since 1950*. New York: Ronald Press, 1956.

————, ed. *An Uncertain Tradition: American Secretaries of State in the Twentieth Century*. New York: McGraw-Hill, 1961.

Grajdanzev, Andrew J. "Korea Divided." *Far Eastern Survey* 14 (Oct. 10, 1945): 281–83.

Grasso, June M. *Truman's Two-China Policy, 1948–1950*. New York: M. E. Sharpe, 1987.

Green, William, and Gordon Swanborough. "The Zero Precursor." *Air Enthusiast* 19 (Aug.–Nov. 1982): 26–43.

Grey, Arthur L., Jr. "The Thirty-eighth Parallel." *Foreign Affairs* 29 (April 1951): 482–87.

Griffith, Robert. *The Politics of Fear: Joseph R. McCarthy and the Senate*. Lexington: Univ. Press of Kentucky, 1970.

Guhin, Michael A. *John Foster Dulles: A Statesman and His Times*. New York: Columbia Univ. Press, 1972.

Gunther, John. *The Riddle of MacArthur*. New York: Harper, 1951.

Gupta, Karunker. "How Did the Korean War Begin?" *China Quarterly* 8 (Oct.–Dec. 1972): 699–716.

Gurtov, Melvin. *The First Vietnam Crisis: Chinese Communist Strategy and United States Involvement, 1953–1954*. New York: Columbia Univ. Press, 1967.

Guttman, Allen, ed. *Korea: Cold War and Limited War*. Lexington, Mass.: Heath, 1972.

Halberstam, David. *The Best and the Brightest*. New York: Random House, 1972.

Hall, Robert B. *Japan: Industrial Power of Asia*. Princeton: Van Nostrand, 1963.

Hamby, Alonzo L. *The Imperial Years: The United States since 1939*. New York: Weybright and Talley, 1976.

Hammer, Ellen Joy. *Vietnam Yesterday and Today*. New York: Holt, Rinehart and Winston, 1966.

Harper, Alan D. *The Politics of Loyalty: The White House on the Communist Issue, 1946–1952*. Westport, Conn.: Greenwood, 1969.

Harrison, James Pinckney. *The Endless War: Fifty Years of Struggle in Vietnam*. New York: Free Press, 1982.

Harrison, Michael M. *The Reluctant Ally: France and Atlantic Security*. Baltimore: Johns Hopkins Univ. Press, 1981.

Hartmann, Susan. *Truman and the 80th Congress*. Columbia: Univ. of Missouri Press, 1971.

Hawes, Grace. *The Marshall Plan for China: The Economic Cooperation Administration, 1948–1949*. Cambridge: Schenkman, 1977.

Hayes, Samuel P. *The Beginning of American Aid to Southeast Asia: The Griffin Mission of 1950*. Lexington, Mass.: Heath Lexington, 1971.

Haynes, Richard F. *The Awesome Power: Harry S. Truman as Commander in Chief*. Baton Rouge: Louisiana State Univ. Press, 1973.

Hayward, Jack. *The One and Indivisible French Republic*. London: Weidenfeld and Nicolson, 1973.

Heinrichs, Waldo. *Threshold of War: Franklin D. Roosevelt and American Entry into World War II*. New York: Oxford Univ. Press, 1988.

Heller, H. Frances, ed. *The Korean War: A 25-Year Perspective*. Lawrence: Regents Press of Kansas, 1978.

Henderson, Gregory. *Korea: The Politics of the Vortex*. Cambridge: Harvard Univ. Press, 1968.

Herman, Edward S. *America's Vietnam Policy: The Strategy of Deception*. Washington, D.C.: Public Affairs Press, 1966.

Herring, George C. *America's Longest War: The United States and Vietnam, 1950–1975*. New York: John Wiley, 1979.

————. "The Truman Administration and the Restoration of French Sovereignty in Indochina." *Diplomatic History* 1 (Spring 1977): 97–117.

Hess, Gary R. *The United States' Emergence as a Southeast Asian Power, 1940–1950*. New York: Columbia Univ. Press, 1987.

Higgins, Marguerite. *Our Vietnam Nightmare*. New York: Harper & Row, 1965.

————. *War in Korea: The Report of a Woman Combat Correspondent*. Garden City, N.Y.: Doubleday, 1951.

Higgins, Trumbull. *Korea and the Fall of MacArthur*. New York: Oxford Univ. Press, 1960.

Hill, Thomas Michael. "Senator Arthur H. Vandenberg, the Politics of Bipartisanship, and the Origins of Anti-Soviet Consensus, 1941–1946." *World Affairs* 138 (Winter 1975–76): 219–42.

Hillman, William, ed. *Mr. President: The First Publication from the Personal Diaries, Private Letters, Papers, and Revealing Interviews of Harry S. Truman*. New York: Farrar, Straus & Giroux, 1952.

Hitchcock, Wilbur W. "North Korea Jumps the Gun." *Current History* 20 (March 1951): 136–44.

Hixon, Walter L. "Containment on the Perimeter: George F. Kennan and Vietnam." *Diplomatic History* 12 (Spring 1988): 149–63.

Hogan, Michael J. *The Marshall Plan: America, Britain, and the Reconstruction of Western Europe, 1947–1952*. Cambridge: Cambridge Univ. Press, 1987.

Hohenberg, John. *Between Two Worlds: Policy, Press and Public Opinion in Asian-American Relations*. New York: Praeger, 1967.

Hoopes, Townsend. *The Devil and John Foster Dulles*. Boston: Little, Brown, 1973.

Hovey, Harold A. *United States Military Assistance: A Study of Policies and Practices*. New York: Praeger, 1965.

Hoyt, Edwin C. "The United States Reaction to the Korean Attack."
    American Journal of International Law 55 (Jan. 1961): 45–
    76.
Hsueh, Chun-tu, ed. *Dimensions of China's Foreign Relations.* New York:
    Praeger, 1977.
Igarashi, Takeshi. "MacArthur's Proposal for an Early Peace with Japan and
    the Redirection of Occupation Policy toward Japan." *Japanese Jour-
    nal of American Studies* 1 (1981): 55–86.
Iriye, Akira. *Across the Pacific: An Inner History of American–East Asian
    Relations.* New York: Harcourt, Brace & World, 1967.
——. *The Cold War in Asia: A Historical Introduction.* Englewood Cliffs,
    N.J.: Prentice-Hall, 1974.
——. *Power and Culture: The Japanese American War, 1941–1945.*
    Cambridge: Harvard Univ. Press, 1981.
Ishizaka, Taizo. "Development of Japanese-American Trade." *Contempo-
    rary Japan* 26 (1960): 405–15.
Jacoby, Neil H. *U.S. Aid to Taiwan: A Study of Foreign Aid, Self-Help, and
    Development.* New York: Praeger, 1966.
James, D. Clayton. *The Years of MacArthur.* 2 vols. Boston: Houghton
    Mifflin, 1970–71.
Jansen, Marius B. "Japan since the Occupation." *Asian and African Studies,*
    18 (1984): 11–40.
Japanese Ministry of Foreign Affairs. *Economic Rehabilitation and Foreign
    Commerce of Japan.* Tokyo: Bureau of Public Information and Cul-
    tural Affairs, 1953.
Jervis, Robert. "The Impact of the Korean War on the Cold War." *Journal
    of Conflict Resolution* 24 (Dec. 1980): 563–91.
Johnson, U. Alexis. *The Right Hand of Power.* Englewood Cliffs, N.J.:
    Prentice-Hall, 1984.
Johnstone, William C. "The United States as a Pacific Power." *Current
    History* 58 (April 1970): 193–96.
Jones, Joseph Marion. *The Fifteen Weeks: Genesis of the Marshall Plan.*
    New York: Harcourt, Brace & World, 1955.
Jung, Yong Suk. "A Critical Analysis on the Cause of Korean War." *Jour-
    nal of Asiatic Studies* 15 (1972): 85–94.
Kahn, E. J., Jr. *The China Hands: America's Foreign Service Officers and
    What Befell Them.* New York: Viking, 1975.
Kai, Miwa. *Political Chronology of Japan, 1885–1957.* New York: East
    Asian Institute of Columbia Univ., 1957.
Kalinov, Kyril. "How Russia Built the North Korean Army." *Reporter* 3
    (Sept. 26, 1950): 4–8.

Kanamori, Hisao. *Exports of Manufactures and Industrial Development of Japan*. New York: United Nations Document, 1964.

Kaner, Norman. "I. F. Stone and the Korean War." In *Cold War Critics: Alternatives to American Foreign Policy in the Truman Years*, ed. Thomas G. Paterson. Chicago: Quadrangle, 1971.

Kattenburg, Paul M. "Vietnam and U.S. Diplomacy, 1940–1970." *Orbis* 15 (1971): 818–41.

———. *The Vietnam Trauma in American Foreign Policy, 1945–1975*. New Brunswick, N.J.: Transaction, 1980.

Kaushik, Susheea. *The Agony of Vietnam: The Origin and Background of American Intervention in Vietnam*. New Delhi: Sterling, 1972.

Keeley, Joseph C. *The China Lobby Man: The Story of Alfred Kohlberg*. New Rochelle, N.Y.: Arlington House, 1969.

Kennan, George F. *American Diplomacy, 1900–1950*. Chicago: Univ. of Chicago Press, 1951.

———. "Japanese Security and American Policy." *Foreign Affairs* 43 (1964): 14–28.

———. *Memoirs: 1925–1950*. Boston: Little, Brown, 1967.

———. "The Sources of Soviet Conduct." *Foreign Affairs* 25 (July 1947): 566–82.

Keylin, Arleen, and Suri Boiangiu, eds. *Front Page Vietnam*. New York: Arno, 1979.

Khrushchev, Nikita. *Khrushchev Remembers*. Translated by Strobe Talbott. Boston: Little, Brown, 1970.

———. *Khrushchev Remembers: The Last Testament*. Translated by Strobe Talbott. Boston: Little, Brown, 1974.

Kim, Chum-kon. *The Korean War: 1950–53*. Seoul: Kwangmyong, 1973.

Kim, Joungwon A. *Divided Korea: The Politics of Development, 1945–1972*. Cambridge: Harvard Univ. Press, 1975.

Kim, Yong-jeung. "The Cold War: The Korean Elections." *Far Eastern Survey* 17 (May 5, 1948): 101–2.

Kirkendall, Richard S. *The Truman Period as a Research Field: A Reappraisal, 1972*. Columbia: Univ. of Missouri Press, 1974.

———, ed. *The Harry S. Truman Encyclopedia*. Boston: G. K. Hall, 1989.

Kolko, Gabriel. *The Politics of War: The World and the United States Foreign Policy, 1943–1945*. New York: Harper & Row, 1968.

Kolko, Joyce, and Gabriel Kolko. *The Limits of Power: The World and United States Foreign Policy, 1945–1954*. New York: Harper & Row, 1972.

Korb, Lawrence J. *The Joint Chiefs of Staff: The First 25 Years*. Bloomington: Indiana Univ. Press, 1976.

LaFeber, Walter. *America, Russia, and the Cold War, 1945–1966*. New York: John Wiley, 1967.

Lasater, Martin L. *The Taiwan Issue in Sino-American Strategic Relations*. Boulder, Col.: Westview, 1984.

Lauterbach, Richard E. "Hodge's Korea." *Virginia Quarterly Review* 23 (June 1947): 349–68.

Leary, William M., Jr. "Aircraft and Anti-Communists: CAT in Action, 1949–1952." *China Quarterly* 52 (Oct.–Dec. 1972): 654–69.

Leckie, Robert. *Conflict: The History of the Korean War, 1950–1953*. New York: Putman's, 1962.

Lee, Chae-Jin, and Hideo Sato. *U.S. Policy toward Japan and Korea: A Changing Influence Relationship*. New York: Praeger, 1982.

Lee, Chong-Sik. *Japan and Korea: The Political Dimension*. Stanford, Calif.: Hoover Institution Press, 1985.

———. "Kim Il-Song of North Korea." *Asian Survey* 7 (June 1967): 349–68.

———. *The Politics of Korean Nationalism*. Berkeley: Univ. of California Press, 1963.

Leffler, Melvyn P. "The American Conception of National Security and the Beginnings of the Cold War, 1945–48." *American Historical Review* 89 (April 1984): 346–81.

Levine, Steven I. "A New Look at American Mediation in the Chinese Civil War: The Marshall Mission in Manchuria." *Diplomatic History* 3 (Fall 1979): 349–75.

Liem, Channing. "United States Rule in Korea." *Far Eastern Survey* 18 (April 6, 1949): 77–80.

Liu, F. F. *A Military History of Modern China*. Port Washington, N.Y.: Kennikat, 1972.

Lowe, Peter. *The Origins of the Korean War*. New York: Longman, 1986.

Mabon, David W. "Elusive Agreements: The Pacific Pact Proposals of 1949–1951." *Pacific Historical Review* 57 (May 1988): 147–77.

MacArthur, Douglas A. *Reminiscences*. New York: McGraw-Hill, 1964.

McAllister, Hohn T. *Vietnam: The Origins of Revolution*. Princeton: Princeton Univ. Press, 1969.

McCullough, David. *Truman*. New York: Simon & Schuster, 1992.

McGlothlen, Ronald L. "Acheson, Economics, and the American Commitment in Korea, 1947–1950," *Pacific Historical Review* 58 (Feb. 1989): 23–54.

McLellan, David S. *Dean Acheson: The State Department Years*. New York: Dodd, Mead, 1976.

———. "Dean Acheson and the Korean War." *Political Science Quarterly* 83 (March 1968): 16–39.

Makinen, G. E. "Economic Stabilization in Wartime: A Comparative Case Study of Korea and Vietnam." *Journal of Political Economy* 79 (Nov.–Dec. 1971): 1216–43.

Manchester, William. *American Caesar: Douglas MacArthur, 1880–1964.* Boston: Little, Brown, 1978.

Mao Tse-tung. *On People's Democratic Dictatorship.* Peking: Foreign Languages Press, 1952.

———. *Selected Works of Mao Tse-tung.* Peking: Foreign Languages Press, 1961.

Marks, John D., and Victor Marchetti. *The CIA and the Cult of Intelligence.* New York: Knopf, 1974.

Martellaro, Joseph A. "The Post-WWII Soviet Economy: A Case of Butter and Guns." *Journal of Political and Military Sociology* 15 (Spring 1987): 73–89.

Martin, Edwin M. *The Allied Occupation of Japan.* Westport, Conn.: Greenwood, 1972.

———. *Divided Counsel: The Anglo-American Response to Communist Victory in China.* Lexington: Univ. Press of Kentucky, 1986.

Mason, Edward S., et al. *The Economic and Social Modernization of Korea.* Cambridge: Harvard Univ. Press, 1980.

Matray, James I. "America's Reluctant Crusade: Truman's Commitment of Combat Troops in the Korean War." *Historian* 3 (May 1980): 437–55.

———. "Captive of the Cold War: The Decision to Divide Korea at the 38th Parallel." *Pacific Historical Review* 50 (May 1981): 145–69.

———. "An End to Indifference: America's Korea Policy during World War II." *Diplomatic History* 2 (Spring 1978): 181–96.

———. *The Reluctant Crusade: American Foreign Policy in Korea, 1941–1950.* Honolulu: Univ. of Hawaii Press, 1985.

———. "Truman's Plan for Victory: National Self-Determination and the Thirty-Eighth Parallel Decision in Korea." *Journal of American History* 66 (Sept. 1979): 314–33.

———, ed. *Historical Dictionary of the Korean War.* New York: Greenwood, 1991.

Matsumura, Yutaka. *Japan's Economic Growth, 1945–1960.* Tokyo: Tokyo News Service, 1961.

May, Ernest R. *The Truman Administration and China, 1945–1949.* Philadelphia: Lippincott, 1975.

May, Ernest R., and James C. Thomson, Jr., eds. *American–East Asian Relations: A Survey.* Cambridge: Harvard Univ. Press, 1972.

May, Gary. *China Scapegoat: The Diplomatic Ordeal of John Carter Vincent.* Washington, D.C.: New Republic, 1979.

Mayer, S. L. "Indo-China and the French." In *History of the Second World War*, ed. Barrie Pitt. London: BPC Publishing, 1966.

Meade, E. Grant. *American Military Government in Korea*. New York: King's Crown, 1951.

Mecklin, John. *Mission in Torment: An Intimate Account of the U.S. Role in Vietnam*. Garden City, N.Y.: Doubleday, 1965.

Melby, John F. *The Mandate Of Heaven: Record of a Civil War, China 1945–1949*. Toronto: Toronto Univ. Press, 1968.

Mesko, Jim. *Armor in Korea*. Carrollton, Tex.: Squadron / Signal, 1984.

Middleton, Harry J. *The Compact History of the Korean War*. New York: Hawthorn, 1965.

Miller, Merle. *Plain Speaking: An Oral Biography of Harry S. Truman*. New York: Berkely, 1973.

Mitchell, C. Clyde. "Land Reform in South Korea." *Pacific Affairs* 22 (June 1949): 144–54.

Mizoguchi, Toshiyuki. "Foreign Trade in Taiwan and Korea under Japanese Rule." *Hitotsubashi Journal of Economics* 14 (Feb. 1974): 38–39.

Mizuno, Soji. *Early Foundations for Japan's 20th Century Economic Emergence: A Short Commercial History of Japan*. New York: Vantage, 1981.

Monat, Pawel. "The Hidden Bosses." *Life*, June 27, 1960, pp. 76–101.

Moore, Ray A. "The Occupation of Japan as History: Some Recent Research." *Monumenta Nipponica* 36 (Fall 1981): 317–28.

Morgenthau, Hans J. *Vietnam and the United States*. Washington, D.C.: Public Affairs Press, 1965.

Mosely, Phillip E. "Soviet Policy and the War." *Journal of International Affairs* 6 (Spring 1952): 107–14.

Motoi, Tamaki. "Close But Distant Neighbors." *Japan Quarterly* 21 (Oct.– Dec. 1974): 349–56.

Murray, Martin J. "The Post-Colonial State: Investment and Intervention in Vietnam." *Politics and Society* 3 (Summer 1973): 437–63.

Nagai, Yonosuke, and Akira Iriye, eds. *The Origins of the Cold War in Asia*. New York: Columbia Univ. Press, 1977.

Nakamura, Takafusa. *The Postwar Japanese Economy: Its Development and Structure*. Tokyo: Univ. of Tokyo Press, 1981.

Nam, Koon Woo. *The North Korean Communist Leadership, 1945–1965: A Study of Factionalism and Political Consolidation*. University: Univ. of Alabama Press, 1974.

Neumann, William L. *America Encounters Japan: From Perry to MacArthur*. Baltimore: Johns Hopkins Univ. Press, 1963.

Neustadt, Richard E. *Presidential Power: The Politics of Leadership.* New York: John Wiley, 1960.

Newman, Bernard. *Background to Viet-Nam.* New York: Roy, 1965.

Ngo Vinh Long. "The New Vietnam Scholarship." *Journal of Asian Studies* 44 (Feb. 1985): 337–43.

Nitze, Paul H. *From Hiroshima to Glasnost: At the Center of Decision: A Memoir.* New York: Grove Weidenfeld, 1989.

O'Ballance, Edgar. *Korea: 1950–1953.* Hamden, Conn.: Archon, 1969.

Okita, Saburo. *The Rehabilitation of Japan's Economy and Asia.* Tokyo: Public Information and Cultural Affairs Bureau, 1956.

Okuda, Yoshio. *Japan's Postwar Industry.* Tokyo: International Society for Educational Information, 1976.

Oliver, Robert T. *Syngman Rhee: The Man Behind the Myth.* New York: Dodd, Mead, 1955.

———. *Why War Came in Korea.* New York: Fordham Univ. Press, 1950.

Oppler, Alfred C. *Legal Reform in Occupied Japan: A Participant Looks Back.* Princeton: Princeton Univ. Press, 1976.

Osbourne, Milton E. *Vietnam: The Origins of Crisis.* Toronto: Baxter, 1965.

Osgood, Robert. *Limited War: The Challenge to American Strategy.* Chicago: Univ. of Chicago Press, 1957.

Paige, Glenn D. "Korea." In *Communism and Revolution: The Uses of Political Violence,* ed. Cyril E. Black and Thomas P. Thornton. Princeton: Princeton Univ. Press, 1964.

———. *The Korean Decision: June 24–30, 1950.* New York: Free Press, 1968.

———. *The Korean People's Democratic Republic.* Stanford, Calif.: Hoover Institution Press, 1966.

———. *1950: Truman's Decision: The United States Enters the Korean War.* New York: Chelsea House, 1970.

Paine, Lauran. *Viet-Nam.* London: R. Hale, 1965.

Panikkar, K. M. *In Two Chinas: Memoirs of a Diplomat.* London: Allen & Unwin, 1950.

Park, Hong-Kyu. "America and Korea, 1945–1953: A Bibliographical Essay." *Asian Forum* 3 (Jan.–March 1971): 57–66.

Paterson, Thomas G. "Presidential Foreign Policy, Public Opinion, and Congress: The Truman Years." *Diplomatic History* 3 (Winter 1979): 1–18.

Patti, Archimedes L. A. *Why Vietnam? Prelude to America's Albatross.* Berkeley: Univ. of California Press, 1980.

Phillips, Cabell. *The Truman Presidency: The History of a Triumphant Succession.* Baltimore: Penguin, 1969.

Pickles, Dorothy. *France: The Fourth Republic*. New York: Barnes & Noble, 1958.

———. *French Politics*. New York: Royal Institute of International Affairs, 1953.

Poats, Rutherford M. *Decision in Korea*. New York: McBride, 1954.

Pogue, Forrest. *George C. Marshall*. 3 vols. New York: Viking, 1963–73.

Poole, Peter A. *The United States and Indochina, from FDR to Nixon*. Hinsdale: Dryden Press, 1973.

Porter, Gareth, ed. *Vietnam: The Definitive Documentation of Human Decisions*. 2 vols. New York: Earl M. Coleman, 1979.

———, ed. *Vietnam: A History in Documents*. New York: New Amsterdam Library, 1981.

Pruessen, Ronald W. *John Foster Dulles: The Road to Power*. New York: Free Press, 1982.

Purifoy, Lewis McCarroll. *Harry Truman's China Policy: McCarthyism and the Diplomacy of Hysteria, 1947–1951*. New York: Franklin Watts, 1976.

Redford, Lawrence H., ed. *The Occupation of Japan: Economic Policy and Reform*. Norfolk: MacArthur Memorial, 1980.

Rees, David. *Korea: The Limited War*. New York: St. Martin's Press, 1964.

Reeve, W. D. *The Republic of Korea: A Political and Economic Study*. London: Oxford Univ. Press, 1963.

Reischauer, Edwin O. *The United States and Japan*. 3d ed. Cambridge: Harvard Univ. Press, 1965.

Ridgway, Matthew B. *The Korean War*. Garden City, N.Y.: Doubleday, 1967.

Riggs, Robert E. *Politics in the United Nations: A Study of United States Influence in the General Assembly*. Urbana: Univ. of Illinois Press, 1958.

Rioux, Jean-Pierre. *The Fourth Republic, 1944–1958*. Translated by Godfrey Rogers. New York: Cambridge Univ. Press, 1987.

Roberts, John G. "The 'Japan Crowd' and the Zaibatsu Restoration." *Japan Interpreter* 22 (Summer 1979): 383–415.

Robinson, Frank M., and Earl Kemp, eds. *Report of the U.S. Senate Hearings—The Truth about Vietnam*. San Diego: Greenleaf Classics, 1966.

Rose, Lisle A. *Roots of Tragedy: The United States and the Struggle for Asia, 1945–1953*. Westport, Conn.: Greenwood, 1976.

Rotter, Andrew J. *The Path to Vietnam: The Origins of the American Commitment to Southeast Asia*. Ithaca: Cornell Univ. Press, 1987.

Rovere, Richard H., and Arthur M. Schlesinger, Jr. *The MacArthur Controversy and American Foreign Policy*. New York: Noonday, 1965.

Rubinstein, Alvin Z., ed. *The Foreign Policy of the Soviet Union.* New York: Random House, 1960.

Rubinstein, Alvin Z., and George Ginsburgs, eds. *Soviet and American Policies in the United Nations.* New York: New York Univ. Press, 1971.

Salisbury, Harrison E. *War between Russia and China.* New York: Norton, 1969.

Sandusky, Michael C. *America's Parallel.* Alexandria, Va.: Old Dominion Press, 1983.

Sarafan, Bertram D. "Military Government in Korea." *Far Eastern Survey* 15 (Nov. 20, 1946): 349–52.

Saxonhoue, Gary R. "Industrial Restructuring in Japan." *Journal of Japanese Studies* 5 (1979): 273–320.

Schaller, Michael. *The American Occupation of Japan: The Origins of the Cold War in Asia.* New York: Oxford Univ. Press, 1985.

———. *Douglas MacArthur: The Far Eastern General.* New York: Oxford Univ. Press, 1989.

———. "MacArthur's Japan: The View from Washington." *Diplomatic History* 10 (Winter 1986): 1–23.

———. "Securing the Great Crescent: Occupied Japan and the Origins of Containment in Southeast Asia." *Journal of American History* 69 (Sept. 1982): 392–414.

———. *The U.S. Crusade in China, 1938–1945.* New York: Columbia Univ. Press, 1979.

Scheer, Robert. *How the United States Got Involved in Vietnam.* Santa Barbara, Calif.: Center for the Study of Democratic Institutions, 1965.

Schnabel, James F. *Policy and Direction: The First Year.* Vol. 3 of *U.S. Army in the Korean War.* Washington, D.C.: Office of the Chief of Military History, U.S. Army, 1972.

Schnabel, James F., and Robert J. Watson. *The History of the Joint Chiefs of Staff: The Joint Chiefs of Staff and National Policy.* Wilmington, Del.: Michael Glazier, 1979.

Schoenbaum, Thomas J. *Waging Peace and War: Dean Rusk in the Truman, Kennedy, and Johnson Years.* New York: Simon & Schuster, 1988.

Schoenbrun, David. *As France Goes.* New York: Harper, 1957.

Schonberger, Howard. *Aftermath of War: America and the Remaking of Japan, 1945–1952.* Kent, Ohio: Kent State Univ. Press, 1989.

———. "American Labor's Cold War in Occupied Japan." *Diplomatic History* 3 (Summer 1979): 249–72.

———. "The General and the Presidency: Douglas MacArthur and the Election of 1948." *Wisconsin Magazine of History* 57 (Spring 1974): 201–19.

———. "The Japan Lobby in American Diplomacy, 1947–1952." *Pacific Historical Review* 46 (1977): 327–59.

———. "U.S. Policy in Post-War Japan: Retreat from Liberalism." *Science & Society* 46 (Spring 1982): 39–59.

———. "Zaibatsu Dissolution and the American Restoration of Japan." *Bulletin of Concerned Asian Scholars* 5 (Sept. 1973): 16–31.

Schulman, Marshall D. *Stalin's Foreign Policy Reappraised.* Cambridge: Harvard Univ. Press, 1963.

Sebald, William. *With MacArthur in Japan: A Personal History of the Occupation.* New York: Norton, 1965.

Service, John S. *The Amerasia Papers: Some Problems in the History of U.S. China Relations.* Berkeley: Univ. of California Press, 1971.

Shaplen, Robert. *The Lost Revolution: The Story of Twenty Years of Neglected Opportunities in Vietnam and of America's Failure to Foster Democracy There.* New York: Harper & Row, 1965.

Sheldon, Walter J. *The Honorable Conquerers: The Occupation of Japan, 1945–1952.* New York: Macmillan, 1965.

Shen, King C. *Vietnam and China, 1938–1954.* Princeton: Princeton Univ. Press, 1969.

Sheridan, James E. *China in Disintegration: The Republican Era in Chinese History, 1912–1949.* New York: Free Press, 1975.

Sherman, William C. "The Evolution of the U.S.-Japan Alliance." *SAIS Review* 5 (1985): 191–200.

Shewmaker, Kenneth E. *Americans and the Chinese Communists, 1927–1945: A Persuading Encounter.* Ithaca: Cornell Univ. Press, 1971.

Simmons, Robert R. *The Strained Alliance: Peking, Pyongyang, Moscow, and the Politics of the Korean Civil War.* New York: Free Press, 1975.

Smith, Beverly. "The White House Story of Why We Went to War in Korea." *Saturday Evening Post,* Nov. 10, 1951, pp. 22–24, 78–79, 86, and 90.

Smith, Gaddis. *Dean Acheson.* Vol. 16 of *American Secretaries of State and Their Diplomacy,* ed. Samuel Flagg Bemis and Robert H. Ferrell. New York: Cooper Square, 1972.

Smith, Robert. *MacArthur in Korea: The Naked Emperor.* New York: Simon & Schuster, 1982.

Spanier, John W. *The Truman-MacArthur Controversy and the Korean War.* New York: Norton, 1965.

Stairs, Denis. "The United Nations and the Politics of the Korean War." *International Journal* 25 (Spring 1970): 302–20.

Stang, Alan. *The Actor: The True Story of John Foster Dulles, Secretary of State, 1953–1959.* Boston: Western Islands, 1968.

Steele, A. T. *The American People and China.* New York: McGraw-Hill, 1966.

Stephens, Michael Dawson. "South Vietnam: New American Frontier." *Contemporary Review* 204 (Dec. 1963): 305–9.

Stuart, John Leighton. *The Forgotten Ambassador: The Reports of John Leighton Stuart, 1946–1949.* Edited by Kenneth W. Rea and John C. Brewer. Boulder, Colo.: Westview, 1981.

———. *Fifty Years in China: The Memoirs of John Leighton Stuart, Missionary and Ambassador.* New York: Random House, 1954.

Stueck, William, Jr. "An Exchange of Opinion (Cold War Revisionism and the Origins of the Korean Conflict: The Kolko Thesis)." *Pacific Historical Review* 57 (1973): 537–75.

———. *The Road to Confrontation: American Policy toward China and Korea, 1947–1950.* Chapel Hill: Univ. of North Carolina Press, 1981.

———. "The Soviet Union and the Origins of the Korean War." *World Politics* 27 (July 1976): 623–35.

———. *The Wedemeyer Mission: American Politics and Foreign Policy during the Cold War.* Athens: Univ. of Georgia Press, 1984.

Suh, Dae-sook. *The Korean Communist Movement, 1918–1948.* Princeton: Princeton Univ. Press, 1967.

———. "A Preconceived Formula for Sovietization: The Communist Takeover of North Korea." In *The Anatomy of Communist Takeovers,* ed. Thomas T. Hammond. New Haven: Yale Univ. Press, 1975.

Sunoo, Hagwon, and William N. Angus. "American Policy in Korea: Two Views." *Far Eastern Survey* 25 (July 31, 1946): 228–31.

Swartout, Robert J. "American Historians and the Outbreak of the Korean War: An Historiographical Essay." *Asia Quarterly* 1 (1979): 65–77.

Temple, Harry. "Deaf Captains: Intelligence, Policy, and the Origins of the Korean War." *International Studies Notes* 8 (1981–1982): 19–23.

Thomas, Nigel, and Peter Abbott. *The Korean War, 1950–1953.* London: Osprey, 1986.

Tint, Herbert. *French Foreign Policy since the Second World War.* London: Weidenfeld and Nicolson, 1972.

Tozer, Warren. "Last Bridge to China: The Shanghai Power Company, the Truman Administration, and the Chinese Communists." *Diplomatic History* 1 (Winter 1977): 64–78.

Trager, Frank N. *Why Viet Nam?* New York: Frederick A. Praeger, 1966.

Truman, Harry S. *Memoirs: Years of Decision.* Garden City, N.Y.: Doubleday, 1955.

———. *Memoirs: Years of Trial and Hope.* Garden City, N.Y.: Doubleday, 1956.

Truman, Margaret. *Harry S. Truman.* New York: William Morrow, 1973.

Tuchman, Barbara W. *Stilwell and the American Experience in China, 1911–1945*. New York: Bantam Books, 1970.

Tucker, Nancy Bernkopf. "American Policy toward Sino-Japanese Trade in the Postwar Years: Politics and Prosperity." *Diplomatic History* 8 (Summer 1984): 183–208.

———. *Patterns in the Dust: Chinese-American Relations and the Recognition Controversy, 1949–1950*. New York: Columbia Univ. Press, 1983.

———. "An Unlikely Peace: American Missionaries and the Chinese Communists, 1948–1950." *Pacific Historical Review* 45 (Feb. 1976): 97–116.

Uchino, Tatsuro. *Japan's Postwar Economy: An Insider's View of Its History and Its Future*. Tokyo: Kodansha International, 1983.

"U.S. Defense Chiefs Back from Orient." *New York Times*, June 25, 1950, p. 18.

Utley, Jonathan G. *Going to War with Japan, 1937–1941*. Knoxville: Univ. of Tennessee Press, 1985.

Vandenberg, Arthur H. *The Private Papers of Senator Vandenberg*. Edited by Walter Millis. Boston: Houghton Mifflin, 1952.

Varg, Paul A. *The Closing of the Door: Sino-American Relations, 1936–1946*. East Lansing: Michigan State Univ. Press, 1973.

Vinacke, Harold M. *The United States and the Far East, 1945–1951*. Stanford: Stanford Univ. Press, 1952.

Wall, Irwin M. *The United States and the Making of Postwar France, 1945–1954*. Cambridge: Cambridge Univ. Press, 1991.

Ward, Robert Edward. *The Allied Occupation of Japan, 1945–1952*. Chicago: American Association, 1974.

Warner, Albert L. "How the Korean Decision Was Made." *Harper's*, June 1951, pp. 99–106.

Warner, Geoffrey. "The United States and Vietnam." *International Affairs* 48 (July 1972): 379–94.

———. "Who Started the Korean War." *Monthly Review* 34 (March 1983): 43–53.

Wedemeyer, Albert C. *Wedemeyer Reports!* New York: Henry Holt, 1958.

Weems, Benjamin. "Behind the Korean Elections." *Far Eastern Survey* 17 (June 23, 1948): 142–46.

Westerfield, H. Bradford. *Foreign Policy and Party Politics: Pearl Harbor to Korea*. New Haven: Yale Univ. Press, 1955.

Whitney, Courtney. *MacArthur: His Rendezvous with History*. New York: Knopf, 1956.

"Who Really Runs the State Department: Businessmen, Lawyers, Foreign

Service Officers, College Professors, and Army Men." *U.S. News & World Report,* May 5, 1950, pp. 32–33.

Wickberg, Edgar. "Japanese Land Policies in Taiwan, 1895–1945." *Agricultural History* 48 (July 1969): 369–79.

Wildes, Harry Emerson. *Typhoons in Tokyo: The Occupation and Its Aftermath.* New York: Octagon, 1978.

Williams, Justin. "Completing Japan's Political Reorientation, 1947–1952: Crucial Phase of the Allied Occupation." *American Historical Review* 73 (June 1968): 1454–69.

———. *Japan's Political Revolution under MacArthur: A Participant's Account.* Athens: Univ. of Georgia Press, 1979.

Willoughby, Charles A., and John Chamberlain. *MacArthur, 1941–1951.* New York: McGraw-Hill, 1955.

Wiltz, John Edward. "The MacArthur Hearings of 1951: The Secret Testimony." *Military Affairs* 39 (Dec. 1975): 166–73.

Wolfe, Robert, ed. *Americans as Proconsuls: United States Military Government in Germany and Japan, 1944–1952.* Carbondale: Southern Illinois Univ. Press, 1984.

"World Policy and Bipartisanship: An Interview with Senator Tom Connally." *U.S. News & World Report.* May 5, 1950, pp. 28 and 31.

Yamamura, Kozo. *Economic Policy in Postwar Japan: Growth versus Economic Democracy.* Berkeley: Univ. of California Press, 1967.

Yanaga, Chitoshi. "Japan." In *The Encyclopedia Americana Annual, 1951.*

GOVERNMENT DOCUMENTS

Acheson, Dean. *American Policy toward China: Statement before a Joint Senate Committee, June 4, 1951.* Washington, D.C.: GPO, 1951.

———. "Crisis in Asia—An Examination of U.S. Policy." *Department of State Bulletin* 22 (Jan. 23, 1950): 111–18.

———. "The Requirements of Reconstruction." *Department of State Bulletin* 16 (May 18, 1947): 991–94.

Blum, Robert M. *The United States and Vietnam: 1944–1947.* Washington, D.C.: GPO, 1972.

Muccio, John J. "Military Aid to Korean Security Forces." *Department of State Bulletin* 22 (June 26, 1950): 1048–49.

Rusk, Dean. "U.S. Concern over Korea's Mounting Inflation." *Department of State Bulletin* 22 (April 17, 1950): 602.

Sawyer, Major Robert K. *Military Advisors in Korea: KMAG in Peace and*

War. Washington, D.C.: Office of the Chief of Military History, 1962.

Truman, Harry S. *Public Papers of the Presidents of the United States: Harry S. Truman*. Washington, D.C.: GPO, 1963.

―――. "Recommendations on Greece and Turkey." *Department of State Bulletin* 16 (March 23, 1947): 534–37.

U.S. Congress. House. *Background Information on Korea: Report of the Committee on Foreign Relations Pursuant to H.R. 206, 81st Cong., 2d sess., 1950*.

U.S. Congress. House. Subcommittee of the Committee on Appropriations. *First Deficiency Appropriations Bill for 1947: Hearings before the Subcommittee of the Committee on Appropriations on H.R. 2849, 80th Cong., 1st sess., 1947*.

U.S. Congress. Senate. Committee on Armed Services and Committee on Foreign Relations. *Military Situation in the Far East: Hearings before the Committee on Armed Services and the Committee on Foreign Relations: An Inquiry into the Military Situation and the Facts Surrounding the Relief of General of the Army Douglas MacArthur from His Assignments in That Area, 3 pts., 81st Cong., 2d sess., 1951*.

U.S. Congress. House. Committee on Foreign Affairs. *Assistance to Greece and Turkey, Hearings before the Committee on Foreign Affairs on H.R. 22616, 80th Cong., 1st sess., 1947*.

―――. *Korean Aid: Hearings before the House Committee on Foreign Affairs on H.R. 5330, 80th Cong., 1st sess., 1949*.

―――. *United States Foreign Policy for a Post-War Recovery Program: Hearings before the Committee on Foreign Affairs on H.R. 4840 and H.R. 4570, 80th Cong., 1st and 2d sess., 1948*.

U.S. Congress. House. Committee on International Relations. *United States Policy in the Far East: Selected Executive Sessions of the House Committee on International Relations: Hearings on the Far East Portion of the Mutual Defense Assistance Act of 1950, 8 vols., 81st Cong., 1st sess., 1976*.

―――. *Economic Assistance to China and Korea, 1949–1950: Hearings Held in Executive Session before the Committee on Foreign Relations on S. 1063, S. 2319, and S. 2845, 81st Cong., 1st and 2d sess., 1974*.

―――. *Executive Sessions of the Senate Foreign Relations Committee of the Senate Foreign Relations Committee, 1947–1948, 2 vols., 80th Cong., 1st and 2d sess., 1976*.

―――. *Legislative Origins of the Truman Doctrine: Hearings of the Committee on Foreign Relations in Executive Session on S. 938, 80th Cong., 1st sess., 1973*.

————. *Reviews of the World Situation, 1949–1950: Hearings Held in Executive Session before the Committee on Foreign Relations*, 2 vols., 81st Cong., 1st and 2d sess., 1974.

————. *The United States and the Korean Problem: Documents, 1943–1953*. Washington, D.C.: GPO, 1953.

————. *The United States and Vietnam: 1944–1947*. Washington, D.C.: GPO, 1972.

U.S. Congress. Senate. Committee on Foreign Relations and the and the Department of State. *A Decade of American Foreign Policy: Basic Documents, 1941–1949*. Washington, D.C.: GPO, 1950.

U.S. Department of Agriculture. *Agricultural Statistics, 1948*. Washington, D.C.: GPO, 1949.

————. *Agricultural Statistics, 1952*. Washington, D.C.: GPO, 1952.

U.S. Department of Defense. *United States–Vietnam Relations, 1945–1967*. 12 vols. Washington, D.C.: GPO, 1971.

U.S. Department of State. *American Foreign Policy, 1950–1955: Basic Documents*. 2 vols. Washington, D.C.: GPO, 1957.

————. *Conflict in Korea*. Washington, D.C.: GPO, 1951.

————. *Foreign Relations of the United States, 1945*. Vol. 6. Washington, D.C.: GPO, 1969.

————. *Foreign Relations of the United States, 1946*. Vol. 1. Washington, D.C.: GPO, 1973.

————. *Foreign Relations of the United States, 1946*. Vol. 8. Washington, D.C.: GPO, 1971.

————. *Foreign Relations of the United States, 1947*. Vol. 1. Washington, D.C.: GPO, 1973.

————. *Foreign Relations of the United States, 1947*. Vol. 3. Washington, D.C.: GPO, 1972.

————. *Foreign Relations of the United States, 1947*. Vol. 6. Washington, D.C.: GPO, 1972.

————. *Foreign Relations of the United States, 1947*. Vol. 7. Washington, D.C.: GPO, 1972.

————. *Foreign Relations of the United States, 1948*. Vol. 1. Washington, D.C.: GPO, 1975.

————. *Foreign Relations of the United States, 1948*. Vol. 6. Washington, D.C.: GPO, 1974.

————. *Foreign Relations of the United States, 1948*. Vol. 7. Washington, D.C.: GPO, 1973.

————. *Foreign Relations of the United States, 1948*. Vol. 8. Washington, D.C.: GPO, 1973.

————. *Foreign Relations of the United States, 1949*. Vol. 1. Washington, D.C.: GPO, 1976.

————. *Foreign Relations of the United States, 1949*. Vol. 4. Washington, D.C.: GPO, 1975.

————. *Foreign Relations of the United States, 1949*. Vol. 6. Washington, D.C.: GPO, 1974.

————. *Foreign Relations of the United States, 1949*. Vol. 7. Washington, D.C.: GPO, 1975.

————. *Foreign Relations of the United States, 1949*. Vol. 8. Washington, D.C.: GPO, 1978.

————. *Foreign Relations of the United States, 1949*. Vol. 9. Washington, D.C.: GPO, 1974.

————. *Foreign Relations of the United States, 1950*. Vol. 1. Washington, D.C.: GPO, 1977.

————. *Foreign Relations of the United States, 1950*. Vol. 2. Washington, D.C.: GPO, 1976.

————. *Foreign Relations of the United States, 1950*. Vol. 3. Washington, D.C.: GPO, 1977.

————. *Foreign Relations of the United States, 1950*. Vol. 4. Washington, D.C.: GPO, 1980.

————. *Foreign Relations of the United States, 1950*. Vol. 6. Washington, D.C.: GPO, 1976.

————. *Foreign Relations of the United States, 1950*. Vol. 7. Washington, D.C.: GPO, 1976.

————. *Foreign Relations of the United States, 1951*. Vol. 6. Washington, D.C.: GPO, 1977.

————. *Foreign Relations of the United States, 1952–1954*. Vol. 13. Washington, D.C.: GPO, 1982.

————. *Hearings on American Foreign Policy, 1950–1955*. 2 vols. Washington, D.C.: GPO, 1957.

————. *Korea's Independence*. Washington, D.C.: GPO, 1947.

————. *North Korea: A Case Study in the Techniques of Takeover*. Washington, D.C.: GPO, 1961.

————. *United States Relations with China*. Washington, D.C.: GPO, 1949.

————. "U.S. Recognizes Viet Nam, Laos, and Cambodia." *Department of State Bulletin* 22 (Feb. 20, 1950): 291–92.

————. Office of Intelligence Research and Analysis. *The Place of Foreign Trade in the Japanese Economy*. Washington, D.C.: GPO, 1946.

————. Office of Media Services. *Aggression from the North: The Record of North Vietnam's Campaign to Conquer South Vietnam*. Washington, D.C.: GPO, 1965.

————. Office of Northeast Asian Affairs. *United States Relations with Japan, 1945–1952*. New York: American Institute of Pacific Relations, 1953.

―――. *The State Department Policy Planning Staff Papers,* 3 vols. New York: Garland, 1983.

―――. *Occupation of Japan.* Washington: GPO, 1946.

―――. *The Record on Korean Unification, 1943–1960.* Washington, D.C.: GPO, 1960.

―――. *United States Relations with China.* Washington, D.C.: GPO, 1949.

Vincent, John Carter. "The Post-War Period in the Far East." *Department of State Bulletin* 13 (Oct. 21, 1945): 644–48.

HISTORICAL MATERIALS IN THE HARRY S. TRUMAN LIBRARY

Presidential Papers:

Appointments Files
General Files
Intelligence Files
Korean War Files
National Security Council Meetings Files
Personal Correspondence Files
Press Conference Transcripts Files
Trip Files

Manuscript Collections:

Papers of Dean Acheson
Papers of John M. Allison
Papers of Max Bishop
Papers of Will L. Clayton
Papers of Clark Clifford
Papers of Matthew J. Connelly
Papers of Rose A. Conway
Papers of George M. Elsey
Papers of Paul G. Hoffman
Papers of John F. Melby
Papers of Frank Pace
Papers of Sidney W. Souers
Papers of Harry S. Truman
Papers of James E. Webb

Oral History Interviews (Transcripts):

Acheson, Dean. Interview with "Messrs: Hillman, Noyes, and Heller" (no first names provided). Feb. 16–17, 1955.

304   BIBLIOGRAPHY

Battle, Lucius D. Interview with Richard D. McKinzie and Theodore A. Wilson. Washington, D.C., June 23, 1971.

Bond, Niles W. Interview with Richard D. McKinzie. Washington, D.C., Dec. 28, 1973.

Bruce, David K. E. Interview with Jerry N. Hess. Washington, D.C., March 1, 1972.

Butterworth, W. Walton. Interview with Richard D. McKinzie and Theodore S. Wilson. Princeton, N.J., July 6, 1971.

Cabot, John M. Interview with Richard D. McKinzie. Manchester, Mass., July 18, 1973.

Clubb, O. Edmund. Interview with Richard D. McKinzie. New York, June 26, 1974.

Griffin, R. Allen. Interview with James R. Fuchs. Pebble Beach, Calif., Feb. 15, 1974.

Hoffman, Paul G. Interview with Philip C. Brooks. New York, Oct. 25, 1964.

Johnson, Joseph E. Interview with Richard D. McKinzie. Princeton, N.J., June 29, 1973.

Lovett, Robert A. Interview with Richard D. McKinzie and Theodore S. Wilson. New York, July 7, 1971.

Melby, John F. Interview with Robert Accinelli, Ontario, Can., Nov. 7, 14, 21, and 28, 1986.

Martin, Edwin W. Interview with Richard D. McKinzie. Washington, D.C., June 3, 1975.

Merchant, Livingston. Interview with Richard D. McKinzie. Washington, D.C., May 27, 1975.

Muccio, John J. Interview with Jerry N. Hess. Washington, D.C., Feb. 10 and 18, 1971.

———. Interview with Richard D. McKinzie. Washington, D.C., Dec. 27, 1973.

Nitze, Paul H. Interview with Richard D. McKinzie. Arlington, Va., June 11 and 17 and Aug. 4, 5, and 6, 1975.

Pace, Frank. Interview with Jerry N. Hess. New York and Washington, D.C., Jan. 17 and 22, Feb. 17 and 25, and June 26, 1972.

Sprouse, Philip D. Interview with James R. Fuchs. Orinda, Calif., Feb. 11, 1974.

HISTORICAL MATERIALS IN THE NATIONAL ARCHIVES

Record Group 16. Records of the Department of Agriculture. Records of Correspondence.

Record Group 59. Records of the Department of State. Decimal Records.
Record Group 218. Records of the Department of Defense. Modern Military Records Division. Records of the Joint Chiefs of Staff and National Security Council.
Record Group 331. Records of the Department of Defense. Modern Military Records Division. Records of the Supreme Commander Allied Powers.
Record Group 353. Records of the Office of the Department of State. Records of the State War Navy Coordinating Committee and the State-Army-Navy-Air Force Coordinating Committee.
Microfilm Series. LM 80. Records of the Department of State on Korean Policy, 1944–47.

INTERVIEWS CONDUCTED BY THE AUTHOR

Battle, Lucius D. Washington, D.C. Interview, 30 May 1990.
Bishop, Max W. S. Ailey, Ga. Interview, 12 April 1988.
Bishop, Max W. S. To Ailey, Ga. Telephone interview, 30 Nov. 1988.
Bishop, Max W. S. To Ailey, Ga. Telephone interview, 12 April 1991.
Bishop, Max W. S. To Ailey, Ga. Telephone interview, 10 April 1992.
Bishop, Max W. S. To Ailey, Ga. Telephone interview, 11 April 1992.
Bishop, Max W. S. To Ailey, Ga. Telephone interview, 20 April 1992.
Bishop, Max W. S. To Ailey, Ga. Telephone interview, 20 June 1992.
Nitze, Paul H. Washington, D.C. Interview, 25 July 1989.
Rusk, Dean. Athens, Ga. Interview, 11 April 1988.
Rusk, Dean. To Athens, Ga. Telephone interview, 6 July 1988.
Rusk, Dean. To Athens, Ga. Telephone interview, 30 Nov. 1988.

CORRESPONDENCE

Battle, Lucius D. Letter to author, Aug. 14, 1989.
Bishop, Max W. S. Letter to author, Dec. 1, 1987.
Bishop, Max W. S. Letter to author, March 18, 1988.
Dupuy, Trevor Nevitt. Letter to author, Aug. 14, 1989.
Kennan, George. Letter to author, Nov. 28, 1988.
Kennan, George. Letter to author, June 13, 1990.
Nitze, Paul H. Letter to author, May 31, 1989.
Nitze, Paul H. Letter to author, July 11, 1989.
Nitze, Paul H. Letter to author, Jan. 29, 1991.

Nitze, Paul H. Letter to author, March 19, 1991.
Nitze, Paul H. Letter to author, Feb. 12, 1992.
Rusk, Dean. Letter to author, June 24, 1987.
Rusk, Dean. Letter to author, Aug. 17, 1987.
Rusk, Dean. Letter to author, April 10, 1989.
Rusk, Dean. Letter to author, Feb. 1, 1991.
Saltzman, Charles E. Letter to author, Oct. 22, 1987.
Webb, James E. Letter to author, March 17, 1986.
Webb, James E. Letter to author, July 21, 1987.

Index

Abbott, George M., 181–82
Acheson, Alice Stanley, 18
Acheson, Dean:
  aid strategy articulated by, 27–28, 54,
    210n, 225n
  Asian expertise of, 182, 210n, 225n,
    267n
  background of, 18–19
  bipartisan foreign policy reestablished
    by, 116
  on comprehensive Asian policy, 73
  congressional dealings with, 20–21, 54–
    55, 58–59, 69–72, 74–75, 93–95,
    108–10, 196–98, 226n, 232n–33n
  critics of, 20–21
  defense budget increase promoted by,
    117
  demeanor of, 20
  document code used by, 208n
  on European recovery vs. Asian issues,
    21, 211n, 218n, 239n
  intelligence of, 19, 67
  Japanese rehabilitation orchestrated by,
    25–28, 29, 30–39, 48–49, 202–3,
    205–6
  Korea policy and, 50–60, 64, 66–85
  loyalty shown by, 19, 20
  mainland China policy and, 135–62,
    266n
  nuclear buildup promoted by, 111
  peace treaty negotiations and, 40–47
  personnel decisions made by, 44, 111,
    114–15, 186, 208n–9n, 219n–20n
  physical appearance of, 20, 111
  PRC diplomatic recognition opposed by,
    152–55, 262n, 264n
  professional respect for, 19–20, 67
  Sino-Japanese trade assessed by, 135,
    140–43

Sino-Soviet relations undermined by,
    157–59
  Southeast Asia policy and, 164–65,
    167–75, 179–201, 267n, 268n,
    271n, 277n
  State Department positions held by, 18–
    19, 25, 27, 29, 32, 59, 66, 172,
    173
  Taiwan policy and, 73, 86–87, 91–134
  Truman Doctrine defended by, 54
  on UN involvement, 73–74, 79–80, 83,
    103, 232n, 256n
  on Vietnam War, 205
Achilles, Theodore C., 181, 182
Advisory Committee on Development of
  Japanese and Korean Trade, 212n,
  222n
Allied Council on Japan (ACJ), 23
Allison, John M., 45, 59–60, 80, 83, 84,
  202, 219n, 227n, 272n
Anderson, USS, 194
Andrews, Stanley, 196
Annam, 169, 176, 177, 192
Army, U.S., 30, 64, 93, 223n, 227n
Asia:
  comprehensive policy adopted for, 17–
    18, 72, 73, 106, 153, 157, 191
  European priority over, 21, 29, 55–56,
    111, 167–68, 211n, 218n, 239n
  see also Southeast Asia
Atcheson, George, 31, 33–34
Auriol, Vincent, 180, 185
Austin, Warren R., 156

Bacon, Ruth E., 156
Bank of China, 138
Bao Dai, 176, 177, 178–79, 180–82, 183,
  185, 188–89, 200–201, 274n
Barkley, Alben, 93

Barr, David G., 160, 266*n*
Barrett, David, 144
Battle, Lucius, 20, 43–44, 46, 47, 210*n*, 229*n*–30*n*, 235*n*
  on European issues vs. Asian concerns, 211*n*, 218*n*, 239*n*
Baudet, Philippe, 174
Beijing Union Medical College, 262*n*
Bevin, Ernest, 42–43, 153, 195, 242*n*
Bidault, Georges, 173
Bishop, Max, 231*n*, 250*n*
  background of, 216*n*, 229*n*, 252*n*
  Communist expansion foreseen by, 66, 83
  DA admired by, 20, 67
  on DA's European emphasis, 21
  on DA's Far Eastern policies, 139, 142, 215*n*, 249*n*, 262*n*, 271*n*
  Japanese peace treaty urged by, 40–41, 42
  Japanese recovery program and, 25, 33, 37–38, 39, 66, 68, 83–84, 89, 122, 202, 213*n*, 214*n*, 216*n*, 236*n*
  Korean policy analyzed by, 66–67, 68, 83–84
  MacArthur's rapport with, 33, 37
  on Rhee as administrator, 229*n*
  State Department positions of, 25, 33, 66, 68, 80, 208*n*, 229*n*, 249*n*, 252*n*
  on Taiwan policy, 89, 91, 122, 238*n*, 252*n*
  on Truman's admiration for Marshall, 228*n*
Blum, Léon, 171, 172
Bollaert, Emile, 173, 174, 177
Bond, Niles W., 62, 66, 67, 228*n*, 237*n*
Bonesteel, Charles, 221*n*
Bonnet, Henri, 171, 193, 195, 198, 274*n*
Borden, William S., 211*n*
Borton, Hugh, 41, 212*n*
Boxer Rebellion, 154
Bradley, Omar N., 43, 68–69, 78, 82, 107, 227*n*, 231*n*, 236*n*–37*n*, 247*n*
Brandeis, Louis D., 18
Bridges, Styles, 90
British Commonwealth:
  Chinese Communist threat and, 119, 195, 255*n*
  Chinese peace negotiations avoided by, 138
  Far Eastern colonies relinquished by, 163, 167, 171

  Japanese trade with, 220*n*–21*n*
  in Japanese treaty negotiations, 42–43
  in postwar Greece and Turkey, 53
  PRC recognized by, 153
Bruce, David K. E., 186–87, 201, 211*n*, 225*n*
Burma:
  British withdrawal from, 163, 171
  civil war in, 76, 183–84, 190–91
  Communist threat to, 188, 193, 272*n*
  economic aid to, 197, 198
  food exported from, 233*n*
  Japanese reparations paid to, 213*n*
  rice production in, 76, 183–84, 190, 200, 273*n*
  U.S. relations with, 163, 164
Burns, James, 116–17
Butterworth, W. Walton, 116, 274*n*
  Chinese Communist contacts viewed by, 143, 145, 259*n*, 261*n*, 263*n*
  French colonialism in Vietnam attacked by, 185–86, 187, 188
  Japanese peace treaty and, 42, 43
  Japanese recovery and, 33, 37, 38, 215*n*
  Korean policy and, 61, 62–63, 64, 65, 66, 228*n*
  policy on Chinese trade developed by, 141, 142
  on Sino-Soviet relationship, 158
  State Department position of, 33, 44, 66, 114–15, 208*n*, 209*n*, 223*n*
  Taiwan policy and, 99–100, 102, 107, 108, 240*n*, 246*n*
Byrnes, James F., 167, 168, 169, 170

Cabot, John M., 90, 145, 148–49, 259*n*
Caffery, Jefferson, 172–73, 174, 178, 180–81, 182
Cairo peace conference (1943), 88, 109, 247*n*
Cambodia:
  French aid against Vietnam solicited by, 177
  French-backed government created in, 192, 193
  as part of French Indochina, 164, 165, 169
  rice production in, 191
Canton, as Nationalist capital, 143
CCP, *see* Chinese Communist Party
Central Intelligence Agency (CIA):
  domino theory developed by, 188
  on Japanese recovery, 216*n*

Korean hostilities predicted by, 69
PRC interrogation transcript obtained
by, 150
on Southeast Asia, 188–89, 192, 193,
194, 272*n*
Taiwan policy analyzed by, 88, 89–90,
91, 103, 106, 113, 118, 129, 130,
155, 255*n*
Chang Chun, 106
Chen Cheng:
as Chiang's ally, 95, 98, 102
economic aid programs and, 91, 92–93,
96
replacements considered for, 96, 97, 99,
101, 104–5, 132, 242*n*
Chiang Kai-shek:
back-channel negotiations with, 125–26
CIA information on, 241*n*
Communist threat and, 112, 113
congressional support for, 88
coup d'état proposed against, 105, 118,
119–21, 123–25, 126–27, 128,
133, 253*n*
economic policies of, 127
Korean War assistance offered by, 129,
255*n*
MacArthur's praise of, 130
military aid policy and, 73, 107, 112–13
monetary reserves expropriated by, 138,
241*n*
Nationalist presidency and, 95, 117–18,
137, 138, 241*n*, 250*n*
political maneuvering by, 95–98, 101,
102, 104–6, 204, 242*n*
repressive policies implemented by, 131
resignation offered by, 122, 123, 126,
127, 128–29, 133, 252*n*
U.S. opposition to, 87, 103–4, 119,
122–25, 132, 133, 134, 204,
252*n*–53*n*
Chiang Kai-shek, Madame, 241*n*
China, People's Republic of (PRC):
anti-American attitudes of, 150, 152,
159
blockade considered against, 151, 262*n*
British interests in, 153
consular officials mistreated by, 150–52
DRV recognized by, 192
economic problems of, 113, 136, 140,
142, 160, 162, 258*n*
food supply in, 160, 194
formal establishment of, 108, 150
iron industry in, 136, 140, 257*n*

Japanese relations with, 42, 43, 48, 76,
135, 157, 159–60, 162, 203, 220*n*,
265*n*, 267*n*
in Korean War, 131, 136, 160–61,
235*n*, 236*n*, 264*n*
Nationalist hostilities with, 113, 114,
118, 122, 128, 129–31, 133–34
population of, 136, 257*n*
Soviet alliance with, 113, 118, 135,
136–37, 151, 157–59, 161
Taiwan invasion planned by, 113
UN membership sought by, 155–56,
198, 203, 264*n*
U.S. trade interests in, 140, 141, 146,
157, 159, 162, 265*n*
Vietnam aided by, 193, 195
Western diplomatic recognition of, 112,
113, 152–55, 262*n*, 264*n*
see also China policy; Chinese Communist Party
China Aid Act (1948), 74, 92, 95, 107,
110, 127, 239*n*, 240*n*–41*n*, 248*n*,
276*n*
China lobby, 88, 90, 91, 93–95, 107,
108–10
China policy:
civil war analysis and, 138–39
diplomatic recognition in, 152–55,
262*n*, 264*n*
first stage of, 135, 136–47
initial formulation of, 88
low strategic priority accorded to, 136,
139–40
McCarthyism and, 115–16
PPS analysis developed for, 136–37,
138, 139
second stage of, 135–36, 147–61
Sino-Russian relationship analyzed for,
136–37
on trade issues, 157, 158–60, 162, 203
two-policy approach undertaken in,
111–12, 248*n*
U.S. diplomatic facilities and, 147–50,
154, 263*n*
China White Paper *(United States Relations with China)*, 107–8
Chinese Communist Party (CCP):
anti-American attitudes expressed by,
143, 145, 146–47, 159
civil war progress and, 87, 95, 137–38,
143
diplomatic status ignored by, 147–50
economic policies of, 146

Chinese Communist Party (*continued*)
Japanese trade with, 76, 135, 140–41,
142–43, 157, 159–60, 162, 258*n*,
265*n*, 267*n*
Marxist-Leninist doctrines espoused by,
146, 147
Nationalist peace negotiations with, 138
private radio transmitters confiscated by,
148
Soviet relationship with, 113, 118, 135,
136–37, 139, 145, 146, 151, 157–
59, 161, 262*n*
Taiwan policy and, 87, 89–90, 92, 99,
103, 106, 107, 245*n*, 246*n*
trade policy developed by, 146, 158–59
see also China, People's Republic of
Chinese Nationalist Army:
Chiang's repressive measures imposed
on, 131, 132
leadership of, 97, 127, 250*n*
size of, 255*n*
U.S. aid program for, 87, 95, 127, 248*n*
Chinese Nationalists (Kuomintang):
capital city moved by, 143
Chiang's leadership of, 95, 98, 117–18,
137, 138, 241*n*, 250*n*
in civil war, 87, 95, 137–38, 143
congressional support for, 88, 90, 91
early Soviet relations with, 146
economic resources of, 127
on French Indochina, 268*n*
Japanese relationship with, 220*n*
military resources of, 106–7, 108–11,
118–19, 127, 130, 132, 251*n*
monetary reserves of, 127, 138
native Taiwanese vs., 90, 91
peace negotiations attempted by, 137–
38, 241*n*
political maneuvering among, 95–98,
101–6, 118, 119–21, 241*n*, 242*n*
PRC attacked by, 114, 122, 128, 129
UN membership of, 155, 156
U.S. recognition of, 153, 155
"Whampoa" military clique of, 138
see also Taiwan; Taiwan policy
Chi Yu-heng, 150, 152
Chou En-lai, 143
anti-American views expressed by, 146–
47, 159
in Chinese Communist factional disputes, 144
secret discussions with, 135, 145–46,
161, 162, 260*n*
Western recognition sought by, 144

Chow, Albert, 125, 253*n*, 255*n*
Chow, William Jack, 125
Chusan Islands, invasion of, 118
Clark, Lewis, 143, 259*n*
Clayton, William L., 26, 29, 211*n*
Clubb, O. Edmund, 144, 148, 150, 154–
55, 255*n*, 262*n*
coal industry, 140, 141, 151
Cochinchina, 169, 173, 177, 179, 180,
186, 192
Cominform, 136
Commonwealth Club, 158
communism, see containment policy; specific countries
Communist Information Bureau, 136
"Condensed Check List on China and Formosa" (Rusk), 129
Congress, U.S.:
China bloc in, 88, 90, 91, 93–95, 107,
108–10
DA and, 20–21, 54–55, 58–59, 69–72,
74–75, 93–95, 108–10, 196–98,
226*n*, 232*n*–33*n*
foreign aid allocated by, 30, 53, 54, 58–
59, 64–65, 69–72, 74–75, 78, 92,
109–10, 129, 196–98, 211*n*, 240*n*,
275*n*
military assistance allocations of, 78,
92, 93–95, 107
partisan control of, 19, 58
Connally, Tom, 72, 79, 95, 110
Consultants on the Far East, 189
containment policy, 18, 72, 112
global economic recovery for, 203
Japanese recovery and, 17–18, 41, 42,
66, 83–84
in Southeast Asia, 188, 189, 193
South Korea and, 60, 79, 80, 83, 84
Taiwan policy and, 102, 112, 121
Cooper, John Sherman, 219*n*
Council of Foreign Ministers, 217*n*
Craig, Loris F., 120
Cumings, Bruce, 236*n*
Czechoslovakia, Japanese peace settlement
rejected by, 47

d'Argenlieu, Thierry, 168, 169, 170, 172,
173
Davies, John P., 41, 90, 148, 149
Deconcentration Review Board, 36
Defense Department, U.S.:
comprehensive Far East strategy of, 72–
73, 106, 157
on military aid to China, 93, 106

military budget and, 117
State Department relations with, 106–7,
    116–17, 157, 196, 218n, 228n
Taiwan policy and, 86, 91, 93, 106, 122
see also Johnson, Louis A.; Joint Chiefs
    of Staff
de Gaulle, Charles, 166, 171, 173
Democratic Liberal Party (Japan), 216n
Democratic National Committee, 231n
Democratic Party, in congressional elec-
    tions of 1946, 19
Dening, M. E., 42
Dewey, Thomas E., 248n
Diem, Ngo Dinh, 205
Dillon, Read, and Company, 35–36
Dodge, Joseph M., 36–37, 39, 215n, 218n
domino theory, 188
Doon, Mrs. W. F., 253n
Dorn, Frank, 124, 125
Draper, William H., Jr., 35–36, 37, 39,
    42, 212n
Dulles, John Foster:
    background of, 44, 219n–20n, 229n
    containment advocated by, 121, 122
    DA's policies vs., 204, 205
    Japanese peace terms and, 44–45, 46,
      220n
    on Southeast Asian trade, 273n
    Taiwan policy and, 121, 122, 124, 131,
      252n
Dupuy, Trevor Nevitt, 227n

Economic Cooperation Administration
    (ECA):
    Chinese communism and, 258n–59n
    directors of, 64, 120, 229n
    Indochinese aid program of, 178, 182
    Korean assistance programs and, 64–65,
      69, 77, 83, 232n, 234n
    on Sino-Japanese trade, 141, 142
    Southeast Asian aid distributed by, 197–
      98, 199
    Taiwan aid administered by, 91–93, 95,
      97–98, 99, 100, 110, 119, 120,
      127, 129, 240n, 247n–48n
    trade relationships and, 189, 238n, 273n
Economic Recovery for Occupied Areas
    Program, 211n
Edgar, Donald D., 93, 98, 105, 106
Eisenhower, Dwight D., 60, 69, 204,
    219n, 221n, 227n
Elysée agreements, 180, 181–82, 185, 186
Erskine, Graves B., 198–99
Europe:

postwar aid to, 28, 29
postwar colonialism and, 164, 166–68,
    172, 184–85, 186–87
Southeast Asia trade with, 189–90
U.S. Asian policy vs., 21, 29, 55–56,
    111, 167–68, 211n, 218n, 239n
European Recovery Program (ERP), 184

Far Eastern Assistance Act (1950), 110
Far Eastern Commission (FEC), 23, 30,
    31–32, 213n
Feary, Robert A., 258n
Formosa, *see* Taiwan
Forrestal, James V., 35, 36, 37, 42, 61,
    93, 231n
Fosdick, Raymond B., 149
France:
    Chinese peace efforts avoided by, 138
    Communist Party in, 175, 270n
    domestic governments of, 171, 172,
      175–76, 270n
    economic recovery of, 167, 175, 187
    Indochina involvement of, 76, 164–88,
      190, 192–93, 195, 197, 198–99,
      200–201
    postwar colonial policies of, 186–88
    Socialist Party in, 171
    U.S. anticolonial pressure on, 184–87,
      188
    U.S. economic aid to, 175, 187
    Vichy government of, 165
Franklin, Benjamin, 186
Franks, Sir Oliver, 153
Freeman, Fulton, 102
French Union, 169, 171, 173, 175, 176,
    177, 178, 180, 186, 187, 192
Fugh, Philip, 144–45

Gay, Merrill C., 148
Germany, postwar rehabilitation of, 28,
    195
Giap, Vo Nguyen, 166
Great Depression, 18
Greater East Asia Co-Prosperity Sphere,
    21, 22, 203–4, 206
Greece:
    postwar aid to, 53, 54, 58, 224n
    Soviet penetration of, 90
Griffin, R. Allen, 93, 100, 197, 275n–76n

Ha Long Bay agreements, 177–78
Harrison, Raymond, 34, 53, 56, 57, 83,
    214n

Harrison Mission, 53, 56, 57, 214*n*, 222*n*, 223*n*, 225*n*
Hart, Liddell, 87
Heath, Donald R., 198
Helmick, Charles, 62, 65
Hiss, Alger, 20
Hitler, Adolf, 131
Hoang Minh Giam, 174
Ho Chi Minh:
    DRV established by, 168
    French effort against, 173
    French negotiations with, 168, 169, 174
    political popularity of, 176, 185
    Provisional Government denounced by, 178
    Soviet ties with, 172, 175, 207*n*
    U.S. relations with, 169, 170, 181, 200, 269*n*
    Vietminh created by, 165–66
Hodge, John, 68, 221*n*
Hoey, Robert, 197
Hoffman, Paul G., 229*n*
    on development of Marshall Plan, 211*n*, 224*n*–25*n*
    on Japanese trade with Korea, 71, 83, 84
    on Southeast Asian trade relationships, 189
    South Korean aid administered by, 64–65, 69, 70
    Taiwan policy and, 97–98, 100
Holland, colonialism of, 163, 164, 184–85, 267*n*
Hong Kong:
    British lease on, 153
    Communist threat to, 119, 255*n*
House of Representatives, U.S.:
    foreign aid appropriations and, 58, 59, 69–71, 74, 109
    see also Congress, U.S.
Howe, Fisher, 252*n*, 253*n*
Huang Ha, 143–45
Hummer, H. R., 227*n*
Huston, Cloyce K., 39

India:
    British withdrawal from, 163
    food shortages in, 184, 273*n*
    PRC recognized by, 153
    U.S. aid sought by, 164
Indochina:
    in rice trade, 76, 190–91, 200
    three nations of, 76, 164, 165; *see also* Cambodia; Laos; Vietnam

U.S. aid to, 83, 107, 178, 180, 182, 193, 194, 195–96, 197, 198, 203, 275*n*
Indochina, French regime in:
    colonial bureaucracy of, 165, 168
    economic benefits gained by, 165, 169, 173, 178, 184
    as French Union, 169, 171, 173, 175, 176, 177, 178, 180, 186, 187, 192
    history of, 76, 165
    military aid to, 188, 193, 194, 195–96, 198–99, 203
    Nationalist agreement on, 268*n*
    U.S. opposition to, 184–87, 188, 200, 201
Indochina Communist Party, 165
Indonesia:
    Dutch control of, 163, 164, 184, 267*n*
    Japanese peace settlement and, 47, 213*n*
    U.S. aid to, 194, 197
Iran, U.S. aid to, 78, 224*n*
iron industry, 136, 140, 257*n*

Jacobs, Joseph, 60, 64
Japan:
    Asian preeminence of, 17–18, 21, 80, 202, 204
    Chinese Communist trade with, 76, 135, 140–41, 142–43, 157, 159–60, 162, 203, 258*n*, 265*n*, 267*n*
    Chinese war with, 146, 160
    Communist threat to, 41, 42, 66, 112
    demilitarization of, 21, 23, 30, 37, 41–42, 220*n*
    economic recovery engineered for, 17–18, 21–22, 202–6; *see also* Japan, reconstruction of
    food supplies in, 25, 34, 56, 75–76, 112, 223*n*, 225*n*, 273*n*
    global trade of, 24–25, 31, 32, 39, 40, 48, 220*n*–21*n*
    industrial growth in, 30–32, 39–40, 216*n*
    peace settlements negotiated for, 26, 40–47, 88, 129, 202, 217*n*, 218*n*, 220*n*
    political stability restored to, 17, 23–24, 39, 41, 42, 216*n*
    population growth in, 25, 32, 56, 70, 75, 112, 213*n*
    in regional trade, 48, 56–57, 70, 76–77, 83–84, 88, 100, 122, 134, 135, 140–41, 142–43, 157, 159–60, 162, 165, 184, 189–92, 194, 196,

199–200, 201, 202–4, 222*n*, 232*n*,
233*n*–34*n*, 238*n*, 239*n*, 265*n*,
266*n*, 272*n*, 273*n*, 274*n*, 276*n*
textile industry of, 24, 221*n*
U.S. military bases in, 41, 43, 46
U.S. occupation of, 23–24, 25, 38, 41
zaibatsu system of, 35–36, 38, 39, 216*n*
Japan, reconstruction of, 23–50
Communist expansion and, 41, 42, 66
economic advisory team for, 33–40, 202
five point plan for, 26
industrial production revived in, 26, 30–
32, 84, 216*n*, 224*n*
Korean links with, 48, 50, 52, 56–57,
68, 70–72, 76, 77, 80, 83–84, 85,
89, 191, 192, 203, 221*n*, 222*n*,
232*n*, 233*n*–34*n*, 266*n*, 272*n*
Sino-Japanese trade and, 135, 140–41,
142–43, 157, 159–60, 162, 265*n*
Southeast Asian trade and, 184, 189–
92, 194, 196, 199–200, 201, 203,
272*n*, 273*n*, 274*n*, 276*n*
Taiwan policy and, 86, 87, 88, 89, 90,
100, 112, 122, 134, 203, 238*n*,
239*n*
U.S. aid for, 17–18, 25, 28, 29–30, 32,
53, 75, 211*n*, 216*n*
U.S.-sponsored program developed for,
26–30, 202
war reparations and, 26, 30–33, 37, 46,
202, 212*n*, 213*n*, 220*n*
JCS, *see* Joint Chiefs of Staff
Jessup, Philip C.:
China policy and, 103, 107–8, 124,
263*n*
on Japanese economy, 75–76, 160,
220*n*
on Nationalist leaders, 112–13, 119,
249*n*
on Southeast Asia, 193, 274*n*
Johnson, Edgar D. J., 232*n*, 234*n*, 266*n*–
67*n*
Johnson, Louis A.:
Defense appointment of, 42, 116, 231*n*
interdepartmental hostilities and, 42,
81–82, 116–17, 196, 250*n*
Japanese peace treaty opposed by, 42,
45
on Taiwan policy, 72–73, 106–7
Johnson, Lyndon B., 20, 205, 277*n*
Joint Chiefs of Staff (JCS):
on China policy, 262*n*
Japanese peace treaty opposed by, 41–
42, 43, 45–46

Japanese recovery program and, 23, 29–
30, 31, 41–42, 43
Korean withdrawal promoted by, 53,
60–65, 69, 227*n*
Pacific Defense Perimeter developed by,
72, 109
on Southeast Asian support, 194, 195,
199
South Korean military aid and, 78–80,
84
Taiwan policy and, 86, 88–89, 91,
102–3, 106–7, 108, 109, 119, 130,
133, 134, 246*n*, 256*n*
see also Defense Department, U.S.
Joint Commission for Rural Reconstruction, 240*n*
Jones, Joseph, 27
Judd, Walter, 90

Kan Chieh-hou, 102
Karkov (Soviet agent), 175
Kee, John, 108
Keizai, Sangyo, 25
Kennan, George F., 148, 228*n*
career of, 61
China report formulated by, 136–37,
138, 139
on Communist expansion, 41, 198
Europe-first strategy promoted by, 29,
55–56, 111
Japanese economy analyzed by, 35, 36,
41, 189–90, 203
on Japanese peace treaty, 41, 43, 217*n*
on Korean commitment, 61, 62, 71, 80,
198, 203
Nitze's advice sought by, 28, 36, 111
nuclear weapons buildup opposed by,
111
Policy Planning Staff headed by, 28–29,
35, 36, 39, 71, 111, 193
PRC UN membership advised by, 198,
203
on Southeast Asia policy, 183, 184,
185, 187, 189–90, 198, 203, 271*n*
Taiwan policy recommended by, 100–
101, 203
Truman Doctrine opposed by, 61
Kennedy, John F., 204–5
Keon, Michael, 144, 260*n*
Khrushchev, Nikita, 235*n*
Kim Il Sung, 79, 235*n*
KMAG (Korean Military Advisory
Group), 78–79
Knowland, William F., 90, 108–9, 110

Koo, Wellington, 105
Korea, 50–85
    economic resources of, 51–52, 56–57
    financial aid granted to, 52, 53, 55, 57–
        58, 64, 69, 74–75, 224n, 226n
    food supply in, 34, 51–52, 56–57, 85
    global strategic view vs. regional eco-
        nomic focus on, 50–51, 60–65
    Japanese trade with, 48, 56–57, 76, 77,
        191, 192, 203, 222n, 223n, 232n,
        233n–34n, 266n, 272n
    Japan linked to, 50, 52, 56–57, 68, 70–
        72, 76, 77, 80, 83–84, 85, 89,
        203, 221n, 232n, 233n–34n, 266n,
        272n
    U.S. inconsistency on, 50, 59–60, 230n
    U.S.-Soviet division of, 51–52, 53, 54,
        59, 198, 203
Korea, North (Democratic People's Repub-
    lic of Korea):
    military capability of, 68, 78, 79, 231n,
        236n
    South Korea invaded by, 45, 69, 73–74,
        79–80, 128, 231n, 235n
Korea, South (Republic of Korea):
    agricultural production of, 56–57, 58,
        70, 76, 77, 84–85, 190, 191
    civilian government vs. military control
        of, 53, 55, 60–64, 229n
    economic assistance for, 69–72, 74–75,
        109, 110, 232n–33n, 234n, 248n
    leadership of, 60, 62, 65, 77
    military assistance for, 68–69, 77–83,
        107, 231n, 236n–37n, 255n
    North Korean invasion of, 45, 69, 73–
        74, 79–80, 128, 231n, 235n
    political stabilization of, 53, 62–65, 76–
        77
    U.S. withdrawal sought from, 53, 60–
        69, 71, 204, 227n, 228n, 230n
Korean Military Advisory Group
    (KMAG), 78–79
Korean War:
    end of, 204
    Japanese trade curtailed in, 201
    onset of, 45, 69, 73–74, 79–80, 128,
        133, 235n–36n
    PRC participation in, 131, 136, 160–61,
        236n, 264n
    Southeast Asian aid package and, 197,
        198
    Taiwan naval protection in, 72, 81, 82,
        87, 128, 129, 133
    UN politics and, 156

Krentz, Kenneth C., 120, 132
Kuomintang, see Chinese Nationalists

Laos:
    French aid against Vietnam solicited by,
        177
    French-backed government created in,
        192, 193
    as part of French Indochina, 164, 165,
        169
Lattre de Tassigny, Jean de, 179
Leclerc, Jean, 166, 168, 170, 173, 176,
    179
Lenin, V. I., 146, 147
Li Tsung-jen, 104, 250n
    background of, 241n
    diminished power of, 105, 117–18, 120,
        243n
    peace settlement sought by, 137–38,
        241n
    political appointments made by, 95–96,
        97, 98, 101–2
Liu An-chi, 105
Liu Shao-ch'i, 144
Lovett, Robert A., 61, 65, 89, 178, 223n

MacArthur, Douglas:
    advisers to, 33, 66, 218n
    economic advisory replacements for,
        33–40, 49, 202
    Japanese reconstruction overseen by,
        23–24, 25, 26, 29, 30, 31, 32, 33–
        40, 56, 202, 213n, 216n, 218n,
        219n, 220n
    Japanese treaty negotiations and, 40, 41,
        42
    Korean military involvement and, 68,
        78, 227n, 235n
    Marshall's rivalry with, 215n
    Pacific Defense Perimeter delineated by,
        72, 73
    Taiwan policy and, 129, 130
McCardle, Carl W., 44, 219n
McCarran, Pat, 90, 95, 241n, 264n
McCarthy, Joseph, 46, 115–16
McConaughy, Walter P., 113, 158
MacDonald, John J., 104
McEvoy, Dennis, 216n
Malaya:
    Communist efforts in, 188
    U.S. aid to, 197
Malaysia, pro-Western orientation of, 163
Mao Tse-tung, 260n, 263n

anti-American position expressed by,
145, 259n–60n, 262n
Chinese Communist factional disputes
and, 144
Korean War and, 235n
on Taiwan, 255n
Marquat, William F., 38
Marshall, George C.:
Asian policy formation delegated by,
26–27, 52
congressional politics employed by, 58,
69, 241n
DA's working relationship with, 19, 28,
223n
foreign aid policy and, 26–27, 29–30
on French Indochina, 172
Japanese recovery program and, 29–30,
31, 34, 215n
Korean policy and, 52, 55, 60–67, 71,
72, 80–81, 83, 84, 228n, 229n–
30n
MacArthur's rivalry with, 215n
at Moscow conference, 26–27, 28, 40,
52, 55, 173
personnel decisions of, 208n
replacement of, 32
Marshall Plan, 29, 48, 55–56, 187, 210n,
211n, 225n, 226n, 241n
Martin, Edwin W., 258n, 277n
Marxism-Leninism, 147
Matray, James I., 222n
Melby, John F., 46, 198–99
Merchant, Livingston T., 96–100, 113–
14, 119, 120, 152, 242n, 273n–
74n
"Military Aid for Indochina," 193
Mitsubishi, 35
Moffat, Abbot, 170
Monnet, Jean, 169
Moutet, Marius, 171
Muccio, John J., 78–79, 227n
Mukden, U.S. consulate in, 148, 150,
151, 161
Mus, Paul, 174
Mutual Defense Assistance Act (1949),
107, 130, 194, 276n

Nanking, Chinese Communist control of,
143
Nash, Frank, 195
Nationalists, Chinese, *see* Chinese Nation-
alists
National Press Club, 73, 109
National Security Council (NSC):

China policy statements of, 137, 138,
141, 265n
on Communist expansion in Southeast
Asia, 193
comprehensive Asia policy of, 153, 157,
191
defense increase advocated by, 117
Japanese reconstruction and, 23, 33, 36,
38, 39, 41, 42
Korean policy formulated by, 63–64,
65–69, 72, 73, 229n, 230n
personnel of, 208n, 229n
SANACC replaced by, 62
on Sino-Soviet relationship, 137
on Taiwan policy, 87, 88, 89, 90–92,
93, 103, 104, 107, 130, 133, 256n
National Union Front, 176
NATO (North Atlantic Treaty Organization), 114, 194, 195
Navy, U.S., Seventh Fleet of, 81, 82, 128,
129, 130, 131
New Deal, 18
Nitze, Paul H., 271n
career background of, 35–36, 204–5,
277n
on China policy, 139–40, 161, 251n,
258n
defense budget recommendations of,
117
on economic recovery as containment
policy, 203
Far Eastern recovery needs analyzed by,
26, 27, 28, 29, 33, 210n, 214n
Indochina military guarantee sought by,
195
Japanese recovery program and, 30, 33,
35, 36, 37, 214n, 223n
on Kennan's PPS reports, 185
on Korean policy, 56, 230n, 231n
nuclear buildup supported by, 111
on political strategy for aid approval, 58
punitive industrial restrictions opposed
by, 30, 224n
reparations curtailment opposed by, 33
on Soviet interests in Southeast Asia,
193
State Department positions held by, 26,
28, 33, 36, 111, 193, 208n, 230n
on Taiwan policy, 111–12, 117, 120–
21, 124
two-China policy developed by, 111–
12, 248n
two-front aid policy advocated by, 27–
29, 55

Nix, Karl W. V., 125–26, 127, 128, 132, 254n, 255n
North Atlantic Treaty Organization (NATO), 114, 194, 195
nuclear weapons, 111
nylon, silk supplanted by, 24, 56

Office of Intelligence Review (OIR), 141, 142
Office of Strategic Services (OSS), U.S., 124, 166
Olive, William M., 149, 161
"On the People's Democratic Dictatorship" (Mao), 145
Operation Lea, 173, 176
Osborn, David L., 101

Pacific Defense Perimeter, 72, 73, 109
Pakistan:
 PRC recognition granted by, 153
 U.S. influence in, 163, 164
Patterson, Robert H., 34, 35, 52, 55
Pauley, Edwin W., 34, 212n
Pei Pein Men, 150
Peng Meng-chi, 102, 105
Pentagon, see Defense Department, U.S.; Joint Chiefs of Staff
Philippines:
 independence achieved by, 163
 Japanese reparations to, 46, 47, 213n
 U.S. economic aid to, 164
 U.S. military aid to, 78, 107
Policy Planning Staff (PPS):
 on Asia food supply, 233n
 China report issued by, 136–37
 defense spending increase backed by, 117
 directorship of, 28, 39, 111, 230n
 Europe-first policy advocated by, 29
 on Japanese rehabilitation, 41
 on Korea, 71
 on Southeast Asia, 182–85
 on Taiwan, 117
Potsdam conference (1945), 109, 247n
PRC, see China, People's Republic of
Prussen, Ronald, 219n

Ramadier, Paul, 172, 173, 174
Reagan, Ronald, 277n
Reed, Charles S., 176, 181
Republican Party:
 Asian policy criticized by, 73, 84, 196

congressional China bloc of, 74, 93, 94–95, 108–10, 241n
congressional control held by, 19, 58
Rhee, Syngman, 60, 62, 65, 68, 77, 229n
rice trade, 56–57, 70, 76–77, 85, 165, 169, 183–84, 190–91, 200, 273n
Roberts, William L., 78
Roosevelt, Franklin D., 18–19
 anticolonial policy of, 166–67, 268n
 on Taiwan leadership, 124–25
Roosevelt, Theodore, 100
Royall, Kenneth, 37
rubber production, 190
Rusk, Dean:
 background of, 115, 116, 125, 190, 221n, 252n
 on China policy, 139, 142, 156, 157, 158, 160
 DA respected by, 20
 on DA's Asian expertise, 182, 210n, 225n
 on diplomatic recognition of PRC, 153, 264n
 on European affairs vs. Asian policy, 21
 on Japanese reconstruction, 22, 41, 44, 45, 47, 76, 80
 on Korean policy, 51, 61, 80, 221n, 230n, 234n, 236n
 Korean War and, 161, 235n, 236n
 on Louis Johnson, 231n, 250n
 Pentagon connections cultivated by, 116–17, 235n
 political abilities of, 116
 on PRC, 152, 153, 262n, 264n
 on Southeast Asian policies, 190, 191, 194–96, 198, 199, 205, 271n, 272n, 273n, 276n, 277n
 State Department career of, 44, 68, 115, 156, 204–5, 208n, 209n, 230n, 252n
 on Taiwan policy, 89, 102, 103, 108, 119, 120, 121–25, 126–27, 128, 129, 130–31, 133, 134, 251n, 252n–53n, 255n
 Truman's decisiveness described by, 81
 UN utilized by, 232n
 U.S.-sponsored coup d'état recommended by, 123–25, 126–27, 128, 129, 133
Russo-Japanese War (1904), 51

Sainteny, Jean, 168, 169
Saltzman, Charles E., 33, 64–65

SANAAC (State-Army-Navy-Air Force
    Coordinating Committee), 62, 63,
    230*n*
San Francisco peace conference (1951),
    40, 46–47
Saul, Eric, 253*n*
SCAP (Supreme Command for Allied
    Powers), 24, 30, 35, 38, 39, 214*n*
Schaller, Michael, 271*n*
Schuman, Robert, 195
Sebald, William J., 24, 42, 218*n*
Senate, U.S.:
    aid programs addressed in, 58, 59, 71–
        72, 73–74, 109–10
    see also Congress, U.S.
silk industry, 24, 56
Singapore:
    pro-Western orientation of, 163
    U.S. aid to, 197
Smith, Alfred E., 18
Smith, Beverly, 237*n*
Smith, H. Alexander, 54, 90, 108–9, 110
Southeast Asia:
    CIA analyses on, 188–89, 192, 193,
        194, 272*n*
    European trade with, 189–90
    FDR's trusteeship proposal for, 166–67
    Japanese trade with, 184, 189–92, 194,
        196, 199–200, 201, 203, 272*n*,
        273*n*, 274*n*, 276*n*
    natural resources of, 183
    political effects on productivity of, 183–
        84
    Soviet interests in, 184, 191, 193, 194,
        276*n*
    U.S. economic program for, 163–64,
        165, 194–98, 201, 276*n*
Soviet Union:
    Chinese Communist alliance with, 113,
        118, 135, 136–37, 139, 145, 146,
        151, 157–59, 161, 262*n*
    full-scale war foreseen with, 112
    Japanese demilitarization desired by, 30,
        224*n*
    on Japanese peace treaty, 40, 42, 43,
        46, 47, 217*n*, 235*n*, 236*n*
    Korean interests of, 51, 53, 54, 55, 58,
        59, 60, 62, 63, 69, 72, 74, 79, 80,
        81, 198, 203
    Mediterranean influence of, 90
    in Nationalist peace negotiations, 138
    Southeast Asian interests of, 184, 191,
        193, 194, 270*n*, 276*n*

Taiwan conflicts and, 123, 131, 246*n*
Tito government denounced by, 136–37
UN affairs and, 62, 74, 82, 123, 131,
    155, 156
U.S. imperialism vs., 108
Vietminh supported by, 175, 192
Sprouse, Philip D., 91, 106, 114, 121,
    249*n*, 263*n*
Stalin, Joseph, 113, 139, 235*n*, 236*n*,
    270*n*
State-Army-Navy-Air Force Coordinating
    Committee (SANACC), 62, 63,
    230*n*
State Department, U.S.:
    administrative structure of, 15, 211*n*
    Advisory Committee on Development
        of Japanese and Korean Trade,
        31
    Defense Department relations with,
        106–7, 116–17, 157, 196, 218*n*,
        228*n*
    European colonialism and, 167–68, 172
    on European interests vs. Far East con-
        cerns, 167–68, 211*n*
    McCarthy's charges of communism in,
        115–16
    Office of Intelligence Review (OIR),
        141, 142
    Office of International Trade, 26, 33
    personnel decisions at, 208*n*–9*n*, 230*n*
    Policy Planning Staff (PPS), 28–29, 39,
        41, 71, 111, 117, 136–37, 182–85,
        230*n*, 233*n*
State-War-Navy Coordinating Committee
    (SWNCC):
    global trade balance studied by, 27,
        210*n*
    Japanese reconstruction and, 23–24, 27,
        29, 31, 35, 36
    Korean policies of, 52, 53, 54, 55, 59–
        60, 64, 224*n*, 230*n*
    SANACC evolved from, 62
Stettinius, Edward R., 167
Stickell, USS, 194
Stilwell, Joseph, 97, 124–25, 253*n*
Stokes, William N., 152
Strategic Bombing Survey, U.S., 214*n*,
    223*n*
Strike, Clifford, 34, 212*n*
Strong, Robert C., 106, 118, 121, 127,
    131–32, 251*n*, 255*n*
Stuart, John Leighton:
    background of, 143, 144

Stuart, John Leighton (*continued*)
   Chinese Communist contacts promoted
      by, 143–47, 259*n*, 260*n*
   Chinese Communist militancy outlined
      by, 147, 259*n*–60*n*
   departure impeded for, 149
   Nationalist Chinese contacts with, 96–
      97, 98, 104, 138, 261*n*
   on Taiwan aid, 93, 114, 130
Stuart, W. W., 119–20
Sun Li-jen:
   background of, 97, 101
   Chiang's efforts against, 97, 98, 102,
      105, 204, 250*n*
   coup d'état planned by, 105, 118, 119–
      21, 123–24, 125, 126–27, 132,
      133, 204, 205, 251*n*
   military abilities of, 97, 105, 113, 124
   U.S. support for, 95, 96–97, 101, 104–
      6, 111, 113, 123–24, 125, 126,
      131, 132, 133, 242*n*, 249*n*, 254*n*,
      255*n*
Sun Yat-sen, 146
Supreme Command for Allied Powers
   (SCAP), 24, 30, 35, 38, 39, 214*n*
SWNCC, *see* State-War-Navy Coordinat-
   ing Committee

tache d'huile, 166, 173
Taft, Robert A. 58, 90
Taiwan, 86–134
   Communist threat to, 86, 89–90, 92,
      99, 101, 103, 106, 107, 114, 133,
      155, 203, 238*n*, 244*n*, 245*n*, 246*n*,
      254*n*, 255*n*
   foreign trade with, 48, 88, 100, 122,
      134, 190, 191, 192, 203, 238*n*,
      239*n*
   indigenous population of, 90, 91, 100
   Japanese claims on, 88, 129
   mainland immigrants to, 92, 99, 106,
      122
   UN involvement in, 89, 95, 99, 100,
      103, 106, 120, 123, 128, 129,
      130–31
   U.S. protection sought for, 37, 112–14,
      122, 128, 129, 132, 133, 203
Taiwan policy:
   for economic assistance, 87, 91–93, 95,
      97–98, 99–100, 119, 127, 239*n*,
      240*n*, 242*n*, 247*n*–48*n*
   five implementation stages for, 86–87
   four approaches to, 88–92

Japanese links with, 86, 87, 88, 89, 90,
      100, 112, 122, 134
   Korean conflict and, 72, 81, 82, 87,
      128, 129, 131, 132, 133
   military assistance and, 72–73, 86, 87,
      88–89, 91, 92, 93–95, 102–3,
      106–11, 114, 118–19, 121, 122,
      130, 133, 247*n*, 248*n*, 249*n*
   Nationalist leadership and, 87, 91–92,
      93, 95–98, 100–106, 117–18,
      119–34, 204, 238*n*, 241*n*, 242*n*,
      249*n*
   two-China policy and, 112
   U.S.-sponsored coup d'état considered
      for, 123–25, 126–27, 128, 129,
      253*n*
Tatsumi, Shiro, 152
Thailand:
   aid to, 194, 197, 198
   Communist threat to, 188, 193
   pro-American orientation of, 163, 164
   rice trade of, 190, 200, 273*n*
Timmerman, T. S., 71
Tint, Herbert, 187
Tito (Josip Broz), 136–37
Todd, W. E., 71–72
Tonkin, 168, 169, 192
Toyota, 35
trans-Siberian Railroad, 81
Treasury Department, U.S., New Deal
      monetary policy of, 18
Truman, Harry S., 253*n*–54*n*
   appointments made by, 23, 32, 36, 37,
      44, 66, 72, 106, 116, 167, 208*n*,
      219*n*, 229*n*, 230*n*, 231*n*, 250*n*,
      254*n*
   bipartisan foreign policy supported by,
      116
   China policies of, 87–88, 93–94, 154,
      157, 259*n*, 262*n*
   comprehensive Asian policy approved
      by, 153, 191
   DA's relationship with, 19, 47, 66,
      250*n*
   decisiveness of, 81
   defense budgets under, 60, 117
   in election of 1948, 66, 231*n*
   foreign aid programs and, 27, 53, 58,
      64, 69, 73, 74, 78, 83, 95, 107,
      130, 194, 197, 211*n*, 226*n*, 232*n*,
      276*n*
   independent diplomatic channels
      employed by, 125–26, 128, 132

Japanese recovery and, 23, 39, 43, 45–46, 216*n*
Korean policies of, 50, 58, 63, 67, 69, 73, 74, 78, 79, 81–83, 226*n*, 228*n*, 230*n*, 232*n*
Korean War and, 79–83, 128, 129, 132, 133, 161
new Southeast Asian governments recognized by, 192–93
Southeast Asia policy of, 167, 191, 194, 197, 199, 268*n*
Taiwan policy of, 83, 87–88, 92, 93, 95, 107–9, 110, 114, 123, 124, 125–27, 128–29, 130, 132, 133, 247*n*, 250*n*, 254*n*–55*n*
treaty negotiations and, 43, 45, 46–47
on U.S. diplomats in PRC, 149, 151, 152
Truman Doctrine, 54, 61, 175, 224*n*
Turkey, postwar aid to, 53, 54, 58, 224*n*
"Two Talks with Mr. Chou En-lai," 146

United Nations:
charter of, 24, 151
Indochina conflict and, 274*n*
Japanese rehabilitation and, 24
Korean hostilities and, 69, 73–74, 79–80, 82, 83, 131, 156, 232*n*
Korean reconstruction and, 52, 53, 59, 60, 61–63, 64, 67
PRC representation in, 82, 155–56, 198, 203, 264*n*
Security Council membership in, 155–56
South Korea recognized by, 65
Taiwan politics and, 89, 95, 99, 100, 103, 106, 120, 123, 128, 129, 130–31, 252*n*–53*n*, 256*n*
U.S. delegation to, 229*n*
on Vietnam, 189, 274*n*
"United States Interests in China," 140
"United States Policy in China," 141
"United States Policy regarding Trade with China," 141
"United States Policy toward Southeast Asia," 183–85
United States Relations with China (China White Paper), 107–8
U.S. News & World Report, 79

Vandenberg, Arthur, 44, 58–59, 72, 93–94, 110, 219*n*, 226*n*, 229*n*
Vietminh (Vietnamese Independence League) *(Viet Nam Doc Lap Minh)*, 165–66
Vietminh Army:
French confrontations with, 166, 171, 173, 176, 179, 274*n*
military strategy of, 166
National Union Front vs., 176
size of, 166, 179, 192
Soviet assistance given to, 175
U.S. ships attacked by, 194
in World War II campaign, 166
Vietnam, 163–201
agricultural production in, 165, 169
as part of French Indochina, 164, 165, 178, 180
in rice trade, 165, 169, 191
three policy stages on, 164
U.S. combat in, 194, 205
U.S. economic aid to, 197, 276*n*
see also Indochina; Indochina, French regime in
Vietnam, Democratic Republic of (DRV):
constitution adopted by, 176
establishment of, 168
French recognition of, 168–69
Provisional Government vs., 177, 178
Soviet support for, 192
Vietnam, French regime in:
autonomy granted to, 192
DRV recognized by, 168–69
French public opinion on, 170, 174–75, 187
military confrontations of, 164, 166, 170, 171, 173, 176, 179, 274*n*
peaceful settlement sought for, 164, 167–75, 179, 200
puppet regime created by, 164, 169, 176–79, 180–82, 200–201
U.S. criticisms of, 185–87
U.S. military aid to, 165, 175, 198–99, 200
withdrawal of, 204
see also Indochina; Indochina, French regime in; Vietnam
Vincent, John Carter:
on French Indochina, 168, 169, 170, 172, 268*n*
Japanese treaty process and, 40
Korean rehabilitation policy and, 52–53, 62, 223*n*
State Department career of, 208*n*
Voorhees, Tracy S., 42, 45, 218*n*–19*n*, 246*n*

Vorys, John, 90

Ward, Angus, 148, 150–52, 262n
Webb, James, 116
  Korean policy and, 70, 80, 81–82
  personnel decisions and, 44, 208n, 250n
  PRC relations and, 151, 262n
  Taiwan policy and, 124, 128, 239n
Wei Tao-ming, 95
West, Robert, 196
"Whampoa" military clique, 138
Wherry, Kenneth, 90
Whitman, R. W., 212n, 222n

Wu, K. C., 101, 104–6, 118, 133, 204, 249n

Xuan, Nguyen Van, 177

Yalta conference (1945), 167
Yenching University, 143, 144–45, 161
Yen Hsi-shan, 106
Yoshida, Shigeru, 46, 47, 216n, 220n
Yugoslavia, 136–37

zaibatsu, 35–36, 38, 39, 216n